"The convoluted spectacle of four Israeli elections within two years poses a forbidding challenge to analysts. In this welcome continuation of The Elections in Israel series, Michal Shamir and Gideon Rahat meet this challenge with resounding success. Not only do the essays in this volume cover the elections themselves authoritatively, but they put this passage of Israeli politics into a data-rich historical and comparative perspective. Of particular note, the elections serve as a laboratory for analysis of the Netanyahu era and the personalization of Israeli politics that it embodies. The book also includes striking insights on challenges to Israeli democracy in the context of worldwide erosion of democracy. This volume should be on the reading list of both experts and casual students of Israeli politics."

Alan Dowty
Past President, Association for Israel Studies

"This is the sixteenth volume in the series The Elections in Israel, an impressive academic endeavor initiated by the late Prof. Asher Arian in 1969. The articles in these volumes propose multi-faceted analysis of the political situation, of voting patterns, and central issues that were on the agenda in each election campaign. But, even more so, they document the changes that have taken place in Israeli society, political culture and its characteristics, and in the essence of Israeli democracy.

These volumes have brought together leading social scientists from Israel and other countries and placed the election results and their analysis under the microscope in order to propose in-depth insights into politics and society in Israel. The latest volume covers the four elections of 2019–2021 which all took place within a two-year span. This was undoubtedly an intellectual and empirical challenge confronting the editors Prof. Michal Shamir and Prof. Gideon Rahat that they have successfully overcome. The final product includes the work of senior and junior scholars highlighting a painful lesson that teaches us much about the fragility of a democracy in crisis, about a divided society, about the radicalization of internal and external conflicts, and about dramatic transformations in Israeli political culture. This is essential reading for all who value democracy and concerned about its future."

Hanna Herzog
Professor Emerita, Tel Aviv University, and co-Director of the
Center for Advancement of Women in the Public Sphere,
Van Leer Jerusalem Institute, Jerusalem

"Four elections in two years is an amazing set of circumstances for any polity to weather. Shamir and Rahat have done a wonderful job, taking us through this landscape. They navigate us through the plus ça change of the increasing personalization of elections and plus c'est la même chose of four elections with similar outcomes and traditional bases of campaigning and voting."

John Aldrich
Pfizer-Pratt University Professor
Department of Political Science
Duke University

The Elections in Israel, 2019–2021

The 16th book in The Elections in Israel series, this book covers an extraordinary political event of having four national elections in two years, which were much (but not all) about one person, "King Bibi."

Analyzing Israel's national elections from 2019 to 2021, this book argues the four elections became, to a large extent, a referendum on Benjamin Netanyahu, the incumbent prime minister and head of the Likud party, facing investigations, a hearing, and indictment on charges of bribery, fraud, and breach of trust. Thus, the first part of the book is dedicated to political personalization and to Netanyahu himself. The second part of the volume covers the traditional actors in parliamentary elections: voters, parties, and the mass media. The book relies on empirical analysis, including extensive use of the Israel National Election Studies data; on theoretical rigor; and on the contextualization of the elections from comparative and long-term perspectives.

The book should interest students and researchers of Israeli politics and society, electoral studies, and the crisis of democracy more generally. Many chapters will be of interest to political science, communications, and sociology students and scholars who study themes that are prominent on the academic and public agenda including political personalization and personalized politics, populism, party decline, and democratic backsliding.

Michal Shamir is the Alvin Z. Rubinstein Professor of Political Science at Tel Aviv University. Her research focuses on democratic politics, including elections, party systems, public opinion, tolerance, and democratic culture.

Gideon Rahat is the chair of the Department of Political Science at the Hebrew University of Jerusalem and holds the Gersten Family Chair in Political Science. He is also a senior fellow at the Israel Democracy Institute. He has been studying the politics of reform, democratic institutions, political parties, candidate and leadership selection, and political personalization.

Routledge Elections in Israel

The Elections in Israel 2015
Edited by Michal Shamir and Gideon Rahat

The Elections in Israel, 2019–2021
Edited by Michal Shamir and Gideon Rahat

For more information about this series, please visit: www.routledge.com/ Elections-of-Israel/book-series/EOITRANS

The Elections in Israel, 2019–2021

**Edited by
Michal Shamir and Gideon Rahat**

First published 2023
by Routledge
4 Park Square, Milton Park, Abingdon, Oxon OX14 4RN

and by Routledge
605 Third Avenue, New York, NY 10158

Routledge is an imprint of the Taylor & Francis Group, an informa business

© 2023 selection and editorial matter, Michal Shamir and Gideon Rahat;
individual chapters, the contributors

The right of Michal Shamir and Gideon Rahat to be identified as the authors of the
editorial material, and of the authors for their individual chapters, has been asserted in
accordance with sections 77 and 78 of the Copyright, Designs and Patents Act 1988.

With the exception of Chapters 8 no part of this book may be reprinted or reproduced
or utilised in any form or by any electronic, mechanical, or other means, now known or
hereafter invented, including photocopying and recording, or in any information
storage or retrieval system, without permission in writing from the publishers.

Chapter 8 of this book is available for free in PDF format as Open Access from the
individual product page at www.routledge.com. It has been made available under a
Creative Commons Attribution-Non Commercial-No Derivatives 4.0 license.

Trademark notice: Product or corporate names may be trademarks or registered trademarks,
and are used only for identification and explanation without intent to infringe.

British Library Cataloguing-in-Publication Data
A catalogue record for this book is available from the British Library

ISBN: 9781032213392 (hbk)
ISBN: 9781032213408 (pbk)
ISBN: 9781003267911 (ebk)

DOI: 10.4324/9781003267911

Typeset in Times New Roman
by Newgen Publishing UK

The OA version of chapter 8 was funded by the European Research Council (ERC Starting
Grant 802990 – PROFECI).

Contents

List of Contributors	ix
Acknowledgments	xiii

Introduction   1

1   Four Elections in Two Years: A Unique Crisis or a
Sign of Things to Come?   3
MICHAL SHAMIR AND GIDEON RAHAT

2   The Four Elections 2019–2021: A Chronological Overview   27
GIDEON RAHAT AND MICHAL SHAMIR

PART 1
Personalization in the Israeli "Parteienstaat"   51

3   Personalization and Personalism in the 2019–2021
Elections: Another Climax of Personal Politics?   53
GIDEON RAHAT

4   King Bibi: The Personification of Democratic Values in
the 2019–2021 Election Cycle   77
LIRON LAVI, NAAMA RIVLIN-ANGERT, CLARETA TREGER,
TAMIR SHEAFER, ISRAEL WAISMEL-MANOR, AND MICHAL SHAMIR

5   A Populist Leader under Neoliberal Logic   99
AVI SHILON

6   Netanyahu and the Very Short History of the
"Right-Wing Bloc"   119
DORON NAVOT AND YAIR GOLDSHMIDT

viii *Contents*

7 Public and Legal Responsibility of Senior Elected
Representatives in the Executive Branch: Benjamin
Netanyahu as a Case Study   139
MORDECHAI KREMNITZER AND DANA BLANDER

PART 2
Voters, Parties, and the Media   161

8 Persistent Optimism under Political Uncertainty:
The Evolution of Citizens' Election Projections
During a Protracted Political Crisis   163
KEREN TENENBOIM-WEINBLATT, CHRISTIAN BADEN,
TALI AHARONI, AND MAXIMILIAN OVERBECK

9 Ethnic Demons and Class Specters: Ethnic and
Class Voting in Israel Revisited   190
GAL LEVY, MAOZ ROSENTHAL, AND ISHAK SAPORTA

10 Joint Lists in Israeli Politics   213
ASSAF SHAPIRA

11 The Arab Electorate and Parties, 2019–2021:
Toward a Non-Zionist Israeli Identity?   238
DORON NAVOT, SAMER SWAID, AND MUHAMMED KHALAILY

12 Three in a (Right-Wing) Boat: Media, Politicians,
and the Public in the Age of Digital Communication   259
ALON ZOIZNER, KEREN TSURIEL, DROR K. MARKUS,
VERED PORZYCKI, GUY MOR-LAN, AVISHAI GREEN,
EFFI LEVI, YARIV TSFATI, ISRAEL WAISMEL-MANOR,
TAMIR SHEAFER, AND SHAUL R. SHENHAV

Index   283

Contributors

Tali Aharoni is a PhD candidate at the Department of Communication and Journalism at the Hebrew University of Jerusalem. Her research interests include journalistic production, news audiences, social media, trust, and the various intersections of media and psychology.

Christian Baden is an associate professor at the Department of Communication and Journalism at the Hebrew University of Jerusalem. His research focuses on framing, discourse dynamics, and the social and psychological process of sensemaking, consensus, and contestation.

Dana Blander is a research fellow at the Israel Democracy Institute and a clinical psychologist. She studies Israeli politics, including the topics of antidemocratic legislation, referendums, private member bills, parliamentary and state investigation committees, and the Israeli electoral committee.

Yair Goldshmidt is a PhD candidate and a research assistant in the School of Political Science at the University of Haifa. His interests include populism, democratic theory, and Israeli politics.

Avishai Green is a PhD student at the Department of Political Science and a doctoral researcher in the DigitalValues project. His main research areas are political epistemology, political communication, and the construction of "political values."

Muhammed Khalaily is a researcher in the Program on Arab Society in Israel at the Israel Democracy Institute. He holds a PhD from the School of Political Science at the University of Haifa. His research focuses on the role and survival of primordial structures in the politics of Arabs in Israel.

Mordechai Kremnitzer is a senior fellow at the Israel Democracy Institute and Professor Emeritus of the Faculty of law at the Hebrew University of Jerusalem. His areas of expertise are criminal law, public law, military law, corruption in government, and proportionality in public policy.

Liron Lavi is an assistant professor at the Department of Political Studies at Bar-Ilan University. Before that, she was a research fellow at the UCLA

x *Contributors*

Y&S Nazarian Center for Israel Studies. Her research interests include elections, representation, democracy, and political communication, and her empirical work has focused on elections in Israel and the United States.

Effi Levi is working on his PhD in the School of Computer Science and Engineering in the Hebrew University of Jerusalem. His main research interests are machine learning, natural language processing, and computer vision.

Gal Levy is a senior teaching faculty and researcher at the Open University, Israel. He has published on the intersection of education and citizenship and on class and ethnic voting in Israel. More recently his research focuses on political activism in the margins of society and on young adults' conceptions of citizenship.

Dror K. Markus is a PhD candidate in the Political Science department at the Hebrew University of Jerusalem. His main research interests are media coverage, public agendas and information-age politics, as well as in computational methodology.

Guy Mor-Lan is a PhD candidate in Political Science at the Hebrew University of Jerusalem. His research lies at the intersection of computational social science methodology, comparative politics, and political communication.

Doron Navot is a senior lecturer and head of the Political Theory and Governance department, the School of Political Sciences at the University of Haifa. His areas of research are political corruption, law and politics, and Israeli politics.

Maximilian Overbeck is a postdoctoral researcher at the Department of Communication and Journalism at the Hebrew University of Jerusalem. His research lies at the intersection of political science, communication, and computational social science, with a focus on religion and politics.

Vered Porzycki is a PhD candidate at the Political Science department at the Hebrew University of Jerusalem. Her research interests include gender, representation, and discourse, as well as comparative politics.

Gideon Rahat is the chair of the Department of Political Science at the Hebrew University of Jerusalem and holds the Gersten Family Chair in Political Science. He is also a senior fellow at the Israel Democracy Institute. He has been studying the politics of reform, democratic institutions, political parties, candidate and leadership selection, and political personalization.

Naama Rivlin-Angert is a PhD candidate in the School of Political Science at Tel Aviv University. Her research interests combine political psychology and communication, and her current research focuses on the deconstruction of political identity.

Contributors xi

Maoz Rosenthal is a senior lecturer at the Lauder School for Government, Diplomacy, and Strategy at Reichman University (IDC Herzliya). He studies political agenda-setting, ethnic voting, and judicial politics.

Ishak Saporta is a senior lecturer in the Faculty of Management at Tel Aviv University. His research interests include ethnic and gender discrimination in employment and education, and employee relations.

Michal Shamir is the Alvin Z. Rubinstein Professor of Political Science at Tel Aviv University. Her research focuses on democratic politics, including elections, party systems, public opinion, tolerance, and democratic culture.

Assaf Shapira is the Director of the Political Reform Program at the Israel Democracy Institute. His research focuses on political parties, political representation, local government in Israel, and Israel's public service.

Tamir Sheafer is a professor in the Department of Political Science and the Department of Communication and Journalism, and the Rector of the Hebrew University of Jerusalem. His research focuses on actor-centered perspectives in political communication, such as information processing and personalization; on the role of political value proximity between actors; on political narratives; and on developing new methods for automated textual analysis.

Shaul R. Shenhav is an associate professor in the Department of Political Science at the Hebrew University of Jerusalem and the incumbent of the Herbert Samuel Chair in Political Science. His research focuses on political narratives and political discourse; on developing new methods for automated textual analysis; and on Israeli politics.

Avi Shilon is a historian who specializes in the field of Israel Studies, and has written books about Menachem Begin, Ben Gurion, and Yossi Beilin. He is a senior lecturer at Tel-Hai College, taught at the Hebrew University of Jerusalem and was a visiting scholar at the Taub Center for Israel Studies at NYU.

Samer Swaid is a postdoctoral researcher at UCL-University College of London. He holds a PhD from the School of Political Science at the University of Haifa. His research focuses on minority politics.

Keren Tenenboim-Weinblatt is an associate professor at the Department of Communication and Journalism at the Hebrew University of Jerusalem. Her research is in the fields of political communication and journalism, with a particular interest in political forecasts and the role of the media in constructing collective pasts and futures.

Clareta Treger is a PhD candidate in the School of Political Science at Tel Aviv University. Her research focuses on public opinion and political behavior. Her dissertation explores experimentally public attitudes toward government paternalism and nudges.

xii *Contributors*

Yariv Tsfati is a Professor in the Department of Communication, University of Haifa. His research focuses on various facets of public opinion, in particular on trust in media, the third person effect, and campaign effects.

Keren Tsuriel is a PhD candidate in the Dan Department of Communication at Tel Aviv University. Her research interests are participation in elections and nonvoters, uses of social media, political communication, and psychological media effects.

Israel Waismel-Manor is a senior lecturer at the School of Political Science, University of Haifa. His research focuses on political attitude formation and its effects on political behavior. His most recent projects explore the ways in which nonverbal communication, physiological stress, institutional settings, and new media influence political preferences and behavior.

Alon Zoizner is an assistant professor at the Department of Communication at the University of Haifa. His research bridges digital technologies, modern information environments, and current political developments, utilizing computational content analysis, experiments, survey analysis, and elite interviews.

Acknowledgments

Our sincere thanks to the Israel Democracy Institute, its President, Yohanan Plesner, and Dorit Shoval, Director of the Administrative Division, for their long-term support for The Elections in Israel series, inaugurated by Asher Arian in 1969; to the Routledge editorial, production, and marketing staff; to Refael Afriat for his invaluable help in the production of the volume; to Tel Aviv University's Alvin Z. Rubinstein Chair of Political Science for its financial support; and to the scholars who agreed to review anonymously the articles submitted to The Elections in Israel series, edited by Asher Arian and by us over the years. We wish to identify them by name and thank them for their important contribution. This is the list of reviewers since *The Elections in Israel—2003* volume to date: Gal Ariely, Nir Atmor, Eli Avraham, Olena Bagno, Meital Balmas, Itai Beeri, Pazit Ben-Nun Bloom, Guy Ben-Porat, Avraham Brichta, Kimmy Caplan, Naomi Chazan, Akiba Cohen, Margit Cohn, Momi Dahan, Abraham Diskin, Gideon Doron, Julia Elad-Strenger, Dani Filc, Daniel Friedmann, Michal Frenkel, Menachem Friedman, Hillel Frisch, Itzhak Galnoor, As'ad Ghanem, Zvi Gitelman, Giora Goldberg, Emanuel Gutmann, Sharon Haleva-Amir, Eran Halperin, Liran Harsgor, Reuven Y. Hazan, Tamar Hermann, Hanna Herzog, Ran Hirschl, Menachem Hofnung, Uri Izhar, Amal Jamal, Elihu Katz, Ilana Kaufman, Ofer Kenig, Orit Kedar, Anthony King, Claude Klein, Sam Lehman-Wilzig, Azi Lev-On, David Levi-Faur, Gilad Malach, Ronen Mandelkern, Moshe Maor, Nissim Mizrachi, Doron Navot, Benny Neuberger, Dganit Ofek, Sarah Osatzky Lazar, Yoav Peled, Yoram Peri, Maoz Rosenthal, Aviad Rubin, Arik Rudnitzky, Tal Sadeh, Itai Sened, Michael Shalev, Jacob Shamir, Tamir Sheafer, Avi Shilon, Yael Shomer, Sammy Smooha, Alberto Spektorowski, Baruch Susser, Yariv Tsfati, Keren Tsuriel, Raphael Ventura, Israel Waismel-Manor, Gabi Weimann, Gadi Wolfsfeld, Ephraim Yaar, Alon Yakter, Moran Yarchi, Yael Yishai, Mina Zemach, and Alan Zuckerman.

Michal Shamir
Gideon Rahat

Introduction

1 Four Elections in Two Years

A Unique Crisis or a Sign of Things to Come?

Michal Shamir and Gideon Rahat

1.1 Introduction

Israel held four general elections between April 2019 and March 2021: three elections in less than a year and four in two years. Such an event is rare but not unprecedented in parliamentary democracies. For example, general elections were held in Spain in April and again in November 2019, following the failure to form a coalition government. These were the third and fourth elections in four years. Since 2015, following the economic crisis, corruption scandals, and mistrust in the traditional parties, the Spanish party system has changed from an essentially two-party system to a multiparty system, and the parties failed to form a stable coalition government. Another example is Greece, which held three elections in June and November 1989, and in April 1990. These elections were held because the party that won the plurality of votes failed to form a government (following an electoral reform). During a year and a half in 1981–1982, Ireland went to the polls three times due to intraparty and coalition crises against the background of budget cuts.

However, the background to the Israeli case is not similar. There was no change in the party system or the electoral system, and there were no new crucial issues on the agenda. There were also no early signs. More than four years have passed between the elections for the 20th Knesset (2015) and for the 21st Knesset (2019). It was the initiative of Prime Minister Benjamin Netanyahu, in power since 2009, to end the 20th Knesset term about seven months before the deadline set by law. The tenure of the 20th Knesset was longer than the average (then) of three and a half years; the tenure of Netanyahu's government was almost four years, compared with an average of about two years (Knesset, 2015).

The elections for the 21st Knesset were held on April 9, 2019. But a new government was formed only after two additional elections: on September 17, 2019 (elections for the 22nd Knesset) and on March 2, 2020 (elections for the 23rd Knesset). The new government was a rotation government based on an agreement between Likud and parts of the Blue and White alliance. Netanyahu headed the government, and Benny Gantz served as an alternate prime minister who was supposed to switch positions with Netanyahu after

DOI: 10.4324/9781003267911-2

4 *Michal Shamir and Gideon Rahat*

18 months. The representatives of the two blocs (right-religious and center-left) won equal veto power. This government was sworn in on May 17, 2020, and lasted only six months. Following the failure to pass the state budget, another election was announced, fourth in number within two years. The elections for the 24th Knesset took place on March 23, 2021. Coalition negotiations led to the establishment of another rotation government. This time its base was the bloc of the parties that opposed Netanyahu. Naftali Bennett; the leader of Yemina headed the government with Yair Lapid of Yesh Atid serving as an alternate prime minister. The government coalition included right-wing, center, and left-wing parties, and for the first time also an Arab party, the United Arab List (Ra'am).

This period of condensed instability was marked by frequent elections; inability to form a government and continued tenure of transitional governments; recurrent change of the rules of the game; lack of governance due to the paralysis of the political system and government ministries; and an incumbent prime minister accused and prosecuted for breach of trust and bribery that allegedly occurred during his tenure. It was, therefore, at the same time, a political, constitutional, and governance crisis. In addition, this event expressed, in a fast-forward focused and dramatic manner, the democratic backsliding in Israel (and the struggle against it). We expound here both – not unrelated – phenomena.

The book analyzes the four elections that Israel experienced in 2019–2021. It opens with two introductory chapters. This chapter provides an overview of this extraordinary episode of four elections over two years. It presents explanations for its occurrence, a comparative analysis of turnout, voting and the structure of the competition, the crisis of political parties, increasing personalization and democratic backsliding, and the meaning and implications of this development for Israeli politics. The second introductory chapter presents a chronological analysis that focuses on each of the four elections: their background, the campaign, and an analysis of their results. The rest of the chapters are grouped into two parts.

The first part examines the personalization of Israeli politics from several angles. It demonstrates how Israel, called in the distant past "parteienstaat" (Akzin, 1955), became a country where politics, in its various manifestations, is exceptionally personalized. This part opens with Rahat's chapter that analyzes political personalization in Israel, and demonstrates that personal politics has reached another peak in these four elections. In the next chapter, Lavi et al. link personalization and support for democracy and point to Netanyahu's role in eroding democratic values. The following chapters in this part focus on Netanyahu, who was at the center of the four elections: Shilon analyzes his leadership patterns; Navot and Goldshmidt examine the relationship between Netanyahu and his support base, particularly in the context of the accusations of his criminal acts; Kremnitzer and Blander offer an analysis of the public and legal responsibility of senior elected officials in the executive branch in light of Netanyahu's case. We purposely devote half of the book

Four Elections in Two Years: A Unique Crisis?   5

chapters to this subject. Beyond Netanyahu's prominence throughout the elections, and beyond his legal affairs, charges, and criminal trial – here lies the explanation for the exceptional events of 2019–2021. Understanding this occurrence is impossible without referring to Israel's high levels of political personalization. And Netanyahu was playing a vital role in it – since entering politics, and specifically in these elections.

The second part presents studies of additional electoral actors: voters, parties, and the media. In the opening chapter of this part, Tenenboim-Weinblatt et al. analyze public opinion throughout this context of political crisis and extreme uncertainty. The next chapter of Levy, Rosenthal, and Saporta analyzes the voting patterns of the Jewish public and updates the study of class and ethnic voting in Israel. In the following chapter, Shapira examines the development of joint lists in Israeli elections. Their number, he demonstrates, peaked in the 2019–2021 elections, and the influence of personalization on them was also evident. In the next chapter, Navot, Swaid, and Khalaily focus on the Arab public and the parties representing it. They point to a change in the outlook of Arab politicians and voters, an aspiration to integrate into the political system through what they call "non-Zionist Israeli identity." In the last chapter, Zoizner et al. compare the agenda of politicians, the media, and the public, and find consistency between them and dominance of the right-wing agenda.

This introductory chapter begins with explanations for the extraordinary occurrence of four elections within two years. It then turns to examine comparatively the election results and voting patterns in the four elections. The following section discusses the crisis of political parties, rising personalization, and the nature of the party system. It then reviews institutional reforms adopted through the crisis, the rotation government, and the ever-expanding "Norwegian law." In the next section, the 2019–2021 elections are linked to the discussion of democratic backsliding in Israel. Finally, the conclusion combines the government instability and democratic aspects of the crisis, revisits the question whether this was a unique crisis, and suggests some propositions and recommendations for future research on the basis of the Israeli extreme case study.

1.2 Explanations for the Crisis: Why Were Four Elections Held in Two Years?

The exceptional occurrence of four elections within two years – three consecutive elections because of the inability to form a government and another one after the formation of a short-lived government – can be explicated in several ways. The personal explanation is the most prominent, mainly focusing on Prime Minister Netanyahu. He was interested in a clear electoral victory to consign his broad popular support as a counterweight to his public corruption indictments. Such a majority could help promote legislation and appointments to assist him in his legal battle. Unable to mobilize

6 Michal Shamir and Gideon Rahat

a clear majority, Netanyahu repeatedly shuffled the cards hoping to achieve his desired result. An explanation at the personal level can also be applied to other politicians, to their refusal to join a government with Netanyahu as a prime minister (but not with the Likud, his party, as they stated). It can also apply to other cases from the right: Lieberman's refusal to join the Netanyahu coalition following the first election in the series in April 2019, thus preventing him from forming a government; Gideon Sa'ar's defection from Likud and the establishment of his party Tikva Hadasha (New Hope); and transitions of various politicians between parties and lists during the turbulent two years of 2019–2021. Even though the personal explanation applies to other parties and personas, it is hard to imagine this event without Netanyahu at the head. And from a broader structural perspective, without the extreme personalization that Israel has gone through and the depth of its personal politics, such an occurrence is inconceivable.

Another explanation may refer to party considerations regarding spatial competition in the party system. These include the detachment of Lieberman and his party, Yisrael Beiteinu, from the right-wing religious bloc, to which they belonged for 20 years (since joining politics in 1999). Similar considerations may also explain the maneuvers of Yemina, led by Bennett, and the establishment of New Hope by Gideon Sa'ar. To this, we can add the behavior of the ultra-Orthodox parties; they adhered to their partnership with Netanyahu, even though they could have disengaged from it. After all, they had done so in the past when there was a majority without their support for the opposing forces. Still, all of these explanations are about personal parties or personal loyalties.

Additional explanations refer to the more latent structural level. According to these, the political crisis and its duration stemmed from the rules of the game and institutional characteristics of the Israeli regime: parliamentarism and the proportional representation (PR) electoral system with its single nationwide constituency, which produce multiple parties, coalition governments, and a two-stage process, in which the citizens elect their representatives to parliament, and they in turn negotiate the new (coalition) government; the relative ease with which the Knesset can be dissolved and new elections proclaimed; the lack of a rigid and codified constitution and the political culture of disrespect for the law and for binding political traditions and norms. Yet all of these elements existed before the current crisis. Possibly, the recent introduction of the rigid mechanism of the "constructive vote of no confidence," made government formation more difficult. This change implies that replacing a government in Israel other than following elections requires presenting an alternative government, and thus reduces the coalition partners' bargaining power after the government has been formed. They are thus required to ensure their gains before the government formation. In the past, in contrast, parties entered the coalition knowing that they could always create a crisis to promote their demands. It can be argued that Yisrael Beiteinu refrained from entering the coalition after the April 2019 election, knowing that after the vote of investiture in the Knesset, its bargaining power would decline. Other parties also refrained from supporting the coalition, knowing that it would be easy for the prime minister to ignore his promises with such an institutional arrangement after forming a new government. Ironically then, a political reform passed for the sake of political stability and governance may have contributed to the occurrence of extreme instability and crisis. We see, however, the acute personalization process Israel has gone through as the major source of the extraordinary event we deal with, and accordingly the first part of the volume covers this phenomenon from different angles.

1.3 Participation, Competition, and Voting in the Four Elections

Table 1.1 compares the four elections of 2019–2021 according to several general criteria used to evaluate the election results, turnout, and competition. Turnout levels in the elections are surprising. Through the first three elections, there was a slight increase in turnout in each, contradicting the expectation that repeated elections would create "voter fatigue." Only in the fourth election, held a year after the third election, following the short and unsuccessful term of the Netanyahu–Gantz government – turnout dropped (by four percentage points). The study by Tenenboim-Weinblatt et al. (Chapter 8) finds a clear link between optimism and the intention to vote in all four rounds. In parallel, optimism grew in the first three elections, but receded in the last one. Indeed, surveys of the Israel Democracy Institute in the run-up to the fourth election showed that it took place in a different climate of public opinion. This climate developed against the background of the prolongation of the

Table 1.1 Comparison between the four elections (2019–2021): General criteria

	April 2019*	Sept. 2019**	2020***	2021 +
Eligible voters	6,339,729	6,394,030	6,453,255	6,578,084
Number of votes	4,340,253	4,465,168	4,615,135	4,436,365
Number of valid votes	4,309,270	4,436,806	4,590,062	4,410,052
Number of invalid votes	30,983	28,362	25,073	26,313
Turnout (%)	68.46	69.83	71.52	67.44
Number and (%) of votes cast for lists that did not pass the electoral threshold	366,016 (8.49)	126,704 (2.86)	36,901 (0.80)	64,752 (1.47)
Electoral volatility	25.16	9.03	7.32	11.61
The number of competing party lists	40	29	29	38
The effective number of party lists	5.24	5.57	5.01	8.52

Source: *Central Elections Committee for the 21st Knesset, 2019. **Central Elections Committee for the 22nd Knesset, 2019. ***Central Elections Committee for the 23rd Knesset, 2020. + Central Elections Committee for the 24th Knesset, 2021.

8   *Michal Shamir and Gideon Rahat*

political crisis, the disappointing experience with Netanyahu and Gantz's rotation government, and the Covid-19 pandemic. A majority of the public estimated that a decisive electoral result was unlikely; gave the rotation government low scores in terms of its impact on strengthening their trust in their leaders and in bringing different social groups together (The Israeli Voice Index, 2020); and only a minority of about a third expressed trust in Prime Minister Netanyahu's management of the Covid-19 pandemic (The Israeli Voice Index, 2021).

There is evidence of a learning curve for both voters and politicians: The number of votes cast for lists that did not pass the electoral threshold dropped sharply between elections (between the third and fourth elections, there was some increase, but it was much smaller than the rates of decline in the first three elections). This pattern can be attributed to both voters who refrained from voting for small party lists and politicians who joined party alliances (Shapira, this volume). A parallel trend occurred with the number of invalid votes. It shrunk throughout the 21st, 22nd, and 23rd Knesset elections, and slightly rose again in the 24th Knesset election.

Electoral volatility (Pedersen, 1979) declined between the first and subsequent elections, as expected from elections held within a minimal time interval (compared to the April 2019 elections, which took place about four years after the previous election). Similarly, the number of lists running in the first three consecutive elections declined, as a result of the withdrawal of tiny lists and the formation of alliances between parties in their attempt to pass the electoral threshold. The first three elections produced a similar effective number of parties (Laakso and Taagepera, 1979). This effective number of parties was lower compared to recent decades because the votes were concentrated in two party lists, Likud and Blue and White. The fourth election produced the highest number of effective parties in Israel's political history, along with the 1999 election. But in 1999, voters had incentives to split their vote (due to the direct election law, in effect then). In 2021, this resulted mainly from the fragmentation in the opposition camp following the fiasco of the Netanyahu–Gantz rotation government.

Table 1.2 presents data on the votes and seats that the party lists won in the four consecutive elections. The support for Likud oscillated across elections: a significant decline in the second election (if we consider its "swallowing" of Kulanu and Zehut), an increase in the third, and again a decline in the fourth. Blue and White demonstrated relative stability in the first three elections and a drastic drop in the fourth, with the disintegration of the alliance. Shas and United Torah Judaism were quite stable in the four elections. Support for the national religious right-wing parties, and even more so the number of their seats, eroded in the first three elections. But in the fourth election, they revived: Their number of seats and votes increased at the expense of the Likud, and to a lesser extent, at the expense of the two ultra-Orthodox parties. All this did not prevent Sa'ar's New Hope party from winning a share of votes and seats similar to what the Likud lost in the 2021 election (compared to 2020). Yisrael Beiteinu became stronger when it reinvented itself after the first election; however, it lost some of that additional support in the next elections. Meretz and Labor – whose support eroded in the first three elections – recovered in the fourth one, getting the support of voters who were disappointed when Hosen Yisrael joined the Netanyahu-Gantz rotation government. The Arab parties and Hadash increased their vote and representation when they ran together in the second and third elections. In the fourth election, after the Joint List fell apart, their support dropped back to its level in the first election.

An analysis of election results by locality, based on data from the Central Elections Committee, indicates consistent voting patterns for parties across the four elections. The highest support for Likud was in localities with a medium socioeconomic ranking. Blue and White (and in the 2021 elections also Yesh Atid) did best in localities with a high socioeconomic rank. In the localities with the lowest socioeconomic ranking, the vote for the Arab parties (the Joint List, Hadash–Ta'al, Ra'am-Balad, and Ra'am in the various elections) stood out in Arab localities, and the vote for the ultra-Orthodox parties (United Torah Judaism and Shas) in Jewish localities with a high concentration of ultra-Orthodox population (Hoffman-Dishon, 2019a, 2019b, 2020). Sociological and political research in Israel emphasizes the strong correlation in the Jewish population between socioeconomic status, ethnicity, and the level of religiosity, while there are different views of the contribution of each to voting patterns. The chapter by Levy, Rosenthal, and Saporta in this volume presents an updated study on this topic. It emphasizes the intersectionality between social identities and analyzes its dynamics, with a focus on the vote of Mizrahim for Blue and White (and see articles on the subject in The Elections in Israel series since 1969).

Changes in turnout in this electoral cycle occurred mainly in low socioeconomic localities. The notable increase in turnout between the first and second elections was in the Arab localities (Hoffman-Dishon, 2019b). It was spurred by the reestablishment of the Joint List and the increasing efficacy felt by Arab citizens and their expectation that they can influence election results and government formation (see Navot, Swaid, and Khalaily in this volume). The increase in turnout in the third election came also mostly from localities with a low socioeconomic ranking. These included this time Arab localities as well as Jewish localities at a low socioeconomic level, including localities in the periphery (Hoffman-Dishon, 2020). Most of the decline in turnout in the fourth election also occurred in localities with a low socioeconomic rating. At the same time, the well-known relationship between socioeconomic status and turnout was evident throughout the election cycle, with turnout being highest in the localities with the highest socioeconomic ranking compared to all others.

Table 1.3 analyzes the power relations between the party blocs in the 2019–2021 elections, defined according to two criteria. First, personal identification with Netanyahu or against him; second, ideological identification

10 *Michal Shamir and Gideon Rahat*

Table 1.2 Results of the 2019–2021 elections (party lists)

21st Knesset elections *				22nd Knesset elections **			
Party-list name	*No. of votes*	*% of votes*	*No. of seats*	*Party-list name*	*No. of votes*	*% of votes*	*No. of seats*
Likud	1,140,370	26.46	35	Likud	1,113,617	25.10	32
Kulanu	152,756	3.54	4				
Zehut	118,031	2.74	0				
Shas	258,275	5.99	8	Shas	330,199	7.44	9
United Torah Judaism	249,049	5.78	8	United Torah Judaism	268,775	6.06	7
Union of Right-Wing Parties	159,468	3.70	5	Yemina	260,655	5.87	7
The New Right	138,598	3.22	0				
				Otzma Yehudit	83,609	1.88	0
Yisrael Beiteinu	173,004	4.01	5	Yisrael Beiteinu	310,154	6.99	8
Blue and White	1,125,881	26.13	35	Blue and White	1,151,214	25.95	33
Labor	190,870	4.43	6	Labor–Gesher	212,782	4.80	6
Gesher	74,701	1.73	0				
Meretz	156,473	3.63	4	The Democratic Camp	192,495	4.34	5
Hadash–Ta'al	193,442	4.49	6	Joint List	470,211	10.60	13
Ra'am–Balad	143,666	3.33	4				
Others	34,686	0.80	0	Others	43,095	0.97	0
Total	4,309,270	100.00	120	Total	4,436,806	100.00	120

Source: *Central Elections Committee for the 21st Knesset, 2019. **Central Elections Committee for the 22nd Knesset, 2019. ***Central Elections Committee for the 23rd Knesset, 2020. +Central Elections Committee for the 24th Knesset, 2021.

23rd Knesset elections***				24th Knesset elections +			
Party-list name	No. of votes	% of votes	No. of seats	Party-list name	No. of votes	% of votes	No. of seats
Likud	1,352,449	29.46	36	Likud	1,066,892	24.19	30
				New Hope	209,161	4.74	6
Shas	352,853	7.69	9	Shas	316,008	7.17	9
United Torah Judaism	274,437	5.98	7	United Torah Judaism	248,391	5.63	7
Yemina	240,689	5.24	6	Yemina	273,836	6.21	7
				Religious Zionism	225,641	5.12	6
Otzma Yehudit	19,402	0.42	0				
Yisrael Beiteinu	263,365	5.74	7	Yisrael Beiteinu	248,370	5.63	7
Blue and White	1,220,381	26.59	33	Blue and White	292,257	6.63	8
				Yesh Atid	614,112	13.93	17
Labor–Gesher– Meretz	267,480	5.83	7	Labor	268,767	6.09	7
				Meretz	202,218	4.59	6
Joint List	581,507	12.67	15	Joint List	212,583	4.82	6
				Ra'am	167,064	3.79	4
Others	17,499	0.38	0	Others	64,752	1.47	0
Total	4,590,062	100.00	120	Total	4,410,052	100.0	120

Table 1.3 Results of the 2019–2021 elections (personal and ideological blocs)

The bloc	No. of votes				% Votes				Seats			
	April 2019	Sept. 2019	2020	2021	April 2019	Sept. 2019	2020	2021	April 2019	Sept. 2019	2020	2021
By personal support[a]												
Netanyahu	2,216,547	2,056,855	2,239,830	1,856,932	51	46	49	42	60	55	58	52
Anti-Netanyahu	1,810,332	2,026,702	2,069,368	2,082,351	42	46	45	47	55	57	55	57
Unidentified	247,705	310,154	263,365	440,900	6	7	6	10	5	8	7	11
Others	34,686	43,095	17,499	29,869	1	1	0	1	0	0	0	0
Total	4,309,270	4,436,806	4,590,062	4,410,052	100	100	100	100	120	120	120	120
By ideological camp[b]												
Right-religious	2,389,551	2,367,009	2,503,195	2,588,299	55	53	55	59	65	63	65	72
Center-left	1,810,332	2,026,702	2,069,368	1,757,001	42	46	45	40	55	57	55	48
Ideologically unidentified	74,701	0	0	34,883	2	0	0	1	0	0	0–	0
Others	34,686	43,095	17,499	29,869	1	1	0	1	0	0	0	0
Total	4,309,270	4,436,806	4,590,062	4,410,052	100	100	100	100	120	120	120	120

Notes

a The Netanyahu bloc included the following lists: in April 2019: Likud, Shas, United Torah Judaism, Union of Right-Wing Parties, Kulanu, The New Right, and Zehut; in September 2019: Likud, Shas, United Torah Judaism, Yemina, and Otzma Yehudit; in 2020: Likud, Shas, United Torah Judaism, Yemina, and Otzma Yehudit; in 2021: Likud, Shas, United Torah Judaism, Religious Zionism.

The anti-Netanyahu bloc included the following lists: in April 2019: Blue and White, Hadash–Ta'al, Labor, Meretz, and Ra'am–Balad; in September 2019: Blue and White, Joint List, Labor–Gesher, and Democratic Camp; in 2020: Blue and White, Joint List, Labor–Gesher-Meretz; in 2021: Yesh Atid, Blue and White, Labor, Yisrael Beiteinu, Joint List, New Hope, Meretz, New Economy.

The unidentified bloc included: in April 2019: Yisrael Beiteinu, Gesher; in September 2019, and in 2020: Yisrael Beiteinu; in 2021: Yemina and Ra'am.

The others category the lists that won 0.33% of the valid votes or less.

b The right-wing religious bloc include the following lists: in April 2019: Likud, Shas, United Torah Judaism, Union of Right-Wing Parties, Kulanu, The New Right, Yisrael Beiteinu, and Zehut; in September 2019: Likud, Shas, United Torah Judaism, Yemina, Yisrael Beiteinu, and Otzma Yehudit; in 2020: Likud, Shas, United Torah Judaism, Yemina, Yisrael Beiteinu, and Otzma Yehudit; in 2021: Likud, Shas, United Torah Judaism, Yemina, Yisrael Beiteinu, New Hope, and Religious Zionism.

The center-left bloc included: in April 2019: Blue and White, Hadash–Ta'al, Labor, Meretz, and Ra'am–Balad; in September 2019: Blue and White, Joint List, Labor–Gesher, and Democratic Camp; in 2020: Blue and White, Joint List, and Labor–Gesher-Meretz; in 2021: Yesh Atid, Blue and White, Labor, Joint List, Meretz, Ra'am.

The ideologically unidentified parties included Gesher in April 2019 and New Economy in 2021.

The others category included the lists that won 0.33% of the valid votes or less.

(right-religious versus center-left). For most parties, there are no qualms regarding the affiliation with personal and ideological blocs. However, the affiliation of Yisrael Beiteinu, a significant actor in these four elections, is less clear. On the one hand, it can be argued that in the April 2019 election, it was clearly associated with the Netanyahu bloc. On the other hand, its refusal to join the Netanyahu-led coalition following the election located it in the "anti-Netanyahu" bloc, certainly in Netanyahu's eyes. That is why we chose to associate it with the non-identified parties. Note that the Netanyahu bloc won the support of the majority of voters in the April 2019 election, even without Yisrael Beiteinu. In the second and third elections, the consistent and rigid line of the party was to call for a unity government and not for the replacement of Netanyahu. Therefore, also in these elections, we classify it as non-identified. The affiliation of Yisrael Beiteinu with the "anti-Netanyahu" bloc became evident only in the run-up to the fourth election in 2021.

The most prominent and significant pattern in Table 1.3 is the overall decline in the support for the Netanyahu bloc and, simultaneously, an increase in the power of the right-religious bloc. The weakening of the Netanyahu bloc and the strengthening of the anti-Netanyahu bloc and the non-identified parties between the April and September 2019 elections is noticeable. At least part of the change was due to the integration of Kulanu in the Likud, which according to the INES (2021) surveys, hardly brought any support for the Likud. In contrast, the 2020 election was characterized by a partial return "home" of voters to Netanyahu's bloc. The 2021 election marked a sharp decline in support for Netanyahu's bloc, a slight increase in support for the bloc of his opponents, and especially an increase in support for parties that refused to identify fully with one of the blocs. In contrast, there was a clear majority for the right-religious bloc in all elections. It is interesting to note that the study of Zoizner et al. in this volume found that throughout this election cycle, the agenda of the news sites largely overlapped the agenda of the political right and the citizens who support it. The right-wing bloc's power peaked in the fourth election of March 2021, when the right wing and religious parties received 59% of the vote and 72 seats. Yet it was then that Netanyahu was ousted. One can thus identify greater differentiation between the composition of the personal and ideological blocs over the two years. It can be argued, then, that paradoxically, it was the adherence to Netanyahu of most of the right that ultimately allowed the center-left minority camp to participate in the government as an equal partner with right-wing parties in the Netanyahu–Gantz and Bennett–Lapid rotation governments. This result can also be seen as an expression of the centrality of personal politics – and specifically of the personal power of Netanyahu – over the blocs, parties, and ideologies (the chapters in the first part examine this from different angles).

The occurrence of four elections in two years and the failure to form a coalition government (at all, or a durable one) obviously indicate acute government instability. At the same time however, we see stability in voting patterns for the ideological camps; overall relative stability in turnout; and stability

14 *Michal Shamir and Gideon Rahat*

in the personal and ideological blocs in the first three elections (Table 1.3). Only the fourth election, with the increasing differentiation between the ideological and personal blocs, brought about a change. This change occurred primarily due to the (personally) non-identifiers and the ideological right anti-Netanyahu parties and politicians, enabled by the high volatility in the configuration of parties and party alliances. The next section casts this period in broader historical and theoretical perspectives.

1.4 Party Decline, Personalization, and the Party System

The crisis of political parties is evident in Israel for several decades (Korn, 1998). This crisis of party democracy inflicts many democracies, but comparative studies found it to be more acute in Israel. Almost everywhere in the democratic world, parties have declined compared to their golden age in the 1950s and 1960s. However, there are democracies where parties' ties with society have weakened only slightly. It can be argued that they have adapted to the changing political, social, economic, cultural, and technological circumstances. Beside them are democracies in which parties declined significantly, and politics became highly personalized. Israel stands out among these cases. In Israel, scholars identified a sharp decline in the parties' relationship with actors who are supposed to mediate between them and society: The number of party members dropped dramatically, the presence of parties in local government decreased significantly, and their relationship with interest groups weakened considerably. As far as voters are concerned, party identification weakened and electoral turnout declined (although in recent years it recovered somewhat); vote switching increased, as did support for new parties (Arian and Shamir, 2002; Kenig and Tuttnauer, 2017; Rahat and Kenig, 2018).

While the parties declined, politics became more and more personalized (Arian and Shamir, 2002; Rahat and Kenig, 2018; Rahat, 2019; Rahat and Sheafer, 2007). Expressions of personalization included, among other things, the rise of personal parties and the strengthening of leaders within other parties at the expense of their party; media coverage that focused, more and more, on politicians, and less and less on parties; individual politicians sending direct messages to the public, especially on social media, bypassing their parties (Zamir and Rahat, 2019); more independent patterns of behavior of politicians; and the increasing weight of candidates in voting considerations (Rahat, 2019).

As Rahat shows in his chapter in this volume, personalization reached new heights in the 2019–2021 elections. The behavior of politicians and voters in the four elections were highly personalized. For example, since 1999, the Israel National Election Studies (INES, 2021) postelection surveys ask the interviewees what they think the elections were about. The data (see Table 3.8 in Rahat's chapter) clearly show the uniqueness of the last four elections, with 50% and more of the respondents saying that the elections were mainly about Netanyahu. A majority perceived the elections in personal terms, whereas in all previous elections, many more people interpreted the elections in terms of issues. In addition, the very occurrence of holding four elections within two years, and the way the coalition negotiations were conducted by the parties elected to the Knesset testify to the prominence of personal politics at the expense of party politics. The attempt to form a government failed twice: After the third election (2020), a rotation government was formed – a new and unique institution, based on personal logic (which lasted after its establishment only a few months). And after the fourth election, a second rotation government was (barely) established. No explanation other than personal considerations can account for this. It was not a matter of allocation of ministerial portfolios, ideological gaps, short-term or long-term partisan interests. It was mainly personal considerations, first and foremost, those of Netanyahu, the incumbent prime minister throughout the crisis; but also those of the other actors, relating to him primarily. In short, if it were not for the high level of personalization – to which Netanyahu himself has contributed in more than a decade of continuous rule since 2009 – this event would not have occurred.

It is important to emphasize that, contrary to a prevailing view, personalization does not necessarily lead to the hollowing of politics from ideology. Like political parties, individuals can be carriers and markers of ideas and ideologies. Lavi et al. demonstrate in this volume that personification has indeed occurred in Israel, where support or opposition to Netanyahu is strongly linked to democratic values. Similarly, the personal interpretation of the elections among the public and the political community does not mean that the elections were not a competition about policy and values; and this is especially the case with regard to the future of democracy in Israel. We will return to this later.

In the past, the Israeli party system was a dominant party system (until 1977) and then a bipolar competitive system (until the 1990s). Since then, its main feature has been instability (Arian and Shamir, 2002; Hazan, 2021; Shamir, 2016). This characterization is closely related to party decline and political personalization. The 2019–2021 elections confirm, demonstrate, and strengthen this claim. The appropriate term to describe the party system today (and valid since the 1990s) is dealignment. This concept stems from a functional model that evaluates parties and party systems according to their relevance to society and politics. Its characteristics are volatility and unpredictability of election results, and the weakening of parties as institutions and of the ties between parties and voters. In such a system, a party cannot become dominant, even if in some elections the gap between the first and the second largest parties is large, such as in the 2003 election, in which the Likud won 38 seats and the next largest party (Labor) won only 19 seats (Arian and Shamir, 2005). In the first three elections in this cycle, the two blocs competed, neck and neck, with two large lists of similar size, Blue and White and Likud. However, the Blue and White alliance split after the 2020

16 *Michal Shamir and Gideon Rahat*

election. In the 2021 election, the Likud became, once again, the largest party (30 seats) by a considerable margin from the second largest party, Yesh Atid (17 seats).

The main quality of this dealigned third party system is being "nonsystemic." It lacks a stable structure that dictates the nature of the interactions between its components. Not only did this party system look different after each election (except for the three elections in 2019–2020), but also the identity of the large party, when there is only one, was not fixed (Likud, Kadima). And while the Likud was always one of the two largest party lists (except in 2006), four party lists on its left have played this role since 2009: Kadima (2009), Yesh Atid (2013, 2021), the Zionist Camp (2015), and Blue and White (2019–2020).

This instability is made possible by Israel's PR electoral system with a single nationwide constituency, which sets low entrance barriers and facilitates the establishment of new lists (even though the electoral threshold was increased several times since the early 1990s). The instability in the behavior of voters and politicians is related to the mistrust and alienation from the parties, and their weakening as a focal point for identification and as political and social institutions. At the same time, personalization intensifies. Politicians contribute to this trend as more and more of them readily move from party to party, form new parties, and change electoral alliances. Many voters change their vote from one election to another and support new parties that do not live long, and this tendency strengthens over time.. Even the relatively low values of electoral volatility between the three consecutive elections of 2019–2020 (see columns 2 and 3 in Table 1.1) are not low compared to the levels of electoral volatility in nonconsecutive elections in other countries (Shapira and Rahat, 2021).

Of 13 "veteran" parties (founded before 1992), 7 survived since 1992, however, their share of the electoral pie shrunk. In the 2019–2021 elections, these parties shared less than 70 seats. Most of them retained their power or even strengthened somewhat; the bulk of the decline in their combined strength is due to the collapse of Labor and the weakening of Meretz (Kenig and Rahat, forthcoming). Center parties have been prominent among the relatively new parties since the 2000s and particularly since 2006, with the establishment of Kadima. Similarly, in this election cycle, center parties, young (Yesh Atid) and infant (Hosen Yisrael), and their joint list, Blue and White, achieved high electoral support.

Dealignment and instability characterize Israeli parties and party system, with movements of both voters and politicians between parties (Kenig and Tuttnauer, 2017; Nikolenyi, 2020). On the other hand, in terms of blocs, stability is evident (Hazan, 2021). The size of the two political camps, the religious right-wing bloc, and the center-left bloc, is relatively stable. The balance of power within these blocs varies across elections, including the 2019–2021 elections (see Table 1.2 here). This dichotomous division is the meaningful one, and the 2019–2021 elections clearly expressed it. Over time, the blocs

Four Elections in Two Years: A Unique Crisis? 17

became more important than parties, and bloc identification in terms of right and left has become pervasive (Arian and Shamir 2002). Since the disintegration of the dominant party system, it replaced the party identification that parents pass on to their children in the process of political socialization (Ventura, 2001).

The coalition for change that was established at the end of this four-election cycle is very complex in terms of identity and ideology, no less and even more so than the opposition. The unifying element is the opposition to Netanyahu and the governing culture he promoted (at least since his victory in 2015). It is not opposition to policy and values. Some members of the coalition share Netanyahu's views on the judiciary, the balance between the Jewish and democratic dimensions, and certainly his views on foreign affairs and security issues. Right-wing parties in the new coalition hold judicial conservative views (meaning limited intervention and conservative rulings), national-Jewish identity, and hawkish stands concerning Judea and Samaria, no less and even more than the Likud. There is no more convincing evidence of the extreme personalization of Israeli politics than this coalition: It was political personalization that led to its formation. At the same time, only breaking the political-ideological logic enabled Israel to exit (temporarily) from the deadlock of four consecutive elections.

In contrast to the claim of bloc stability, some refer to the center that developed and grew in the last two decades as a third and distinct bloc. Yakter and Tessler (forthcoming) maintain that a center bloc exists, defined on the central cleavage in Israeli politics, the Israeli–Palestinian conflict. According to this interpretation, it would be wrong to talk about bloc stability. This relates to whether the Israeli party system has undergone realignment or dealignment (Arian and Shamir, 2002, 2005; Shamir, 2016). The concept of realignment stems from the social cleavage model and involves fundamental changes in the power of party coalitions and their ideological and social bases. In our view, there has been only one realignment in the Israeli party system, that of 1977. This realignment crystalized in the first half of the 1980s and endures since. The dealignment of the party system has merged with the realignment, and together they define the current party system. A deep and multidimensional cleavage of collective identity that involves policy dilemmas and values with a sociological basis for voting patterns defines this alignment.

This collective identity cleavage has an external and an internal dimension. The external dimension refers to Israel's geographical borders and relations with the world in general, and with the Arabs and the Palestinians in particular. It is expressed through stands on the Israeli–Palestinian conflict, the peace process, and issues of annexation, territorial compromise, and a Palestinian state. The internal dimension of collective identity defines commonalities within the community. It refers to the meaning of Zionism, nationalism, citizenship, religion–state relations, and the tension between a Jewish and democratic state (Shamir and Arian, 1999). Of these two dimensions, the external dimension (about territory and security) is more dominant in

18 *Michal Shamir and Gideon Rahat*

politics. Nationalism and religiosity are the main sociological pillars of the cleavage, and to a lesser extent, ethnicity and class among Jews. Obviously, this alignment is not frozen but dynamic. Levy, Rosenthal, and Saporta's study in this volume exemplifies it when they identify changes in ethnic and class voting. Yakter and Tessler (forthcoming) point to changes and differences in policy positions in light of changing reality. They emphasize the formation of a group of voters they call "Skeptical Doves" prepared in principle to compromise territory, but distrustful of the Palestinian side. They constitute the political center. From our perspective, however, the most significant changes are the increasing importance and momentum of the internal dimension of the collective identity cleavage versus the external one and the shift in emphasis in the internal dimension, where the attitude toward democracy takes precedence over religion and state (Shamir, Dvir-Gvirsman and Ventura, 2017; Talshir, forthcoming). Public discourse, Knesset debates, legislative initiatives, and actual legislation reflect this change, and it was very noticeable in this election cycle. When asked in the INES (2021) postelection surveys what the elections were mostly about, the attitude toward democracy lead over all other policy issues, in all but the first election. We will return to this subject later.

1.5 Institutional Reform: The Rotation Government and the "Norwegian Law"

The political crisis, manifested in the frequent elections, spawned unusual institutional reforms. Because of a lack of trust, the arrangement that Netanyahu and Ganz adopted to form a rotation government following the third election was anchored in Israeli Basic Laws.[1] This arrangement could have been inscribed in a coalition agreement, as was the case in Israel in 1984–1988 and Ireland in 2020. However, it was not a first or unique case where the negotiations over the formation of the government led to changes in basic laws for immediate, more or less worthy, political needs. This practice expresses a lack of respect for constitutional arrangements, typical of Israeli political culture (the Basic Laws are the Constitution in the making). This disrespect is part of what Sprinzak (1986) called a culture of illegality. It does not necessarily negate the rule of law yet does not see it as a supreme principle but rather as a practice that can be ignored. According to Sprinzak, this culture existed in Israel even before the establishment of the state, and is rooted in Jewish tradition that developed in the Diaspora, a tradition of a minority that has to survive facing hostile rulers.

This reform added a new type of government – the rotation government – to the standard one of a government headed by a single prime minister. It is based on an equal distribution of power reflected in the division of the tenure of the two prime ministers, the composition of the government, and even in the ministerial committees. This distribution of power is expressed: (1) In having, in addition to the prime minister, an alternate prime minister who is supposed to replace the incumbent prime minister according to a rotation rule that is enshrined in law. This rotation is not considered a change of government. In other words, the alternate prime minister receives the support of the Knesset for his government in the investiture vote for the government headed by the (first to lead) prime minister and does not need an additional vote upon taking office; (2) Identification of the affiliation of every minister and deputy minister with one of these two prime ministers, who can appoint or dismiss only the ministers that are affiliated with him/her; (3) An equal division of power in government even in a situation where there is no equality in the number of ministers identified with the two prime ministers; (4) In a clear reflection of the mistrust between the parties, the law prevents the replacement of the government without elections by one of the two prime ministers. It also sets additional rules designed to prevent a breach of the rotation agreement.

Netanyahu's rotation government (the 35th government, with Gantz serving as an alternate prime minister) did not survive because it did not pass the state budget (see details in the next chapter). However, the new constitutional structure remained and was reused following the 2021 election to establish another rotation government. This time, the agreement determined that Bennett (who headed a party list of seven seats) would be the prime minister, while Lapid would be the alternate prime minister. The platform prepared to allow Netanyahu to continue to rule served his opponents to seize the prime minister position. It gave them a ready-made mechanism to balance power relations within the government and to obligate the parties to carefully consider their moves before overthrowing the government.

At the same time, and mainly to satisfy political needs, the law known in Israel as the "Norwegian law" was expanded. This alternate member law allows Ministers and Deputy Ministers to resign from the Knesset and vacate their seats, thus allowing additional candidates from their list to become Members of Knesset (MKs). It also guarantees that if they quit the government or are fired, they will return to take their place as MKs.[2] The law was stitched according to the needs of the coalition members, with the formation of the rotation governments of both Netanyahu–Ganz and Bennett–Lapid. It includes complex quotas of resigning Ministers that are derived from the number of seats that parties hold.

Interestingly, these two rules, which originated from an immediate political need under conditions of severe distrust on both sides, brought about an institutional reform that may be desirable and worthy. Even if the existing structure of the rotation government is shaky, and even if the "Norwegian law" is a patchwork, both may be a blessing for Israeli politics in its current state. The rotation government is probably the almost exclusive path (and perhaps preferred over all other alternatives) to forming a government in the polarized and fragmented political situation. Moreover, it brings together conflicting forces and allows them to rule together. In doing so, it creates a consensus government that faces the majoritarian-populist approach that characterized the tenure of the fourth Netanyahu government (2020–2015) and the 2019–2021

20 *Michal Shamir and Gideon Rahat*

election campaigns. It has the elements that Lijphart (2012) identified with a consensus government: mutual veto, autonomy for every political camp, and, even more important, the division of power beyond majority logic. The partial "Norwegian law," which public discourse perceives as simply intended to "provide jobs" for more politicians, is a suitable provision in the opinion of experts, who claim that the Knesset is too small to fulfill its role, especially that of scrutinizing the executive branch (Friedberg and Atmor, 2013).

1.6 The 2019–2021 Elections and the Crisis of Democracy in Israel

Political Science sees elections as central instruments of democracy (Powell, 2000). They are thus particularly appropriate for examining the state of democracies, certainly in an era where the crisis of democracy is widely discussed and claims of democratic backsliding are frequently made. All the more so when it comes to a sequence of four elections within two years. This episode in Israel's political history involved a multidimensional crisis, which was all at once a political, constitutional, and governance crisis.

We identify the background to this crisis in political personalization, especially the centralized type, and party decline. These worsened the problem of the source of political authority since democracy is the rule of law and institutions and not the rule of man; centralized (personal) power collided with (liberal) democracy's stipulation for power dispersion, amidst a political culture characterized by weak norms of governance and disrespect for basic laws and court rulings, in a democracy that lacks a rigid and codified constitution.

The inability to reach a decision, and two years without an elected government most of the time (having a transitional government) and without a functioning government during all of this period, is undoubtedly a cause for concern among supporters of democracy. The repeated attempts and actual change of the rules of the game during the game, in the hope to give victory to one of the sides; and more generally, the behavior of many politicians and political parties during these two years also contribute to such concern.

To all of the above – and not unrelatedly – we should add a populist leader who faces criminal investigations that have matured over the two years into criminal charges and a criminal trial, enslaving the public interest in favor of his personal considerations (see Kremnitzer and Blander; Navot and Goldshmidt in this volume). Netanyahu won substantial support even when he did not achieve the desired electoral victory and challenged key elements of liberal democracy (see Shilon; Navot and Goldshmidt; and Kremnitzer and Blander in this volume). At the peak of the current global populist wave, in the second half of the second decade of the 21st century, Netanyahu was part of a large group of populist leaders who headed democracies (Donald Trump in the United States, Yair Bolsonaro in Brazil, Andrej Babiš in the Czech Republic, Victor Orbán in Hungary, Mateusz Morawiecki in Poland, Narendra Modi in India,) and non-democracies (Vladimir Putin in Russia, Recep Tayyip

Erdoğan in Turkey, Rodrigo Duterte in the Philippines). Netanyahu's loss of his prime ministerial position, along with Trump's election loss and Babiš's downfall, marked the (temporary?) halt of the populist wave.

The ongoing crisis concerned not only the liberal component of Israeli democracy, which was its weaker dimension from its inception. It also touched the majoritarian and formal aspect of democracy, in a similar manner to countries that call themselves illiberal democracies and democracies in the world in general (V-DEM, 2019). A notable example was the refusal of Knesset Speaker Yuli Edelstein in March 2020 to allow the gathering of the Knesset to elect a new Knesset Speaker from the opposing camp. This refusal occurred when his challenger had a majority in the Knesset. In addition, there were attempts to delegitimize the election process, reminiscent of the U.S. 2020 Presidential election. Netanyahu's supporters raised unsubstantiated allegations about ballot fraud, attacked the Central Elections Committee, and raised doubts about the election results. Nevertheless, the attempt to challenge the fairness of the elections and their results did not succeed. According to polls of the Israel Democracy Institute, public trust in the fairness of the elections did not change between February 2019 (just before the first election) and March 2021, shortly after the last election.[3] In the run-up to the September 2019 election, it did drop significantly, following the Likud allegations regarding election fraud and demands to place cameras in the polling stations (see the next chapter). But by the end of this election cycle, confidence in the election process returned to its previous level. Most importantly, throughout the crisis, the possibility of replacing the government other than through democratic elections did not come up at all.

As to the public, we point to several patterns. First, turnout did not decline despite expectations for voters' fatigue. There were even signs of persistent optimism regarding election results and their consequences (Tenenboim-Weinblatt et al., in this volume). Political participation was not limited to election day, and during this period, tens of thousands of citizens took part in the ongoing protests near the prime minister's residence and elsewhere. The restriction of mass protest activity due to the Covid-19 pandemic did not bring its demise. Instead, dozens and even hundreds of small protests arose across the country. Netanyahu's supporters were also in the streets, albeit in much smaller numbers. In the electronic and social media, a polarized discourse intermixed support or opposition to democratic values with support or opposition to Netanyahu. At the same time, the level of public support for democratic values did not decline over these turbulent two years (see Figure 4.1 in Lavi et al. in this volume). However, alarming patterns of personification and politicization of democratic values emerged beneath the surface, where Netanyahu embodied authoritarian, antidemocratic, and anti-liberal values (ibid.).

Much of the contemporary literature on democratic backsliding focuses on political elites, even if it is clear that it is the interaction between political elites and the general public that nurtures this process. The Israeli case

22 *Michal Shamir and Gideon Rahat*

concurs with this focus. In their influential book, written following Trump's election as president of the United States in 2016, Levitsky and Ziblatt argue that "[d]emocratic backsliding today begins at the ballot box" (2018, 5). In our time, they claim, democracies break down through the electoral road, the deed of elected representatives. And such leaders also rise in old and established democracies. The test of these democracies is not in the existence of such leaders, but in preventing them from coming to power, and in case they do, in being able to prevent them from harming democratic institutions. Levitski and Ziblatt assign a special role to political parties and to the commitment to democratic norms of toleration and restraint, beyond political polarization. However, Israel does not excel in these. During 2019–2021, we witnessed the failure to act and the submission of the representative institutions, the Knesset and political parties, in the face of personal politics and concentrated power. Nevertheless, individual politicians and political parties were the ones to halt this intense episode of democratic backsliding in 2021.

1.7 Conclusion

The 36th government of Israel, the Bennett–Lapid "government of change," was sworn in on June 13, 2021. In early November, the Knesset passed the 2021–2022 state budget, the first budget in over three years. This achievement was perceived at the time as cementing the coalition's stability, ensuring its survival and thus putting an end to the two-year-long political crisis. However, a year following its formation, after the coalition lost its bare majority of 61 and with the growing number of rebel MKs within its ranks, the government reached a dead end, and the Knesset dissolved itself, with a new election scheduled for November 1, 2022.

To summarize the two-year severe crisis and its four elections, we emphasize the blending of government instability, constitutional crisis, and accelerated democratic backsliding. Government instability and recurrent elections are not a unique event; neither is democratic backsliding. It is the combination of them that renders this case unusual or extreme. In case study research design terms, our study of the four-election two-year crisis is defined as the extreme case method. It is seen as exploratory, and often serves "as an entrée into a subject, a subject which is subsequently interrogated with a more determinate (less open-ended) method" (Seawright and Gerring, 2008, 302). In this sense we do not regard the Israeli case as unique; such crises are possible in the future, in Israel and in other countries as well. As a matter of fact, given the collapse of the Bennett-Lapid government and the announcement of yet another election, the fifth in four years, one can say that Israel is still within this unfolding political crisis. Therefore, there is much to learn from it. Political scientists should expand the study of severe political crises in democracies through systematic comparative research.

We note that the "government of change" eventually established after the fourth election is also not exclusive to Israel. It was an alliance of political parties and politicians from the right, left, and the center against an incumbent populist leader who was perceived as a danger to democracy. Indeed, essential parts of the coalition see themselves as having mobilized and even compromised to save democracy.[4] We find similar such political alliances against a populist leader likewise perceived as antidemocratic in 2021 in the Czech Republic and in 2022 in Hungary.

The analyses in this volume point to political personalization, and in particular centralized personalization, as a major factor standing behind the political crisis Israel has gone through. It appears to be the best explanation for the recurrent elections and for the unsuccessful or aborted coalition negotiations between them. It is also the crucial factor in accounting for the constitutional crisis and for the nondemocratic moves in the electoral arena and beyond it during this period. The literature on political personalization is concerned with its implications for democracy, with no consensus among scholars. The Israeli case study provides strong evidence for the negative potential of (centralized) political personalization in threatening democracy (see Rahat in this volume; see also Frantz et al., 2021). Its relationship with governmental instability should also be further investigated.

Throughout the crisis, government turnover occurred as a result of elections and coalition agreements, formulated by elected party representatives, as is customary in parliamentary democracy. The Israeli case study points also to the need to study in depth the impact of regime and electoral system variables upon crisis initiation and resolution. On the one hand, most Parliamentary systems, unlike Presidential ones, allow to call early elections, which necessarily makes for shorter duration of governments (commonly regarded as an indicator of government instability). Moreover, the Proportional Representation electoral system that is used in Israel fosters multiparty systems, fragmentation, and coalition governments. On the other hand, one may posit that the flexibility afforded to elected representatives in Israel – a parliamentary regime with the most extreme PR electoral system, which facilitates the establishment of new lists and alliances – helped pave a (temporary) way out of the crisis in 2021. This conjecture is worth pursuing through systematic comparative research.

Coming back to Israeli politics, we point out in closing some subtleties and by-products of the way the political crisis developed. First, the formation of the 2021 rotation government with the support of eight parties from the right and left, including an Arab party, did not change the personalized nature of politics; it only rendered it more decentralized. This means that personalization is still alive and well in Israel, on its wide-ranging manifestations and repercussions. For students of personalization, this opens the way to systematic comparison of the impact of centralized versus noncentralized personalization on different dimensions of politics. Second, while the change in the rules of the game in the form of the rotation government may have been born in sin and for answering immediate political needs, it gave birth to an inherently restrained government, built on a broad agreement, facing a Knesset with somewhat greater ability to act and counterbalance the executive.

24 *Michal Shamir and Gideon Rahat*

Finally, special attention should be given to the inclusion of Ra'am in the coalition. The inability to break the electoral deadlock led Netanyahu to legitimize the participation of an Arab party in government, or at least that the government would rely on its support. This development met at the appropriate timing with the "non-Zionist Israeli identity" of the Arab public and its representatives (see Navot, Swaid, and Khalaily in this volume). Netanyahu's opponents reaped the fruits in what may be a vital step on the way to integrate the Arab citizens into Israeli politics. However, at the time of writing, and following the announcement of another election within four years, it is undoubtedly too early to assess the developments we have surveyed.

Only time will tell where Israeli democracy is headed: Will the consensus government exemplified by the Bennett-Lapid government take hold? Will it allow for reasonable governance? Will the populist wave subside or revitalize? Will personalization be halted, and will the political parties regain a suitable role and status? Will the standing of the Knesset be strengthened and that of the court maintained? Will Israel use the opportunity to integrate Israeli Arabs, or will Israel miss it? The answers depend on what will happen in the world, in the region, and in Israel, but the future of Israeli democracy is in our hands.

Notes

1 The new version of Basic Law: The Government, see: https://m.knesset.gov.il/Activ ity/Legislation/Documents/yesod6.pdf
2 This is an amendment to the Basic Law: The Knesset, which was adopted on June 16, 2020. It was first adopted as a temporary provision and was first implemented during the 20th Knesset (2015–2019). (https://fs.knesset.gov.il/23/law/23_lsr_573 903.pdf).
3 The question that was asked was: "To what extent do you have or do not have trust in the fairness of elections, that is, that the published results will exactly reflect the vote?" (The Israel Democracy Institute, Israeli Voice Index, www.idi.org.il/centers/ 1123/26883).
4 See, for example, Lapid's speech in the Knesset at the special meeting on the 26th anniversary of the assassination of Yitzhak Rabin (https://news.walla.co.il/item/ 3465941).

References

Akzin, Benjamin. 1955. "The Role of Parties in Israeli Democracy." *Journal of Politics* 17 (4): 607–645.
Arian, Asher, and Michal Shamir. 2002. "Candidates, Parties and Blocs." In *The Elections in Israel 1999*, edited by Asher Arian and Michal Shamir, 11–32. Albany: State University of New York Press.
Arian, Asher, and Michal Shamir. 2005. "On Mistaking a Dominant Party in a Dealigning System." In *The Elections in Israel 2003*, edited by Asher Arian and Michal Shamir, 13–32. New Brunswick and London: Transaction Publishers.
Central Elections Committee for the 21st Knesset. 2019. Results of the 21st Knesset elections. https://votes21.bechirot.gov.il [Hebrew].

Central Elections Committee for the 22nd Knesset. 2019. Results of the 22nd Knesset elections. https://votes22.bechirot.gov.il [Hebrew].

Central Elections Committee for the 23rd Knesset. 2020. Results of the 23rd Knesset elections. https://votes23.bechirot.gov.il [Hebrew].

Central Elections Committee for the 24th Knesset. 2021. Results of the 24th Knesset elections. https://votes24.bechirot.gov.il [Hebrew].

Frantz, Erica, Andrea Kendall-Taylor, Carisa Nietsche, and Joseph Wright. 2021. "How Personalist Politics is Changing Democracies." *Journal of Democracy* 32 (3): 94–108.

Friedberg, Chen, and Nir Atmor. 2013. "The Size of Legislatures: How it is Determined, Whether it Changes and Under Which Circumstances." In *Reforming Israel's Political System*, edited by Gideon Rahat, Shlomit Barnea, Chen Friedberg, and Ofer Kenig, 606–630. Jerusalem: The Israel Democracy Institute. [Hebrew].

Hazan, Reuven Y. 2021. "Parties and the Party System of Israel." *In The Oxford Handbook of Israeli Politics and Society*, edited by Reuven Y. Hazan, Alan Dowty, Menachem Hofnung, and Gideon Rahat, 351–366. Oxford: Oxford University Press.

Hoffman-Dishon, Yaron. 2019a. The *21st Knesset Elections: Analysis of the Vote by Socio-Economic Cluster*. Adva Center, April 14, 2019. https://adva.org/he/bchirot2019-socioeconomic/ [Hebrew].

Hoffman-Dishon, Yaron. 2019b. *The 22nd Knesset Elections: Analysis of the Vote by Socio-Economic Cluster of Localities and Neighborhoods*. Adva Center, September 25, 2019. https://adva.org/he/bchirot2019b-socioeconomic/ [Hebrew].

Hoffman-Dishon, Yaron. 2020. *Analysis of the Vote for the 23rd Knesset Elections by Socio-economic Ranking of Localities and Neighborhoods*. Adva Center, March 10, 2020. https://adva.org/he/elections23-social-economic/ [Hebrew].

INES. 2021. Israel National Election Studies www.tau.ac.il/~ines/

Kenig, Ofer, and Gideon Rahat. Forthcoming. *Political Parties in Israel Since 1992*. Jerusalem: The Israel Democracy Institute. [Hebrew].

Kenig, Ofer, and Or Tuttnauer. 2017. "The Decline of the Large Mainstream Parties," In *The Elections in Israel 2015*, edited by Michal Shamir and Gideon Rahat, 21–46. New York: Transaction Publishers.

Knesset. 2015. Press Release, March 31, 2015. https://main.knesset.gov.il/News/PressReleases/Documents/01042014.pdf [Hebrew].

Korn, Dani, ed. 1998. *The Demise of Parties in Israel*. Tel Aviv: Hakibbutz Hameuchad. [Hebrew].

Laakso, Markku, and Rein Taagepera. 1979. "Effective Number of Parties: A Measure with Application to Western Europe." *Comparative Political Studies* 12 (1): 3–27.

Levitsky, Steven, and Daniel Ziblatt. 2018. *How Democracies Die*. New York: Crown.

Lijphart, Arend. 2012. *Patterns of Democracy*, 2nd edition. New Haven: Yale University Press.

Nikolenyi, Csaba. 2020. "The End of Kalanterism? Defections and Government Instability in the Knesset." *Israel Studies* 25 (2): 95–114,

Pedersen, Mogens N. 1979. "The Dynamics of European Party Systems: Changing Patterns of Electoral Volatility." *European Journal of Political Research* 7 (1): 1–26.

Powell, G. Bingham, Jr. 2000. *Elections as Instruments of Democracy*. New Haven: Yale University Press.

Rahat, Gideon. 2019. *The Decline of the Group and the Rise of the Star(s): From Party Politics to Personal Politics*. Jerusalem: The Israel Democracy Institute. [Hebrew].

Michal Shamir and Gideon Rahat

Rahat, Gideon, and Ofer Kenig. 2018. *From Party Politics to Personalized Politics? Party Change and Political Personalization in Democracies.* Oxford: Oxford University Press.

Rahat, Gideon, and Tamir Sheafer. 2007. "The Personalization (s) of Politics: Israel 1949–2003." *Political Communication* 24 (1): 65–80.

Seawright, Jason, and John Gerring. 2008. "Case Selection Techniques in Case Study Research: A Menu of Qualitative and Quantitative Options" *Political Research Quarterly* 61 (2): 294–308.

Shamir, Michal. 2016. "'Ladies and Gentlemen,' Mahapach': The 1977 Realignment from a Political Historical Perspective." In *The Handbook of Israel: The Major Debates*, edited by Eliezer Ben-Rafael, Julius H. Schoeps, Yitzhak Sternberg, and Olaf Glöckner, 479–488. Berlin and Boston: De Gruyter Oldenbourg.

Shamir, Michal, and Asher Arian. 1999. "Collective Identity and Electoral Competition in Israel." *American Political Science Review* 93 (2): 265–277.

Shamir, Michal, Shira Dvir-Gvirsman, and Raphael Ventura. 2017. "Taken Captive by the Collective Identity Cleavage: Left and Right in the 2015 Elections." In *The Elections in Israel 2015*, edited by Michal Shamir and Gideon Rahat, 139–164. New York: Transaction Publishers.

Shapira, Assaf, and Gideon Rahat. 2021. "Electoral Behavior in Israel." In *The Oxford Handbook of Israeli Politics and Society*, edited by Reuven Y. Hazan, Alan Dowty, Menachem Hofnung, and Gideon Rahat, 617–635. Oxford: Oxford University Press.

Sprinzak, Ehud. 1986. *Each One Does as He Sees Fit: Illegalism in Israeli Society.* Tel Aviv: Hapoalim Library. [Hebrew].

Talshir, Gayil, forthcoming. "Which '*Israel Before All*'? From Israeli-Palestinian Conflict to Jewish/Democratic Left-Right Axis" *Israel Affairs.*

The Israeli Voice Index. December 2020. www.idi.org.il/media/15513/israeli_voice_ind ex_2012_heb-final-004.pdf [Hebrew].

The Israeli Voice Index. January 2021. www.idi.org.il/media/15680/israeli_voice_ind ex_2101_heb-final.pdf [Hebrew].

V-DEM. 2019. *Democracy Facing Global Challenges: V-DEM Annual Democracy Report.* https://www.v-dem.net/static/website/files/dr/dr_2019.pdf

Ventura, Raphael. 2001. "Family Political Socialization in Multiparty Systems." *Comparative Political Studies* 34 (6): 666–691.

Yakter, Alon and Mark Tessler. forthcoming. "The Long-Term Electoral Implications of Conflict Escalation: Doubtful Doves and the Breakdown of Israel's Left-Right Dichotomy". *Journal of Peace Research.*

Zamir, Shahaf, and Gideon Rahat. 2019. *Online Political Personalization: A Comparative Study of Parties and Politicians in Israel.* Jerusalem: The Israel Democracy Institute. [Hebrew].

2 The Four Elections 2019–2021

A Chronological Overview

Gideon Rahat and Michal Shamir

The fourth Netanyahu government began its term on May 14, 2015, less than two months after the elections to the 20th Knesset. At its establishment, the government was based on a minimal winning coalition of 61 Members of Knesset (MKs). In addition to the Likud, the coalition included the ultra-Orthodox and religious parties (United Torah Judaism, Shas, and the Jewish Home) and Kulanu, founded by Moshe Kahlon, a former Likud MK and minister. Yisrael Beiteinu (except for MK Orly Levy-Abekasis, who remained in the opposition) entered the coalition in 2016 and widened its base to 66 MKs, until it left in 2018. This government lasted four years between elections and then an additional year as a transitional government.

At the end of 2016, Donald Trump was elected to the presidency of the United States. This had much impact on Israel, both internationally and domestically. Internationally, Netanyahu and his government reaped political achievements when the United States recognized Jerusalem as the capital of Israel (an issue that had been frozen since the UN partition plan in 1947), moved the U.S. embassy to Jerusalem, and recognized Israeli sovereignty over the Golan Heights. Internally, the Basic Law: Israel – the Nation State of the Jewish People was adopted. This controversial law (primarily because it does not include the principle of civic equality) was debated politically for years, but was not promoted, among other reasons, for fear of the American response during Obama's Presidency.

This government was characterized by an acceleration of the movement from a liberal conception of democracy toward a populist one that emphasized the rule of the (Jewish) majority (see Shilon in this volume). The "nation-state law" stood out in particular,[1] but there were various other legislation attempts and laws to that effect. The 20th Knesset accelerated the trend of legislation perceived as restricting democratic freedoms (evident since the 18th Knesset), pertaining to the freedom of speech and legitimacy of civic associations, and a law that allowed the Knesset to remove an incumbent MK by a super-majority of 90 MKs (Fuchs, 2019). Another feature of Netanyahu's fourth term in office as prime minister was the increase in his personalized power and his becoming the undisputed leader of the right-religious bloc. The next five

DOI: 10.4324/9781003267911-3

28 *Gideon Rahat and Michal Shamir*

chapters analyze these processes and their ramifications from various points of view.

The investigations of corruption allegations against Netanyahu (that eventually led to indictments) created a rift between his supporters and opponents. However, the right had a solid majority that could ensure its rule for years to come. It was unclear whether and to what extent these allegations would undermine this majority. For example, the coalition crisis at the end of 2018 did not stem from these allegations. Defense Minister Avigdor Lieberman resigned and his party Yisrael Beiteinu left the coalition amid criticism of Netanyahu's compromising security policy toward Hamas in Gaza and controversy over the conscription of ultra-Orthodox youngsters.

This chapter looks at the four Knesset elections held in the years 2019–2021 chronologically. It examines each election from the moment it was announced through the submission of the candidate lists, the election campaign, election results, and consequent politics of government formation.

2.1 The Elections to the 21st Knesset, April 9, 2019

After Lieberman resigned and Yisrael Beiteinu left the coalition in November 2018, Netanyahu's government was left with a minimal coalition of 61 MKs. In the second half of December 2018, the State Attorney, Shai Nitzan, announced that a recommendation to prosecute Netanyahu for bribery and breach of trust was passed to the Attorney General, Avichai Mandelblit. At the same time, the coalition disagreed on the formula for amending the Military Service Act, which the High Court of Justice ordered the Knesset to amend. On December 24, Prime Minister Benjamin Netanyahu announced that the 21st Knesset election would be held on April 9, 2019. Two days later, the Knesset adopted a law that shortened its term by about seven months and scheduled the new elections.

In almost each of the 45 polls (Hamichlol, 2019a) conducted between the announcement of the election and the submission of the candidate lists, a clear majority emerged for the right-wing religious bloc (that included Likud, the ultra-Orthodox and religious parties, and according to the common perception that was refuted only after the election, also Yisrael Beiteinu). It was short of a majority in several polls in which one or more of its parties failed to pass the electoral threshold. This led to efforts to form party alliances. The competing center and left parties, could not be seen as a coherent bloc. The Arab parties and Hadash were not considered acceptable coalition partners. In addition, the bloc affiliation of Orly Levy-Abekasis's Gesher party was unclear.

Netanyahu was the undisputed leader of Likud. The last time he competed for the Likud leadership was in 2014. Even then (and in general since 2006), no senior politician challenged him. In 2016, the primaries were canceled because no candidate challenged Netanyahu. At the beginning of February 2019, Likud held primaries to choose its Knesset candidates. Several candidates

The Four Elections 2019–2021: A Chronological Overview 29

who did not serve as Likud MKs in the outgoing Knesset won top positions on the list: Yoav Galant of Kulanu, Nir Barkat, former mayor of Jerusalem, and Gideon Sa'ar, who returned to politics. From the day that elections were announced to the Election Day, polls predicted that Likud would win around 30 seats. The comparison with actual election results (the Likud won 35 seats) indicates that voters turned in the last days of the election campaign to support the Likud, the large party in their bloc.

In the run-up to the election, the party alliance that contained the Likud's national-religious partners disintegrated. The Jewish Home leaders Naftali Bennett and Ayelet Shaked left the party and established a new party, The New Right. This shook the balance of power within the Jewish Home alliance, and power sharing was renegotiated with The National Union-Tkuma, the junior partner in the alliance. Far-right Otzma Yehudit and Zehut, founded by Moshe Feiglin (formerly a Likud MK who challenged Netanyahu's leadership several times), joined the race for the national-religious electorate. Fearing that if one or more of them would not pass the electoral threshold, the bloc would be short of a majority, Netanyahu pressured these parties to run on a joint list. Eventually, and through Netanyahu's active mediation, Jewish Home, The National Union-Tkuma, and Otzma Yehudit allied and established the Union of the Right Parties. To facilitate it, Netanyahu took an unprecedented step and allocated one slot in the Likud list to a Jewish Home candidate.

The Jewish Home abandoned the primaries method. Its central committee approved the recommendation of the public council it established to select Rafi Peretz as the party leader and to place another female candidate in a top position; it also selected the additional candidates for the Knesset. Naftali Bennett, who brought the primaries to the Jewish Home, did not stick to it in his new party (The New Right). He and his co-leader, Ayelet Shaked, nominated the party candidates. The central committee of The National Union-Tkuma selected the party leader and the candidates for the Knesset. It ousted its incumbent leader Uri Ariel and replaced him with MK Bezalel Smotrich (German, 2019).

Kulanu was considered to be the moderate partner of the Likud-led coalition. It watered down legislative initiatives aimed to restrict various democratic freedoms and limit the judicial system. Kulanu, perceived as a party with a social message, surprisingly won 10 seats in the 2015 election, and its leader, Moshe Kahlon, served as finance minister. The polls indicated that the party lost its charm and glamor, predicting it to win between 0 and 6 seats. In December 2018, Kulanu experienced the departure of several MKs; Yoav Galant, one of its most prominent members, joined the Likud. However, Kahlon's status as the founding leader was not challenged, and he continued to have full control of the nominations to the candidate list.

For the solid partners of the right-wing religious bloc, the ultra-Orthodox parties Shas and United Torah Judaism (an alliance composed of Agudat Yisrael and Degel HaTorah parties), most polls predicted 4–6 seats and 6–7 seats, respectively. Both did better in the election, winning eight seats each. In these parties, rabbinical councils, influenced by politicians and activists, continued to be the selectors of the leader and the candidates. In Shas, Aryeh Deri established his status as the undisputed party leader. In United Torah Judaism, there were no changes in the identity of the top candidates but the division of slots between Agudat Yisrael and Degel HaTorah changed and became equal.

Yisrael Beiteinu (after the defection of MK Orly Levy-Abekasis) held five seats in the outgoing Knesset. Since the announcement of the election and until the submission of the lists, most polls predicted that it would retain its power or lose one seat. Even though in the last few weeks, many polls indicated that the party would not pass the electoral threshold, it ended up winning five seats and maintained its power. Relying mainly on distinct groups, of immigrants (in the case of Yisrael Beiteinu) and the ultra-Orthodox (United Torah Judaism and Shas), seems to be a key to electoral stability.

Former Yisrael Beiteinu MK Orly Levy-Abekasis established her own party in December 2018. It was named after the Gesher party that her father, David Levy, founded when he defected from Likud in 1995. Like him, she emphasized the social agenda. It was not clear to which bloc Gesher belonged, and Levy-Abekasis herself refrained from clarifying it. It was however common to see her as part of the center-left bloc (which turned out to be a mistake). The first polls after her announcement predicted that Gesher would win 4–6 seats, but over time most of them (correctly) indicated that it would not pass the electoral threshold.

The day after the dissolution of the 20th Knesset, Benny Gantz, former Chief of Staff of the IDF (Israel Defense Forces), registered his party, Hosen Yisrael, with the Parties Registrar. Polls published a week later – when only the leader's identity was known but not who would join the party and what would be its platform – predicted it would win 10–16 seats. This level of support remained stable until the end of January 2019, when Hosen Yisrael allied with Moshe "Bogie" Ya'alon's new party, the National Statist Movement (Telem). This party did not receive much support in the polls but provided Hosen Yisrael with genuine right-wing candidates who in their past were close to Netanyahu (see below). After creating the alliance, the polls indicated an increase in support (19–24 seats). Close to the deadline for submitting the Knesset candidate lists (February 21, 2019), Hosen Yisrael and Telem joined with Yesh Atid into the Blue and White alliance. The polls predicted that Yesh Atid will win between 9–17 seats, less than Hosen Yisrael (Hamichlol, 2019a). But Yesh Atid added to the alliance, as a relatively veteran and established party, a network of activists spread throughout the country. Thus, the places on the candidate list were divided equally between Hosen Yisrael and Yesh Atid. An agreement was also signed between the two party leaders, Gantz and Lapid, stipulating that in the event of an election victory, Gantz would serve first as prime minister and then Lapid would replace him.

The Four Elections 2019–2021: A Chronological Overview   31

The partners in the Blue and White alliance were all personal parties. In Hosen Yisrael, Gantz was the one who determined the composition of the list. Among the personalities that Gantz recruited were Gabi Ashkenazi, also a former IDF Chief of Staff, and Avi Nissenkorn, who served as the chairperson of the Histadrut, Israel's largest federation of workers' unions. Yair Lapid continued to be the undisputed leader of Yesh Atid and to nominate its candidate list, as did Bogie Ya'alon in Telem. Yesh Atid recruited several new candidates who held high ranks in the police (Yoav Segalovich), military (Orna Barbivai), and Mossad (Ram Ben Barak). The prominent candidates in Telem were former close associates of Netanyahu who later became his fierce opponents: Its leader Ya'alon was a Likud defense minister in Netanyahu's government; Zvi Hauser, served as the government secretary (2009–2013); Yoaz Handel served as the Director of Communication and Public Diplomacy in the Prime Minister Office (2011–2012).

In the outgoing Knesset, the Zionist Camp alliance, which included Labor and the Hatnu'a party, held 24 seats. Labor experienced leadership turnover through closed primaries as early as July 2017. The incumbent party chairperson, Yitzhak Herzog, was ousted in the first round of elections, in which none of the candidates received more than the 40% needed to win. In the second round, the two leading candidates from the first round competed: Amir Peretz, who previously served as the party's chairperson (2005–2007), and Avi Gabay, who left Netanyahu's government where he served as a Kulanu representative and joined Labor less than a year before the race. Gabay won and led Labor in the April 2019 election. At the beginning of January 2019, when the polls predicted 9–10 seats for the Zionist camp, Gabay surprisingly announced on a live TV broadcast, standing next to Tzipi Livni, Hatnua's leader, that he ends the partnership with Hatnu'a. Support for Labor did not change after this announcement nor after Hatnu'a announced on February 17 that it would not run in the election as most polls predicted that it would not pass the electoral threshold. On February 11, Labor held primaries for its candidate list. Its members chose two MKs who were former leaders of the 2011 social protest and two former chairpersons for its top places. The party chairperson, Avi Gabay, appointed retired general Tal Russo to the reserved second slot.

Meretz held five seats in the outgoing Knesset. Its leader was Tamar Zandberg, who was selected in primaries that were held in March 2018, after the retirement of former party leader Zehava Galon. The party also used a similar method to select its candidate list for the April 2019 election, and two Arab candidates won the realistic fourth and fifth places.

The Joint List, composed of four parties (Hadash, Ra'am, Balad, and Ta'al), had 13 seats in the outgoing 20th Knesset. Polls predicted that it would sustain its power. Internal disagreements within The Joint List led to its split and the creation of two separate alliances (see the chapter by Navot, Swaid, and Khalaily in this volume). On the day of submitting the candidate lists,

32   *Gideon Rahat and Michal Shamir*

Ta'al and Hadash submitted a joint list, with Ayman Odeh from Hadash at the head and Ahmad Tibi from Ta'al in second place. Balad and Ra'am submitted a joint list, with Ra'am's leader Mansour Abbas at the top, followed by Balad's leader, Mtanes Shehadeh.

Along with the multiplicity of personal parties, the election campaign was also very personal. It was framed as a horse race between the two leading candidates, Prime Minister Netanyahu and Gantz, the contender for the crown. Accusations of corruption against Netanyahu received ample coverage. They became even more central following the Attorney General's announcement that he is considering criminal prosecution on suspicion of bribery, fraud, and breach of trust. The Likud did not consider replacing its leader due to these accusations but adhered to him. Already before the announcement, Likud published the message that "Netanyahu's investigations=an attempt of political assassination." Part of the Likud campaign was devoted to taking a populist line that claimed that there is a systematic persecution campaign of the legal and media elites against the candidate whom most people support and that Netanyahu is innocent (see the chapters by Shilon and by Navot and Goldshmidt in this volume). At the same time, political corruption was not a major issue in the election campaign, neither in the media nor among politicians and the electorate, compared to socioeconomic and security and foreign affairs policies (see the chapter by Zoizner et al.).

As in previous elections, the Central Elections Committee experienced ritualistic attempts to disqualify non-Zionist, Arab, and racist candidates and parties (Shamir and Weinshall-Margel, 2015). The committee disqualified the Ra'am–Balad list and the candidate Ofer Kasif from Hadash–Ta'al. It rejected the requests for the disqualification of Hadash–Ta'al, the Union of the Right Parties, and of Michael Ben-Ari and Itamar Ben-Gvir from Otzma Yehudit. The High Court of Justice, which has the final say, practiced its traditionally liberal doctrine, and disqualified only the candidacy of Michael Ben-Ari from Otzma Yehudit, claiming that "in Dr. Ben-Ari's actions and statements there is an incitement to racism as a dominant and central goal of his doctrine" (Election appeal 1867/19).

According to the polls, the right-wing religious bloc increased its support from 61 seats on the day the candidate lists were submitted to an average of 64.5 seats a few days before the election (Hamichlol, 2019a). The Likud's support was stable during this period and averaged 29 seats. The power of Blue and White averaged 31.5 seats, but a downward trend of a few seats over the period was evident. The polls indicated that the national-religious parties would win an average of 13 seats, Labor 9 seats, and Meretz 5–6. Comparing these predictions to the actual election results indicates that in the last days before the election, when no publication of polls is allowed, the horse race between the Likud and Blue and White (or in the language of personal politics, between Bibi and Gantz) moved voters from small to the large parties within each bloc (amounting to 8 seats on the right and about 5

The Four Elections 2019–2021: A Chronological Overview 33

in the center-left camp). As usual, the polls underestimated the power of the ultra-Orthodox parties and Yisrael Beiteinu.

The ability of small parties to pass the electoral threshold became crucial because it affected the power of the blocs. Most polls were accurate in predicting that Gesher would not pass the electoral threshold, but inaccurate in their prediction that Zehut would pass. And there was a party that all polls predicted would pass the electoral threshold but ended up missing by less than 1,500 votes to overcome it – The New Right. According to the polls, another party alliance, Ra'am–Balad, was also in danger, and indeed it passed the electoral threshold by the hairline. Yisrael Beiteinu, which according to the polls was on the verge of the electoral threshold, won five seats, a result that later turned out to be critical in forming a government.

Likud and Blue and White won 35 seats each (see Table 2.1). Taking a historical perspective, this is a comparatively high number of seats: Not even the victorious list achieved this since the 2003 election, when Likud, led by Ariel Sharon, won 38 seats. The combined number of seats of the two largest party lists, 70, was the highest since 1992. Based on previous election results and INES (2021) polls, those who paid the price were mainly Labor and the national-religious right. A majority of those who voted for Labor in 2015 supported Blue and White in these elections; many of the voters (and potential supporters) of the national-religious right voted for Likud. Kulanu lost much of its support, and some of its previous voters supported Blue and White. In contrast, the ultra-Orthodox parties and Yisrael Beiteinu maintained their power. On the left, Meretz lost its power among Jewish voters, primarily to Blue and White. The Joint List that split into two party alliances lost support mainly due to the decline in Arab turnout, and also, to some extent, to Meretz, which placed Arab candidates close to the top of its candidate list.

The election results looked like a clear-cut victory for Netanyahu. Although two parties from his bloc did not pass the electoral threshold and wasted about 6% of the vote (The New Right and Zehut), there was still a majority of 65 seats for the lists that were perceived to belong to his bloc: Likud, Shas, United Torah Judaism, The Union of Right-Wing Parties, Yisrael Beytenu, and Kulanu.[2] The draw in the number of seats between the Likud and Blue and White stemmed mainly from movements within the center-left camp, not from voters who crossed the lines between blocs.

After the election, all 65 MKs of the right-wing religious bloc, including Yisrael Beiteinu, recommended to the President that Netanyahu should form the government. However, what appeared to be a clear victory for the right-religious bloc led by Likud and Netanyahu did not produce a coalition and a government. Netanyahu was unable to close the gaps between the demands of the ultra-Orthodox parties and those of Yisrael Beiteinu. On May 30, 2019, the extension that Netanyahu received from the President to form a government expired. On the same day, the 21st Knesset passed the law for its dissolution by a majority of 74 MKs from the right-religious bloc, Hadash and the Arab parties, with opposition only from the Zionist parties of the center-left

34 *Gideon Rahat and Michal Shamir*

Table 2.1 Results of the 21st Knesset elections (April 2019)

Party-list name	Votes	Percentage	Seats
Likud	1,140,370	26.46	35
Blue and White	1,125,881	26.13	35
Shas	258,275	5.99	8
United Torah Judaism	249,049	5.78	8
Hadash–Ta'al	193,442	4.49	6
Labor	190,870	4.43	6
Yisrael Beiteinu	173,004	4.01	5
Union of the Right Parties	159,468	3.70	5
Meretz	156,473	3.63	4
Kulanu	152,756	3.54	4
Ra'am–Balad	143,666	3.33	4
The New Right	138,598	3.22	0
Zehut	118,031	2.74	0
Gesher	74,701	1.73	0
Social Security	4,618	0.11	0
Arab List	4,135	0.10	0
Social Justice	3,843	0.09	0
Magen	3,394	0.08	0
Justice for All	3,281	0.08	0
Tzomet	2,417	0.06	0
Yashar	1,438	0.03	0
Our rights in our Voice	1,316	0.03	0
Veteran Citizens	1,168	0.03	0
Kol Yisrael Achim	1,140	0.03	0
Pirates	819	0.02	0
Just Love	733	0.02	0
Eretz Yisrael Shelanu	701	0.02	0
N Nach	624	0.01	0
From the Beginning	603	0.01	0
Hope for Change	562	0.01	0
Green Economy	556	0.01	0
Education	518	0.01	0
Responsibility for the Founders	428	0.01	0
Men Dignity	404	0.01	0
Equals	401	0.01	0
Social Leadership	385	0.01	0
You and Me	368	0.01	0
Biblical bloc	353	0.01	0
Ichud Bnei Habrit	265	0.01	0
Brit Olam	216	0.01	0
New Horizon	0	0.00	0
Together	0	0.00	0
Reform Party	0	0.00	0

Source: Central Elections Committee for the 21st Knesset, 2019.

Note: 6,339,729 eligible voters; number of votes: 4,340,253; valid votes: 4,309,270; disqualified votes: 30,983; turnout: 68.46%.

camp. For the first time in the history of Israel, the elections did not lead to the formation of a government, and the Knesset decided to dissolve itself about a month after its inauguration. As a result, the President was denied the possibility of allotting the mandate to form a government to another MK. The transitional government that served from the end of the 20th Knesset continued to serve throughout the tenure of the 21st Knesset.

2.2 The Elections to the 22nd Knesset, September 17, 2019

With the decision to hold new elections, Netanyahu reshuffled his transitional government. He fired ministers Naftali Bennett and Ayelet Shaked who were not elected to the 21st Knesset because their New Right party did not pass the electoral threshold. He nominated a minister from his own party as the minister of justice and allotted two ministries to the representatives of the national religious parties.

In the run-up to the September 2019 elections, the parties demonstrated their ability to learn their lessons. They established alliances (see Shapira's article in this volume) and candidates joined larger parties in the face of failures to cross the electoral threshold (The New Right, Zehut, Gesher). Parties such as Ra'am–Balad, Kulanu, and Meretz, which experienced dangerous proximity to the electoral threshold, established new alliances. Already at the end of May, Kulanu allied with the Likud. Its candidates, except for one, were nominated as Likud candidates. Hadash and the Arab parties (Ra'am, Balad, Ta'al) succeeded to reach an agreement on running in a joint list, as in the 2015 election (see Navot, Swaid and Khalaily in this volume). Gesher created a joint list with Labor. At the same time, Meretz added Stav Shafir, a reinforcement actress from the Labor Party who ran on behalf of the Green Movement Party, and Yair Golan, a former IDF Deputy Chief of Staff, who ran on behalf of Democratic Israel. This alliance was called the Democratic Camp. Netanyahu managed to convince Zehut to withdraw from competing in the elections in exchange for his promise to nominate its leader, Moshe Feiglin, as a minister and to fulfill several additional requirements. Four parties of the national-religious right (The Jewish Home, The National Union-Tkuma, The New Right, and Otzma Yehudit) negotiated to establish a joint list. The negotiations ended in a tripartite alliance (Yemina) that did not include the extreme partner, Otzma Yehudit. Ayelet Shaked, a non-religious woman, was placed at the head of this national-religious right-wing alliance.

Most parties did not replace their leaders nor their candidate lists ahead of the forthcoming election. While Labor froze its list (yet two of its MKs retired), the resignation of its leader Gabay, following what was perceived as an electoral failure, opened a competition for his position. Amir Peretz, who previously served as party leader, won in his contest with two of the veterans of the 2011 social protest, Itzik Shmuli and Stav Shafir. Meretz held internal elections for the party leader and candidate list, this time by the delegates of the party conference and not by the party members. MK

Nitzan Horowitz ousted the incumbent leader, Tamar Zandberg. Non-Jewish candidates won this time lower positions on the list, which contributed (along with the reestablishment of The Joint List) to a sharp decline in Arab support for the party.

Election polls (Hamichlol, 2019b) indicated that competition focuses again on Likud and Blue and White. Support for the ultra-Orthodox parties, Shas, and the United Torah Judaism, remained stable. This was the case also for Labor, with no apparent sign that running together with Gesher increased its support. As in the previous election, the religious right-wing alliance, Yemina, and the Democratic Camp, led by Meretz, lost support as the election approached. Otzma Yehudit shuffled around the electoral threshold, and according to most polls, was not expected to pass it. The polls predicted that Yisrael Beiteinu, who chose a new path and announced that it would support a unity government without the ultra-Orthodox parties, would increase its support to 10–11 seats. Eventually, its support grew to 8 seats. It was also evident that the alliance of Hadash and the Arab parties, The Joint List, was growing stronger.

In the election campaign, Blue and White highlighted the criminal allegations against Netanyahu. Lieberman and Yisrael Beiteinu raised issues of religion and state. Netanyahu, for his part, tried, along with dismissing the accusations against him, to create a foreign affairs-security agenda. He declared his intention to apply Israeli sovereignty over the Jordan Valley and the northern Dead Sea, claiming that this was a "one-time opportunity" to do so. At the same time, as in the first election campaign, the most critical issues on the public's agenda remained the socioeconomic issues, followed by foreign affairs and security. The issue of corruption was far behind, as were state and religion issues, and this was also reflected in the media agenda (Zoizner et al., this volume).

During the election campaign, the Likud, apparently due to the revitalization of the Arab sector following the reestablishment of The Joint List, tried to promote quick legislation that would allow placing cameras at the polling stations, claiming that this would ensure the integrity of the election. The counterclaim was that the initiative intended to suppress the Arab vote. The Knesset rejected the bill, but the Central Elections Committee responded to the call to ensure election integrity when it recruited 3,000 cameras-equipped inspectors to tour the polls during Election Day.

In the run-up to these elections, an attempt was made in the Central Elections Committee to disqualify The Joint List and the far-right party Otzma Yehudit and some of its candidates. The High Court of Justice (Election Appeal 5487/19; Election Appeal 5506/19) qualified the parties but disqualified two of the candidates of Otzma Yehudit, Baruch Marzel and Ben-Zion Gopstein, accepting the claims that they were indeed racist.

The results of the September 17, 2019 elections (Table 2.2) were not much different from those of April 2019. Blue and White and the Likud won similar support (this time Blue and White had slightly more votes), and with

The Four Elections 2019–2021: A Chronological Overview 37

Table 2.2 Results of the 22nd Knesset elections (September 2019)

Party-list name	Votes	Percentage	Seats
Blue and White	1,151,214	25.95	33
Likud	1,113,617	25.10	32
Joint List	470,211	10.60	13
Shas	330,199	7.44	9
Yisrael Beiteinu	310,154	6.99	8
United Torah Judaism	268,775	6.06	7
Yemina	260,655	5.87	7
Labor–Gesher	212,782	4.80	6
The Democratic Camp	192,495	4.34	5
Otzma Yehudit	83,609	1.88	0
Tzomet	14,805	0.33	0
Popular Unity	5,946	0.13	0
Red and White	4,358	0.10	0
Justice	3,053	0.07	0
The Secular Right	2,395	0.05	0
Respect and Equality	1,545	0.03	0
Our Rights in Our Voice	1,473	0.03	0
Pirates	1,236	0.03	0
Economic Power	1,193	0.03	0
Progressive	1,033	0.02	0
Kama	994	0.02	0
New Order	928	0.02	0
Democtatura Party	736	0.02	0
North	725	0.02	0
The Christian Liberal Movement	610	0.01	0
Daa'm	592	0.01	0
Man Dignity	542	0.01	0
Biblical Bloc	497	0.01	0
Social Leadership	434	0.01	0
Zehut	0	0.00	0
Kol Yisrael Ahim	0	0.00	0
Noam	0	0.00	0

Source: Central Elections Committee for the 22nd Knesset, 2019.

Note: 6,394,030 eligible voters; number of votes: 4,465,168; valid votes: 4,436,806; disqualified votes: 28,362; turnout: 69.83%.

more than 30 seats each, they finished again as the two major parties. The status of kingmaker was this time even more clearly in Lieberman's hands. His party, Yisrael Beiteinu won eight seats and could provide a majority for the right or the center-left (if such a possibility existed in the face of the reluctance to cooperate with The Joint List). Running together under the banner of The Joint List significantly enhanced the power of Hadash and the Arab parties. This stemmed from the large increase in Arab turnout and a further decrease in the vote for the Zionist left parties (for details, see Navot, Swaid, and Khalaily in this volume). The two Jewish left-wing parties, Meretz and Labor, did not increase their power despite their running in alliances. The ultra-Orthodox parties achieved similar results as in the previous election, while Yemina, the national-religious alliance (whose composition was supposed to improve the sector and the bloc achievements) weakened. In terms of the power balance between the camps, the middle of the political map, the 60th and 61st seats, moved left in this election, falling into the hands of Yisrael Beiteinu, in particular due to the increase in the support for The Joint List.

The INES (2021) September 2019 election data reveal high stability of the vote for the party alliance of the Arab and Hadash lists and the ultra-Orthodox Shas and United Torah Judaism; over 70% stability in the vote for the Likud and Blue and White; and stability of about two-thirds in the vote for Meretz/the Democratic Camp and the national-religious right parties. Many votes passed to and from Labor–Gesher (to and from Blue and White) as only a third of Labor voters in the April election continued to vote for it. The alliances of Likud with Kulanu and Zehut and of Labor with Gesher did not pay off. The voters of Zehut, Kulanu, and Gesher in the previous election were highly volatile and dispersed among various parties, even in the competing bloc. Thus, if the Likud and Kulanu won 39 seats combined in April 2019, in September, when they ran in an alliance, they won only 32. As to the other parties, the characteristic stability of the blocs was evident, and vote transitions occurred primarily between parties within the blocs.

Fifty-five MKs (Likud, Shas, United Torah Judaism, and Yemina) recommended to the president that Netanyahu form the government, while 54 MKs (Blue and White, Labor-Gesher, the Democratic camp, and The Joint List except for three MKs from Balad) recommended Gantz. Yisrael Beiteinu and the three Balad MKs from The Joint List refrained from recommending a preferred candidate. The President decided to nominate Netanyahu to form a government, but he (who at the time faced a hearing concerning the corruption allegations against him) failed to form a government, and after a month the task was handed to Gantz, who also failed. After failing to identify another MK who could fulfill the task, the Knesset automatically disbanded. Israel again faced new elections. While the composition of the Knesset changed, the 34th government, which began its term in 2015, continued to rule as a transitional government. The elections for the 23rd Knesset were scheduled for March 2, 2020.

2.3 The Elections to the 23rd Knesset, March 2, 2020

Political personalism and the fluidity of the party system continued to be salient features also in the third election (see Rahat and also Shapira, in this volume). Immediately after the September 2019 election, the Yemina Knesset faction split into its components (Jewish Home, National Union-Tkuma and The New Right). In light of the danger of not passing the electoral threshold and wasting votes, there was a need to recreate a party alliance for the

The Four Elections 2019–2021: A Chronological Overview 39

religious right-wing parties. The negotiations between them ended only about an hour before the deadline for submitting the lists to the Central Elections Committee. The Jewish Home announced that it would join the alliance, canceling an early agreement to run jointly with Otzma Yehudit. The latter ended up running, again, independently. On the other side of the political map, the Democratic Camp alliance ceased to exist in December 2019, following the retirement of Stav Shafir from the list and the transfer of Yair Golan from Democratic Israel to Meretz. In January 2020, the Labor–Gesher alliance and Meretz, given their dangerous proximity to the electoral threshold, announced a joint run.

In general, the parties froze their candidate list and did not conduct contests for their leadership. The Likud remained with the same list, except for the retirement of Moshe Kahlon, the former finance minister, and the inclusion of Gadi Yabarkan who defected from Blue and White. Likud recruited Yabarkan, an immigrant from Ethiopia, hoping to draw the support of Ethiopian immigrants after many of them voted Blue and White in the September 2019 election in protest of police violence against members of their community. To strengthen Netanyahu's legitimacy and stir up the grassroots, Likud conducted primaries for the party leadership on December 26. Netanyahu defeated Gideon Sa'ar by a considerable margin (73% to 27%). Lapid, in a move that was supposed to strengthen Blue and White, announced that he gives up on his rotation agreement with Gantz, leaving him as the sole candidate for prime minister.

Until the submission of the candidate lists, the polls (Hamichlol, 2020) indicated stability in the support for Likud and a slight increase in that of Blue and White, apparently at the expense of the parties on its left. The strength of the ultra-Orthodox parties, Yisrael Beiteinu and The Joint List also seemed stable.

The election campaign continued to be focused on the criminal allegations against Netanyahu (Navot and Goldshmidt in this volume). On January 28, 2020, when the Knesset plenary session was scheduled to decide on the establishment of a committee to discuss Netanyahu's request for immunity, and while he was in the United States ahead of the publication of President Donald Trump's peace plan, he withdrew his immunity request. On the same day, the Attorney General, Mandelblit, filed the indictment against Netanyahu for bribery, fraud, and breach of trust in the Jerusalem District Court. Netanyahu's critics claimed that he withdrew the request because he did not have a majority in the Knesset to approve it. Netanyahu claimed that he did so because he could not get a fair chance to present his case and did not want to harm President Trump's "Deal of the Century." His announcement came hours before the publication of U.S. President Donald Trump's political program. It demonstrated how the election campaign was a mix of foreign policy, domestic policy, diplomatic, political, and personal-judicial issues and considerations.

U.S. President Trump presented his peace plan, the "Deal of the Century," at the White House in the presence of Prime Minister Benjamin Netanyahu. It

40   *Gideon Rahat and Michal Shamir*

instilled hope in the right wing for promoting unilateral annexation of 30% of the West Bank, while the danger that the Palestinians would get 70% of it as part of the plan was seen as improbable because the Palestinians rejected the plan. The center received it with mixed feelings because, although it addressed Israeli interests, it did not seem applicable given the Palestinian solid opposition. The left opposed the plan, claiming that it ignored Palestinian stands and interests. Despite the publication of the peace plan during the election campaign, there was no noticeable increase in foreign and security issues on the public and media agendas (See Zoizner et al., this volume).

As before, attempts were made to disqualify candidates for the Knesset at the Central Elections Committee. The High Court of Justice (Election Appeal 852/20; Election Appeal 922/20) decided not to disqualify the party of the wife of Yigal Amir, Prime Minister Yitzhak Rabin's assassin. A majority of 5 to 4 barely approved Hiba Yazbek's (Balad) candidacy.

Two difficulties arose in the administration of these elections. One was breaches of privacy. In February 2020, an information security breach was discovered in an application that the Likud used to store the list of voters. A few days later, another loophole was uncovered that allowed access to the complete database of the Israeli electorate. The second difficulty was the outbreak of the Covid-19 pandemic. A solution had to be found to allow the few thousands ill and quarantined citizens to exercise their right to vote.

Election polls conducted from the date of submission of the candidate lists until the date of the election (Hamichlol, 2020) again indicated a close competition between Blue and White and Likud (each expected to win 31–36 seats). The ultra-Orthodox parties and Yisrael Beiteinu demonstrated stability. In all polls, there was no majority for the bloc that supported Netanyahu. However, the unwillingness of the right within the bloc opposing Netanyahu to form a government with the support of The Joint List meant that it would also be unable to form a government.

On March 2, 2020, the Likud won a significant electoral achievement with 36 seats (Table 2.3). Since the 2003 election – in which the Likud (with Ariel Sharon at its head) won 38 seats – it did not reach such an achievement. It was also the largest number of votes the Likud ever won. This accomplishment was attributed mainly to Netanyahu's election campaign, which included many meetings with voters in various parts of the country, and to the energy that the Likud gained from conducting its internal leadership selection. The bloc that supported Netanyahu increased its representation by 3 seats to 58 seats, still short of the needed majority, while the bloc that opposed him won 62 seats.[3] The Joint List gained two seats, mainly due to a further increase in Arab turnout (Rudnitzky, 2020). The ultra-Orthodox lists maintained their power, while Yisrael Beiteinu, which emphasized its anti-ultra-Orthodox approach, lost some of its support. The right-wing religious Yemina alliance and the left-wing alliance of Labor, Gesher, and Meretz, lost support. Their potential votes were again "sucked in" by the large parties in their bloc, Likud and Blue and White, respectively.

Table 2.3 Results of the 23rd Knesset elections (March 2020)

Party-list name	Votes	Percentage	Seats
Likud	1,352,449	29.46	36
Blue and White	1,220,381	26.59	33
Joint List	581,507	12.67	15
Shas	352,853	7.69	9
United Torah Judaism	274,437	5.98	7
Labor–Gesher–Meretz	267,480	5.83	7
Yisrael Beiteinu	263,365	5.74	7
Yemina	240,689	5.24	6
Otzma Yehudit	19,402	0.42	0
Liberal Power	3,781	0.08	0
Voice of Women	2,773	0.06	0
Pirates	1,473	0.03	0
Mishpat Tzedek	1,375	0.03	0
Israelist	980	0.02	0
I and You	812	0.02	0
Union of Alliance and Partnership	677	0.01	0
New Order	677	0.01	0
The Power to Influence	667	0.01	0
Progressive	622	0.01	0
Daa'm	612	0.01	0
The Jewish Heart	516	0.01	0
Shma	442	0.01	0
The Biblical Bloc	389	0.01	0
Kama	350	0.01	0
Red and White	342	0.01	0
The Vision	308	0.01	0
Social Leadership	271	0.01	0
Human Dignity	222	0.00	0
Action for Israel	210	0.00	0
Tzomet	0	0.00	0

Source: Central Elections Committee for the 23rd Knesset, 2020.

Note: 6,453,255 eligible voters; number of votes: 4,615,135; valid votes: 4,590,062; disqualified votes: 25,073; turnout: 71.52%.

Contrary to expectations for "voter fatigue" (but in line with the electorate's optimism that Tenenboim-Weinblatt et al. found, see in this volume), there was a further increase in turnout. A learning process was evident in the decline in wasted votes – the votes given to parties that fail to pass the electoral threshold. Party lists that failed to pass the electoral threshold got less than 1% of the vote, the lowest in the history of Israeli elections (see Shamir and Rahat in this volume).

According to the INES (2021) surveys, the patterns of electoral volatility between the September 2019 and March 2020 elections remained similar to those of the previous elections: very high stability for The Joint List and the ultra-Orthodox parties and high stability for Likud, with 85% of its voters

42 *Gideon Rahat and Michal Shamir*

in September 2019 declaring that they stayed loyal. Among Blue and White voters, about 75% remained loyal, but it is worth noting that a small but significant portion of about 8% stated that they decided to support Likud. In the other parties, the level of loyalty was lower. In these elections, in which Kulanu, Zehut, and Gesher did not run independently, very few voters crossed the lines between the blocs, and when they did, they mainly crossed to the right.

After consulting the parties, the President assigned the government formation to Gantz, who was recommended by 61 MKs (compared to 58 for Netanyahu). In a surprising move, Gantz formed a unity government that included Netanyahu, the Likud, and most of its allies. Many voters of the center-left bloc, for whom the election was a referendum for and against Netanyahu, perceived this move as a breach of promise. At the same time, this act also received a great deal of support due to several reasons: the fatigue after three consecutive elections without decision; the understanding that the bloc that recommended Gantz would be unable to form a stable government because it included non-Zionist/Arab and right leaning parties; and the challenge of the Covid-19 pandemic that was predicted to cause severe health and economic crises. Thus, while not falling in line with the prevailing right-left cleavage, the two sides could justify their joint government in the name of an emergency.

This development undermined the political blocs and changed the composition of the party alliances in the Knesset. It even led to splits and defections within party alliances and parties in the bloc of Netanyahu's opponents.[4] On March 29, Telem and Yesh Atid split from the Blue and White alliance and merged into one faction. At the same time, Yoaz Handel and Zvi Hauser from Telem defected and established a new faction (Derech Eretz). On April 6, the Labor–Meretz faction split into two separate factions.

After feverish coalition talks, a new government came to power on May 17. It was a unity government established in the name of the emergency that the Covid-19 pandemic caused. It was based on arrangements to ensure mutual veto and parity despite the size differences between its components. The government included from the right-religious bloc, in addition to Likud, the ultra-Orthodox parties, Shas and United Torah Judaism, Gesher that crossed sides, and Rafi Peretz from The Jewish Home. From this bloc, only the representatives of The New Right and The National Union-Tkuma remained in opposition. Of the bloc that opposed Netanyahu, 15 MKs from Hosen Yisrael joined the government coalition (except for one MK who joined the Yesh Atid faction, plus one Yesh Atid MK who joined Hosen Yisrael), and also Derech Eretz (two MKs) and Labor (three MKs). The lack of trust between the parties led to the creation of a new mechanism, a "rotation government," and its anchoring in amendments to Basic Law: The Government. These amendments intended to entrench the coalition agreement between the sides, even without numerical equality, including a mutual veto, determination of a special status for an "alternate prime minister," and an attempt

The Four Elections 2019–2021: A Chronological Overview   43

to ensure that the parties have no interest in violating the prime ministers rotation agreement. Netanyahu was to serve as prime minister for 18 months, to be followed by Gantz as prime minister for the next 18 months (see also Shamir and Rahat in this volume).

2.4 The Elections to the 24th Knesset, March 23, 2021

The pairing between Netanyahu and Gantz in the framework of the rotation government failed. From its inception, it was burdened by difficulties and disagreements in matters of appointments to senior positions and of policy. For example, on the day that the new government met for the first time, Netanyahu and senior Likud officials appeared in court at the opening of his trial, and attacked the prosecution and the media, which Gantz and Blue and White claimed to defend. After a six-month term, following the failure to pass a state budget (and after a compromise that postponed the deadline for its submission by four months, which required another amendment of the Basic Law: The Knesset), new elections were scheduled. The "rotation government" became a transitional government.

The fourth election within two years focused again on Netanyahu's continued tenure as prime minister. But the battleground for these elections was different this time. The Netanyahu camp (the Likud and its loyal allies, ultra-Orthodox United Torah Judaism and Shas, and the alliance of religious Zionist parties) did not face a challenge from a large party list. Rather, several parties and joint lists challenged it from the right, center, and left. From the right came a challenge from Gideon Sa'ar, who founded a new right-wing party called New Hope (Tikva Hadasha). It consisted of three MKs from the Likud, two MKs from Derech Eretz (who retired from Boogie Ya'alon's Telem, when they joined the Netanyahu-Gantz government), and other personalities (including former MK Benny Begin, son of the legendary Likud leader, Menachem Begin). Yemina, led by Naftali Bennett, ran as a government alternative, receiving support from The Jewish Home, which refrained from running in this election. New Hope and Sa'ar pledged in the election campaign that they would not join a Netanyahu-led government. Bennett and Yemina committed to refrain from supporting a center-left government. Lieberman and Yisrael Beiteinu continued to hold right-wing positions on foreign affairs and security issues but belonged to the camp that challenged Netanyahu in light of their opposition to his continued tenure and their stern positions regarding the participation of the ultra-Orthodox parties in the government.

Gantz, the alternate prime minister, headed the Blue-and-White list. Many prominent politicians withdrew from his party, including former IDF Chief of Staff, Gabi Ashkenazi, who had served as foreign minister, and Avi Nissenkorn, who had served as justice minister in the short-lived rotation government.[5] Telem withdrew after the polls showed that it did not pass the electoral threshold. Yesh Atid ran with no partners this time, presenting its leader, Yair Lapid, as the main alternative of the center-left bloc. The alliance

44   Gideon Rahat and Michal Shamir

between Labor and Meretz disintegrated, and the two parties decided to run separately. The Joint List also disintegrated, when Ra'am decided to run on its own, while its other three components (Hadash, Ta'al, and Balad) remained together. Several other ventures arose during this election campaign as part of the challenge to Netanyahu. One of them was headed by Tel Aviv mayor Ron Huldai, who decided not to run after the polls indicated that his venture was doomed to fail. The polls initially predicted him to win 8–9 seats, but when the time came to submit his party list, they indicated that he would not pass the electoral threshold and would thus hurt the bloc of Netanyahu's opponents. Another venture was that of MK Ofer Shelach. After the rejection of his demand for an internal contest for the leadership of Yesh Atid, he established a new party. Eventually, he refrained from running in the election after failing to gain sufficient support. Yaron Zelicha ran on the economic ticket (like Moshe Kahlon and Kulanu in 2015); he refused to withdraw although the polls consistently indicated that he would not pass the electoral threshold. He ended up receiving less than 1% of the vote, wasting about 35,000 votes.

Most parties' candidate lists stayed intact, and only Labor and Balad conducted contests for party leadership. Labor used a very open primaries method, in which thousands of members could join just a few days before the selection contest. It selected a new leader, Merav Michaeli, and a new list for the Knesset. Two representatives of the party, Peretz and Shmuli, who joined the Netanyahu–Gantz government and served as ministers, resigned from the party when it decided to leave the government. In Balad, the party center replaced its chairman, Mtanes Shehadeh, with Sami Abu Shehadeh. The few significant changes in the candidate lists resulted from retirements and defections of several senior members of Blue and White who criticized the foundation and conduct of the rotation government. In Yesh Atid, Lapid recruited new candidates, some of them defectors from Hosen Yisrael. At the same time, one of the party's senior members, Ofer Shelach, resigned due to Lapid's refusal to compete for party leadership. In Likud, Netanyahu nominated several candidates, including Orly Levy-Abekasis from Gesher (who joined Likud) and Ofir Sofer, a candidate from the Religious Zionist alliance. This last nomination was part of the deal with The National Union-Tkuma party that agreed in return to run in a joint list with two other far-right parties, Otzma Yehudit and the anti-LGBT and anti-feminist Noam. Meretz reserved a slot for a female Arab candidate, hoping to attract Arab votes, to no avail. In United Torah Judaism, a "revolution" occurred when Degel HaTorah, a junior partner in the alliance, became its senior partner. Not only that it got half of the list slots, but its candidates appeared first in every pair of candidates. In the parties that Sa'ar, Huldai, and Zelicha formed, there were no internal elections; the party leader determined the composition of the candidate lists.

The fourth election took place amid the Covid-19 pandemic. It affected the agenda of the election campaign and the work of the Central Elections Committee, especially its preparations for Election Day. In terms of the agenda, socioeconomic issues, in particular in the context of the Covid-19, came up at the expense of foreign affairs and security issues, and there was an exceptionally high overlap between the agendas of the public, the media, and the politicians (Zoizner et al., this volume). At the same time, the election campaign focused again on Netanyahu. He emphasized his success in leading Israel to achieve the highest anti-Covid-19 vaccination rate in the world, in addition to his other achievements that included normalization and peace agreements with Arab countries ("Abraham Agreements"). The ultra-Orthodox parties emphasized their support for Netanyahu; they claimed that a vote for them was a vote for Netanyahu plus an emphasis on the state's Jewish character. Netanyahu's opponents continued to address his criminal charges. They also criticized his Covid-19 policy – especially the selective enforcement of the imposed restrictions, aspects of the economic policy, and the failure to control entry to Israel. Netanyahu tried to focus the election campaign on a single rival candidate, Yair Lapid. He wanted to have a focused personal and negative campaign against a single main rival like his previous election campaigns. However, this strategy failed because he faced additional personal challenges from within his ideological camp, from both Sa'ar and Bennett.

Another significant change in the fourth round of elections was the change in Netanyahu's approach to the Arab population. Instead of presenting them as archenemies, he tried to address them and gain their vote. He visited Arab localities and made promises for programs and budgets for pressing issues, such as crime eradication. He also met with the leader of Raa'm, Mansour Abbas, in order to establish a possible coalition pact. These developments fit the climate of opinion that developed among many Arab citizens who wanted to take a more influential part in the political game (see Navot, Swaid, and Khalaily, this volume). This change of mindset matured after the election and was expressed in the attempts of the two camps to form a coalition with the support of Arab MKs and in the composition of the coalition that was eventually formed (ironically, by Netanyahu's rivals, who could credit him for legitimizing this move).

In the polls conducted until the submission of the candidate lists (Hamichlol, 2021), Likud support declined compared to previous elections, from 36 to about 30 seats and even less. Yesh Atid, which left the Blue and White alliance with the joining of Hosen Yisrael Netanyahu's rotation government, maintained its power, which stood at about 15 seats. Following Arab disappointment with the inability of The Joint List to utilize its power and influence government formation, polls predicted that The Joint List would decline from 15 to about 10 seats. Shas, United Torah Judaism, and Yisrael Beiteinu once again enjoyed stable support. The challengers from the right, New Hope and Yemina, started off with 14–21 and 10–14 seats in the polls, respectively. Fragmentation and the more or less equal power of the camps of Netanyahu's opponents and supporters, focused interest once more in the predictions concerning parties that would fail to pass the electoral threshold.

46 Gideon Rahat and Michal Shamir

The polls indicated that there were several parties very close to the electoral threshold, and others failing to pass it. The religious Zionist parties were in such danger, and Netanyahu pressured them to run together, (again) reserving a place for their candidate on Likud's list. Labor did not pass the electoral threshold in any poll until it held internal elections, replaced its leader, and elected a new candidate list. From that moment on, it moved away from the electoral threshold. Meretz was still close to this danger at the time.

Central Elections Committee members attempted again to disqualify lists and candidates. The change in Netanyahu's orientation toward the Arab voters seemingly led to a change in the effort to disqualify their lists by the majority of the representatives of the right-wing parties in the Committee. The only motion for dismissal that reached the High Court of Justice concerned a candidate from Labor, Ibtisam Mara'ana-Menuhin; eight judges to one rejected this disqualification.

In polls conducted after the submission of the lists (Hamichlol, 2021), support for Likud remained stable, around 28 seats, as was that of Yesh Atid, the largest party in the opposing camp (around 17 seats). Support for Shas (about 8 seats), United Torah Judaism and Yisrael Beiteinu (about 7 seats) also remained stable. Polls predicted that Labor would win around 6 seats. The Religious Zionism alliance (which included The National Union-Tkuma, Otzma Yehudit, and Noam), Meretz, and especially Ra'am seemed to be close to the electoral threshold. New Hope suffered from decline in the polls during this period, from about 15 seats to less than 10. Yemina also dropped from 12 seats to less than 10. The Joint List declined from 9–10 seats in the more optimistic polls at the beginning of the period to only 7 on election eve.

If in the March 2020 election, the Covid-19 pandemic was in its infancy, in the March 2021 election, this was a much more acute problem, especially in the administration of Election Day. This led to an increase of the election budget by 50%. It was used, among other things, to increase the number of polling stations to about 15,000 (from about 11,000 in previous elections). These included regular polling stations intended to reduce turnout queues, polling stations in hospitals and sheltered housing, and unique and separate polling stations for quarantined and infected citizens (Kenig, 2021).

During the vote count, groups of Netanyahu's supporters (including his son) claimed that members of the Central Elections Committee falsified election results to harm Netanyahu. These were similar claims to those raised by Trump and his supporters in the United States. These claims, however, did not find many believers. The general view of the election conduct under the shadow of the Covid-19 pandemic was positive (Kenig, 2021).

With the publication of election results (Table 2.4), it became clear that the polls were accurate regarding Likud, Yesh Atid, Shas, United Torah Judaism, and Yisrael Beiteinu. They were also right in identifying the drop in support for Yemina, New Hope, and The Joint List. These declines continued in the last days before the election, when it is not allowed to publish poll results. What was surprising was the rate of support and the dispersal of votes among

Table 2.4 Results of the 24th Knesset elections (March 2021)

Party-list name	Votes	Percentage	Seats
Likud	1,066,892	24.19	30
Yesh Atid	614,112	13.93	17
Shas	316,008	7.17	9
Blue and White	292,257	6.63	8
Yemina	273,836	6.21	7
Labor	268,767	6.09	7
United Torah Judaism	248,391	5.63	7
Yisrael Beiteinu	248,370	5.63	7
Religious Zionism	225,641	5.12	6
Joint List	212,583	4.82	6
New Hope	209,161	4.74	6
Meretz	202,218	4.59	6
Ra'am	167,064	3.79	4
New Economic Party	34,883	0.79	0
Rafa	17,346	0.39	0
Pirates	1,309	0.03	0
Me and You	1,291	0.03	0
Hope for change	1,189	0.03	0
Social Bang	811	0.02	0
Mishpat Tzedek	729	0.02	0
Tzomet	663	0.02	0
Am Shalem	592	0.01	0
New Order	514	0.01	0
Kama	486	0.01	0
The Impossible is Possible	463	0.01	0
Jewish Heart	443	0.01	0
Ourselves	441	0.01	0
Biblical Bloc	429	0.01	0
New World	429	0.01	0
Partnership Alliance	408	0.01	0
Israelis	395	0.01	0
Shma	395	0.01	0
Daa'm	385	0.01	0
Social Leadership	256	0.01	0
Maan (Yachad)	253	0.01	0
Hetz	226	0.01	0
We	220	0.00	0
Human Dignity	196	0.00	0
Democratit	0	0.00	0

Source: Central Elections Committee for the 24th Knesset, 2021.

Note: 6,578,084 eligible voters; number of votes: 4,436,365; valid votes: 4,410,052; disqualified votes: 26,313; turnout: 67.44%.

parties that were perceived to be close to the electoral threshold: The Religious Zionism on the right, and Blue and White, Labor, Meretz, and Ra'am from the center and left. All of these parties passed the electoral threshold at a considerable distance from it.

48 *Gideon Rahat and Michal Shamir*

The Likud lost much support (5% and six seats) compared to the 2020 election. According to INES (2021) polls, these votes went mainly to other right-wing parties, New Hope, Yemina, and The Religious Zionism, or were attributed to those who chose not to vote. New Hope, the challenging force from within, won less than 5% of the vote and six seats. This prevented it from appearing as a ruling party but was enough to fulfill its mission to prevent Netanyahu from forming a government. Yesh Atid won 17 seats, as expected. Its former partner, Blue and White, did weaken but won many more seats than expected (eight seats). Shas, United Torah Judaism, and Yisrael Beiteinu maintained their power. Yemina, which presented itself as an alternative ruling party, was very disappointed with the result (seven seats). However, compared to the failure to pass the electoral threshold in the April 2019 election and its electoral record when running in an alliance with other religious right parties in September 2019 and 2020, this could be seen as a success. Labor showed signs of recovery with higher support than in previous elections, and so did Meretz, which feared that it would not pass the electoral threshold. Both were able to reclaim voters who had migrated in previous elections to Blue and White. The Religious Zionist alliance was also successful. It won six seats in its own right (four for The National Union-Tkuma, one for Noam, and one for Otzma Yehudit), and another seat on the Likud list. The Joint List and Ra'am, which represent the Arab electorate, declined from 15 to 10 seats. The sharp decline in Arab turnout – according to Rudnitzky (2021), from 65% in the 2020 election to 45% in the 2021 election – explains this weakening.

Following the elections, 52 MKs recommended to President Rivlin that Netanyahu form the government, 45 MKs recommended Lapid, and 7 recommended Bennett. Netanyahu failed to form a government because he did not succeed in attaching to the right-wing religious bloc, which together with Yemina held 59 seats, a single additional party. The attempt to include the Ra'am party in the coalition – which was open to this idea – met with stubborn opposition from The Religious Zionism. The other parties clung to their opposition to his continued tenure (including the right-wing parties, Yisrael Beiteinu and New Hope).

After another round of consultations, the President assigned the task of forming the government to Yair Lapid, Yesh Atid leader, now recommended by 56 MKs (This time the 6 MKs of New Hope and 5 of the 6 MKs of The Joint List recommended him). During the time allotted to Lapid to form a coalition, Israel experienced another round of fighting against Hamas in Gaza (operation "Wall Guard") and violent clashes between Arabs and Jews within Israel, especially in the mixed cities and around the Al-Aqsa Mosque. These developments seemed to thwart the effort of Netanyahu's opponents to form a coalition government because it had to include a variety of parties from the left (Meretz and Labor), the center (Yesh Atid, Blue and White), the right (Yisrael Beiteinu, New Hope, and Yemina), and at least have the support of an Arab party. However, at the end of the operation and the riots, the move succeeded. These parties formed a government that included the Arab party

Ra'am. The government was a rotation government, like that of Netanyahu and Gantz. It included the mutual veto mechanism and an alternate prime minister who would replace the acting prime minister after two years (see Shamir and Rahat, this volume). The agreement was that the first to hold the prime minister post would be Naftali Bennett, who headed a party with only seven MKs but held a strategic position from which he could prevent the formation of the government and lead to a fifth election. After two years, Lapid, the leader of the largest party in this coalition (17 seats), would replace Bennett. This, as evident, did not happen. After one year, the Bennett-Lapid government collapsed and new elections were scheduled.

Notes

1 The High Court of Justice, by a majority of ten against one, rejected a petition that was submitted against the law (HCJ 5555/18). The Judges argued that the law does not negate Israel's democratic character and does not violate the principle of equality in its legal system.
2 Even without the votes of Yisrael Beiteinu, which turned out to be a problematic partner, a majority of the voters (51.5%) supported the parties of Netanyahu's right-religious bloc. But 6% were not translated into seats because they were given to parties that did not pass the electoral threshold.
3 Even with the votes of Otzma Yehudit, which did not pass the electoral threshold, Netanyahu's bloc did not win a majority of the vote in this election.
4 In addition, on March 23, 2020 Orly Levy-Abekasis (Gesher) defected from the Labor–Gesher–Meretz alliance and joined the Netanyahu right-religious bloc.
5 Nissenkorn retired after joining the new list that Ron Huldai, the mayor of Tel Aviv, established.

References

Central Elections Committee for the 21st Knesset, 2019. *Results of the 21st Knesset Elections.* https://votes21.bechirot.gov.il [Hebrew].
Central Elections Committee for the 22nd Knesset, 2019. *Results of the 22nd Knesset Elections.* https://votes22.bechirot.gov.il [Hebrew].
Central Elections Committee for the 23rd Knesset, 2020. *Results of the 23rd Knesset Elections.* https://votes23.bechirot.gov.il [Hebrew].
Central Elections Committee for the 24th Knesset, 2021. *Results of the 24th Knesset Elections.* https://votes24.bechirot.gov.il [Hebrew].
Election Appeal 1867/19. *High Court of Justice. "Ben-Ari and Others against the Central Elections Committee."* https://supremedecisions.court.gov.il/Home/Download?path=HebrewVerdicts%5C19%5C060%5C018%5Cv04&fileName=19018060.V04&type=2 [Hebrew].
Election Appeal 5487/19. "Segal and Others against Ben-Gvir and Others." https://supremedecisions.court.gov.il/Home/Download?path=HebrewVerdicts%5C19%5C870%5C054%5Cv06&fileName=19054870.V06&type=4
Election Appeal 5506/19. "Otzma Yehudit and Others against The Joint List and Others." https://supremedecisions.court.gov.il/Home/Download?path=HebrewVerdicts%5C19%5C870%5C054%5Cv06&fileName=19054870.V06&type=4

50 Gideon Rahat and Michal Shamir

Election Appeal 852/20. High Court of Justice. "MK Ofir Katz and Others against MK Hiba Yazbek and Others"; https://supremedecisions.court.gov.il/Home/Download?path=HebrewVerdicts/20/520/008/v09&fileName=20008520.V09&type=2

Election Appeal 922/20. '"Mishpat Tzedek, Lereforma Bemarechet Hamishpat Veleshihrur Yigal Amir,' against the Central Elections Committee for the 23rd Knesset." https://supremedecisions.court.gov.il/Home/Download?path=HebrewVerdicts/20/520/008/v09&fileName=20008520.V09&type=2.

Fuchs, Amir, 2019. "2010–2019 – A Decade of Anti-Democratic Legislation." Israel Democracy Institute, December 25, 2019. www.idi.org.il/articles/29388. [Hebrew].

German, Atara, 2019. "Those were Elected to the List of the National Union for the Knesset," *Srugim Website*, January 14, 2019. [Hebrew].

Hamichlol, 2019a. *The 21ˢᵗ Knesset Elections*. www.hamich lol.org.il/הבחירו_ת_לכ נסת_העשרים_ואחת [Hebrew].

Hamichlol, 2019b. *The 22nd Knesset Elections*. www.hamichlol.org.il/הבחירות_לכנסת_הע שרים_ושתיים [Hebrew].

Hamichlol, 2020. *The 23rd Knesset Elections*. www.hamich lol.org.il/הבחירות_לכנסת_ה עשרים_ושלוש [Hebrew].

Hamichlol, 2021. *The 24th Knesset Elections*. www.hamich lol.org.il/הבחירות_לכנסת_ה עשרים_וארבע [Hebrew].

HCJ 5555/18. *MK Akram Hasson and others v. the Knesset of Israel and Others*. https://supremedecisions.court.gov.il/Home/Download?path=HebrewVerdicts/18/550/055/v36&fileName=18055550.V36&type=4 [Hebrew].

INES. 2021. Israel National Election Studies. www.tau.ac.il/~ines/

Kenig, Ofer, 2021. *Covid-19 and the 2021 Elections in Israel: Challenges and Opportunities, Case Study*, August 18. Stockholm: International Institute for Democracy and Electoral Assistance. www.idea.int/sites/default/files/covid-19-and-the-2021-elections-in-israel-en.pdf

Rudnitzky, Arik, 2020. *Arab Voter Turnout in Knesset Elections: The Real, the Ideal, and Hope for Change*. Policy Research 148. Jerusalem: The Israel Democracy Institute. [Hebrew].

Rudnitzky, Arik, 2021. "The Vote of the Arab Citizens in the Elections to the 24th Knesset, March 2021." Israel Democracy Institute, April 4. www.idi.org.il/articles/34241 [Hebrew].

Shamir, Michal, and Keren Weinshall-Margel, 2015. "'Your Honor, Restrain Us': The Political Dynamics of the Right to Be Elected in the Israeli Democracy." In Michal Shamir (ed.), *The Elections in Israel – 2013*. 59–84. New Brunswick, NJ: Transaction.

Part 1

Personalization in the Israeli "Parteienstaat"

3 Personalization and Personalism in the 2019–2021 Elections

Another Climax of Personal Politics?

Gideon Rahat

Israel has undergone a profound process of *political personalization*, whereby the political weight of individual actors increases over time, while the centrality of the party decreases. As a result, *political personalism* – the situation in which the political weight of a single actor is relatively high in comparison to that of the party, is particularly pronounced in Israel, compared to other countries.

This chapter asks whether the level of political personalism in Israel reached a new height in the 2019–2021 four-election cycle. To answer this, personalism in 2019–2021 elections is analyzed and compared to the past in the institutional, media and behavioral arenas. The first section presents the conceptualization of personalization and personalism, the research question and the hypothesis. The next section outlines the research methodology and the indicators of personalism in the three arenas, followed by the findings.

The 2019–2021 election cycle indeed marks a new record in personal politics. Most of the evidence points to greater personalization; some indicators suggest the preservation of high levels of personalism; and there is no indication whatsoever of de-personalization. The concluding part integrates the evidence, pointing to a focus on party leaders and especially the prime minister (presidentialization) and personalization in the 2019–2021 coalition politics. It also proposes explanations for these processes and discusses the consequences of personalization for democracy.

3.1 Conceptualization, Research Question, and Hypothesis

Political personalism and personalization are all about the balance of power between individual politicians and their groups or organizations, where political personalization is a process, and personalism refers to a situation.

Political personalization can be identified in three arenas:[1]

1 Institutional personalization is seen in the adoption of laws and rules that emphasize the individual and weaken the status of the group, such as the concentration of power in the party in the hands of its leader.

DOI: 10.4324/9781003267911-5

54 *Gideon Rahat*

2   Personalization in the media: (a) In the controlled media, where the messengers control the content and timing of the delivery of the messages, messages are sent more by individuals and less by parties, and their content emphasizes the individual over the group; (b) In the uncontrolled media, the messengers do not control the content or timing of the delivery of the messages; here, politics is increasingly presented as competition and cooperation between individuals rather than parties.
3   Behavioral personalization pertains to: (a) politicians, where their actions as team players decline, and an increase in individual action is seen; (b) among voters, there is an increase in the perception of politics as a competition between personalities and not between parties.

All the above types of personalization are relevant for the classification of personalism. For example, personal parties (Hosen Yisrael, Yesh Atid, Kulanu) are more personalized than parties in which collegial bodies make decisions (Labor, Meretz, Hadash). When the personal activity of individual politicians on social networks is greater than their parties', this is a manifestation of personalism in the controlled media. Media coverage that focuses on politicians rather than their parties is a manifestation of personalism in the uncontrolled media. A speech by a politician who uses the word "I" more frequently than words referring to a group (for example, "we") is an example of a politician's behavioral personalism, and when more voters attest that they vote for the party leader or its candidates rather than due to party identification, that would be considered personalism in voters' behavior.

Personalization and personalism can also be differentiated by varying levels: Centralized personalization and personalism relate to the strengthening and strength of those at the top, especially prime ministers, presidents and party leaders, versus the weakening or weakness of the group (government, party, etc.). Decentralized personalization and personalism are about the strengthening and strength of many politicians, including backbenchers, compared to the weakening and weakness of the group.

Research in Israel (Rahat, 2019; Rahat and Sheafer, 2007; Balmas et al., 2014) identified high levels of political personalization and personal politics in the 21st century, in all three arenas: institutionally, in the way mayors are elected and candidates and party leaders are selected; in patterns of media coverage of election campaigns, election propaganda and social network activity; and behaviorally, in the speeches of prime ministers and the behavior of legislators, in the weight of personal considerations in voting behavior, and in the patterns of consumption of politicians' and political parties' messages on social networks.[2] A comparative study of 26 democracies (almost all of them parliamentary) found that the level of personalization is extremely high in Israeli politics, and that it developed in parallel with a particularly sharp decline in the linkage between parties and society (Rahat and Kenig, 2018).

Here I focus on the question whether personal politics in Israel reached new heights in the 2019–2021 elections. Previous studies create an expectation for a positive answer, and several of the chapters in this volume appear to concur. Navot and Goldshmidt, in their chapter on Netanyahu and the justice system, contend that "the criminal proceedings against Netanyahu led to an overlap of his personal interest in escaping the clutches of the law and the aspiration of the parties that compose the right-wing-religious bloc..." Kremnitzer and Blander devote their chapter to (Netanyahu's) personal matter that has become a constitutional quandary for Israel: how to deal with an incumbent prime minister facing indictments and refusing to relinquish his position. Lavi et al. address the personification of democratic values in the 2019–2021 elections, where personalities (and in particular Netanyahu) signified and symbolized worldviews.

3.2 Methodology

The chapter explores institutional developments, patterns of communication, media content and behavioral patterns of politicians and voters on the eve of and during the 2019–2021 elections. The analysis is not intended to identify developments between the four elections (although it may reveal such differences). The main goal of the analysis is to systematically examine distinctive and valid indicators of personal politics in order to identify the level of personalized politics and enable its comparison to the findings of previous studies (see Table 3.1).

3.2.1 The Institutional Arena

Candidate and leader selection are major events in the life of parties. The nomination of candidates for public office distinguishes them from all other

Table 3.1 Personalism indicators by arena

Arena	Type	Indicator
Institutional	In parties	Leader selectorate type
		Candidate selectorate type
Media	Controlled media	Appearance of the leader's name in the names of the competing lists
		Comparison of the activities of parties and their politicians on social networks
		Comparison of consumption patterns thereof[a]
	Uncontrolled media	Emphasis on persona versus parties in the coverage of election results by major newspapers
Behavioral	Politicians	Use of words in speeches by party leaders following exit polls
	Citizens	Voting motivations
		Perception of elections

Note: a This indicates both personal politics in the controlled media arena and in the behavior of (potential) voters.

56   Gideon Rahat

groups and organizations. This study systematically examines, for the period prior to each election, the patterns of candidate selection and selection of the party leader, and how these patterns have evolved since 1992.[3] In cases where no reselection was held in the run-up to the September 2019, 2020 or 2021 elections, the way in which the candidates and party leader were previously selected was coded. The data are drawn from Kenig and Rahat (forthcoming), who coded them using party regulations and news reports.

The differentiation is between selection by party institutions (council of sages, secretariat, central committee, conference), the leader (who selected him/herself or in cases where party regulations set rules for leadership selection but the leader is approved automatically, as long as the founding leader was not challenged), and party members (primaries). The selectorate is considered more partisan if its overall perception is likely to be partisan and competition for the vote of its selectors is within the party (Rahat and Sheafer, 2007; Rahat and Kenig, 2018). Such a method entrusts the party elite ("nominating committee") with the selection of the candidates and the leader. Selection by delegates of party institutions (central committee, conference, council) renders the competition more public, but is still largely contained within the party and is therefore also classified as partisan. In contrast, primaries (where party members are the selectorate, as in the Israeli case) transfer personal competition to the wide public and are thus perceived as a personal (decentralized) method. The most personal method is selection by a single leader (centralized personalism).

3.2.2 The Media Arena

Personalism in the controlled media is examined in two ways. First, in the way the party presents itself on the ballot paper: does only the name of the party appear, or is the leader's name also included? One of the manifestations of the personalization of Israeli politics is the addition of the leader's name to the party name on the ballot and the increase in the number and centrality of the parties that have done this over the years (Rahat, 2019). The second way is by comparing (a) the extent of politicians' activity to that of parties on social networks and (b) their consumption (Zamir and Rahat, 2019). On the supply side, this means assessing the number of parties' Facebook posts and Twitter tweets and measuring them against those of their leaders and of three senior politicians from their ranks (average outputs of candidates in positions 2–4 on the candidate list). On the consumption side, the number of likes to the parties' Facebook pages and of their Twitter followers are compared to those of their leaders and three senior politicians (average consumption of content presented by candidates in positions 2–4 on the candidate list).

Personalism in the uncontrolled media was examined by analyzing the top front-page headlines (the headline and the subhead that appear in the largest fonts combined) of five daily newspapers (*Haaretz*, *Yedioth Ahronoth*, *Maariv*, *Israel Hayom*, and *The Jerusalem Post* print versions) in the two days after the election. Here, the number of mentions of the names of politicians, parties and blocs are compared. These headlines encapsulate the representation of politics by the media – as interpersonal, interparty or perhaps inter-bloc competition.

3.2.3 The Behavioral Arena

Personalism in the behavior of politicians was examined by analyzing the speeches on election night, following the publication of exit polls, of the leaders of the two largest parties: Netanyahu (2019a, 2019b, 2020, 2021), Benny Gantz (2019a, 2019b; Karni, 2020), and Yair Lapid (2021). It is then compared to speeches of winning leaders in past elections: Menachem Begin in 1977 (Begin, 1977), Yitzhak Rabin in 1992 (Karpel, 1993), Ehud Olmert in 2006 (Itim, 2006), and Netanyahu (2009, 2015). These speeches represent the party leaders' concluding remarks on the election campaign and the assumed outcome: Is it (and to what extent) their own personal success or failure or that of the party?

The frequency of the repeated use of keywords that express party and group, and personal politics, were coded.[4] The analysis counts the number of mentions of the Hebrew word for "I," *ani*, as a marker of personalism and references to the leader's family members as a separate marker of "privatization."[5] In contrast, group references included the use of the word *anachnu* (we) as well as mentions of the names of the lists. The word "party" was counted but not in relation to the speaker's party because it usually referred to other parties.[6] Words that signified a populist gesture of the leader to his followers (various iterations of the pronoun "you," namely, *atem, otchem, lachem, shelachem, kulchem*) were also examined.

Voters' behavior and perceptions were also analyzed, in two ways. First, by examining voting motivations in the Israel National Election Studies (INES, 2021) for elections 1977–2021. The share of those who stated that they voted mainly based on party identification was compared to the share of those who cited personalized reasons – voting for the leader or the party candidates. Second, I evaluated the distribution of respondents to the postelection question: "In your opinion, what were the last elections most of all about?," asked in INES (2021) postelection surveys since 1999. Here I compared the share of respondents who claimed that the elections denoted an evaluation of the prime minister across the elections.

3.3 Findings: A New Highpoint in Personal Politics

3.3.1 Institutional Personalization and Personalism

Figure 3.1 presents the number of Members of Knesset (MKs) – in each Knesset at the time it was elected – according to the selectorates that chose them to be their party candidates. It extends back to 1992 (when primaries

58 *Gideon Rahat*

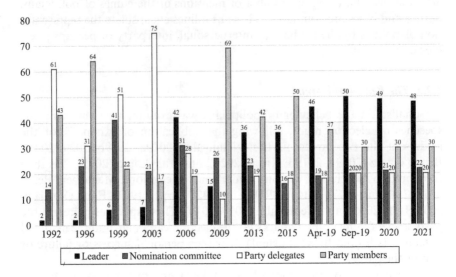

Figure 3.1 Number of MKs (immediately after each election), according to the selectorates that chose them to be candidates of their parties, 1992–2021.

Source: Kenig and Rahat, forthcoming.

were first adopted by an established party, Labor). Clearly, after the single peak in their use in 2003, the selection by party delegates was abandoned. Selection by party members (a marker for decentralized personalism) was the most common alternative in 2009–2015, while in 2019–2021 it was selection by the most exclusive selectorate, a single leader (a marker for centralized personalism).

A significant share of the party leaders who competed in 2019–2021 never faced a selection contest in their party (a minority of them may have been reapproved without competition). They held the top position in their capacity as the party founder: Yair Lapid (Yesh Atid), Benny Gantz (Hosen Yisrael), Moshe (Boogie) Ya'alon (Telem – the National Statist Movement – Hatnu'a Haleumit Hamamlachtit), Ahmad Tibi (Ta'al–Hatnu'a Ha'Aravit Lehitchadshut), Avigdor Lieberman (Yisrael Beiteinu), Moshe Kahlon (Kulanu), Naftali Bennett and Ayelet Shaked (The New Right – Hayamin Hehadash and Yemina), Orly Levi-Abekasis (Gesher), and Gideon Sa'ar (New Hope – Tikva Hadasha). In short, about 40% of Knesset seats in the 21st–24th Knessets were held by personal parties or parties with an undisputed leader (see Table 3.2). Moreover, while personal parties around the world usually refrain from formally determining the status of the leader in their regulations, personal parties in Israel (Yesh Atid, Yisrael Beiteinu, Kulanu, Telem) explicitly proclaim this status.[7] This signifies that they are personal parties, which characterizes centralized personal politics.

Table 3.2 Party leaders' selectorates 1992–2021, by number of parties and their Knesset representation

	Election year Selectorate											
	1992	1996	1999	2003	2006	2009	2013	2015	2019[a]	2019[b]	2020	2021
Party institutions	9 (63)	10 (46.5)[b]	11 (59)	10 (49)	11 (68)	8 (31)	8 (38)	8 (31)	8 (29)	10 (35)	9 (34)	10 (36)
Members	1 (44)	3 (58.5)	2 (42)	3 (58)	3 (35)	5 (72)	4 (45)	3 (55)	3 (44)	2 (36)	2 (38)	2 (36)
Leader[a]	3 (13)	4 (15)	7 (18)	6 (13)	4 (17)	2 (16)	4 (37)	5 (34)	6 (46)	9 (49)	8 (48)	7 (47)
Total parties	13 (120)	17 (120)	20 (119)	19 (120)	18 (120)	15 (119)	16 (120)	16 (120)	17 (119)	21 (120)	19 (120)	19 (119)

Source: Kenig and Rahat, forthcoming.

Notes:
a Includes cases where there was no significant challenge to the founding leader.
b The cases of Shinuy and Mapam, in which both the members and the delegates of a party institution participated in selecting number one on the list, were divided between the two categories.

60   *Gideon Rahat*

In the Likud, Netanyahu's leadership was not seriously challenged since 2006. Primaries for the Likud leadership that were scheduled on 2016 were canceled because Netanyahu was the sole candidate. In the run-up to the September 2019 elections, Netanyahu himself initiated a leadership selection contest; he faced off Gideon Sa'ar and won 73% of the Likud members' votes. Thus, even in the Likud – which, in the two decades following Begin's retirement (1983), was characterized by internal democracy and fierce competition for leadership – centralized personalism gained ground. In the Shas party, the dominant status of Aryeh Deri is evident; he became the undisputed leader when he ousted his opponent Eli Yishai in 2015 from the top position and from the party altogether. Other parties, like Meretz and Labor, where there was competition and even turnover of leadership, survived but significantly weakened.

Table 3.2 describes the selectorates of the leaders of the parties represented in the Knesset since 1992. It presents the number of parties that used each selectorate (party institutions, member or leader) and (in parentheses) those parties' share of Knesset seats. There is a relative and absolute increase in the number of parties led by a self-appointed leader from 2009 to the September 2019 elections, as well as in the number of seats of these parties. The share of parties whose leaders were selected by a party institution shrank already in 2009, which marked a record in terms of the use of primaries. In the 2019–2021 elections a record share and number of parties employed personal methods, due to an increase in selection by the party leader. These trends are similar to those identified for candidate selection.

3.3.2 *Personalism in the Media*

The name of the candidate list that appears on the ballot is a marker for the content of communication between parties and voters and an obvious indicator for personalism. In the April 2019 election, 16 lists (out of 40) added the name of the party leader(s) to their name; in the following September 2019 election, 11 (out of 29) did so; in March 2020 elections, 13 lists (out of 29); and in March 2021, 20 (out of 38). In 6 of the 11 lists that won representation in the Knesset in April 2019, the party leaders' name appeared on the ballot; in September 2019 – seven out of nine; in 2020, four out of eight; and in the 2021 election, 9 out of 13. Likud and Blue and White, the two large parties, included the leaders' names in all four elections.

Until 1973 there was just a single case of a marginal party, in which the party leader's name appeared on the ballot paper ("Abie Nathan to the Knesset," 1965). Since 1977 the practice has grown (though not in a continuous and linear way). Since 1999, 7 (2003) to 20 lists (2021) have contested each election with the name of their leader (or leaders in certain cases) on the ballot (Rahat, 2019). A comparison of 2019–2021 to 1999–2015 reveals that this practice has become established, but there is no indication of increased personalization. From a global perspective, this is an extreme expression of

Personalization and Personalism in the 2019–2021 Elections 61

personalism. According to Rahat and Kenig's comparative study (2018), in most (16 out of 25) democracies, parties do not put the leader's name on the ballot; in the remainder (nine) there were a few such cases, usually of small parties.

Another practice that developed, particularly in the last decade, is the inclusion of the party leader's name in the name of the party when registering with the Parties Registrar (this is a separate procedure from registration with the Central Elections Committee for the purpose of running in elections). This applies not only to marginal parties but also to prominent ones that have won Knesset seats: "*Yesh Atid*-headed by Yair Lapid" (registered in advance of the 2013 election); "*Kulanu* headed by Moshe Kahlon" (registered before the 2015 election); and on the eve of the April 2019 elections, "*Telem* – the National Statist Movement, led by Moshe (Boogie) Ya'alon" and "*Gesher*-headed by Orly Levi-Abekasis."

Table 3.3 provides an additional point of view on controlled media patterns. It compares parties' activity on Facebook and Twitter with that of their leaders and the average activity of their three senior politicians in 2019. These data do not refer specifically to election periods. In nonelection periods parties tend to be less active on social networks (Zamir and Rahat, 2019) and we thus expect to identify a relatively high level of personalized politics. In the absence of relevant data for election periods, we will use these data, with the necessary caution.

On Facebook the output of the party leaders is greater than that of their parties (The ultra-Orthodox parties are not included in the following discussion due to their limited use of social media). In contrast, in four out of six

Table 3.3 Party and personal outputs on social networks: Facebook posts and Twitter tweets, 2019

Name of party/list	Posts per month (Facebook) (15.1.2019–14.2.2019)			Tweets per month (Twitter) (From the date each account was opened until 16.7.2019)		
	Party	Leader	Average 3 seniors	Party	Leader	Average 3 seniors
Likud	39	131	24	25	38	42
Yesh Atid	41	48	11	16	36	11
Blue and White	0	55	31	37	73	52
Shas	26	15	0	16	14	14
United Torah Judaism	0	0	0	117	0	2
Labor	25	94	44	32	39	75
Yisrael Beiteinu	46	52	15	37	16	5
Hadash	19	25	14	93	20	15

Note: Thanks to Shahaf Zamir for providing the data.

62   *Gideon Rahat*

cases party activity exceeds the average of their three senior politicians, while in two cases the opposite is true. In terms of output on Facebook, then, we see mostly centralized personal politics. On the other hand, on Twitter, only in Yesh Atid and Blue and White the leaders demonstrate the highest level of activity. In two cases the party's output is the highest, while in two, the three senior politicians' is. In short, on Twitter the output of parties and politicians is fairly balanced. However, a reasonable expectation is that parties – organizations that are supposed to be the basic organizing unit of politics, especially in parliamentary regimes with a closed-list electoral system – will produce output eclipsing that of the politicians who compose them.[8] From this perspective personalism is evident on this indicator as well.

A comparison with data from the eve of the 2015 elections (Zamir and Rahat, 2019)[9] – shows that Facebook posts in 2015 were more numerous in six of eight parties than those of their leaders, compared to none of the six in 2019. The average monthly Twitter output of the parties was higher in five out of eight cases in 2016 than their leaders', while leaders tweeted more than their parties in four out of six cases in 2019. Parties' output in comparison to their top three politicians remains similar on Facebook, where the parties are more active in general. On Twitter the overall comparison between a party and its senior politicians was and remains balanced, with examples on both sides. Thus, stability is identified in personal politics in general and we see an increase in centralized personalism that concerns leaders. However, this may be attributed to the fact that data for 2019 are not from the election period; so we will be content with stating that the levels of centralized personalism remain high.

Table 3.4 compares the consumption of the parties' outputs on Facebook and Twitter with that of their leaders and their three senior politicians. The

Table 3.4 Consumption of parties and politicians on social networks: Facebook likes and Twitter followers, 2019

Name of party/list	Number of Facebook likes (24.6.2019–26.6.2019)			Number of Twitter followers (16.7.2019)		
	Party	Leader	Average 3 seniors	Party	Leader	Average 3 seniors
Likud	64,193	2,436,331	97,702	30,209	1,626,199	44,912
Yesh Atid	32,203	437,487	24,169	3,124	156,999	4,229
Blue and White	17,159	149,693	187,306	10,798	35,022	79,380
Shas	3,373	62,183	0	195	93,821	3,749
United Torah Judaism	5,348	0	0	281	30	517
Labor	75,708	78,735	121,034	10,703	82,267	143,690
Yisrael Beiteinu	47,999	224,068	5,063	3,572	91,219	2,127
Hadash	64,693	201,081	24,285	11,941	62,117	2,666

Note: Thanks to Shahaf Zamir for providing the data.

data reflect the number of people exposed at a specific point in time to the content that parties and politicians produce. In the case of Facebook there is a preference for party leaders in five cases, and two for senior politicians. In five cases the party has more likes than its three senior politicians, and in one case (in which the leader has no Facebook page) it has more followers than its leader.

Facebook consumption is personalized, and usually of the centralized type. The same applies to Twitter. A preference for party leaders is evident in five cases, while in three there is a preference for senior politicians. Only in one case does the party have more followers than its three senior politicians, and only in one case the party has more followers than its leader. There is considerable personalism of both kinds but the centralized kind is more pronounced. These patterns were identified in previous studies that compared Israel to other countries (Zamir and Rahat, 2019).

A comparison to data from the eve of 2015 elections (Zamir and Rahat, 2019) confirms that the supremacy of party leaders was maintained, but the gaps in terms of absolute numbers only expanded. The average number of Facebook page likes and Twitter followers for the three senior politicians was high in five out of eight parties in 2015; in 2019, this was so in three out of six cases on Facebook and four of six on Twitter. To conclude, this indicator of personalism either intensified (in the case of party leaders) or maintained its high levels (for senior politicians).

The indicator for personalism in the uncontrolled media looks at how election results (in the context of a parliamentary system with a closed-list electoral system!) were described: as a contest between individuals, parties or blocs. Table 3.5 presents the number of times politicians (by name), parties (by name) and blocs were mentioned in the headlines of five newspapers in the two days after the elections. Personalism is evident, as personalities garnered 106 mentions compared to 69 references to parties in these headlines. The term bloc is mentioned 31 times, and in the context of these elections it is a concept that combines the individual (Bibi and anti-Bibi) with the group (the parties associated with each bloc).

The gap between the number of times that politicians and parties were mentioned shrank in the September 2019 and March 2020 elections, but grew again in March 2021. The term bloc (*gush*) received significantly more mentions in September 2019 and 2020; and this term was used even after the 2021 elections in which bloc identification was somewhat less clear than before. It seems that the concept of bloc was used as a bridge between the institutional reality of a parliamentary regime and its closed-list electoral system and the perception of an election as being primarily a competition for the premiership.

A comparison to past data (Rahat, 2019) – which included only the newspapers *Haaretz*, *Yedioth Ahronoth*, and *Maariv* – reveals the process of personalization in the uncontrolled media: in 1965, the ratio was 29 mentions of parties to 4 for personalities; in 1984, it was 30:14; in 2003, 17:13; while the

64　*Gideon Rahat*

Table 3.5 Number of mentions of parties and politicians in the headlines of five major daily newspapers in the two days following the elections

Election		Haaretz	Israel Hayom	The Jerusalem Post	Maariv	Yedioth Ahronoth	Total
April 2019	Personality	10	8	3	6	3	30
	Party	7	4	0	3	2	16
	Bloc	1	0	0	1	1	3
September 2019	Personality	8	4	3	5	3	23
	Party	7	2	2	5	4	20
	Bloc	2	3	0	3	2	10
2020	Personality	6	1	4	5	2	18
	Party	9	0	1	3	0	13
	Bloc	3	1	2	4	0	10
2021	Personality	5	7	4	8	11	35
	Party	7	2	1	9	1	20
	Bloc	3	0	1	2	2	8

Note: Analysis of the two headlines that appear in the largest fonts (main headline and sub-headline) on page one.

total for the four elections of 2019–2021 was 57:72. However, in September 2019 the ratio for the headlines of these three newspapers was equal (16:16) and in March 2020 almost equal (12:13). Thus, the main difference in comparison to 2003 was in the April 2019 and March 2021 elections. The concept of blocs in this election cycle (which was not used in the past – see the Appendix in Rahat, 2019) evidently combined the individual (Bibi and anti-Bibi) with the group (the parties associated with each bloc).

3.3.3 Behavioral Personalization and Personalism

The first part of Table 3.6 presents the analysis of the 2019–2021 election-night speeches of the leaders of the two largest lists. There are several signs of personalism. First, the pronoun *ani* (I) is widely used in what are perceived as victory speeches[10] – especially Netanyahu in April 2019 and March 2020 and Gantz in September 2019 – and less so in other election-night speeches. It seems that instead of saying that "success has many fathers and failure is an orphan," in the case of centralized personalism, from the leader's point of view "success has a single father and failure has many fathers." Second, in most cases, Netanyahu displayed further privatization in his frequent reference to his family members. Third, in 2019–2020, the word *miflaga* (party) was almost absent; only once was it attributed (by Gantz) to the leader's own party. All other references were general or referred to other parties. Likud was mentioned several times by Netanyahu, while Gantz rarely mentioned Blue and White, the name of the alliance he headed. This changed in the 2021

Table 3.6 Analysis of leaders' election night speeches: Use of pronouns as % of all words in a speech (in parentheses, total number of pronouns in the speech)

Election night speeches 2019–2021

The speech (in parentheses, the number of words in the speech)	Personal words		Group words		Ratio ani:anachnu (we)+speaker list name	The word miflaga (party)	Distinctive reference to the audience		
	Ani (I)	Family and its members	Anachnu (we)	Name of the speaker's list (including allies in the list)			Atem (you)	Otchem (you)	Lachem/ Shelachem/ kulchem (For you/ Your/All of you)
Gantz April 2019 (830)	1.45 (12)	0.84 (7)	2.17 (18)	0.24 (2)	**0.60** **(12:20)**	0.36 (3)	0.24 (2)	0.00 (0)	1.32 (11)
Netanyahu April 2019 (771)	*4.80* *(37)*	*1.43* *(11)*	*0.26* *(2)*	*0.91* *(7)*	*4.11* *(37:9)*	*0.13* *(1)*	*1.69* *(13)*	*0.26* *(2)*	*3.37* *(26)*
Gantz September 2019 (660)	*3.18* *(21)*	*0.30* *(2)*	*0.91* *(6)*	*0.61* *(4)*	*2.10* *(21:10)*	*0.00* *(0)*	*0.91* *(6)*	*0.15* *(1)*	*0.76* *(5)*
Netanyahu September 2019 (524)	2.23 (12)	1.15 (6)	2.10 (11)	1.34 (7)	**0.67** **(12:18)**	0.57 (3)	1.34 (7)	0.38 (2)	1.15 (6)
Gantz 2020 (723)	3.04 (22)	0.00 (0)	3.32 (24)	0.69 (5)	**0.76** **(22:29)**	0.00 (0)	0.00 (0)	0.00 (0)	1.11 (8)
Netanyahu 2020 *(1496)*	*3.14* *(47)*	*1.00* *(15)*	*1.07* *(16)*	*0.74* *(11)*	*1.74* *(47:27)*	*0.00* *(0)*	*0.67* *(10)*	*0.27* *(4)*	*1.80* *(27)*
Lapid 2021 (293)	2.05 (6)	0.34 (1)	3.75 (11)	0 (0)	**0.55** **(6: 11)**	1.37 (4)	0 (0)	0 (0)	0.34 (1)
Netanyahu 2021 (703)	*1.99* *(14)*	*0.14* *(1)*	*1.99* *(14)*	*0.28* *(2)*	*0.88* *(14:16)*	*0.43* *(3)*	*0.14* *(1)*	*0.28* *(2)*	*1.28* *(9)*

(continued)

Table 3.6 Cont.

Election night speeches 1977–2015

The speech (in parentheses, the number of words in the speech)	Personal words		Group words		Ratio ani:anachnu (we)+speaker list name	The word miflaga (party)	Distinctive reference to the audience		
	Ani (I)	Family and its members	Anachnu (we)	Name of the speaker's list (including allies in the list)			Atem (you)	Otchem (you)	Lachem/ Shelachem/ kulchem (For you/ Your/All of you)
Begin 1977 (695)	1.87 (13)	0.86 (6)	0.00 (0)	1.73 (12)	**1.08** **(13:12)**	0.86 (6)	0.00 (0)	0.00 (0)	0.00 (0)
Rabin 1992 (407)	3.19 (13)	0.00 (0)	0.98 (4)	0.64 (3)	**1.86** **(13:7)**	0.98 (4)	0.00 (0)	0.00 (0)	0.25 (1)
Olmert 2006 (1347)	0.97 (13)	1.26 (17)	0.15 (2)	0.37 (5)	**1.86** **(13:7)**	0.07 (1)	0.00 (0)	0.00 (0)	0.52 (7)
Netanyahu 2009 (467)	2.14 (10)	0.43 (2)	1.50 (7)	0.86 (4)	**0.91** **(10:11)**	0.43 (2)	0.21 (1)	0.00 (0)	0.86 (4)
Netanyahu 2015 (425)	4.00 (17)	2.35 (10)	0.94 (4)	1.65 (7)	**1.55** **(17:11)**	0.24 (1)	0.47 (2)	0.47 (2)	3.53 (15)

Note: Italics are used for speeches in the 2019–2021 elections perceived as victory speeches.

election – the party returned to the speeches, especially to indicate its size compared to other parties, lending an enhanced sense of success. With that, the use of the pronoun *anachnu* (we) returned, even in the ostensible winner's speech (Netanyahu). Finally, in all elections Netanyahu prominently used the pronouns *atem* (you) and *lachem/shelachem/kulchem* (you, yours, all of you) in comparison to Gantz, reflecting a populist relationship between the leader and "his" collective (when implicitly there are also "they" who are not part of "you").

A comparison of the ratio between the number of uses of *ani* (I) and of *anachnu* (we) plus the name of the list shows that the degree of personalism in victory speeches was higher in the Netanyahu April 2019 speech and Gantz's September 2019 speech than in previous victory speeches (second part of Table 3.6). This ratio is lower though in Netanyahu's March 2020 election speech compared to Olmert's in 2006 and similar to his own speech from 2015 and Rabin's speech from 1992, but the absolute number of mentions of *ani* (I) is the highest. The process of personalization was already identified in the analysis of the speeches of prime ministers when they presented their governments to the Knesset from the establishment of the state (1948) until 2009 (Balmas et al., 2014). Thus, we can determine that personalization persists. Second, as far as family members are concerned there is no systematic pattern of privatization. Third, there is a clear decline in the use of the word *miflaga* (party) when comparing Rabin's (1992) and Begin's (1977) speeches to later speeches (except for speeches after the 2021 election, when party size was framed as a significant achievement). Targeting words directly to the party leadership and prominent activists physically present – and indirectly to television viewers who consider themselves aligned with that group – is prominent for Netanyahu from 2015 (although less so in September 2019 and 2021), signifying the populist discourse between Netanyahu and his audience (see Shilon in this volume).

The broad support for personal parties (the Blue and White alliance parties) and parties that seem to have become almost personal parties (Likud) is a marker for personalism in voting behavior. In past elections, such parties were not as successful as in the 2019–2021 elections. At the same time, parties with functioning collegial institutions were in decline (though they adorned themselves with unselected personalities like Tal Russo in Labor, Yair Golan in Meretz or those who headed personal mini-parties like Orly Levi-Abekasis).[11] Indeed, in the 2019–2021 elections, for every three to six respondents who testified that their primary voting motivation was party identity, there were ten who said that their vote was based on the identity of the party's candidate for prime minister and its candidates (see Table 3.7). When asked following the elections, "In your opinion, what were the last elections mainly about?" in the four elections held in 2019–2021, a large majority claimed that they were centered on whether or not Netanyahu could be trusted. The percentage of voters that chose the personal over the thematic was even higher than in 1999, when the direct election of the prime minister was practiced (see Table 3.8). Interestingly, in the 2021 elections the ratio between voting for partisan versus

Table 3.7 Voting motivation in Knesset elections, 1977–2021 (%)[a]

Year	Partisan motivation	Personalized motivation		Ratio partisan: personalized motivations	Other reasons	
	Party identification	The party's candidate for prime minister	The party's candidates for Knesset		Party positions on certain issues	Whether the party is in power or in the opposition
1977	27.9	15.8	0	**1.77**	50.1	6.3
1981	32.3	20.1	0	**1.61**	39.4	7.9
1984	33.0	9.6	0	**3.44**	53.6	3.8
1988	32.5	21.7	0	**1.50**	42.5	3.3
1992	29.1	12.0	0	**2.43**	56.0	2.8
1996	22.9	16.8	0	**1.36**	57.0	3.3
1999	19.0	0	11.7	**1.62**	64.0	5.3
2003	23.7	0	12.7	**1.87**	57.4	6.2
2006	20.7	0	20.8	**1.00**	50.6	7.9
2009	19.2	0	24.0	**0.80**	49.8	7.0
2015	13.1	19.2[b]	10.0	**0.45**	53.9	3.8
2019 April	10.7	18.2[b]	13.0	**0.34**	53.2	4.5
2019 Sept.[c]	0	0	0	**0**	0	0
2020	12.1	17.1[b]	11.6	**0.42**	53.0	6.1
2021	17.6	20.4[b]	8.1	**0.62**	52.4	1.6

Source: Based on INES 1977–2021.

Notes:
a The share of those who chose one of the categories in the survey. Those who did not respond, and the few who suggested other categories or claimed that all motivations had the same weight are not included.
b The category in these surveys was the party leader.
c In September 2019 the question was not asked.

Table 3.8 Distribution of respondents to the question: "In your opinion, what were the last elections mainly about?" (1999–2021)

Election year	Personal	Policy	Don't know/No answer/Refusal
1999	39	59	2
2009	22	63	15
2013	12	80	8
2015	28	59	13
2019 April	50	34	16
2019 September	56	38	6
2020	51	40	7
2021	62	33	5

Note: Based on INES 1999–2021 (postelection surveys).

personalized motivations decreased, yet the share of those who thought that they had been primarily about the continuation of Netanyahu's rule peaked.

Table 3.7 presents the distribution of voting motivations in the 1977–2021 Knesset elections, according to the INES (2021) surveys. The data are based on self-testimony and may reflect "social desirability": the large proportion of citizens who claim that their vote was motivated by party positions may reflect, at least in part, the perception that this is the "right answer" for citizens in a democracy. However, from changes under the guise of "social desirability" much can still be learned about citizens' views on politics. Also, there are slight changes over the years in the wording of the questions, and in some years, in the response categories. However, a distinct decline over time can be observed (with a few slight temporary spikes) in the choice of party identification as a main motive for voting. It is difficult to identify a trend in the proportion of those who choose personalized motivations (and it should be noted that the number and type of response categories varied between surveys, see Table 3.7). It is clear, however, that there is no decline in the proportion of those who indicated that their vote was based on such motives. From this it follows that the ratio between a party motive and a personal motive changed over time toward the non-partisan personal direction (bold fifth column in Table 3.7).

Table 3.8 presents the distribution of responses to the question on what the elections have primarily been about since 1999. The response categories to this question varied over the years, including the grounds for the assessment of the prime minister (his character and functioning, suitability to the position, leadership, trust and continued tenure). The thematic categories varied in response to changes in the political agenda. Nevertheless, this question can tell whether the personal was central in the interpretation of the elections by the citizenry. This does not exclude the possibility that themes were important, but may be reflected in the persona that embodies them (see Lavi et al. in this volume). The share of those who viewed the elections in personal terms was

70   *Gideon Rahat*

relatively high in 1999 under the direct elections for prime minister (abolished in 2001). Thereafter it was much lower (but not negligent), ranging between 12% and 28%. In the 2019–2021 election cycle the majority and up to 62% in the last election in this cycle chose this option.

3.4 Summary and Conclusions

All indicators in the institutional, media and behavioral arenas point to high levels of personal politics. But did we witness intensified personalization?

Table 3.9 summarizes the main findings of this study. The changes in leadership selection (self-appointment) and candidate selection (selection by a leader) do mark further institutional centralized personalization. The addition of the leader's name(s) to the name of the candidate list (and sometimes to the name of the registered party) is a practice that became established but did not significantly change in the 2019–2021 elections. Comparing the social network activity of politicians to that of parties did not reveal much change,

Table 3.9 Summary of findings: Personalism and personalization in the 2019–2021 elections

Arena	Type	Indicator	Magnitude of personalism	Additional personalization in elections 2019–2021
Institutional	Non-governmental institutions – parties	Candidate selection methods	High	Yes
		Leadership selection methods	High	Yes
Media	Controlled media	Candidate list names	High	No
		Social network activity	High	No
		Social network consumption	High	Yes (centralized)
	Uncontrolled media	Coverage of election results in major newspapers'	High	Yes, with differences among elections
Behavioral	Politicians	Party leaders' speeches following exit polls	Especially high in the winners' speeches	Yes (regarding the winners)
	Vote	Motives for voting and perception of elections	High	Yes

but consumption patterns provided signs of centralized personalization in the controlled media. Newspaper headlines that report election results, which are rather like an epilogue, attested to additional centralized personalization in the uncontrolled media in the April 2019 election. After that there was a change of direction in favor of more frequent use of the term "bloc" for the next two elections, but personalism reappeared in the headlines after the 2021 election. Netanyahu and Gantz speeches following elections that they deemed a success marked further centralized personalization in the behavior of politicians. An analysis of voters' motivations indicated a clear increase both in the relative weight of the personal versus partisan factor in the vote and in the perception of elections as being about the prime minister. To conclude, in this four-election cycle, Israel experienced further political personalization.

Party leaders have become the dominant figures in the political arena. Parties are becoming merely the platforms that carry them. Parties may have to exist out of necessity, due to the electoral system and the law. They also still constitute a solution to the problems of collective action. But they are becoming secondary actors. This is reflected in their organization, their media activities, the behavior of their leaders and voters' perception of them. Israeli politics also reached a new peak in presidentialization, where its patterns of action as well as its perception gradually resemble that of a presidential regime without any substantial change being made in the system of government (Poguntke and Webb, 2005, 2018).

How did the "parteienstaat" (Akzin, 1955) become the state of personal politics (a title that Israel shares with Italy, according to Rahat and Kenig, 2018)? One possible explanation is the decline in the parties' linkages with society in Israel, found to be one of the three steepest declines in a comparison of 26 democracies (Rahat and Kenig, 2018). Another explanation may lie in the mutual influence of the different types of personalization (in institutions, media and behavior) that have increasingly fed each other (Rahat and Sheafer, 2007). To this we can add the style of leadership of the Israeli prime minister in the last dozen years, Benjamin Netanyahu, as analyzed in this volume by Shilon and by Navot and Goldshmidt.

Personal politics does not begin and end at election time. In the two years of this four-election cycle between 2019 and 2021, it was also a significant factor in coalition politics. Forming a coalition is a matter of finding a formula for divvying up governmental jobs, resources, and policies. What was so unusual about the first two elections in 2019 that made it impossible to find the redeeming formula, which had been previously found even in conditions of an inter-bloc tie (following the 1984 election)? The key to the answer is not in the behavior of the parties; they could have found the formula, experience shows. The ideological distance between them on key issues was not greater than in the past. It can be argued that it is even narrower because today the Palestinian issue – a key topic on the Israeli political agenda – is "stuck" between the Hamas administration in Gaza and the Palestine Liberation Organization (PLO) administration in the West Bank, meaning it is currently

72   *Gideon Rahat*

somewhat less pressing for Israel while the Palestinians are split. Nor are positions on social and economic issues fundamentally different among Israeli politicians. In retrospect, it can be argued that the solution to the 2019–2020 deadlock was an agreement between two of the following three personalities: Netanyahu, Gantz and Lieberman. When Lieberman changed his mind and refused to compromise and join the government of the right-wing bloc to which he belonged, and when Netanyahu and Gantz could not agree on the formation of a government, new elections were scheduled. When Gantz and Netanyahu did reach an agreement, following the third election in 2020, a government was formed. Both have parties and representatives in the Knesset that they had to sway. But in Gantz's party, Hosen Yisrael, all but one MK joined the coalition, and in Netanyahu's Likud all MKs did what they were told. The solution to the postelection deadlock revolved around the establishment of a new, personalized, one-of-a-kind institution in the democratic world of an "alternate prime minister." This was not a precedent per se: the 1984 and 1988 unity governments were also built on the principle of equal distribution of posts and rotation; but these remained in the agreement. In 2020, a fundamental constitutional change has created a distinct (personal) status of an "alternate prime minister."

Another interesting development in this cycle of elections concerns the blocs. These are usually seen as combinations of ideologically close parties that could form a governing coalition together if they garner enough seats. There is nothing new in the description, understanding and interpretation of Israeli politics (and perhaps of any multiparty coalition politics in other democracies) in terms of blocs. What was new in 2019–2021 is that the right-religious bloc was perceived as Netanyahu's bloc (almost institutionalized when in an interparty agreement these parties pledged to support only Netanyahu for prime minister) and the rest (including the right-wing parties Yisrael Beiteinu, Telem, which was part of the Blue and White alliance, and New Hope) as an anti-Netanyahu bloc. The 2021 election created another rift between the personal and the ideological, when Gideon Sa'ar, a senior Likud right-wing politician, broke away to form New Hope (Tikva Hadasha). The deal for the formation of a new government, following the fourth election in 2021, was in the hands of many party leaders; thus, personalized politics became somewhat more decentralized in comparison to 2019–2020, when Gantz was the one leading candidate in the anti-Netanyahu bloc.

The 2019–2021 elections brought personal politics to a new peak. It is unclear whether we are still in the midst of a process; toward its end, with the creation of a new balance of power between the personal and the party; or perhaps at the pinnacle, after which the pendulum will move in the direction of "partyness." In any case, the rise of personal politics in Israel to such high levels is cause for concern. Political personalization does much more harm than good (Rahat, 2019). Personal politics can (though it does not have to) flatten the political discourse, reinforce negative political coverage and propaganda, and undermine the status of women in politics. Also, even if

Personalization and Personalism in the 2019–2021 Elections 73

personal politics creates a clearer focus for personal responsiveness, in the long run parties remain a more stable alternative for political responsiveness. Similarly, there can be personal politics that enhance political trust in the short term by lending politics a human face. But ultimately this weakens trust because heroes rise and fall, while democracy is supposed to stay with us even after the heroes leave. There may be talented and charismatic leaders with democratic-liberal and non-populist views who can meet the expectations of democratic audiences and are even better suited to the age of personal politics, but history has taught us that the test of the resilience of a democratic regime is precisely in times when it is headed by less successful and worthy leaders. In such times the rule of law and the sturdiness of the institutions are critical. Of particular concern today is the strong (though not absolute) connection between personal politics and populism, the shift to an emphasis on charismatic authority rather than on the rule of law and institutions (the legal-rational source of authority), and the damage to the structure of checks and balances caused by centralized personalization. In light of this, personal politics can and should be seen as a threat to democracy and certainly to its quality.

It is impossible, and undesirable, to return to a past of party dominance. The solution is to create a new balance (perhaps also by creating some incentives for decentralized personalism) and to direct personal politics in a way that will enhance group and party collective action. After all, groups in general and parties in particular are made up of individuals who want to progress, succeed and win and are together because they understand that only in collaboration can they achieve those goals.

Notes

1 The review below is based on Pedersen and Rahat (2021).
2 Particularly notable is research in the online realm: Haleva-Amir (2011); Zamir and Rahat (2019); Bar-Ilan, Bronstein, and Aharony (2015); Haleva-Amir (2016); Lev-On (2011); Lev-On and Haleva-Amir (2018); Livak, Lev-On, and Doron (2011); Samuel-Azran, Yarchi, and Wolfsfeld (2018). On the behavior of legislators, see Friedman and Friedberg (2021). On media in general, see Markowitz-Elfassi, et al. (2021). On the uncontrolled media, see Greenwald and Lehman-Wilzig (2019); Shenhav and Sheafer (2008); Van Aelst et al. (2017). On perceiving the phenomenon as part of the Americanization of Israeli politics, see Aronoff (2000).
3 In the event that there was no clear leader (e.g., Agudat Yisrael), the selection of number one on the list was examined.
4 Some applicable words were rarely used and therefore were not included in the final analysis: *oti, otanu, banu, bachem*.
5 References that were coded include *mishpachti* (my family) and family members either by name or affiliation to the speaker, for example, my father, my mother and so forth (*avi, imi, horay; bni, biti, banay, bnotay; ishti, ra'ayati, bat zugi, em habanim; achi, achia, achoti, achyotai, nechaday, savi, savati*).
6 The phrase *miflagtenu* (our party) was used only once (Gantz, 2019a).

74   *Gideon Rahat*

7 This claim is based on a comparison with other parties in a database encompassing over 200 parties in more than 30 democracies. See PPDB R2.
8 Zamir and Rahat (2019) suggest that parties should be expected to produce at least twice the amount of any politician, and demonstrate that this is indeed the case in most countries.
9 Also excluding the ultra-Orthodox parties.
10 The speeches were presented and perceived as victory speeches at the time, either because of the election results or because the leader wanted to create a momentum for the coalition negotiations.
11 Kadima of 2006 may be regarded as an early manifestation of the phenomenon. But Kadima changed and became far less personalized under Olmert's leadership.

References

Akzin, Benjamin. 1955. "The Role of Parties in Israeli Democracy." *Journal of Politics* 17 (4): 607–645.

Aronoff, Myron J. 2000. "The 'Americanization' of Israeli Politics: Political and Cultural Change." *Israel Studies* 5 (1): 92–127

Balmas, Meital, Gideon Rahat, Tamir Sheafer, and Shaul Shenhav. 2014. "Two Routes to Personalized Politics: Centralized and Decentralized Personalization." *Party Politics* 20 (1): 37–51.

Bar-Ilan, Judith, Jenny Bronstein, and Noa Aharony. 2015. "Israeli Parties and Party Leaders on Facebook During the 2013 Election Campaign." *iConference 2015 Proceedings (online).* www.ideals.illinois.edu/bitstream/handle/2142/73671/23_ready.pdf

Begin, Menachem. 1977. "Election Victory Speech 1977, The Night of the Upheaval, at Zeev Fortress." *Personal Archive – Begin Heritage Center*, May 17 [Hebrew]. https://db.begincenter.org.il/article/נאום-ניצחון-הבחירות--1977ליל-המהפך-במצודת/

Friedman, Avital, and Chen Friedberg. 2021. "Personalized Politics and Weakened Parties – An Axiom? Evidence from the Israeli Case." *Party Politics* 27 (2): 258–268.

Gantz, Benjamin. 2019a. "Gantz in His Post-Election Speech: 'I Will Be Everyone's Prime Minister'." April 9 [Hebrew]. www.youtube.com/watch?v=yjawUTuGJ0o

Gantz, Benjamin. 2019b. "Following the Results of Exit Polls: Speech by Blue and White Chairman Benny Gantz." September 17, 2019 [Hebrew]. www.youtube.com/watch?v=c8ec9N8Ft9c

Greenwald, Gilad, and Sam Lehman-Wilzig. 2019. "Is she Still 'the Legendary Jewish Mother'? A Comparative Look at Golda Meir's and Tzipi Livni's Election Campaign Coverage in the Israeli Press." *Israel Affairs* 25 (1): 42–64.

Haleva-Amir, Sharon. 2011. "Present-Absent: The Use of Personal Internet Tools among Knesset Members." In *Connected: Politics and Technology in Israel*, edited by Erez Cohen and Azi Lev-On, 211–260. Tel Aviv: The Israeli Political Science Association.

Haleva-Amir, Sharon. 2016. "Talking to Themselves: Classification of Facebook's Political Usages and Representatives' Roles among Israeli Members of Knesset." In *Forms and Functions of Political Participation in a Digital World*, edited by Alex Frame and Gilles Brachotte, 13–24. New York: Routledge.

INES. 2021. Israel National Elections Study. www.tau.ac.il/~ines/

Itim. 2006. "Ehud Olmert's Victory Speech." *Haaretz*, March 29 [Hebrew]. https://www.haaretz.co.il/misc/2006-03-29/ty-article/0000017f-dc1a-d3ff-a7ff-fdba98350000

Karni, Yuval. 2020. "Gantz in a Speech After Exit Polls: I Share the Disappointment and Pain'." *Ynet*, March 3 [Hebrew]. www.ynet.co.il/articles/0,7340,L-5687 807,00.html

Karpel, Dalia. 1993. "I Will Navigate." *Haaretz Supplement*, January 1, p. 27 [Hebrew].

Kenig, Ofer, and Gideon Rahat. Forthcoming. *The Parties in Israel Since 1992*. Jerusalem: The Israel Democracy Institute [Hebrew].

Lapid, Yair. 2021. "Yair Lapid on Election Night: 'No Government Will Be Formed in Israel on the Basis of Kahanist Voices'." Match 23 [Hebrew]. www.youtube.com/watch?v=hFLuI70yO50

Lev-On, Azi. 2011. "Campaigning Online: Use of the Internet by Parties, Candidates and Voters in National and Local Election Campaigns in Israel." *Policy & Internet* 3 (1): 1–28.

Lev-On, Azi, and Sharon Haleva-Amir. 2018. "Normalizing or Equalizing? Characterizing Facebook Campaigning." *New Media & Society* 20 (2): 720–739.

Livak, Lior, Azi Lev-On, and Gideon Doron. 2011. "MK Websites and the Personalization of Israeli Politics." *Israel Affairs* 17 (3): 445–466.

Markowitz-Elfassi, Dana, Tamir Sheafer, Yariv Tsfati, Gabriel Weimann, and Gadi Wolfsfeld . 2021. "Political Communication and Israeli Politics." In *The Oxford Handbook of Israeli Politics and Society*, edited by Reuven Y. Hazan, Alan Dowty, Menachem Hofnung, and Gideon Rahat, 637–651. Oxford: Oxford University Press.

Netanyahu, Benjamin. 2009. "Netanyahu's Speech at Ganey HaTa'arucha." February 11 [Hebrew]. www.youtube.com/watch?v=jvf15-oP5jU

Netanyahu, Benjamin. 2015. "Benjamin Netanyahu's Victory Speech at Ganey HaTa'arucha." March 17 [Hebrew]. www.youtube.com/watch?v=6eC41fPlFZo

Netanyahu, Benjamin. 2019a. "2019 Elections: Prime Minister Benjamin Netanyahu's Victory Speech." April 9 [Hebrew]. www.youtube.com/watch?v=1GsjFsjc82g

Netanyahu, Benjamin. 2019b. "Prime Minister Benjamin Netanyahu's Speech After the Exit Polls." September 17 [Hebrew]. www.youtube.com/watch?v=32vHVVR-8Cw

Netanyahu, Benjamin. 2020. "Netanyahu's Election Night Speech: 'Huge Victory'." March 2 [Hebrew]. www.youtube.com/watch?v=e3c-hu2No0s

Netanyahu, Benjamin. 2021. "I Do Not Rule Out Anyone." March 24 [Hebrew]. www.ynet.co.il/news/article/H1a5YgdNO

Pedersen, Helene H., and Gideon Rahat. 2021. "Introduction: Political Personalization and Personalized Politics within and beyond the Behavioral Arena." *Party Politics* 27 (2): 211–219.

Poguntke, Thomas, and Paul Webb, eds. 2005. *The Presidentialization of Politics: A Comparative Study of Modern Democracies*. Oxford: Oxford University Press.

Poguntke, Thomas, and Paul Webb. 2018. "Presidentialization, Personalization and Populism: The Hollowing out of Party Government." In *The Personalization of Democratic Politics and the Challenge for Political Parties*, edited by William P. Cross, Richard S. Katz, and Scott Pruysers, 181–196. London: ECPR.

PPDB R2. Political Parties Database Round 2 (data would be released online to www.politicalpartydb.org

76 *Gideon Rahat*

Rahat, Gideon. 2019. *The Decline of the Group and the Rise of the Star(s). From Party Politics to Personal Politics*. Jerusalem: The Israel Democracy Institute [Hebrew].

Rahat, Gideon, and Ofer Kenig. 2018. *From Party Politics to Personalized Politics? Party Change and Political Personalization in Democracies*. Oxford: Oxford University Press.

Rahat, Gideon, and Tamir Sheafer. 2007. "The Personalization(s) of Politics: Israel 1949–2003." *Political Communication* 24 (1): 65–80.

Samuel-Azran, Tal, Moran Yarchi, and Gadi Wolfsfeld. 2018. "Rhetoric Styles and Political Affiliations during Israel's 2013 'Facebook Elections'." *International Journal of Politics, Culture, and Society* 31 (1): 15–30.

Shenhav, Shaul R., and Tamir Sheafer. 2008. "From Inter-Party Debate to Inter-Personal Polemic: Media Coverage of Internal and External Party Disputes in Israel, 1949–2003." *Party Politics* 14 (6): 706–725.

Van Aelst, Peter, Tamir Sheafer, Nicolas Hube, and Stylianos Papathanassopoulos. 2017. "Personalization." In *Comparing Political Journalism* edited by Claes de Vreese, Frank Esser, and David Nicholas Hopmann, 112– 130. London: Routledge.

Zamir, Shahaf, and Gideon Rahat. 2019. *Online Political Personalization: A Comparative Study of Parties and Politicians in Israel*. Jerusalem: The Israel Democracy Institute [Hebrew].

4 King Bibi

The Personification of Democratic Values in the 2019–2021 Election Cycle[1]

Liron Lavi, Naama Rivlin-Angert,
Clareta Treger, Tamir Sheafer,
Israel Waismel-Manor, and Michal Shamir

4.1 Introduction

The 2019–2021 unprecedented four-election cycle revolved much around Benjamin Netanyahu, the (then) incumbent prime minister since 2009. Not only was Netanyahu dominant in its instigation and in setting its agenda, eventually he himself became the election agenda. Indeed, according to the Israel National Election Studies (INES) data, following each of the four elections, at least half of the Israeli electorate – and in the fourth election close to two thirds – stated that the elections were mostly about Netanyahu.[2] This was far beyond any policy issue, and more than ever before. In fact, the last time Netanyahu loomed high on the election agenda was in 1999, following his first term in office, in what was the second out of three direct elections of prime minister conducted in Israel. Then, the leading response to "what were the elections most of all about" was Netanyahu (40%), still far from his perceived centrality in the 2019–2021 election cycle.[3] Indeed, this election cycle had concluded in 2021 with an unprecedented coalition that brought together diverse parties: Jewish and Arab, religious and secular, right and left, with one common aim – to end Netanyahu's tenure.

The second most common issue that Israelis stated that these elections were about by the end of the cycle was the "future of democracy" (14%).[4] This is not surprising in light of the political and constitutional gridlock that led to four elections within less than two years. This was accompanied by Netanyahu's investigations, indictment, and court case on charges of bribery, fraud, and breach of trust (see Navot and Goldshmidt in this volume), looming high on the public agenda during this period. The political turbulence coupled with Israelis' concerns over the future of democracy tap into the prominent academic discussion about a global "crisis of democracy," and especially the extent to which this crisis has extended to a decline in diffuse democratic support to the most fundamental "rules of the game," that is, the support for democratic values and principles.

DOI: 10.4324/9781003267911-6

78 *Liron Lavi et al.*

In light of Netanyahu's centrality in these elections and against the back-drop of "democratic backsliding," we build on the literature of political personalization to examine whether and how Netanyahu himself embodied attitudes toward democratic principles in this election cycle. Political personalization is a globally salient process, and Israel exhibits high levels of political personalization and (current) personalism (see Rahat in this volume). However, little is known about the role of personalism in support for or rejection of democratic values and principles.

This chapter goes beyond politicization of democratic values and claims that political personalization – especially when it revolves around one person such as is the case in Israeli politics – may further challenge (or enhance) democratic values. This can happen when these values become *personified*, namely attached to and identified with a politician. This *personification*, we claim, is a distinct manifestation of personalization, whereby values and ideas become embodied in a persona.[5] We thus address the question of whether democratic values are associated with the appraisal of Netanyahu in this election cycle, beyond their politicization by left-right leaning.

We identify two dimensions of democratic values: liberal and regime support. We find that affection for Netanyahu has a significant effect on these values in an authoritarian and illiberal direction that goes beyond the effect of political leaning. These findings suggest that Netanyahu's personification may thus erode support for democratic values. The chapter concludes with a discussion of the possible ramifications of personification for Israeli democracy and democracies in general in the context of the role of citizens and political elites in democracy's backsliding.

4.2 Public Support for Democracy – Israel from a Global Perspective

The importance of public support for democracy is captured by Mattes's (2018) quote: "democracy requires democrats." A flourishing democracy requires a democratic – or civic – culture to function (Almond and Verba, 1963). This culture constitutes a shared vision of democracy and wide support for democratic values and principles. Support for democratic values is part of what Easton (1965, 1975) terms "diffuse support for democracy" and what Norris (2011) identifies as "support for regime principles." It underscores the collective meaning-making of democracy, "a pluralistic culture based on communication and persuasion, a culture of consensus and diversity, a culture that permitted change but moderated it" (Almond and Verba, 1963: 8). This diffuse support for democracy, is paramount in helping democracies survive (Easton 1965). Recently, Claassen (2020) demonstrated that support for democracy in 135 countries over a period of 29 years has been significantly and positively associated with subsequent changes in democracy, especially with the endurance of democracy, once it has been established.

The Personification of Democratic Values 79

In the ongoing discussion over democratic backsliding, the jury is still out concerning the verdict on democratic deconsolidation. Already half a century ago, political scientists identified declining trust in institutions and disenchantment with representative democracy in established democracies. These were first noticed in the United States in the late 1960s and through the 1970s, and then also in many other established democracies. These findings spurred debates on the nature of public discontent and the level at which the decline in democratic support occurred: the diffuse support for democracy, or only at the specific, less consequential concrete level (Citrin, 1974; Dalton, 2004; Miller, 1974a, 1974b; Norris, 1999, 2011; Pharr et al., 2000). Recent studies by Mounk (2020) and Foa and Mounk (2016, 2017, 2019) established a connection between deconsolidation of political regimes and deconsolidation of democratic culture, suggesting the crisis has reached the diffuse levels of support for democracy. They demonstrate that the erosion in democratic support (measured by World Values Survey data) is associated with subsequent declines in the actual extent of democratic governance and system-level democratic backsliding (measured by downgrades in Freedom House scores) as well as increase in support for nondemocratic alternatives (such as "strong leader," "military rule," and "experts' rule"), especially among younger generations. Still, their findings are disputed (*Journal of Democracy*, 2017). Other research concludes that there is no consistent cross-national evidence for a decline in democratic support, and that support for democratic principles is almost universally high (Van Ham et al., 2017).

In Israel, a cursory overview of survey indicators for diffuse democratic support shows fluctuations over a 40-year period but no apparent consistent downward (or upward) trend since 1980. Available questions from different research projects include such democratic norms as support for free speech, equality before the law, and opposition to authoritarian rule (Israeli Democracy Index, 2003–2020; Peres and Yuchtman-Yaar, 1992; Shamir and Sullivan, 1983; Yuchtman-Yaar and Peres, 2000). Historically, support for equality before the law and freedom of speech in the abstract has been relatively high and stable, although dropping under security threats, when attached to specific groups, or juxtaposed with other values. Principled opposition to an authoritarian leader was weaker and oscillated the most.[6]

As to system-level indicators of the quality of Israeli democracy – in spite of contradictory assessments and lively debates over it (e.g., Ben-Rafael et al., 2016; Ariely, 2021) – international indices, such as Freedom House, the Economist, Varieties of Democracy (V-Dem), and the Election Integrity Project, have consistently rated Israel (within the 1967 borders) as a democracy. Over the years, Israel ranks relatively high on these scales compared to the majority of the countries in the world, but relatively low compared to OECD countries (Hermann et al., 2020). However, Freedom House (2021a) aggregative score indicates a decline in Israeli democracy, dropping consistently from 84 (out of 100) in the first decade of the 2000's down to 76 in 2020.

80 *Liron Lavi et al.*

Israel thus joins a global trend of democratic backsliding. According to one of Freedom House's (2021b) latest reports, 2020 was the 15th consecutive year of decline in global freedom and democracy. Seventy-three countries experienced deterioration in their political rights and civil liberties, while only 28 experienced improvements. The last decade – and especially the dramatic 2016 Brexit referendum and U.S. Presidential elections – heightened the discussion on the global state of democracy. It focused on the questions of whether, how, and why democratic regimes may be backsliding to the extent that they may actually deconsolidate even in well-established democracies. This scholarship entertains explanations such as political elite (mis)behavior, institutional failures, technological developments, economic crises, and growing inequality (Corbett, 2020). Working within the personalization perspective, we focus here on the political elite, and more specifically on its apex.

We set out to examine the inner workings of democratic support in Israel, which in this election cycle, we contend, were not only structured by political affiliation, but also by centralized personalization focused on Netanyahu. Understanding whether and to what extent diffuse democratic support is conditioned on political leanings and appraisals of a focal political figure will provide a more nuanced account of the state of democratic culture in Israel. We will return to this, and to the implications on the prospects of democratic backsliding, in the conclusion.

4.3 Personification of Democratic Values

The 2019–2021 election campaigns exhibited centralized personalism (Rahat in this volume) with a distinct spotlight on Benjamin Netanyahu, the (then) Israeli prime minister in office for over a decade. This political context – coupled with the long-lasting polarized nature of the Israeli political system – led to the *personification* of democratic values in this election cycle. We thus expect to find that at this point in time, these values are associated with the appraisal of Netanyahu.

Before delving into the personification of democratic values in Israel, it is important to acknowledge that support for democratic values and principles is politicized in the sense that it varies by political left-right leanings. In Israel this is documented at least since 1980 (Shamir and Sullivan, 1983: 923, interestingly to a similar extent as in the United States). It has also been abundantly shown that support for democratic values and principles in Israel varies by levels of education, religiosity, and country of origin (e.g., Canetti-Nisim, 2004; Yuchtman-Yaar and Peres, 2000). Furthermore, the Israeli party system has been long characterized as politically polarized and subjugated by the collective identity cleavage (Canetti, Frant and Pedahzur, 2002; Shamir, Dvir-Gvirsman and Ventura, 2017), that has been found to foster affective polarization (Gidron, Adams and Horne, 2020).

Politicization and polarization reinforce one another. Politicization is a process in which representatives make competitive claims around a certain issue.

The Personification of Democratic Values 81

In this process, opinions, interests, and values become associated with political affiliations, and increasingly diverge along these lines (De Wilde, 2011). In this turbulent four-election cycle, contestants made competing claims along the lines of the very basic values of democracy, which became a subject of partisan political debate. Beyond this politicization, the question of democracy was tied strongly to Prime Minister Benjamin Netanyahu's indictment and court case. It reached such an extent that the center-left bloc placed Netanyahu himself at the heart of its election campaign, aiming all its efforts to remove him from office, claiming that he is "a danger to democracy" (Arlosoroff, 2019; Binyamin, 2020). As a result, the already politicized democratic values were intertwined in the election campaign with an intensified personal focus.

Political personalization refers to the process of increased personal focus, where the centrality of the individual actor in the political process increases over time while that of the political party declines (Rahat and Sheafer, 2007). Israel, together with Italy, is heading the list of 26 democracies in Rahat and Kenig's (2018) wide-scale comparative study of political personalization (see also Zamir and Rahat, 2019). If political personalization is a process, personalism is a situation in which the political weight of the individual actor is high in comparison to that of the political party (Pedersen and Rahat, 2019; see also Rahat in this volume). As stated, this chapter focuses on a specific form of personalism, that is, personification of values in the 2019–2021 election cycle.

Also relevant to our study is the distinction between centralized and decentralized personalization (Balmas et al., 2014). The former pertains to the centrality of a single politician while the latter pertains to several individuals who are on the rise. Taken to the extreme, centralized personalization may amount to presidentialization (Poguntke and Webb, 2005, 2018), especially when the entire focus is on one dominant person, the head of the country's executive branch in non-presidential political systems. Of the three facets of personalized politics – the institutional, media and behavioral (see Rahat in this volume), we focus on the latter. For politicians it entails "playing solo," where the "me" overrides the "we." Citizens, on their part, perceive politics as a game between competing individuals rather than teams.

Personalization scholars hold the view that personalization and personalism need not necessarily be apolitical or constitute a shift away from issues to persons. In fact, Wattenberg argues that since the 1980s the key to understanding the rise of "candidate-centered politics" in the United States is not personality politics, but rather the increasing importance of candidate-centered issues (2013). He refers to this as the second stage of candidate-centered politics, where the candidate "takes over" the party.[7] He predicts this shift to issue-focus within personalization to occur in parliamentary systems as well, with the changes in political communication. Political communication scholars indeed suggest that personalization in media coverage of politicians can include "their ideas, capacities and policies" (Van Aelst, Sheafer, and Stanyer, 2012), as opposed to a focus on politicians' personal characteristics or personal lives. Moreover, personalization can be a suitable strategy to

82 *Liron Lavi et al.*

communicate complex content, where politicians confer to it a face and a voice (Brettschneider, 2008).

We add to this perspective, taking centralized personalization and personalism beyond dominant politicians' ability to set the agenda and speak for substantive policy issues. Our claim is that the leader, especially in a presidentialized political system, may *stand for*[8] identities, ideas, and values. We term this representation or embodiment of an idea by an individual *personification*.

4.4 Hypotheses

We posit that in this election cycle, the Israeli presidentialized context exceeded the representation of policy by politicians and amounted to personification of key democratic values. Many in the political community, as well as citizens, consider the 2019–2021 elections as being concentrated on "Only-Bibi" vs. "Just-Not-Bibi." Indeed, as mentioned above, between a half and two thirds of Israelis, more than ever before, stated that the elections were mostly "about Netanyahu." At the same time, in the course of this election cycle "the future of democracy" had become the first policy issue the elections were about (see also Alpher, 2020; Shavit, 2019). These two are not disconnected. In line with the literature we reviewed, we argue that political personalism around Netanyahu did not void the elections of substance. To the contrary. The focus on Netanyahu brought the very fundamental values of Israel's democracy to the center stage. And Netanyahu embodied the rejection of these values.

Our primary interest lies in whether and to what extent renunciation vs. support for democratic values in this election cycle was personified by Netanyahu, and not only politicized by left-right affiliation. We begin our empirical exploration with replication of the well-established explanations for support in democratic values. We expect it to be grounded in citizens' socio-economic background and in their political affiliation. In terms of direction, and based on the surveyed literature, we expect that right-wing affiliation, as well as lower education, high religiosity, and former Soviet Union and Mizrahi ethnic origin will be associated with low support for democratic values (H1).

The personification thesis leads us to expect to find a distinct personification effect by Netanyahu above and beyond the politicization effect (H2), but in the same direction (H2a). Following the presidentialization and personalization thesis, and given Netanyahu's long-lasting dominance in Israeli politics, we expect that this personification of democratic values will be associated with Netanyahu, but not with his major rival in three out of the four rounds, Benny Gantz (H2b).

4.5 Data and Measurement

To test our hypotheses, we rely on the 2019–2021 INES data, utilizing the April 2019, March 2020, and March 2021 pre-electoral waves.[9] All samples were representative of the Israeli electorate, but we use Jewish respondents only (n=1,347; 729 and 1,498 respectively) since we presume that the processes we study here operated differently among Jews and Arabs, and thus require separate and different analysis. The fieldwork was carried out by Tel Aviv University's B. I. and Lucille Cohen Institute for Public Opinion Research.

The three elections are examined to study the extent to which support for democratic values was politicized and personified. By *democratic values* we mean support for democratic principles and rejection of nondemocratic alternatives and values. We evaluate democratic values using six items pertaining to attitudes toward a strong leader; adherence to the democratic rules of the game; commitment to the democratic regime; freedom of speech; equal rights; and trust in the Supreme Court.[10] All the items, except for the last one, were taken from or based on items in studies that measure diffuse democratic support (see Foa and Mounk, 2016, 2017; *Journal of Democracy*, 2017; Norris, 2011: 44–45). The survey items are listed in Appendix 4.1, and their dimensional analysis is presented in Table 4.1.

The analyses include all sociodemographic variables that were associated in past research with support for democratic values: gender, age group, education level, religiosity, country of origin, density of living (as indicator for socioeconomic status), and political interest. They are part of the replication effort (H1), and in the other analyses they are included as control variables. Their measures are listed in Appendix 4.2.

To measure whether and to what extent these values were *politicized* along the political left-right continuum (H1), we differentiate between voters of two political blocs. First, the right that was led by the Likud and Benjamin Netanyahu and included additional smaller right-wing and religious parties. Second, the center-left that was led by Benny Gantz and Blue and White party (Kahol-Lavan) in the first three elections and included additional smaller left parties. In the 2021 election – following the disintegration of the Blue and White alliance as a result of Gantz joining Netanyahu's coalition as the alternate prime minister – the center-left bloc was highly fragmented, and Yair Lapid of the Yesh Atid party became its leader. Nevertheless, its composition has hardly changed.[11] Our independent variable here is vote intention, dichotomized into these two blocs, coded 1 for right and 0 for center-left.

To explore our major thesis of *personification*, we employ party leaders' love–hate thermometers, scaled between 0 and 10 (in conjunction with the vote variable), and examine how affection for the leader is associated with support for democratic values. Personification is manifested in the *relation* between affect for the leader and democratic support. The main variable of interest is the Netanyahu love–hate thermometer (H2, H2a), and as control, we use the Gantz thermometer (in the March 2020 election). We dichotomize these scales, with 0–4 scores indicating the hate pole, and 6–10 the love pole.[12]

The literature conceptualizes personalization and personalism in terms of the balance between party and person (Pedersen and Rahat, 2019). Indeed, empirical explorations commonly employ such comparisons (see, for example, Aarts, Blais, and Schmitt, 2013). When it comes to public opinion, the strong overlap between vote and leader affect is well-known. In order to establish our personification thesis, we need therefore to corroborate an independent role of Netanyahu's appraisal, beyond political affiliation. Thus, in order to test the personification of the democratic values hypothesis, we juxtapose it to its partisan sources.

4.6 Analysis

4.6.1 Democratic Values in the 2019–2021 Election Cycle

Figure 4.1 presents support for democratic values and principles in the April 2019, March 2020, and March 2021 elections. There is much variation in levels of support for these principles, but on the whole, they are quite stable over the election cycle, with an average of 66% across the six items in each survey. Over 80% are committed to democracy and support political equality; attitudes toward democratic leadership and the adherence to the rules of the democratic game are at 60%; and less than 60% support freedom of speech for critics of Israel, the item which fluctuates the most.

Given this variation, to what extent do democratic values in Israel cluster? A factor analysis reveals that these measures comprise two dimensions (see Table 4.1). The first dimension pertains to regime support, including rejection of authoritarian leadership and adherence to the democratic rules of the game. The second dimension pertains to liberal values, comprised of support for equal rights, freedom of speech, and trust in the Supreme Court. The factor structure holds across the elections. The only exception is commitment

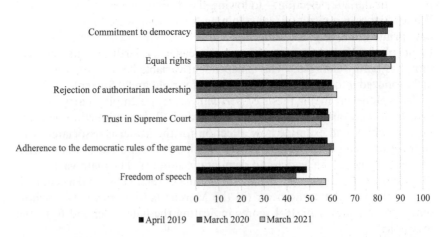

Figure 4.1 Support for democratic values, 2019–2021. Percentage of those who "agree" and "strongly agree" with claims in support for democratic values.

The Personification of Democratic Values 85

Table 4.1 Factor analysis of democratic values and principles, 2019–2021

	April 2019		March 2020		March 2021	
	Regime support	*Liberal values*	*Regime support*	*Liberal values*	*Regime support*	*Liberal values*
Rejection of authoritarian leadership	**.78**	.19	**.84**	.16	**.84**	.08
Adherence to the democratic rules of the game	**.83**	.07	**.87**	.07	**.47**	.21
Commitment to democracy	**.49**	.13	.08	**.58**	.16	**.42**
Equal rights	.03	**.80**	−.06	**.75**	.02	**.71**
Freedom of speech	.20	**.62**	.15	**.57**	.19	**.41**
Trust in Supreme Court	.17	**.63**	.26	**.57**	.11	**.42**

Note: Factor solution was obtained with Varimax rotation. Bolded entries signify which variables load on which factor.

to democracy that loads on the regime support dimension in April 2019 and on the liberal dimension in 2020 and 2021. While both dimensions are part and parcel of democratic support, they are distinct, reflecting different aspects of democracy.

Based on these results we constructed three (additive) scales, which serve as our dependent variables:

1 *Democratic support six item scale*, which combines the two following value scales, and the commitment to democracy item, which oscillates between the two factors in the surveys. (Cronbach alpha: April 2019 = .62, March 2020 = .59, March 2021 = .60).
2 *Regime support scale*, made up of the variables that indicate rejection of authoritarian leadership and adherence to the democratic rules of the game (Cronbach alpha: April 2019 = .64, March 2020 = .69, March 2021 = .57).
3 *Liberal values scale*, which includes the support for equal rights, freedom of speech, and trust in the Supreme Court variables (Cronbach alpha: April 2019 = .47, March 2020 = .46, March 2021 = .51).

The first scale is the most inclusive. It measures a wide range of democratic values, including both liberal and regime support components. The two additional scales indicate the regime support and liberal subdimensions of democratic culture. All dependent variables have been rescaled to range between 0 and 3 – where 0 is no support for democracy and 3 is full support for democracy – in order to allow meaningful comparison between the models.

86   *Liron Lavi et al.*

4.6.2 Personification of Democratic Values

We begin with the replication of recognized sources of democratic support. Table 4.2 presents the results of the regression models for each of the dependent variables for the April 2019 election, incorporating the standard predictors of democratic support from the literature (H1). The results validate previous findings concerning the effect of political affiliation and sociodemographic variables. As expected, voters' education, religiosity, and ethnic origin are associated with attitudes toward democratic values, as well as political interest. Secular, educated, and those who are interested in politics also tend to support democratic values. However, most important for our purpose is the strong impact of political affiliation, an indication for the politicized nature of support for democracy. A vote for the right bloc significantly reduces support for democratic values, as hypothesized, on both dimensions.[13] The difference in support for democracy between right-wing and left-wing supporters is larger than all other variables (across their full range), with one exception (the difference between respondents without matriculation diploma and those with academic degree on regime support). In addition, the bloc vote adds significantly to the explanation of democratic support above and beyond the sociological model (the R^2s of the sociological models are .241, .125, and .181, all smaller than the R^2s of their respective models in Table 4.2).[14]

Next, we turn to our main hypotheses and test whether and what role personification plays in the support for democratic values (H2, H2a, H2b). We estimate three regression models for each dependent variable. They include all the control variables listed above, but for ease of display, we present in Tables 4.3 and 4.4 only the coefficients of the leader appraisal and bloc vote variables. The first column for each dependent variable includes only the leader appraisal; the second column – only the bloc vote; and the third column, both, indicating the unique effect of each.[15]

Table 4.3 presents the results regarding personification in April 2019, March 2020, and March 2021. We know already that democratic values are politicized. Now we can add the personification effect. Across the three elections, for the three dependent variables – overall democratic support (I) and its subdimensions – democratic regime support (II) and liberal values (III), this effect is significant and substantial. The personification effect is displayed in the first row in the table, and all coefficients are statistically significant, most of them of similar size to the bloc vote coefficients, and in some of the models even larger. As hypothesized, voters' sentiment toward Netanyahu affects their orientation toward democracy (H2); support for Netanyahu – like right-wing affiliation – is associated with less support for democratic values and their two subdimensions (H2a).

To evaluate personification *beyond politicization*, and given the strong association between them, we conduct the analysis in two stages. First, for each democratic support indicator, we estimate the Netanyahu effect in the first

Table 4.2 The effect of political affiliation and sociodemographic variables on support for democratic values and principles, April 2019

	Overall democratic support	Regime support	Liberal values
Bloc vote (1=right)	−.430***	−.444***	−.621***
	(.060)	(.100)	(.072)
Gender (1=Female)	−.045	.091	−.099
	(.056)	(.094)	(.065)
Age group	.012	.004	.028
	(.022)	(.035)	(.028)
Education	.095***	.174***	.034
	(.025)	(.041)	(.029)
Religiosity	−.077*	.002	−.112*
	(.035)	(.056)	(.046)
Origin			
Asia/Africa	.004	−.042	−.032
	(.077)	(.128)	(.095)
Europe/America	.095	.091	.024
	(.079)	(.129)	(.090)
Former Soviet Union	−.234*	−.355*	−.182
	(.095)	(.164)	(.113)
Density of living	−.015	−.035	.021
	(.078)	(.127)	(.095)
Political interest	.101***	.109*	.058
	(.028)	(.047)	(.037)
Constant	1.757***	1.343***	2.015***
	(.138)	(.259)	(.168)
Observations	359	382	383
R-squared	.370	.198	.314

Notes: Standard errors in parentheses.
*** p<.001, ** p<.01, * p<.05.
The three categories in italics are three categories of the Origin variable. The base category includes the respondents whose father was born in Israel.

column, where it appears alone in the model, without the vote; this provides an estimate as to its maximum effect that incorporates its joint effect with the vote (beyond the controls). Then, the Netanyahu coefficient in the models that include the bloc vote *and* Netanyahu's appraisal together (the third column for each dependent variable) provides an estimate of its unique effect, beyond the bloc vote. All these coefficients are significant, and in several of the models, larger in size than the bloc vote coefficients. Support for democratic values in Israel is thus not only politicized, but also personified by Netanyahu, in particular with regard to the regime support dimension in April 2019 and March 2020. In the March 2021 election, politicization and personification balance out, but the unique effect of personification with respect to illiberal values gains in strength, whereas politicization is somewhat weakened. In this last election, the interconnection between the bloc vote and the Netanyahu

Table 4.3 Personification by Netanyahu of democratic values and principles: April 2019, March 2020, and March 2021

	(I) Overall democratic support			(II) Regime support			(III) Liberal values		
April 2019 – Netanyahu									
Netanyahu's Appraisal	−.377***		−.221*	−.417***		−.393*	−.517***		−.215*
	(.054)		(.087)	(.092)		(.157)	(.064)		(.101)
Bloc vote		−.430***	−.272**		−.444***	−.135		−.621***	−.482***
		(.060)	(.092)		(.100)	(.160)		(.072)	(.106)
R-squared	.329	.370	.371	.187	.198	.195	.275	.314	.314
N	437	359	312	468	382	334	464	383	331
March 2020 – Netanyahu									
Netanyahu's Appraisal	−.382**		−.259**	−.522***		−.381*	−.427***		−.230*
	(.056)		(.081)	(.105)		(.176)	(.066)		(.105)
Bloc vote		−.442***	−.282***		−.619***	−.348		−.526***	−.392***
		(.067)	(.085)		(.117)	(.182)		(.079)	(.114)
R-squared	.319	.334	.360	.156	.176	.186	.281	.293	.319
N	497	426	382	523	447	400	527	453	406
March 2021 – Netanyahu									
Netanyahu's Appraisal	−.350***		−.252**	−.383***		−.285*	−.429***		−.365***
	(.056)		(.085)	(.089)		(.139)	(.067)		(.100)
Bloc vote		−.353***	−.242**		−.430***	−.313*		−.409***	−.234*
		(.068)	(.089)		(.113)	(.145)		(.081)	(.107)
R-squared	.300	.286	.320	.150	.145	.183	.253	.244	.288
N	425	331	283	445	342	294	455	355	304

Notes: OLS regressions; control variables not presented. Standard errors in parentheses.

*** $p<.001$, ** $p<.01$, * $p<.05$.

The Personification of Democratic Values   89

sentiment is somewhat weaker than in the previous elections (Pearson correlation of .73, compared to .80 and .83 in 2019 and 2020). This finding is especially interesting given the changes in the political map in the March 2021 election, as some right-wing parties joined forces with center-left parties against Netanyahu such that the right-left dimension became less associated with Netanyahu appraisal.

In order to determine whether the personification effect is, indeed, as we conjecture (H2b), unique to Netanyahu, we use as "control" the (dichotomized) thermometer measure for Benny Gantz, the leader of the Blue and White alliance and Netanyahu's major opponent in the first three elections (Table 4.4). The results are unequivocal.[16] When the "Gantz affect" is alone in the model, it is meaningful and statistically significant (.32, .39, and .34), but consistently lower in absolute value than the comparable March 2020 Netanyahu coefficients (−.38, −.52, and −.43). In terms of direction, affection for Gantz increases support for democratic values, in contrast to affection for Netanyahu (stronger and negative). However, when Gantz's appraisal is combined with the bloc vote in the model, its effect declines dramatically (remaining statistically significant only in the inclusive democratic support scale), and political leaning takes almost all of the effect. In all of these models, when Gantz's appraisal and bloc vote are combined, the political affiliation has a strong effect, but the personification is non – or barely – significant. Particularly telling is the regime support subdimension model (II): the Netanyahu appraisal coefficient is −.52, and compares to Gantz's .39, when alone in the model; adding the bloc vote makes Gantz appraisal nonsignificant, while Netanyahu turns the bloc vote coefficient nonsignificant. These results confirm hypothesis H2b, and thus our *personification* claim, which revolves around the political figure in the apex of the "presidentialized" system.

We found clear evidence for personification of (anti)democratic values by Netanyahu, by far the most dominant political figure in Israel. Personification of democracy occurs beyond political affiliation, and takes place in both subdimensions, but more through the regime support dimension which measures the (anti)-authoritarian facet, embodied in a strong leader. This is the thrust of Netanyahu's personification of democratic values in this election cycle.

4.7 Conclusion

The 2019–2021 election cycle was unique in many ways, not the least of, its focus on the (then) incumbent prime minister and the leading candidate, Benjamin Netanyahu. This is well captured in the following quote from one survey respondent to the question about right-left self-identification: "I don't know 1 Right, 7 Left; we are 'Bibi'. Write whatever you want." The election cycle was also about Israeli democracy, as this period in Israel's electoral history constituted simultaneously a political crisis and a constitutional one.

Table 4.4 Personification by Gantz of democratic values and principles: March 2020

	(I) Overall democratic values			(II) Regime support			(III) Liberal values		
March 2020 – Gantz									
Gantz's Appraisal	.317***		.158*	.394***		.224	.339***		.102
	(.053)		(.067)	(.103)		(.142)	(.067)		(.085)
Bloc vote		−.442***	−.377***		−.619***	−.417**		−.526***	−.538***
		(.067)	(.078)		(.117)	(.160)		(.079)	(.093)
R-squared	.306	.334	.373	.164	.176	.193	.250	.293	.334
N	462	426	352	482	447	365	488	453	373

Notes: OLS regressions; control variables not presented. Standard errors in parentheses.

*** $p<.001$, ** $p<.01$, * $p<.05$.

Therefore, we set out to examine the relation between the high personalism in Israeli politics and diffuse democratic support. We focused on an understudied aspect of political personalization, which we term *personification* – the embodiment of values and ideas in a dominant political figure. We found evidence for this distinct phenomenon that goes beyond the politicization of democratic values. This personification was concentrated on Netanyahu and was manifested in *both* antidemocratic authoritarian values and illiberal values. This pattern was most pronounced on the regime support dimension in April 2019 and March 2020. Netanyahu's dominance, his long-lasting incumbency, and the state of presidentialization of the Israeli political system play a key role in this personification. This is indicated by the fact that we do not find such personification for his major political rival in 2019–2020, Benny Gantz, even though he framed his electoral effort as defense of Israeli democracy.[17]

Is Israeli democracy under threat? Israel is part of the global democratic backsliding trend. While citizens' support for democracy in Israel has been stable over the years, our study has uncovered that "under the hood" it is politicized and personified. Netanyahu personifies the strong leader notion, fostering and facilitating antidemocratic authoritarian, and to a lesser extent, also illiberal views. That being said, the March 2021 election resulted, eventually, in an unprecedented coalition that included right, center, left, Jewish, and Arab parties, who joined forces to oust Netanyahu. The jury on the state of democracy in Israel is still out, then, as the long-term effects of Netanyahu's personification on democratic deconsolidation in Israel – as well as counterefforts to curb them – continue to unfold.

We focused here only on personification of democratic values in Israel during this stormy and personalized election cycle. Whether this has been a long-term process, when it began, and whether it occurred with prominent Israeli leaders in the past are questions worth further exploration. However, there is nothing unique about this case – consider the parallel developments in the Unites States, Hungary, Turkey, or Brazil. These findings expand the personalization literature and also support the claim that personalized politics need not be content-free. We showed that fundamental values become embodied in a leading politician and are brought to the forefront of the political contest. Our findings also corroborate the interconnectedness of- and changing balance between leaders and political parties. They suggest that even as parties lose salience and appeal, political affiliations and identities do not disappear but may become more candidate-centered. The two latter points combined underscore the crucial role of politicians in personalized and presidentialized systems with respect to democratic culture.

What do our findings imply regarding the global "democratic backsliding" debate? These findings join the growing public and academic concerns about possible democratic crisis, and the role of political elites in it. Much of the recently growing scholarship on democracy deconsolidation examines those elites. Levitsky and Ziblatt (2018), for example, blame political elites who are

92 *Liron Lavi et al.*

not fulfilling their role to uphold basic democratic norms. McCoy and Somer (2019) similarly emphasize the role of political leaders in harming democracy by bringing to the forefront of the national agenda or even manufacturing what they call "pernicious" polarization. Frantz et al. (2021) connect between the personalization trend in democracies and democratic backsliding, suggesting it allows "[p]oliticians [to] erode checks and balances and incrementally consolidate power, even when public support for democracy remains high" (2021: 106). In democratic political systems, politics always involves interaction between the citizenry and its leadership. These studies as well as our research turn on its head "the elitist theory of democracy" (Peffley and Rohrschneider, 2007) by showing that political elites cannot be trusted as gatekeepers or defenders of democracy. To the contrary, they may be the instigators of nondemocratic policy and broader democratic deconsolidation.

We contribute to this claim the notion of *personification* as a mechanism for democratic erosion, showing that a dominant political leader can stand for antidemocratic notions and embody rejection of democratic norms. We believe that such personification is much more likely in presidential and in presidentialized systems, and that it might be intensified where "strong leadership" is long-lasting and the leader's term in office is unlimited. A prolonged rule of a single democratically elected leader probably facilitates such a process of personification, thereby intensifying the political debate around already contested principles of democracy.

Given the reciprocal nature of the relationship between the public and its leadership, we should ask when and how strong leaders affect citizen values, and in particular democratic support, and when and how public opinion gives rise to such leaders. Perhaps it is convergence between authoritarian tendencies of leaders and of parts of the electorate that brings these leaders into power. These leaders, in turn, hammer at democratic representative and liberal institutions, values, and practices. The invasion of Trump supporters into the U.S. Capitol on January 6, 2021, is a case in point (Washington Post Staff, 2021). As Poguntke and Webb (2018: 196) emphasize, personalization and presidentialization "set free" or lead the way for voters and strong executive leaders alike in this direction. Indeed, while personification could be harmful for democratic support, the other side of the coin should also be considered – can personification *enhance* democratic support? German Chancellor Merkel might be a promising case for such an examination. All these conjectures call for multilevel, multi-method, and cross-national studies, that bring together publics and leaders, in the search for answers about deconsolidation (and also consolidation) of democratic culture and regimes.

Notes

1 This study was funded by a grant (No. 2315/18) of the Israel Science Foundation to the Center of Excellence "Looking Beyond the Crisis of Democracy: Patterns of Representation in Israeli Elections." The authors acknowledge the valuable comments of Gidi Rahat, Mark Peffley and the anonymous reviewers.

2 Israel National Election Studies 2019–2021: www.tau.ac.il/~ines/2019.html
3 The question asks "What were the elections most of all about" in the postelection surveys. In 2015, about a third of respondents said the election was about Netanyahu, more than any other option presented to them, but very close to "social issues." In 2013, the choice of the Netanyahu option was much more marginal (12%) compared to policy issues; in 2009 less than a quarter chose the personal response of who should be prime minister (in that election the leading candidates were Netanyahu and Livni). In 1999, 40% chose the Netanyahu option, followed by a quarter who chose "the socioeconomic situation" (www.tau.ac.il/~ines/elections.html).
4 Following the first election in the cycle (April 2019) this option obtained 10%, tied with "security threats and how to handle them" and "conflict with the Palestinians."
5 This implies that personalization does not necessarily entail politics void of substance. To the contrary, it may highlight and bring to the fore substantive issues of utmost importance – here, democratic values. We develop this point further in the next sections.
6 While diffuse democratic support seems to be stable, trust in political institutions, a standard indicator of more specific support for democracy, exhibits a steep decline. Questions about trust in the Knesset, government, Supreme Court, and politicians are available since the mid-1980s and show a consistent decline (Israeli Democracy Index, 2003–2020; Peres and Yuchtman-Yaar, 1992; Sapanov, 2002).
7 Unlike the first stage in which candidates tried to differentiate themselves from the party (Wattenberg 2013: 76–81).
8 In her classic exploration of representation, Pitkin (1967) contrasts the notion of representation as "standing for" with "acting for" the represented. Our case is an example of the former.
9 The April 2019 pre-electoral wave was in the field between February 24 and April 8, 2019; The March 2020 pre-electoral wave between January 29 and March 1, 2020; And the March 2021 pre-electoral wave between February 21 and March 22, 2021. In September 2019, not all support for democracy items were included.
10 While trust in institutions is usually associated with more specific support for democracy, the Supreme Court is a symbol of liberal democracy in Israel and was often referred to as such in the election discourse. Factor analysis indicates that trust in the Supreme Court does not load on the same factor with trust in other democratic institutions, but rather with the liberal values (see Table 4.1).
11 The right bloc included in the April 2019 election: Likud, The New Right, The Union of Right-Wing Parties, United Torah Judaism, Shas, Kulanu, Yachad, and Zehut. In the March 2020 election: Likud, Yemina, Otzma Yehudit (Jewish Power), United Torah Judaism, and Shas. In the March 2021 election: Likud, Yemina, The Religious Zionism, New Hope, United Torah Judaism, and Shas.
   The center-left bloc included in the April 2019 election: Blue and White, Labor, Meretz, Hadash–Ta'al, Ra'am–Balad, and Gesher. In the March 2020 election: Blue and White, Labor–Gesher–Meretz, and The Joint List. In the March 2021 election: Yesh Atid, Blue and White, Labor, Meretz and The Joint List.
   Over the four rounds, some right-wing parties dissociated themselves from the "Netanyahu bloc" (e.g., New Hope). Since our aim is to identify a personification effect beyond right-left affiliation, we coded these parties according to their political orientation (i.e., as right) rather than their attitudes toward Netanyahu. The only party that did not clearly fit into one of these camps over this election cycle was Avigdor Lieberman's Yisrael Beiteinu. We therefore left it out of the analyses.

94 *Liron Lavi et al.*

12 We excluded the middle category, 5, from the analysis. As a result, for Netanyahu 179 respondents were excluded in April 2019, 80 in March 2020, and 192 in March 2021. For Gantz, 59 respondents were excluded in March 2020.

13 The results of these models in March 2020 and March 2021 are similar with slight variations.

14 The full models upon which these results are based are not reported here. They will be provided upon request by the authors. This applies also to other such results in this section.

15 Since the sample size decreases from the first model to the second and third, we ran, as a robustness test, the same regressions with respondents for whom we have all data, and obtained the same results. As an additional robustness test, we also used the left-right self-identification 7-point scale, dichotomized into right (coded as 1) and center-left (coded as 0), instead of the bloc vote; the results remain robust, with slight changes.

16 In the April 2019 study, the questionnaire was split into two versions administrated randomly to two samples, and the evaluations of party leaders other than Netanyahu were not included in the same version as the democratic support variables.

17 The Likud headed by Netanyahu obtained 35, 32, and 36 seats in the April 2019, September 2019, and March 2020 elections respectively, compared to the 35, 33, and 33 seats obtained by the Blue and White alliance headed by Gantz. In March 2021, the Likud received 30 seats, while the components of the Blue and White combined gained 25 seats: 17 for Yesh Atid and 8 for Gantz's party that kept the Blue and White label.

Sources: https://votes21.bechirot.gov.il/; https://votes22.bechirot.gov.il/; https://votes23.bechirot.gov.il/; https://votes24.bechirot.gov.il/

References

Aarts, Kees, André Blais, and Hermann Schmitt, eds. 2013. *Political Leaders and Democratic Elections.* Oxford: Oxford University Press.

Almond, Gabriel A., and Verba Sidney. 1963. *The Civic Culture: Political Attitudes and Democracy in Five Nations.* Princeton: Princeton University Press.

Alpher, Rogel. 2020. "Why Just-Not-Bibi After All." *Haaretz*, www.haaretz.co.il/opinions/.premium-1.9058683 [last access: 29/09/20] [Hebrew].

Ariely, Gal. 2021. *Israel's Regime Untangled: Between Democracy and Apartheid.* Cambridge: Cambridge University Press.

Arlosoroff, Meirav. 2019. "Clear and Immediate Danger: It Is Time to Limit the Term of Office of the Prime Minister of Israel." *The Marker*, November 24. www.themarker.com/news/politics/.premium-1.8168827 [Hebrew].

Balmas, Meital, Gideon Rahat, Tamir Sheafer, and Shaul Shenhav. 2014. "Two Routes to Personalized Politics: Centralized and Decentralized Personalization." *Party Politics* 20 (1): 37–51.

Ben-Rafael, Eliezer, Julius H. Schoeps, Yitzhak Sternberg, Olaf Glöckner, and Anne Weberling, eds. 2016. *Handbook of Israel: Major Debates.* Berlin: de Gruyter Oldenbourg.

Binyamin, Idan. 2020. "Bending the Rules: Kahol Lavan Also Leads Moves that Crumble Democracy." *Shakuf*, August 29. https://shkifut.info/2020/08/bendthelaw/ [Hebrew].

The Personification of Democratic Values   95

Brettschneider, Frank. 2008. "Personalization of Campaigning." In *The International Encyclopedia of Communication*, edited by Wolfgang Donsbach, 3583–3585. Malden: Blackwell Publishing.

Canetti, Daphna, Howard L. Frant, and Ami Pedahzur. 2002. "The Triumph of Polarization." In *The Elections in Israel 1999*, edited by Asher Arian and Michal Shamir, 165–178. Albany: State University of New York Press.

Canetti-Nisim, Daphna. 2004. "The Effect of Religiosity on Endorsement of Democratic Values: The Mediating Influence of Authoritarianism." *Political Behavior* 26 (4): 377–398.

Citrin, Jack. 1974. "Comment: The Political Relevance of Political Trust." *American Political Science Review* 68 (3): 973–988.

Claassen, Christopher. 2020. "Does Public Support Help Democracy Survive?" *American Journal of Political Science* 64 (1): 118–134.

Corbett, Jack. 2020. "The Deconsolidation of Democracy: Is It New and What Can Be Done About It?" *Political Studies Review* 18 (2): 178–188.

Dalton, Russell J. 2004. *Democratic Challenges, Democratic Choices: The Erosion of Political Support in Advanced Industrial Democracies*. New York: Oxford University Press.

De Wilde, Pieter. 2011. "No Polity for Old Politics? A Framework for Analyzing the Politicization of European Integration." *Journal of European Integration* 33 (5): 559–575.

Easton, David. 1965. *A Systems Analysis of Political Life*. New York: J. Wiley.

Easton, David. 1975. "A Re-Assessment of the Concept of Political Support." *British Journal of Political Science* 5 (4): 435–457.

Foa, Stefan R., and Yascha Mounk. 2016. "The Danger of Deconsolidation: The Democratic Disconnect." *Journal of Democracy* 27 (3): 5–17.

Foa, Stefan R., and Yascha Mounk. 2017. "The Signs of Deconsolidation." *Journal of Democracy* 28 (1): 5–15.

Foa, Stefan R., and Yascha Mounk. 2019. *Democratic Deconsolidation in Developed Democracies, 1995–2018*. CES Open Forum Series 2018–2019. [Working Paper].

Frantz, Erica, Andrea Kendall-Taylor, Carisa Nietsche, and Joseph Wright, 2021. "How Personalist Politics Is Changing Democracies." *Journal of Democracy* 32 (3): 94–108.

Freedom House. 2021a. Israel. https://freedomhouse.org/country/israel/freedom-world/2021

Freedom House. 2021b. Democracy Under Siege. https://freedomhouse.org/report/freedom-world/2021/democracy-under-siege

Gidron, Noam, James Adams, and Will Horne. 2020. *American Affective Polarization in Comparative Perspective*. Cambridge: Cambridge University Press.

Hermann, Tamar, Or Anabi, Ayelet Rubabshi-Shitrit, Avraham (Rami) Ritov, and Ella Heller. 2020. *The Israeli Democracy Index 2020*. Jerusalem: Israel Democracy Institute.

Israel National Election Studies (INES). 2021. www.tau.ac.il/~ines/

The Israeli Democracy Index, 2003–2020. www.idi.org.il/centers/1123/1340

Journal of Democracy. 2017. Online Exchange on "Democratic Deconsolidation." www.journalofdemocracy.org/online-exchange-democratic-deconsolidation/

Levitsky, Steven, and Daniel Ziblatt. 2018. *How Democracies Die*. New York: Crown.

Mattes, Robert. 2018. "Support for Democracy." In *Oxford Research Encyclopedia in Politics*, edited by William Thompson. New York: Oxford University Press. Online

96 *Liron Lavi et al.*

Publication. https://oxfordre.com/politics/view/10.1093/acrefore/9780190228 637.001.0001/acrefore-9780190228637-e-622

McCoy, Jennifer, and Murat Somer. 2019. "Toward a Theory of Pernicious Polarization and How It Harms Democracies: Comparative Evidence and Possible Remedies." *The ANNALS of the American Academy of Political and Social Science* 681: 234–271.

Miller, Arthur H. 1974a. "Political Issues and Trust in Government." *American Political Science Review* 68 (3): 951–972.

Miller, Arthur H. 1974b. "Rejoinder." *American Political Science Review* 68 (3): 989–1001.

Mounk, Yascha. 2020. "The End of History Revisited." *Journal of Democracy* 31 (1): 22–35.

Norris, Pippa. 1999. *Critical Citizens: Global Support for Democratic Governance.* Oxford: Oxford University Press.

Norris, Pippa. 2011. *Democratic Deficit: Critical Citizens Revisited.* Cambridge: Cambridge University Press.

Pedersen, Helene H., and Rahat Gideon. 2019. "Introduction: Political Personalization and Personalized Politics within and beyond the Behavioural Arena." *Party Politics* https://doi.org/10.1177/1354068819855712

Peffley, Mark, and Robert Rohrschneider. 2007. "Elite Beliefs and the Theory of Democratic Elitism." In *The Oxford Handbook of Political Behavior*, edited by Russell J. Dalton and Hans-Dieter Klingemann, 193–212. Oxford: Oxford University Press.

Peres, Yochanan, and Ephraim Yuchtman-Yaar. 1992. *Trends in Israeli Democracy: The Public's View.* Boulder and London: Lynne Rienner Publishers.

Pharr, Susan J., Robert D. Putnam, and Dalton J. Russell. 2000. "A Quarter-Century of Declining Confidence." *Journal of Democracy* 11 (2): 7–25.

Pitkin, Hannah. 1967. *The Concept of Representation.* Berkeley: University of California Press.

Poguntke, Thomas, and Paul Webb. 2005. *The Presidentialization of Politics: A Comparative Study of Modern Democracies.* New York: Oxford University Press.

Poguntke, Thomas, and Paul Webb. 2018. "Presidentialization, Personalization and Populism: The Hollowing Out of Party Government." In *The Personalization of Democratic Politics and the Challenge for Political Parties*, edited by William P Cross, Richard S. Katz, and Scott Pruysers, 181–196. London: Rowman & Littlefield Publishers/ECPR Press.

Rahat, Gideon, and Ofer Kenig. 2018. *From Party Politics to Personalized Politics? Party Change and Political Personalization in Democracies.* Oxford: Oxford University Press.

Rahat, Gideon, and Sheafer Tamir. 2007. "The Personalization(s) of Politics: Israel 1949–2003." *Political Communication* 24 (1): 65–80.

Sapanov, Shiri. 2002. Political Efficacy in Israel: Comparative and Historical Perspectives. M.A. Thesis, Tel Aviv: Tel Aviv University.

Shamir, Michal, Shira Dvir-Gvirsman, and Raphael Ventura. 2017. "Taken Captive by the Collective Identity Cleavage: Left and Right in the 2015 Elections." In *The Elections in Israel 2015*, edited by Michal Shamir and Gideon Rahat, 139–164. New Brunswick: Transaction Publ.

Shamir, Michal, and John Sullivan. 1983. "The Political Context of Tolerance: A Cross-National Perspective from Israel and the United States." *American Political Science Review* 77 (4): 911–928.

Shavit, Ari. 2019. "Just Not Just-Not-Bibi." *Makor-Rishon*, October 17. www.mako rrishon.co.il/opinion/178317/ [Hebrew].

Van Aelst, Peter, Tamir Sheafer, and James Stanyer. 2012. "The Personalization of Mediated Political Communication: A Review of Concepts, Operationalizations and Key Findings." *Journalism* 13 (2): 203–220.

Van Ham, Carolien, Jacques J. Thomassen, Kees Aarts, and Rudy Andeweg, eds. 2017. *Myth and Reality of the Legitimacy Crisis: Explaining Trends and Cross-National Differences in Established Democracies.* New York: Oxford University Press.

Washington Post Staff, 2021. "Woman Dies After Shooting in U.S. Capitol; D.C. National Guard Activated After Mob Breaches Building." January 7. www.was hingtonpost.com/dc-md-va/2021/01/06/dc-protests-trump-rally-live-updates/

Wattenberg, Martin P. 2013. "US Party Leaders: Exploring the Meaning of Candidate-Centred Politics." In *Political Leaders and Democratic Elections*, edited by Kees Aarts, Blais André, and Schmitt Hermann, 76–90. Oxford: Oxford University Press.

Yuchtman-Yaar, Ephraim, and Yochanan Peres. 2000. *Between Consent and Dissent: Democracy and Peace in the Israeli Mind.* Lanham: Rowman & Littlefield.

Zamir, Shahaf, and Gideon Rahat. 2019. *Online Political Personalization: A Comparative Study of Parties and Politicians in Israel.* Policy Paper 124. Jerusalem: Israel Democracy Institute. www.idi.org.il/media/12563/political-personalization.pdf [Hebrew].

APPENDIX 4.1

Democratic Values Indicators

Indicator name	Survey item
Adherence to the democratic rules of the game	There are times when it seems it would be preferable to deviate from the democratic rules of the game in order to achieve significant change.
	Note: Reversed scale
Rejection of authoritarian leadership	In order to take care of Israel's unique problems, there is a need for a strong leader who doesn't take the Knesset or the elections into consideration.
	Note: Reversed scale
Commitment to democracy	You feel committed to the democratic regime in Israel, even if there are times when you don't like the decisions.
Equal rights	The state has to ensure full and equal social and political rights to all citizens, regardless of religion, race, or sex.
Freedom of speech	We must secure the freedom of speech of people who speak out against the state.
Trust in Supreme Court	How much trust do you have in the Supreme Court?

Note: Likert 4-point response scale.

98   *Liron Lavi et al.*

APPENDIX 4.2

Control Variables

The control variables used in the OLS regressions presented in the paper were coded as follows:

1   Gender
    0   male
    1   female
2   Age group
    1   18–29
    2   30–39
    3   40–49
    4   50–59
    5   60+
3   Education level
    1   High school education with no matriculation and lower
    2   High school education with matriculation
    3   Post high school education (non-academic)
    4   Academic education
4   **Religiosity** – "In terms of religion how do you define yourself?"
    0   Secular
    1   Traditional
    2   Religious
    3   Very religious
5   **Origin** – Four dummy variables based on the place of birth of the respondent if not born in Israel, and on the place of birth of the respondent's father for Israel-born respondents. The categories are as follows:
    1   **Israel** – Respondents whose father was born in Israel (base category).
    2   **Asia or Africa** – Respondents whose father was born in Asia or Africa.
    3   **Europe or America** – Respondents whose father was born in Europe or America.
    4   **Former Soviet Union** – Respondents whose father was born in the former Soviet Union.
6   **Density of living** – Number of people living in the household divided by the number of rooms, truncated so that respondents with density of .25 and lower were grouped into the .25 value and respondents with density of 2 and higher were grouped into the 2 value.
7   **Political interest** – "To what extent do you tend to discuss political issues with your friends and family?"
    0   Not at all
    1   To small extent
    2   To a certain extent
    3   To a great extent

5 A Populist Leader under Neoliberal Logic

Avi Shilon

On May 17, 2012, *Time* magazine crowned the prime minister of Israel, Benjamin Netanyahu, with the title "King Bibi" (Stengel, 2012). At the time, he was well into his second term as prime minister and headed Israel's 32nd government. Both in Israel and in the international media, Netanyahu, popularly known as Bibi, was perceived as an established leader, who shrewdly calculated his steps vis-à-vis his political rivals.

In hindsight, it is clear that his behavior during his second term was the result of lessons learned from his first term (1996–1999), which began against the background of a stormy ideological conflict between the right and left over the Oslo Accords (1993) and in the shadow of the national trauma following the assassination of Yitzhak Rabin (1995). During this term, Netanyahu had conflicts with many Likud ministers, who left or were dismissed from his government. The term ended after only three years, with the disintegration of his right-wing–religious coalition, the opening of a police investigation concerning gifts he had received as prime minister and defeat in the 1999 election to Ehud Barak, head of the Israel Ahat [One Israel] list. Following his defeat, Netanyahu took a break from politics.

During his second term (2009–2013), Netanyahu preferred to establish a unity government, which included, intermittently, the central-left parties Labor and Kadima. Many of the Likud ministers were members of what was known as the "second generation of the fighting family." They saw themselves as the carriers of the original Revisionist ideology that combined strident nationalism and liberal values. Though potentially a coalition fraught with tension, at the top of this government's agenda was a consensual issue: preventing Iran from developing nuclear weapons. Netanyahu was even able to quell the issue that had been a permanent conflictual part of Israel's political agenda since 1967 – the future of the Occupied Territories. In his 2009 "Bar-Ilan speech," he agreed, on the one hand, to the establishment of a Palestinian state but, on the other, he saddled it with conditions that eliminated this possibility, which were expected to be firmly rejected by the Palestinians. Thus, he satisfied both right and left, as well as the U.S. administration of President Barack Obama.

The *Israel Hayom* daily newspaper was founded in 2007 by the American billionaire Sheldon Adelson and designed to support Netanyahu. Two of its

DOI: 10.4324/9781003267911-7

100   *Avi Shilon*

most prominent journalists, Mordechai Gilat and Dan Margalit, were known for their support for a strong and independent judicial system and expressed this in their columns. Following the disclosure of what is known today as Case 2000 (Weitz, 2019),[1] we know that the editorial line of *Israel Hayom* was dictated by Netanyahu's office. Thus, there is no doubt that the prominence of journalists who supported an independent judicial system was not by chance. In light of this, it can be claimed that when Netanyahu returned to the premiership in 2009, he chose, intentionally, to avoid conflicts with the judicial system and sought to create a broad consensus around his government and policies. In other words, he was determined to avoid what he considered to be the mistakes of his first term.

This chapter begins by recalling aspects of Netanyahu's first and second terms in order to demonstrate that the blunt populism and polarizing manner in which he operated during the four rounds of elections that took place in Israel between 2019 and 2021 did not directly derive from his personality or worldview; neither were they features of his original political path. Rather, the claim is that Netanyahu's populist conduct in this period, and indeed before, was calculated and then invigorated by the election of Donald Trump as president of the United States in 2016. Netanyahu, who was quoted as claiming in his police interrogations that the United States is the only important country in the world (*The Marker*, 2019), is well known for his Americanist orientation. It appears that his political confidence increased following his victory in the 2015 election (which he won despite predictions to the contrary). As a result of this victory, and following Trump's entry into the White House, Netanyahu adopted the U.S. president's populism as the appropriate updated template for a political leader. The fact that prior to the Trump era Netanyahu prevented the passage of the controversial Nation State Law (Basic Law: Israel – the Nation State of the Jewish People), yet promoted it after Trump was elected, is telling. This is additional evidence that Netanyahu's pattern of leadership during the 2019–2021 campaigns was planned and that it was anchored in varied global and domestic political contexts.

Another event that may explain the change in Netanyahu's pattern of leadership is related to the Joint Comprehensive Plan of Action that the superpowers signed with Iran around that time, in July 2015. After the agreement was drafted, and subsequently accepted by the international community, Netanyahu lost a central component in his political agenda, that is, keeping the military option against the Iranian nuclear project alive. Losing this card may have led him to reconsider his leadership pattern and choose a revamped populist path.

5.1 Generational Change in Israel's Right Wing

In order to understand Netanyahu's political behavior in the 2019–2021 elections and more generally, the generational change in Israel's right wing during his time in office warrants a look. Here, a comparison can be made

A *Populist Leader under Neoliberal Logic* 101

between the development of Netanyahu's political path and that of the founder of the Revisionist Movement, Ze'ev Jabotinsky.

In *Jabotinsky's Children,* Daniel Heller (2017) sought to clarify why, during the 1930s, Jabotinsky made statements that contradicted the liberal and socialist values that he had expressed earlier. Heller argued that Jabotinsky did not necessarily change his ideas but rather adjusted himself to the processes of radicalization that had taken place among his young supporters. He needed to maneuver between his desire for their support and his original liberal positions. Indeed, examining the changes that take place in the inner circle and the audience of a leader, any leader, is an important tool to understand changes in their political behavior. It is critical in Netanyahu's case as well.

When joining the Israeli political arena at the end of the 1980s, Netanyahu was surrounded by national religious figures from the founding generation of Gush Emunim, descendants of the Revisionist Movement and advisers from the American neoconservative camp (Pfeffer, 2018: 215–252). In recent years, these were replaced by a new, younger generation that included, among others, Netanyahu's son, Yair, members of the ultraright Im Tirtzu movement, and national-religious journalists such as Shimon Riklin and Erel Segal. They fervently challenged what they consider to be the "ruling elite" and "the hegemony." During the 2015 election, for example, Netanyahu's chief campaign strategist was Gil Samsonov, who held Jabotinsky's liberal nationalist ideals. In 2019, in contrast, his senior communications adviser was Erez Tadmor, a founder of Im Tirtzu and the author of *Why Do I Vote Right and Get Left?*. The book's main thrust is that former Likud leaders, including Menachem Begin and Yitzhak Shamir, did not take advantage of opportunities after 1977 to boldly reorganize the political system. Rather, they "surrendered" to continued left-wing dominance within the establishment, despite the right wing's victory in elections (Tadmor, 2017).

Tadmor is a typical example of the younger right-wing figures who grasp the impact and tactics of the new media and who choose to distance themselves from the generation of the Revisionist Movement that surrounded Netanyahu in previous years. Many of Netanyahu's blunt speeches against the left and the judicial system were written by Tadmor or advisers with a similar agenda (Schneider, 2018). Netanyahu's opponents on the left, and members of the older generation of the Revisionist right wing too,[2] have criticized his unrestrained attacks on the judicial system. They compare Likud's current position to that of the Begin era. But the critics ignore the fact that figures such as Begin, and definitely Jabotinsky, are not role models for the younger right-wing generation. Instead, they are examples of what must be fixed.

This new right-wing generation, aged mostly between 20 and 40 years old today, was inspired by Naftali Bennett's forthright slogan from the 2013 elections, "No Apologies" (Bennett, ironically in this respect, succeeded Netanyahu in 2021). The terrorist attacks of the Second Intifada (Palestinian uprising) in the early 2000s influenced their worldviews much more than

102 *Avi Shilon*

Jabotinsky's writings or Begin's leadership style (Del Sarto, 2017). Like Jabotinsky's response to the radicalization of the young guard of Betar (the Revisionist youth movement) in the 1930s (including Begin!), Netanyahu is sometimes dragged along by the younger generation; sometimes he restrains them, but at other times he sides with them to provoke his rivals.

The right wing's intellectual base has also changed during Netanyahu's years in office. During his first term, Netanyahu had the backing of Shalem College, which insisted on relatively moderate statist conservatism.[3] Over the last decade, new frameworks have emerged, including Im Tirtzu, the Mida website, and the Shibolet publishing house. All are characterized by more aggressive, nationalist and populist positions (Sagiv, 2020).

Netanyahu's populist leadership style, which reached its peak during the 2019–2021 elections, was influenced by political trends, both local and international, as well as sociological and technological (new media) developments that occurred over the course of the last decade. The change in Netanyahu's politics – from nationalist conservativism to blatant populism should be analyzed against this background.

5.2 A Decline of the Old Statism and the Rise of Neoliberal Logic

On the eve of the first day of his trial for bribery and breach of trust, Netanyahu summarized the position that he had expressed throughout the election campaigns in a simple statement:

> What is on trial today is the attempt to thwart the will of the people… For more than a decade, the Left has not succeeded in doing so at the polls. In recent years it has found a new invention. Actors in the police and the Attorney General's office have joined forces with the Leftist newspapers to invent groundless and hallucinatory cases against me.
>
> (Eichner and Zimuki, 2020)

It is possible to read these words as populist posturing and an attempt to directly represent the people in their struggle against the elites in democratic institutions. But it should also be noted that Netanyahu was attacking statist institutions. His indictment opens in formal language – "The State of Israel vs. Benjamin Netanyahu." Beyond his personal interest to pressure the judicial system, his readiness to bluntly attack state institutions can be understood in the context of long and meaningful processes in Israel's history of statism (*mamlachtiut*) – and its decline.

The notion of *mamlachtiut*, led by David Ben-Gurion, was originally accepted by "all of the Jewish groups in the country" (Bareli and Keidar, 2011: 9), despite deep political disagreements. Statism – which placed the state's institutions above all sectorial-political interests and considerations – declined in favor of what can be termed "neo-Zionism" (Ram, 2011). State institutions have lost their prestige while the individual and sectorial considerations of various groups that claim to be the genuine representatives of Zionism have gained traction.[4] With this decline, it has become convenient to attack such entities. A typical example of this are settlers in the Occupied Territories who confront, from time to time, the representatives of the state, IDF (Israel Defense Forces) soldiers, claiming that it is they, the settlers, who embody the essence of current Zionism (Dayan, 2020: 87–123). The prime minister, however, is meant to represent these very state institutions, so for him to belittle them warrants attention.

But a closer look suggests that in the "neo-Zionist" era, it is no coincidence that Netanyahu is the first prime minister to come out against Israel's traditional (and problematic) position in his calling to open the classified files concerning the Yemenite Children Affair[5] (Bender, 2016); nor had any previous prime minister dared to contradict the position of the IDF chief of staff as Netanyahu did when he supported IDF soldier Elor Azaria[6] before and during his trial (Levinson, Lis, and Cohen, 2017). These two incidents expose part of the deeper political process that characterizes the right in Netanyahu's era: support for the interests of groups or individuals, even when they are in conflict with perceived state interests or the collective interests of Israeli society as a whole.

Since neoliberal logic has succeeded "in assimilating itself into the emotional blood circulation of the general public" (Shenhav, 2006), the public accepts the attempt to weaken the institutions that are responsible for the necessary checks and balances. It is enabled with attitudes that range from indifference to active support, because the neoliberal logic leads to a process of "marketization of democracy." In this situation, regulatory institutions are also seen as "commodities" that should be examined in accordance with market demands, and not according to moral and idealistic values, which cannot be measured in terms of their immediate and concrete "profit" to the citizen (Brown, 2017: 17). Thus, if the judicial system damages the successful "merchandise" that the prime minister provides to the "consumers" – the public – one can demand that the judicial system adapt itself to "market demands," that is, to the will of the people-consumers. Therefore, for example, the IDF chief of staff's position that it was necessary to put Azaria on trial would have been perceived in the past as justified, requiring an individual soldier to pay a price for his actions to preserve the "values" of the state, the military, and the public. Under neoliberal logic, the need to "get 'our' boy out of jail" becomes more important.

The extensive literature on neoliberalism – both as a global phenomenon (Zuidhof, 2016; Cornel, 2016) and in the Israeli context (Filc and Ram, 2014; Krampf, 2015) – conceptualized it in various ways. For the purposes of this chapter, I relate to its basic meaning: an ideology that relates to various fields of public life (which were not conducted exclusively according to the logic of the market), based on decisions that seek maximum efficiency and celebrate the ideal of competition as an organizing principle of life, while the state shrinks or changes its role in relation to society (Davies, 2014).

104   *Avi Shilon*

Netanyahu's criticism of the judicial system can be understood, therefore, in light of the processes of sectorialization and privatization. These emerged as a result of the rise of the neoliberal approach in Israel. Indeed, in certain cases, the anti-majoritarian character of judicial review assists in advancing neoliberal policies (Gross, 2000). But this is not necessarily clear to the wider public, which is ready to accept attacks on the court if it perceives its position as endangering what appears to be a more profitable formula, the continued rule of Netanyahu.

5.3 The 2019–2021 Elections

5.3.1 Netanyahu's Claim, and How He Made His Case

Netanyahu focused on four major claims during the 2019–2021 election campaigns. The first highlighted his status as leader. "Netanyahu, A League Apart" was the central slogan that opened the campaign of April 2019. With these words, Netanyahu sought to differentiate himself from other politicians as an international statesman who can personally guarantee the high status of Israel and its future.

The second major claim was developed in the campaign for the September 2019 election, which followed Netanyahu's failure to form a government. It emphasized that any alternative to a Netanyahu-led right-wing government would be illegitimate because it would be forced to rely on the support of the Arab party alliance (The Joint List), which was presented, in the public-political jargon, as "the Arabs." This time, the slogan "Bibi or Tibi" – a play on words between Netanyahu's nickname and the family name of Ahmed Tibi, leader of the Arab Ta'al party, who held the third spot on The Joint List's candidate roster – became a catchphrase in the Likud propaganda. Essentially, it differentiated between the "real Israel," that is, Jewish citizens, and the others, that is, Arabs.

The third major claim centered on the struggle with the media, which were presented by Netanyahu's aides as an arm of the left-wing elite that constructs an alternative reality, whose aim is to control the consciousness of Israel's citizens. For example, the words, "They Won't Decide" captioned images of senior journalists, while Netanyahu often repeated the claim that media reports were "fake news" (Tucker, 2020).

The fourth major claim emerged in response to the Attorney General's decision to adopt the recommendations of the police to indict Netanyahu. "Investigate the investigators!" (Schneider, 2019) was aimed squarely at the prosecution system. Netanyahu argued that by indicting him, which he claimed was based on political and personal considerations, the prosecution was preventing the will of the people from being fulfilled. He thus presented himself as embodying the will of the people and as the defender of "real" democracy. In doing so, he sought to obscure the fact that he was referring to a narrow democratic model, based on one element, majority rule, while weakening the values and institutions of checks and balances that are essential to the functioning of a liberal democracy.

In the 2021 campaign, which began following the dissolution of the Netanyahu–Gantz government, Netanyahu (2021) touted his personal part in the success of the Covid-19 vaccination rollout. He credited himself for securing the deal with Pfizer (Hilai, 2021). This argument echoed the slogan, "Netanyahu, A League Apart." But this time, in addition to again emphasizing his image as a leader who possesses abilities not found in his opponents, as in the April 2019 campaign, he now surprised with conciliatory rhetoric toward the Arab citizens. Having learned a lesson, this time around he intended to win their votes, not to paint them as the "others" (Salameh, Shaalan, and Azulay, 2021).

In what follows, I will demonstrate how Netanyahu's claims were linked to his style as a populist leader who operates in the context the neoliberal logic that has found its way into Israeli society. This, together with the common conception among the public that Israel has benefited – in terms of economy and security – under his leadership, serve as the main factors that explain his political power. And powerful he was, indeed still is as these lines are being written, even if he is (temporarily?) out of power.

5.3.2 Populism and Neoliberalism in the Service of Netanyahu

Explaining the rise of populism around the world is beyond the scope of this chapter. However, one of the central explanations for it – which relates also to the Israeli case – is that it arises as a response to instability and trends of competition created by a neoliberal economy. The tendency toward massive privatization flourished in many countries during the 1990s (and in the Israeli case was vigorously promoted by Netanyahu during his term as minister of finance, 2003–2005). Social-democratic movements failed to present a relevant alternative to the sectorialization of society (Tariq, 2015). Neoliberalism strengthens populist trends and fits to them since, just as advocates of neoliberalism view institutions and regulations as constraints on the development of the economy, populist leaders tend to accuse statist institutions of limiting their freedom to personally represent the will of the people (Weyland, 1999).

Populism, in contrast with its common unidimensional image in the public discourse, is a complex concept (Canovan, 2005). For example, Likud leaders Begin and Netanyahu can both be characterized as populists. However, the populism of Begin, Likud's founding father, is of an inclusive type: by emphasizing the "Jewish" narrative as an alternative to the pioneering-socialistic narrative of the Labor movement, Begin included the Mizrahim[7] and the religious sector within "we the Israelis." His government even used distributive economic policies that created a high rate of inflation in order to "benefit the people." In contrast, Netanyahu's populism is exclusionary in character. Under his leadership, the ethnic–cultural–Jewish conception of Israel has become still more extreme, to the point of rhetorically separating between "the real Jews,"

106 *Avi Shilon*

that is, supporters of the right, and Arabs and even liberal Jews who oppose Netanyahu. This has found expression in legislation like the Basic Law: Israel – The Nation State of the Jewish People and the law denying the entry of Boycott, Divestment and Sanctions (BDS) activists into Israel (Filc, 2018: 154–155).

Thus, Netanyahu's late and sudden attempt, in the 2021 campaign, to include the Arab citizens in "the people of Israel" was perceived as a cynical maneuver and did not win him the votes he sought (Verter, 2021). Yet, unintentionally, Netanyahu did contribute eventually to a new political atmosphere that soon after allowed cooperation between the Zionist parties and the Arab party Ra'am in the new government that was formed in 2021 without him.

The organizing principles of populism include the placement of the "people" and their rights at the center of the ideological and political discourse, while differentiating between "them," the elites, and "us," the real/ ordinary people; a special status for the leader, who by the power of his charisma can bypass democratic institutions; polemical and polarizing rhetoric, in a boorish language; and a tendency to address the nation's mythic past, which serves as a role model for the present.

Researchers of this phenomenon disagree on whether to define populism as an ideology, discourse, rhetoric, policy, or a thin ideology, a platform that can borrow from here and there. Mudde and Kaltwasser (2017) suggest defining the populist model of democracy as a direct expression of the sovereignty of the people, or what Rousseau famously defined as the "general will."

I relate to Netanyahu's populism primarily as an expression of rhetoric and thin ideology that borrows from here and there, alongside a claim to directly represent the will of the people (who are defined according to the circumstances). Thus, for example, when he was in the opposition, Netanyahu opposed deals to release terrorists, due to the need, he claimed, to safeguard public security. But as a prime minister, under the pressure of the social protest in the summer of 2011 and the public desire to see the kidnapped soldier Gilad Shalit freed from Hamas' captivity, he acquiesced to such a deal. His justification was that in doing so he was demonstrating his concern for safeguarding the security of IDF soldiers. In the same manner, as a populist who is not committed to a solid ideology, he could also change his rhetoric toward the Arab public when their votes were needed.

As noted earlier, there is a strong linkage between neoliberalism and populism (Frank, 2000). Within the framework of the neoliberal project, the accumulation of capital among economic elites has increased, and with it inequality has deepened. This has led to two contradictory political trends: on the one hand, a call for renewed support for socialist ideologies (Bernie Sanders in the United States and Jeremy Corbyn in the United Kingdom, to name two); on the other, a flourishing of nationalist and anti-institutional ideologies that revolve around a charismatic leader who seeks to directly represent the people – like Trump and Netanyahu in his later years. Thus, the primary focus of the recent election campaigns centered on Netanyahu's claim to represent the will of the people, who ostensibly want him to continue to serve their interests; this, against the interests of the elites that sought to replace him through various mechanisms (the media, the police, and the judicial system). In his own words, this translated to claiming:

> The Left knows that…they cannot beat us at the polls. They are hunting me and trying to bring down the right wing government that I lead… It falls to the Attorney General to say that he is considering indicting me, when there is nothing.
>
> (*Haaretz*, 2019)

Netanyahu's expressions are characteristic of populism – a perception of democracy as the unmediated expression of the will of the people and resentment toward anti-majoritarian mechanisms.

5.3.3 *"Us and Them"*

Likud and Blue and White both won 35 seats in the April 2019 elections. However, Netanyahu was prevented from securing the necessary majority to form a coalition because Avigdor Lieberman and his party, Yisrael Beiteinu, refused to join a right-wing-religious government – and its five seats were crucial to achieve such a goal. Lieberman also refused to join a government led by Benny Gantz, because it too lacked a majority, without including the seats of the non-Zionist and Arab parties. However, Netanyahu was concerned that Lieberman might change his mind and agree to join a government that is supported by these parties. Thus, Likud's campaign for the September 2019 elections emphasized the difference between "us and them" – the "real people," based on Likud's own ethnic–cultural meaning, that is, the Jews, and "the citizens of Israel," which included Israel's Arabs. This alleged contradiction was pushed far, to the extent that at a Likud members' event Netanyahu compared the possibility of a government led by anyone other than him to a terrorist attack (Calcalist, 2019).

The differentiation between Jews and Arabs is typical of populism, because populism is an "ideology that claims that the state's population must be made up of those who belong to the native nation and is suspicious and hostile of non-native elements" (Mudde, 2007: 9).

However, it is important to note that in the Israeli context populism makes "nativism" a contested element. From a historical perspective, the Arabs could actually be seen as the natives, and the Jews as the immigrants. Yet, from an epistemological perspective, the Zionist conception identifies the Jews as the original natives of the land.

5.3.4 *Identity Politics in the Service of Netanyahu's Populism*

Neoliberalism also strengthens engagement with identity politics. At its core, there is an inherent tension between the ideal of a competitive market in which

108   *Avi Shilon*

"every person acts for himself" and the political representation of collective interests (Amable, 2011). Because the economic sphere influences the social sphere, competition between various groups within a society serves as fertile ground for a populist politician, who can maneuver between them.

Indeed, in addition to the religious/ethnic divide between Jews and Arabs, Netanyahu also sought to address the Jewish population by sectors.

The class dimension of voting in Israeli elections is well-known. Hoffmann-Dishon (2019) of the Adva Center analyzed the breakdown of votes in the April 2019 election in various communities in Israel that were categorized in ten socioeconomic clusters. Blue and White received more votes than Likud in the well-off communities – clusters 10, 9, 8; in cluster 7 there was parity; and Likud received a majority in clusters 6, 5, 4 (as well as a slight advantage in the lowest clusters, where there was a high rate of ultra-orthodox and Arab voters who usually vote for "their" own parties). This voting pattern was also evident in the 2015 election (Kashti, 2015). Mizrahim, who tend to be more traditional than Ashkenazim (Yadgar, 2010), have been a serious element of Likud and the right wing's voter base since 1973 (Shapira, 1989). Right-wing-religious governments are based on the support of the lower socioeconomic class within the Jewish population, while members of the higher socio-economic class tend to support center-left governments.

Because of the way that Israeli society was shaped in its formative years, the class element overlaps, to a great extent, with the Mizrahi/Ashkenazi divide and with the traditional/secular divide (Shamir and Arian, 1982). As a result, the populist discourse in Israel is fertile ground for the expression of identity politics. Ironically, Netanyahu, who is rather a typical example of Israel's elite (Ashkenazi man, born in a well-to-do Jerusalem neighborhood to a father who was a professor, educated in the United States, and a soldier in the elite IDF unit, Sayeret Matkal) adopted polarizing rhetoric on these issues.

Two prominent examples of Netanyahu's use of identity politics were seen in his response to a statement by Yoaz Hendel (then a member of Blue and White) during the third round of elections, in March 2020. Hendel claimed that "in Israel there are people who came with a mentality of *darbukas* [goblet drum, A.S.], and others who came with the mentality of concert halls" (Hecht, 2020). Drumming on darbukas is identified as part of Mizrahi Jews' folklore and culture. Hendel's words were used to frame him as a "privileged" Ashkenazi who feels superior to "ordinary" people. Netanyahu retorted: "This is how he [Hendel] relates to the people who came home, to the Land of Israel, with a rich and magnificent culture. He should be ashamed!" (Rut-Avneri, 2020).

Netanyahu subsequently provided a less direct and more sophisticated response to this incident, which demonstrated how his populism plays on the nationalist-traditionalist-Mizrahi identity, in contrast to what is perceived to be the universalist-secular-Ashkenazi identity of the "other" side (Grinberg, 2004). A week after Hendel's statement, Netanyahu was filmed with three right-wing journalists, Shimon Riklin, Erel Segal, and Yinon Magal, singing and playing guitars to the song "Shabechi Jerusalem" [Praise Jerusalem]. At

A Populist Leader under Neoliberal Logic   109

the end of the song Netanyahu asked, "Wait, you didn't bring darbukas?" to the on-cue laughter of the others (YouTube, 2020.) The musical clip quickly went viral. While the media were primarily occupied with the fact that journalists took an active role in political propaganda, the clip served to address the collective subconscious of the public in the context of identity politics: the song "Praise Jerusalem" is a clear expression of religion, nationalism, and Mizrahi identity. The words are taken from the Book of Psalms, and thus connect to the traditional image that Netanyahu sought to attach to himself; the subject of the song is Jerusalem, a symbol of Israeli-Jewish nationalism; and the melody, to which Netanyahu wanted to add the sound of *darbukas*, is wholly Mizrahi. Netanyahu thus connected himself to three important identity issues, which highlighted the divide between his supporters and his rivals according to origin, tradition, and nationalist stands.

The use of the song (Praise Jerusalem became a sort of campaign anthem in the third round of elections) was meant to underscore the difference between the left and the right in terms of identity politics, their relationship with religion, national identity, and ethnicity. The attitude toward tradition is an acute subject for most Israeli Jews, as is demonstrated by surveys that have been conducted since the 1990s (Levi, Levinson, and Katz, 1994; Hermann et al., 2013). But in this way, Netanyahu was actually seeking to divert the public discourse from the question of his legal woes and trial to the question of identity.

It is worth noting that identity politics originated in the "New Left" and developed in the 1960s to seek cultural pluralism and to challenge intergroup hierarchies. However, in Israel identity politics was mainly adopted by the populist right to serve as an agent of nationalism and sometimes also for the suppression of the "other." Similar to the way that the right adopted postmodernist relativism and related to the truth according to its needs, Netanyahu's use of identity politics distorts the progressive agenda. In the context of national, ethnic, and religious Jewish supremacy in Israel, his emphasis on the discrimination of Mizrahim and traditional Jews by the left is not meant to expand the Mizrahi discourse that could encompass – at least from a historical perspective – inclusive possibilities relating to Jewish–Arab coexistence; on the contrary, identity politics of the right is intended to deepen the Jewish ethnonational hegemony, to reinforce the "us and them" attitude.

5.3.5 "Sour [Pickles] Theory"[8] as a Leadership Principle

So far, we have dealt with the Netanyahu's leadership style, primarily with how he engages with his rivals: his use of identity politics, exclusion of the Arab population and castigation of statist anti-majoritarian institutions. However, the question remains: What is the worthwhile "merchandise," if we stick to the neoliberal terminology, that Netanyahu offers the public? According to the 2019 Israel Democracy Index, the public still demonstrated a relatively high level of confidence in the judicial system.[9] If most people do not support

110   *Avi Shilon*

his belief that the judicial system is plotting against him, on what basis did Netanyahu's electoral support remain strong, and how is it that, in the 2019 elections, 64% of Israelis declared that the indictment against him had no influence on their vote (Orkabi, 2019)?

The answer lies in additional findings published in the same 2019 Index: 50% of the public believes that Israel's state under Netanyahu was good to very good (Hermann et al., 2020). In other words, half the public believes that irrespective of Netanyahu's claims against the judicial system, the country has nevertheless benefited from his continued leadership. It can be argued that Netanyahu did not win support as a result of his attacks on the judicial system (although his attacks are accepted as legitimate, following neoliberal logic); rather, his gains were the result of a widespread public feeling – which is also influenced by the same neoliberal logic, and is of course open to factual debate – that Netanyahu provides Israel with achievements. The appreciation of his accomplishments can be seen as an expression of the internalization of neoliberal logic (which examines reality by gains and losses). A different public mindset could have led to an inverse situation, to broad opposition to Netanyahu: despite appreciation for his accomplishments, his (still alleged) corruption could have led to moral reservations.

This point is well illustrated in a speech Netanyahu delivered in the Knesset in October 2017, nicknamed by the media the "Sour Pickles Speech" (*Neum Hahamutsim*). The central claim of the speech is that his government provided achievements to the satisfaction of the majority of the public and therefore criticism of him has no basis. This was the "trump card" that Netanyahu played to strengthen and justify the necessity of his holding on to power (YouTube, 2017):

> This is Israel's Golden Age. Israel is experiencing unprecedented diplomatic and economic momentum ... within a decade we will become a state of 10 million citizens and have a GDP of half a trillion dollars. This will give us power to ensure our future...even though, the depression industry still exists ... Recently there is a renewal, a new stream of them – a stream of sour [people] ... it's hard for them, the pickles.

The speech serves as a key to understanding Netanyahu, especially because it lacks ideology or any other principle, except for details on materialistic success. It fits the populist model of Mudde (2017) that perceives populism as a thin ideology, whose essence is policy, not loyalty to a solid worldview. As noted, it also enabled him to change his attitude toward the Arab citizens in the fourth campaign.

In this speech, Netanyahu emphasized that in 2017, more than three million Israelis (about a third of the population) traveled abroad over the summer and during the month of Jewish holidays, suggesting that they had the disposable cash to do so. He also highlighted the low unemployment rate (around 3%); referred to the Happy Planet Index (World Happiness Report) surveys

A Populist Leader under Neoliberal Logic   111

that give Israelis a high global ranking; pointed to the peace that was being maintained on the northern border; and claimed that Israel's diplomatic dominance helped to convince President Trump to nix the nuclear deal between the world powers and Iran. There was no mention of values or ideology – just a list of achievements in the name of a good and secure life.

An examination of Israel's situation of under Netanyahu is beyond the scope of this chapter. However, if we stick to the neoliberal logic, which boils down to the evaluation of a state according to its economic growth, we can agree that the last decade, at least until the Covid-19 pandemic, was indeed good for Israel. According to the International Monetary Fund, in 2009, the year that Netanyahu entered office, Israel's GDP per capita was $27,512; in 2017, it was $36,250 (Israel Democracy Institute, 2017a). Israel experienced an increase of 40% while during the same period, GDP per capita of OECD countries grew at an average rate of 30%. A decade ago, Israel's GDP was 23.5% lower than the OECD average. In 2019, it was lower than the OECD average by only 13.9% (*Globes*, 2019). In addition, in 2019, labor participation and employment rates were high (81% and 78%, respectively), and unemployment stood at only 3.8%, while real wages continued to increase, although at a slower pace than previous years (Fox and Epstein, 2019).

It is not just economic growth that expressed "Israeli success" under Netanyahu. His immediate predecessors Ehud Barak (1999–2001), Ariel Sharon (2001–2006), and Ehud Olmert (2006–2009) dealt with the Second Intifada (2001–2005), a war in Israel's north (2006) and a broad military operation in the south (2008), which took the lives of hundreds of soldiers and citizens. In contrast, Netanyahu led Israel through a decade with only limited confrontations, primarily military operations in Gaza, which were considered by most Israelis as unavoidable and he led them almost without "boots on the ground," favoring air strikes in an attempt to avoid the loss of soldiers' lives.

On the diplomatic front, the forecasts that lack of progress in the peace talks with the Palestinians would lead to Israel's diplomatic isolation were disproved. Moreover, during the Trump era, even ideas that once sounded radical, like annexation, began to be seen by many as possible and legitimate. They were removed from the agenda in exchange for excitement over the economic possibilities that peace agreements with Bahrain and the United Arab Emirates opened up for Israelis, agreements that Netanyahu also pushed as personal achievements.

Of course, the answer to the question of Israel's "health" under Netanyahu is relative. The data presented do not calculate for values or morals, or the damage that some policies are likely to cause in the future, due to the continued occupation. Economic growth comes at the expense of widening social and economic gaps. In terms of the Gini Index, which examines inequality, Israel, with an index of 42.8, was ranked 102 out of 150 countries for 2017 (Israel Democracy Institute, 2017b). Moreover, as a result of structural and demographic factors, the future growth of Israel's economy is not certain (Rosenberg, 2018: 231–245). Even Israel's moniker of a "start-up

112   *Avi Shilon*

nation" was a bit of a collective fantasy, as the technology-entrepreneurial sector contributed only 6% of Israel's national GDP.

Still, the fact remains that the general sentiment of Israeli citizens was positive, according to surveys conducted by both the Israel Democracy Institute (2018) and the New Economics Foundation (NEF). Israel was ranked 13th in the NEF's Happy Planet Index for 2019, while in the previous two years, it had been ranked 11th (*Ynet*, 2019). This positive feeling – despite many people's disappointment with Netanyahu's behavior – can be explained, as Dayan (2020: 100) suggests, by the internalization of neoliberal logic:

> [Even if the socio-economic gaps widen,] the promise of solidarity and an egalitarian Zionist society in the original paradigm of Israel's founding fathers was replaced by the country's economic success story, which is measured by global "common sense": a country is measured by its growth rate and its ability to encourage investment, not by its ability to shrink gaps and solve social and moral problems.

One can also offer an additional conclusion. The areas that are weakening, such as education, health, welfare, and the rule of law, may define the standard of living according to a social-democratic vision; in the neoliberal era, Israelis prefer – as demonstrated by the above data on the satisfaction of the Israeli public – to measure their standard of living by the possibility of going abroad, studying in academic colleges (which have thrived under Likud's rule), and buying goods cheaply online.

5.3.6 The Fourth Campaign as a Continuation of the Populist Pattern under Neoliberal Logic

According to a public opinion survey (Israeli and Deitch, 2020), the Covid-19 crisis exposed the fragility and the weaknesses of Israeli society, as well some inabilities of the government in handling it and the absence of moral leadership in the governing echelons. In this context, neoliberal logic led Netanyahu, in the 2021 campaign, to focus on his personal role in the success of the vaccination operation, since according to this logic, those who bring "results" are worthy of victory (Netanyahu, 2021).

An additional element in Netanyahu's 2021 strategy well illustrates his embrace of populism: if in previous campaigns he accused his opponents of collaborating with the Israeli Arabs, this time Netanyahu expressly called on the Arab public to grant him support, and even promised a future peace agreement with Saudi Arabia that would open the possibility of flying directly to Mecca, the most holy city for the Muslims (Charish-Hazony, 2021). At the same time, he encouraged voters to support the Religious Zionism, a party whose members explicitly advocate discrimination against Arab citizens.

In other words, Netanyahu seems to have adopted a contradictory strategy – for and against the Israeli Arab public. In fact, the "change" and

A Populist Leader under Neoliberal Logic   113

"contradiction" in his attitude are themselves another expression of populism; as Mudde (2007) suggest, populism is not bound by ideology but by policies that borrow from here and there according to need.

Moreover, the attribution of his political success to the adoption of neoliberal logic by the public can help us understand why his change of approach was accepted without significant protest by his electoral base.[10] When citizens are consumers who participate in a profit-maximizing competition, all means are "kosher" to achieve political victory (Brown, 2017).

5.4 Instead of a Summary: Hobbes, Locke, Netanyahu, and Israeli Society

The characteristics of populist leadership and the adoption of the neoliberal logic that explain Netanyahu's political success integrate, and in fact expand, the Hobbesian logic that characterizes the Netanyahu era (Navot and Rubin, 2016). Hobbesian logic is based on the familiar social contract theory: in exchange for providing personal security to citizens (in the Israeli case, both physical and economic), the leader's rule is ensured (Hobbes, [1651] 2003). It follows, then, that Netanyahu succeeded in convincing many Israelis that he can ensure their security against the dangers that they perceive in their harsh Middle Eastern environment, which may reflect the "state of nature" in the Hobbesian theory.

The extent to which Netanyahu focused on security and economics says a lot about his leadership style. In contrast to his passionate rhetoric against Iran and Hamas, Netanyahu avoids, almost in principle, military operations that are likely to endanger Israeli soldiers. This also explains his readiness to adopt the strict policies of the Ministry of Health since the emergence of Covid-19 in March 2020 (unlike his fellow populist leaders around the world) and also his subsequent resoluteness to obtain the vaccines, to the point where Albert Burla, the CEO of vaccine producer Pfizer, described him as "obsessive" (Ahimeir, 2021).

Hobbes' conception of the "state of nature" was the source of John Locke's liberal philosophy. In turn, this was the source of neoliberalism as a worldview, though in a process that does not naturally fit Locke's approach. This helps in creating the linkage between the Hobbesian logic that characterizes Netanyahu's leadership and the neoliberal logic that allowed him to present his policies as a "success."

5.5 Epilogue

If the fourth campaign, running up to the 2021 election, should be understood as the continuation of the same leadership pattern as the previous campaigns, then how can one explain that this time King Bibi lost his throne?

First, this time around four party leaders ran against him, some of them from right-wing parties. It became difficult for him to run a successful populist

114   *Avi Shilon*

campaign, which required a clear distinction between "us" and "them." Second, the Likud lost six seats to Gideon Sa'ar's Tikva Hadasha (New Hope) party. The politicians of this party and its supporters left the Likud, and represented a minority of right wingers who concluded that Netanyahu's attacks on the judicial system and his populist conduct overshadowed his claim for success.

The third reason concerns the very logic on which he based his status, neoliberal logic. If Netanyahu was supported because he could "deliver the goods," the fact that he went to the polls four times in two years without the ability to provide a stable government – and no one saw the repeated elections as an achievement – in fact harmed his image. In terms of this logic, he was transformed from a "successful leader" to "damaged goods."

Notes

1 In Case 2000, Netanyahu is accused of attempting to broker a deal with *Yedioth Ahronoth* publisher Arnon Mozes to garner positive media coverage for himself in exchange for legislation that would somewhat weaken *Israel Hayom*, ensuring *Yedioth*'s place as Israel's largest daily.
2 In an interview, Dan Meridor, a second-generation Revisionist, declared that for the first time in his life he will not vote Likud but for the Blue and White party alliance instead (*Haaretz* Podcast, 2019). Benny Begin (son of renowned Likud leader Menachem Begin) went even further, declaring, "It is clear to people who have been raised to put 'Mahal' [the official acronym of the Likud party] in the ballot box, that he [Netanyahu] cannot be the prime minister" (Meet the Press, 2020).
3 As can be seen in *Azure*, an elitist journal for conservative thought, that it published.
4 On the developing relationship between Netanyahu and various sectors see Navot and Goldshmidt in this volume.
5 The Yemenite Children Affair refers to the alleged mysterious disappearance of babies of (mainly) Yemenite Jewish immigrants to Israel during its formative years, 1948–1954.
6 Azaria, an Israeli soldier, was tried in a military court for shooting and killing a Palestinian who was already severely wounded after stabbing a soldier in Hebron in March 2016. While being perceived by many Israelis as a hero, others blamed him of murder, or at least of behavior that contradicted the IDF ethos.
7 Mizrahim are Jews who immigrated from Middle Eastern and North African countries, in contrast to Ashkenazim, who immigrated from Europe.
8 In Hebrew, the same word is used for sour and pickles.
9 Hermann et al., 2020. According to the data, despite the attacks on Israel's Supreme Court, public confidence in the court rose from 52% in 2018 to 55% in 2019. Public confidence in the government and the Knesset was lower, standing at around 30%.
10 He even adopted the nickname "Abu Yair," or Yair's father, following the custom in Arab culture of naming a man as the father of his oldest child, on his Arabic-language Facebook page.

References

Ahimeir, Yaakov. 2021. "Thoughts following the interview with the CEO of Pfizer." *Israel Hayom*, March 13. www.israelhayom.co.il/opinion/860563 [Hebrew].

Amable, Bruno. 2011. "Morals and Politics in the Ideology of Neo-Liberalism." *Socio-Economic Review* 9 (1): 3–30.

Bareli, Avi, and Nir Keidar. 2011. *Israeli Statism*. Jerusalem: Israel Democracy Institute. [Hebrew].

Bender, Arik. 2016. "Netanyahu on the Yemenite Children Affair: 'I don't Understand Why It Is Classified." *Ma'ariv*, June 21. www.maariv.co.il/news/politics/Article-546417 [Hebrew].

Brown, Wendy. 2017. *Undoing the Demos: Neoliberalism's Stealth Revolution*. New York: Zone Books.

Calcalist. 2019. "Netanyahu at Right Wing Conference: Minority Government – National Historic Terrorist Attack." *Yedioth Ahronoth*, November 17. www.calcalist.co.il/local/articles/0,7340,L-3773890,00.html [Hebrew].

Canovan, Margaret. 2005. *The People*. Cambridge: Polity.

Charish-Hazony, Hoodia. 2021. "What Lies Behind Netanyahu's Promise of Direct Flights to Mecca?" *Makor Rishon*, March 21. www.makorrishon.co.il/news/327783 [Hebrew].

Cornel, Ban. 2016. *How Global Neoliberalism Goes Local*. Oxford: Oxford University.

Davies, William. 2014. *The Limits of Neoliberalism: Authority, Sovereignty and the Logic of Competition*. London: Sage.

Dayan, Hilla. 2020. "Neo-Zionism: A Sociological Portrait." *Theory and Criticism* 52: 87–113 [Hebrew].

Del Sarto, Raffaella. 2017. *Israel Under Siege: The Politics of Insecurity and the Rise of the Israeli Neo-Revisionist Right*. Washington: Georgetown University Press.

Eichner, Itamar, and Tova Zimuki. 2020. "Netanyahu's Attack Speech and the Facts from the Other Side." *Ynet*, May 25. www.ynet.co.il/articles/0,7340,L-5736092,00.html [Hebrew].

Filc, Dani. 2018. "Populism." *Mafteach – Lexical Periodical for Political Thought* 13: 143–158 [Hebrew].

Filc, Dani, and Uri Ram eds. 2014. *Rule of Capital: Israeli Society in a Global Era*. Jerusalem and Tel Aviv: Van Leer Institute and Hakibbutz Hameuchad. [Hebrew].

Fox, Hadas, and Gil Epstein. 2019. "Labor Market, An Overview." In *State of the Nation Report, Society, Economy and Policy in Israel*, edited by Avi Weiss, 139–162. Jerusalem: Taub Center for Social Policy Studies in Israel. www.taubcenter.org.il/wp-content/uploads/2020/12/snr2019english.pdf

Frank, Thomas. 2000. *One Market Under God: Extreme Capitalism, Market Populism, and the End of Economic Democracy*. New York: Anchor Books.

Globes. 2019. "Is GDP in Israel Higher or Lower than OECD Countries?" *Globes*, April 9. www.globes.co.il/news/article.aspx?did=1001281523 [Hebrew].

Grinberg, Lev. 2004. "Postmortem of the Ashkenazi Left." In *Who's Left in Israel?* edited by Dan Leon, 85–99. Portland: Sussex Academic Press.

Gross, Eyal. 2000. "How Did 'Free Competition' Become a Legal Right? In the Weeds of the Right to Business Freedom." *Iyunei Mishpat* 23: 229–261 [Hebrew].

Haaretz. 2019. "The Left Is Hunting My Government, the State Attorney Is Persecuting Right-Wingers." *Haaretz,* February 28. www.haaretz.co.il/news/law/1.6980735 [Hebrew].

116   *Avi Shilon*

Haaretz Podcast. 2019. "Dan Meridor: There Are No False Persecutions in Israel. A Prime Minister Cannot Serve While Indited." *Haaretz*, November 19. www.haar etz.co.il/digital/podcast/weekly/.premium-PODCAST-1.8152148 [Hebrew].

Hecht, Ravit. 2020. "I Think that Arabic Culture Around Us Is a Jungle." *Haaretz*, February 6. www.haaretz.co.il/news/elections/.premium-MAGAZINE-1.8503437 [Hebrew].

Heller, Kupfert Daniel. 2017. *Jabotinsky's Children: Polish Jews and the Rise of Right Wing Zionism*. Princeton: Princeton University Press.

Hermann, Tamar, Or Anabi, William Cubbison, and Ella Heller. 2020. *The 2019 Israel Democracy Index*. Jerusalem: Israel Democracy Institute. www.idi.org.il/books/29414

Hermann, Tamar, Nir Atmor, Ella Heller, and Yuval Lebel. 2013. *The 2013 Israeli Democracy Index*. Jerusalem: Israel Democracy Institute.

Hilai, Sivan. 2021. "Petition: Netanyahu Uses the Ministry of Health's Vaccine Slogan." *Ynet*, March 10. www.ynet.co.il/news/article/BkAck00IQd [Hebrew].

Hobbes, Thomas. [1651] 2003. *Leviathan* (trans. Hugo Bergman), Jerusalem: Magnes.

Hoffmann-Dishon, Yaron. 2019. "The Election to the 21st Knesset; An Analysis According to Socio-Economic Clusters," April 14. https://adva.org/he/bchirot2019-socioeconomic/ [Hebrew].

Israel Democracy Institute. 2017a. "GDP per Capita." www.idi.org.il/policy/world-comparison/indexes/gross-domestic-product/ [Hebrew].

Israel Democracy Institute. 2017b. Gini Index. www.idi.org.il/policy/world-comparison/indexes/gini-coefficient/ [Hebrew].

Israel Democracy Institute. 2018. Abstract of the Israel Democracy Index. www.idi.org.il/media/11558/takzir-index-hebrew.pdf [Hebrew].

Israeli, Zipi, and Mora Deitch. 2020. "The Israeli Public and the Effects of the Coronavirus: Findings from a Public Opinion Poll in the Second Wave of the Crisis." *INSS Poll*, September 29, 2020. www.inss.org.il/publication/coronavirus-inss-survey/

Kashti, Or. 2015. "Voting Analysis: Vast Majority for Netanyahu in the Periphery and among the Middle Class," *Haaretz*, March 19. www.haaretz.co.il/news/elections/EXT.premium-EXT-MAGAZINE-1.2594125 [Hebrew].

Krampf, Arieh. 2015. *National Sources of Market Economy: Economic Development during the Formation of Israeli Capitalism*. Jerusalem: Magnes and Hebrew University [Hebrew].

Levi, Shlomit, Hana Levinson, and Elihu Katz. 1994. *Beliefs, Keeping Mitzvot, and Social Relations among Jews in Israel*. Jerusalem: Guttman Israel Institute of Applied Social Research. [Hebrew].

Levinson, Haim, Jonathan Lis, and Gili Cohen. 2017. "After Rejection of the Appeal: Netanyahu Called for a Pardon for Elor Azaria." *Haaretz*, July 30. www.haaretz.co.il/news/politi/.premium-1.4302198 [Hebrew].

Meet the Press. 2020. *Channel 2*, January 4. www.mako.co.il/news-politics/2020_q1/Article-29258ebf9917f61026.htm [Hebrew].

Mudde, Cas. 2007. *Populist Radical Right Parties in Europe*. Cambridge: Cambridge University Press.

Mudde, Cas, and Cristobal Rovira Kaltwasser. 2017. *Populism: A Very Short Introduction*. Oxford: Oxford University Press.

Navot, Doron, and Aviad Rubin. 2016. "Likud's Success in the 2015 Elections: Netanyahu's Hobbesian Moment." *Israel Affairs* 22 (3–4): 628–640.

Netanyahu, Benjamin. 2021. "I Brought Vaccines, Now I'll Open the Economy. Listen to Albert!" *Netanyahu's Facebook page*, March 17. www.facebook.com/watch/?v=164754372147946 [Hebrew].

Orkabi, Eitan. 2019. "64%: Indictment Won't Change Our Vote." *Israel Hayom*, November 24. www.israelhayom.co.il/article/709597 [Hebrew].

Pfeffer, Anshel. 2018. *Bibi: The Turbulent Life and Times of Benjamin Netanyahu*. London: Basic Books.

Ram, Ori. 2011. *Israeli Nationalism: Social Conflicts and the Politics of Knowledge*. London: Routledge.

Rosenberg, David. 2018. *Israel's Technology Economy*. London: Palgrave Macmillan.

Rut-Avneri, Daniel. 2020. "There are People with the Mentality of a Concert, or of a Darbuka." *Israel Hayom*, February 7. www.israelhayom.co.il/article/731677 [Hebrew].

Sagiv, Asaf. 2020. "The Strange Case of Radical Conservativism." *Hazman Hazeh* https://hazmanhazeh.org.il/conservatism/ [Hebrew].

Salameh, Daniel, Shaalan Hassan, and Azulay Moran. 2021. "Netanyahu Courtesy of the Arab Voice: 'Opportunity for a New Future'." *Ynet*, January 13. www.ynet.co.il/news/article/BkF74whCw [Hebrew].

Schneider, Tal. 2018. "Netanyahu's Hive: The People Behind the Prime Minister." *Globes*, December 24. www.globes.co.il/news/article.aspx?did=1001266020 [Hebrew].

Schneider, Tal. 2019. "A Strong Response of Netanyahu to his Corruption Indictment: "Interrogate the Interrogators." *Globes*, November 21. www.globes.co.il/news/article.aspx?did=1001308187 [Hebrew].

Shamir, Michal, and Arian Asher. 1982. "The Ethnic Vote in Israel's 1981 Elections." *Electoral Studies* 1 (3): 315–331.

Shapira, Yonatan. 1989. *We Have Been Chosen to Rule – The Path of the Herut Movement: A Sociological-Political Explanation*. Tel Aviv: Am Oved. [Hebrew].

Shenhav, Yehuda. 2006. "Economics Are Just the Method; the Goal Is to Design the Soul." *Haaretz,* March 22. www.haaretz.co.il/literature/1.1092710 [Hebrew].

Snir, Itai. 2012. "Common Sense." *Mafteach – Lexical Periodical for Political Thought* 5: 179–214. [Hebrew].

Stengel, Richard. 2012. "King Bibi." *Time Magazine*, May 28. http://content.time.com/time/covers/0,16641,20120528,00.html

Tadmor, Erez. 2017. *Why You Vote Right and Obtain Left?*. Jerusalem: Sela-Meir. [Hebrew].

Tariq, Ali. 2015. *The Extreme Centre: A Warning*. London: Verso.

The Marker. 2019. "Mozes-Netanyahu recordings." *The Marker*, October 27. www.themarker.com/law/1.8029360 [Hebrew].

Tucker, Nati. 2020. "Netanyahu Stopped Attacking the Media (and He Knows Why)." *The Marker*, March 6. www.themarker.com/advertising/1.8632733 [Hebrew].

Verter, Yossi. 2021. "Netanyahu's Cynical Show in Nazareth Was Intended Not Only for Arabs, But Also for Likud Members." *Haaretz*, January 14. [Hebrew].

Weitz, Gidi. 2019. "Case 2000: "Changing Versions, Judgment Day, and 'Keyser Söze'. Behind the Scenes of Netanyahu and Mozes' Testimony." *Haaretz*, June 13. www.haaretz.co.il/news/elections/.premium-1.7367106 [Hebrew].

Weyland, Kurt. 1999. "Neoliberal Populism in Latin America and Eastern Europe." *Comparative Politics* 31 (4): 379–401.

Yadgar, Yaakov. 2010. *Masortim in Israel.* Jerusalem: Keter, Shalom Hartman Institute and Bar-Ilan University. [Hebrew].

Ynet. 2019 "Israel Is Number 13 on the Happiness Index, Finland Is the Happiest of All." *Ynet*, March 20. www.ynet.co.il/articles/0,7340,L-5481839,00.html [Hebrew].

YouTube. 2017. "*Neum Hahamutsim* of Prime Minister Netanyahu." October 24. www.youtube.com/watch?v=yigG-NCDtog [Hebrew].

YouTube. 2020. "Exciting! The Prime Minister Sings "Praise Jerusalem." February 13. www.youtube.com/watch?v=dIPydB5SDKk [Hebrew].

Zuidhof, Peter-Wim. 2016. "Towards a Post-Neoliberal University: Protest and Complicity." *Krisis: Journal for Contemporary Philosophy* 2: 49–55.

6 Netanyahu and the Very Short History of the "Right-Wing Bloc"

Doron Navot and Yair Goldshmidt

In late January 2020, shortly before the elections for the 23rd Knesset, Attorney General Avichai Mandelblit filed an indictment against Benjamin Netanyahu, the prime minister and chairman of the Likud party. He charged him with breach of trust and bribery during his tenure as prime minister and as minister of communications. Contrary to earlier evaluations (Benn, 2018; Segal, 2020), the indictment did not lead to Netanyahu's ouster; on the contrary, two weeks before election day, the leaders of Shas, Yemina, and United Torah Judaism signed a letter in which they pledged their future support for a government headed by him (Barsky, 2020). Then, in the election held about a month after the indictment was filed, the Likud was the leading vote-getter.

In the 2021 elections, that took place two weeks before Netanyahu appeared in the opening of the evidence phase in his trial, the Likud lost six seats. Yet Netanyahu was recommended as the candidate to form a coalition by the largest number of Members of Knesset (MKs). When giving Netanyahu the mandate to form a government, President Reuven Rivlin noted "I know the position held by many that the President should not give the role to a candidate who is facing criminal charges," and that this was "not an easy decision" (Lis, 2021). When Netanyahu failed to form a government, Rivlin gave Yair Lapid the mandate to form a coalition. In June 2021, Israel's 36th government, comprised of eight parties and headed by Prime Minister Naftali Bennett, unseated Netanyahu's interim government and won a majority in the vote of investiture in the Knesset. The present chapter explains the logic behind these political developments.

The main argument presented here is that the criminal proceedings against Netanyahu led to an overlap of his personal interest in escaping the clutches of the law and the aspiration of the parties that compose the right-wing-religious bloc—the Likud, the ultra-Orthodox, and national religious parties—to rein in the courts. Netanyahu was perceived as almost the only one willing to take the personal risk of waging war against the judicial system (Friedmann, 2019), because he has comparatively little to lose (he was already facing serious criminal charges) and much to gain (staying out of jail). Netanyahu was also perceived as having the ability, thanks to his unexcelled political talents, to remake the judicial system. Given the specific nature of the charges against

DOI: 10.4324/9781003267911-8

Netanyahu and his rhetorical skills, his indictment and trial amplified his voters' feeling that the judicial system is unfair and must be revamped—a change that he and he alone can and wishes to make. In addition, the Netanyahu trial had symbolic weight; it bolsters his status as the representative of the "real people" and embodies the injustice of the courts and the legal system.

The proceedings against Netanyahu contributed to his status as the leader of the bloc, because it fitted into the battle that the right wing was waging against the Israeli legal system, highlighted the alleged need to reform the system (and thus enhanced the right's legitimacy), gave credibility to Netanyahu's declarations that he will work to this end, and, in addition, turned him into a symbol of the alleged prejudice against the right. Moreover, because the indictment of Netanyahu had been seen as discriminatory and as an attempt to harm the right, the ultra-Orthodox and the national religious parties could not support a coalition led by anyone but him. Support for another candidate would have been perceived as playing into the enemy's hand and, ultimately, illegitimate. This limited the right-wing parties' room for maneuver to such an extent that they committed themselves before the elections to support him and only him in forming a coalition government. In other words, it was the prosecution of Netanyahu that produced the dynamics that led to the creation of Netanyahu's right-religious bloc. At the same time, the criminal trial, that started a month after the election to the 23rd Knesset (April 2020), undermined the status of Netanyahu in his own party, and gave some opponents within it the excuse to challenge him, defect, and form a new party named New Hope (Tikva Hadasha).

The first section of this chapter is devoted to the presentation of its conceptual framework. The second section traces the changes in Netanyahu's attitude toward the legal system. The third section focuses on the patterns of escalation in Netanyahu's approach to the justice system. The fourth section exemplifies how the findings of the police investigation and the decision of the Attorney General were incorporated into the Likud's election campaigns, serving as "proof" that there is no alternative but to modify the judicial system. The final section concludes.

6.1 Conceptual Framework: Support for a Defendant and the Nexus of Democracy, Populism, and Political Economy

In what situation can a politician reap political benefit from the fact that he is facing criminal charges? Although studies of the relations between politics and the judicial system and of Israeli political culture have not directly answered this question, we can extract possible explanations from them. Sprinzak (1986) maintained that Israel had been, and continued to be, marked by a culture of illegalism (see also Galnoor and Blander, 2013). Following this logic, Netanyahu's run-ins with the law could contribute to his image as a "bulldozer" who operates on behalf of "his" public and shares its culture

Netanyahu and the Very Short History of the "Right-Wing Bloc"   121

of illegalism. The weakness of this analysis is that it ignores the fact that Israel is home to well-developed judicial activism, especially with regard to the treatment of high-ranking persons suspected of corruption (Gur-Arye, 2014). A second theory postulates just the opposite. It claims that there was an increase in judicial activism in Israel since the 1970s, attributed to the weakness of the party system since the end of the 1970s (Barzilai, 1998; Friedmann, 2019; Mautner, 2020) or to the "upheaval" of 1977 (the change of government) that triggered the anxiety of the ousted liberal elite. According to this theory, it is possible that an indictment does not damage a defendant because the allegedly hyperactive judicial system itself is severely criticized and faces a crisis of legitimacy. Still, this does not mean that facing criminal charges is an advantage.

An alternative theory claims that questionable behavior is paying off at the polls because the people protest against the existing order and its rules that are considered to be directed against them (Kremnitzer, 2020). Without denying the value of these explanations, we must remember that Netanyahu had been the existing order; that is, when Netanyahu's entanglement with the law began, he had already been prime minister for eight consecutive years; So, it is possible that, more than a rejection of the existing order, the support for Netanyahu expressed support for the continuation of the existing order. An explanation of a different sort links the public's attitude toward Netanyahu's trial with its attitude toward the media, as Netanyahu himself already did in the 2015 election campaign (Tsfati, 2017), and continued in the 2019–2021 campaigns (see Shilon in this volume). An explanation in this line (but more general) is proposed here.

We argue that a populist regime has emerged in Israel (Filc, 2018; Rogenhofer and Panievsky, 2020). Populism is a form of democratic politics marked by a dichotomous approach that differentiate "the real/pure people" (on whose side its carriers allegedly stand) and "the elite" and by animosity toward the institutions that embody the liberal order, including the mainstream media (Finchelstein, 2017, 103–4). The impact of Netanyahu's case on his political standing is examined through the lens of the literature that examines the link between populism and constitutional battles (Arato, 2016; Blokker, 2019; Roznai and Hostovsky-Brandes, 2020). It also draws on Gutwein's (2019) studies of the evolvement of Netanyahu's rule.

Legal restrictions may be perceived as frustrating popular sovereignty (Blokker, 2019), which is the life's breath of populism. Over time, the battle against the judicial system—changing judges' selection procedures, selecting close associates as judges, modifying the powers of the judiciary, and the like— is essential for instituting a populist regime (Arato, 2016). This is especially the case when the courts actively promote liberal values, and constrain the ability to selectively allocate resources to those who are perceived as "the real people." Indeed, populists try to exploit the constitution as a way to increase their power; not to limit it, as constitutions are supposed to do (Roznai and Hostovsky-Brandes, 2020).

122   *Doron Navot and Yair Goldshmidt*

Netanyahu's campaign against the judicial system is similar to that of other populist leaders in the world. On the one hand, Netanyahu's confrontations with the law could grant him an electoral advantage. Just like Netanyahu, who is liable to be deprived of his freedom as a result of a criminal trial, so too the sovereignty of the people is threatened by the courts. Accordingly, Netanyahu has sought to limit the powers of the courts and supported the attempts of former Justice Minister Ayelet Shaked to appoint conservative Supreme Court judges and to change the composition of the Judicial Appointments Committee.

On the other hand, Basic Law: Israel – Nation-State of the Jewish People enacted in 2018 is an example of the use of constitutional methods in order to consolidate a populist regime (Gutwein, 2019). This law defined "the people" as a counterweight to other Basic Laws that defined equal individual rights for all Israeli citizens.

Another important dimension in our analysis is Netanyahu's economic policy, and its relation to the judicial system. Most of the literature on populism (see, for example, Filc 2010, 2018) glosses over the possibility that populists provide a material value to its supporters. In contrast, the claim here is that the populist regime that Netanyahu established did so. We further assert that because these benefits are not compatible with liberal values, and because the courts have ruled again and again that various practices of budget allocation are illegal, this regime was in an inherent conflict with the judicial system.

The new order that emerged in Israel under Netanyahu focuses on the allocation of budgets to specific sectors and local authorities, as a function of their political support. This is, to a large extent, a substitute for the universal public services that have been cut back or privatized as part of the neoliberal project that has taken place since 1985. Thus, the main beneficiaries of the populist regime are those who are organized on a sectorial basis, some of them from lower classes in terms of income or education. Such a compensatory mechanism is the practice of allocating funds to members of the ruling coalition—known as the distribution of "coalitional funds"—beyond those that were allocated through the national budget. This took place, even when the practice has become less legitimate over time and was criticized by the public, the media, and the courts. For example, in September 2020, the government distributed approximately a billion shekels, mainly to settlers and the ultra-Orthodox, who received a share far exceeding their proportion in the population (Milman and Zerahia, 2020).

As far as Netanyahu is concerned, the populist style has been even more effective electorally in the face of the opposition's rejection of the compensatory mechanisms and its attempts to eliminate them, without proposing universal alternatives, such as an expansion of the welfare state. One example is a bill sponsored by Yair Lapid in 2018 to ban the practice of the allocation of "coalitional funds" (*Knesset News*, 2018). Another example that sheds light on the gulf between Netanyahu's populist and sectorial politics and his rivals'

Netanyahu and the Very Short History of the "Right-Wing Bloc" 123

liberal-universal politics is provided by Tzipi Livni's failure to form a government in 2008, following Prime Minister Olmert's resignation. She rejected the demand by ultra-Orthodox Shas to increase child benefits by 600 million shekels (Levi, 2019). Netanyahu, by contrast, promised the ultra-Orthodox whatever they wanted; this paved the way for him to establish a government following the election in 2009, with coalition agreements that added 1.4 billion shekels for child allowances and granted other demands (Weissman, 2009).

From that time on his economic policy became "generous" and selective (unlike his years as finance minister, 2003–2005), and budgets were used to pay for supporting him. Since then, this trend has only accelerated. Under the 35th Government (2020–2021), for example, the allocation for the residential facilities of yeshivot increased by more than 300%. The budget for ultra-Orthodox culture, which is distributed to various organizations that are close to the ultra-Orthodox parties and to organizations that convince people to become religious observants, has also tripled, from 25 million shekels in 2014 to 75 million shekels in 2019 (Ilan, 2019a). Similarly, the budget of the Ministry of Religious Services grew from 376 million shekels in 2014 to 736 million shekels in 2019 (Ilan, 2019b).

The High Court of Justice ruling in 2014 that the state must stop funding the studies of yeshiva students who had received a military deferment exemplifies the tension between the populist sectorial regime and the courts. So does the High Court of Justice decision that same year that the state must no longer provide guaranteed income payments to married adult yeshiva (Kollel) students, on the grounds that the regulation is contrary to equality and discriminates against secular university students. This ruling followed an earlier decision by the High Court of Justice, in 2010, which annulled the budgetary preference for Kollel students over university students. In practice, that ruling cut some 120–140 million shekels that had been allotted to Kollel students (Yoez, 2014). These cases exemplify the tension between the liberal and universal principles of the judicial system and the particularistic nature of budgets for ultra-Orthodox institutions, which are the linchpin of the cooperation between Netanyahu and the ultra-Orthodox. Accordingly, ultra-Orthodox trust in the judicial system, and especially the High Court of Justice, is very low (Hermann, Heller, Cohen, Bublil, and Omar, 2016).

There is also fierce tension between the settlers and the courts. The growing strength of the settler sector in recent decades was fueled by the fact that settlement construction functions as a key mechanism to provide land and services at reduced prices. This serves as a compensation for their relative scarcity within the Green Line and contributes to the consolidation of the settlement project with the passage of time. This has generated an increasing contradiction between the principle of civic equality that is the foundation of the judicial system and the discrimination on which the settlement project is based (Gutwein, 2016). Meanwhile, the increased legitimacy of the settlements in the Israeli discourse has contributed to the settlers' growing assertiveness. This, in turn, augmented their friction with the judicial system.

124   *Doron Navot and Yair Goldshmidt*

An example of this tension is the case of the Dreinoff Apartment Buildings in Beit El. In 2015 the High Court of Justice ruled that the buildings must be razed, because they had been constructed on privately owned Palestinian land. In response to the court's ruling, MK Moti Yogev of The Jewish Home party said, "We need to send D9 bulldozers to the Supreme Court building and demolish it" (Bender, Somberg, and Eldad, 2015). He expressed, in perhaps the most brutal form, how the public he represents feels about the Supreme Court. Similarly, over the past decade, the High Court of Justice has ordered the state to evacuate a long series of outposts (Magid, 2020). Still another example was the High Court of Justice ruling that struck down the Regularization Law that intended to legalize post factum the forced and illegal seizure of usage rights and land titles and to legitimize the expropriation of Palestinian land. The High Court of Justice ruled that the law was unconstitutional in that it infringed the right of the Palestinian residents to property and equality, while granting clear priority to the interests of the Israeli settlers (Dolev, Adamker, and Horodniceanu, 2020). The High Court of Justice also struck down a plan by Culture Minister Miri Regev to make government grants to cultural, music, theater, and dance groups for performances in Judea and Samaria—grants that were officially intended to support the periphery, but, according to the court, actually had a discriminatory character (Gorali, 2020).

In addition, the High Court of Justice blocked government distribution policies that were not universal and focused on lower and lower middle-class Jews in the periphery. These, according to an analysis of voting patterns by socioeconomic clusters, constitute the Likud's base (Hoffmann-Dishon, 2019). The most prominent issue may be the attempt to exploit the definition of "national priority areas" for the allocation of budgets. The High Court of Justice blocked the government's attempts to define specific towns and local councils as national priority areas as a way to provide them with tax benefits. For example, in 2014 the government decided to add five Jewish localities to the map of national priority areas: Arad, Beit She'an, Hatzor ha-Gelilit, and the settlements of the Central Arava Regional Council and of the Ayalot Regional Council. The High Court of Justice ruled that they must be removed from the map, because the benefits were discriminatory and had not been granted on the basis of clear criteria (*Knesset News*, 2014). Another allocation policy that gave an advantage to the Jewish right wing (over Arabs and the Jewish left) was the enactment of "loyalty-citizenship" legislation, that "makes civic and social rights conditional on ostensible loyalty to the state, and in practice to the right wing" (Gutwein, 2016). That is, those who support the Likud-led coalition are depicted as belonging to the "people"—loyal, Zionist, authentic Jews, and the like—and thus eligible to receive more than those who oppose the Likud, and especially left wingers. This paves the way for an unequal allocation of resources that benefits the right.

Netanyahu is very important for the populist order. First of all, his political skills and his experience enabled him to identify the electoral potential of the populist discourse, and to implement it with great skill and success. Second, and building on this, as Netanyahu's populism increased, so did his importance as a leader who represents "the people." Third, the distributional mechanisms that grounded his power were contrary to procedural justice, transparency, and equality before the law. Netanyahu continued to develop these mechanisms even when their legal legitimacy declined and they became the focus of public debate. Last and perhaps most important, because the judicial system is powerful, a politician will avoid coming into conflict with it (Friedmann, 2019), unless he has an extra reason to do so. Netanyahu is among the very few who were willing to confront a judicial system that has actively worked against the allocation of resources he promoted (Mautner, 2020); and, as we will see below, he has had very strong personal grounds for doing so.

6.2 Netanyahu and the Legal System: Statist (*Mamlachtit*) Rhetoric and an Ambivalent Attitude Toward the Courts

Netanyahu's view of the Israeli courts was and is complex. While he supports, in general, the separation of powers and the system of checks and balances (Prime Minister's Office, 2018), he also believes that the Israeli courts do not always respect these principles. Zooming in beyond his general view, we can identify four different periods in Netanyahu's attitude about the judicial system; the fourth and current phase will be the focus of the next section.

Netanyahu's attitude toward the judicial system in the first period, which lasted until the end of his first term as prime minister (1999), can be described as reserved. It was manifested in a series of dismissals and appointments he and his right-hand man at the time, Avigdor Lieberman (Navot, 2012), initiated. In addition, during the mass demonstrations of the ultra-Orthodox against the High Court of Justice, Netanyahu did not stand forthrightly alongside Chief Justice Aharon Barak (Levitsky, 2001). Were this not enough, Netanyahu found himself enmeshed in a police investigation and drew the scathing criticism of the Attorney General, who nevertheless closed the case against him (Leshem, 2017).

The second period began with his second tenure as leader of the opposition (2006–2008), and continued throughout his second term as prime minister (2009–2013). As the leader of the opposition he demanded the resignation of Prime Minister Ehud Olmert who faced a criminal investigation into his conduct. Later, during the election campaign, he endeavored to return Benny Begin and Dan Meridor to the Likud, since, from his perspective, they constituted a sort of certificate of integrity (Leshem, 2017). During this term he praised the courts and torpedoed legislative initiatives that would have reduced their powers (Weissman, 2011; Azoulay and Glickman, 2011). Netanyahu spoke in favor of complying with High Court of Justice rulings even when the court reached decisions against his agenda (Kamm and Freidson, 2015). But his second term as prime minister was also marked by the appointment of several senior officials who were known in their opposition to judicial activism.

126 *Doron Navot and Yair Goldshmidt*

After the end of the 2015 elections campaign, and more so during the term of his fourth government (2015–2002), a clear change in Netanyahu's attitude toward the courts became evident. When the 2015 election results were published, the chair of the Knesset Foreign Affairs and Defense Committee, MK Yariv Levin—who had been seen as a leading candidate for the post of justice minister in that government and was known to be close to Netanyahu—declared that he would promote legislation to change the face of the Supreme Court (Ha'artez, 2015). In early May, even before Netanyahu's fourth government was installed, *The Economist* (2015) published an article "Netanyahu v the Supreme Court." Its author predicted that Netanyahu would severely curtail the powers of the High Court of Justice. Netanyahu was unable to appoint a justice minister from the Likud and had to accept Ayelet Shaked of The Jewish Home party. She too was critical of the judicial system (Sadeh, 2020). While in office, Shaked worked vigorously to appoint conservative judges, to curtail the power of the court system, and to redefine the position of the Attorney General and the authority of the legal advisors in the government ministries. Already in the first year of that term, Netanyahu rarely reacted to the harsh criticism of the High Court of Justice uttered by members of his government. Instead, his Finance Minister Moshe Kahlon became the "defender" of the High Court of Justice (Tadmor, 2017). Netanyahu himself ramped up his criticism of the High Court of Justice, for instance after its ruling about the natural gas arrangement (Pulver, 2016), and publicly backed ministers such as Justice Minister Shaked who were highly critical of its decisions (Ravid, 2016). There were also repeated attempts to promote legislation that would reduce the powers of the High Court of Justice and of the Attorney General, on which Netanyahu kept a reserved position. In the next section we will see how the progress in the processing of the criminal allegations against him influenced his rhetoric and attitude toward the law enforcement system.

6.3 The Cases Against Netanyahu

In the first half of 2016, the police received information that raised suspicions that Netanyahu was involved in fraud, breach of trust, and reception of personal favors. In July, the Attorney General announced, without providing details, that an investigation concerning Netanyahu was in progress. In November, a prominent journalist, Raviv Drucker, exposed the ties between the billionaire James Packer and Netanyahu's son, and claimed that Netanyahu's personal attorney tried to arrange permanent resident status for Packer. A week after this report, Netanyahu took part in the business conference sponsored by an ultra-Orthodox newspaper identified with the then-deputy Minister of Health, Yaakov Litzman of the United Torah Judaism party. He received a warm welcome: "The Prime Minister is going through difficult times," said Litzman and added:

He has opponents at home and abroad, but he knows that his ultra-Orthodox partners are at his side. [...] We are in the Prime Minister's coalition, vote with him even on matters that are of no concern to us, such as the [establishment of the Israel Broadcasting] Corporation, and foreign affairs and defense, and we ask and receive his support for matters that are important to us, such as the Sabbath, the needs of the yeshivas, and repeal of the Conscription Law. Who knows better than I how busy the Prime Minister is, but nevertheless he decided to be here with us. This is insurance for the positive bond he sees in the ultra-Orthodox community.

(Adamker, 2016)

On January 2, 2017, the Justice Ministry announced that Netanyahu was being investigated on suspicion of having received favors from two businessmen—Arnon Milchan and Packer (Bizportal, 2017). This affair was known as Case 1000. A week later, another journalist broke the story that "Case 2000" focused on negotiations between Netanyahu and the publisher of *Yedioth Ahronoth*, so that the latter, Noni Moses, would guarantee extremely favorable coverage of Netanyahu in return to curtailing the circulation of the free daily *Israel Hayom*, Israel's most widely distributed newspaper (often nicknamed "*Bibiton*," due to its unremitting support of Netanyahu) (Peleg, 2017). Several weeks after the Attorney General's announcement about the investigations, Netanyahu was asked to relate to these matters during question time in the Knesset. In his response he emphasized that he was the only one who had worked to torpedo the bill that was aimed to curtail the circulation of *Israel Hayom*, and asked: "And they're investigating me?." So far as he was concerned, Case 1000 embodied "the same hypocrisy." He went further and asserted that "there is an unprecedented campaign of a witch hunt and persecution... The goal is to replace the government by means of media pressure on the Attorney General, so that he will file an indictment at any cost" (Knesset Channel, 2017).

In mid-2017, it was revealed that several persons close to Netanyahu had been arrested in connection with the "submarine affair," a defense procurement deal that was suspected to be corrupted. In July 2017 Netanyahu was interviewed on Channel 20 (a right-wing pro-Netanyahu outlet) and declared: "it's a fake news campaign with a soviet style" (Nir, 2017). At this stage, Netanyahu's criticism was directed only at the media.

On February 13, 2018, the Israel Police announced that it gathered sufficient evidence to ground suspicions against Netanyahu of bribery, fraud, and breach of trust with regard to his relations with Milchan and his conversations with Moses, and fraud and breach of trust in his dealings with Packer (*Ha'aretz*, 2018). Netanyahu announced in a press conference that "ever since I was elected Prime Minister, there has hardly been a single day when slander and false charges were not hurled at me." He said he was confident that the legal authorities would drop these charges (*Israel Hayom*, 2018).

6.4 The Cases Against Netanyahu, the Election Campaigns, and the Formation of the Right-Wing-Religious Bloc: The Objections to the Trial as a Battle "For Democracy"

6.4.1 Toward the April 2019 Election

On December 2, 2018, the police announced its conclusions in an additional affair, known as Case 4000 (the Bezeq-Walla! case). It claimed that Netanyahu received a bribe and acted with a conflict of interest when intervening in regulatory decisions that benefited the Bezeq telecommunications corporation and its holder of controlling interest, Shaul Elovitch. In return, he requested, directly and indirectly, that Elovitch intervene to procure him favorable coverage on the *Walla!* website that was also under his control. Netanyahu released a statement that the police recommendations and their timing (on the last day of the police superintendent term) "don't surprise anyone." He again expressed his confidence that the Attorney General would reach the conclusion that "there was nothing" (Hoval, 2018). In a speech to the Likud convention, Netanyahu repeated the main points of his statement to the Knesset during question time. But now his tone was much harsher (Wootliff, 2018).

On December 24, 2018, about three weeks after the police announcement and following the earlier (November) departure from the coalition of Avigdor Lieberman as defense minister and his party, the leaders of the coalition factions unanimously decided to reschedule the forthcoming election date, so it will take place seven months early. This occurred before the Attorney General's decision about indicting Netanyahu (Azoulay, 2018). Netanyahu's lawyers stated that "to announce a hearing during an election campaign without listening to the other side distorts the voters' will and strikes a severe blow to the democratic process" (Peleg, 2019). Mati Tuchfeld (2019)—a journalist whose views generally reflect those of Netanyahu—wrote that his campaign strategy would be to keep the investigations in view so that when the Attorney General will publish his decision it would already be a nonissue; to highlight the contamination of the investigations; and to make it clear that it was not about bribery in any conventional sense. Then, after the Attorney General published his decision, Netanyahu planned to present the election as a "vote of confidence" in him.

In early 2019, Netanyahu issued a statement, which he labelled "dramatic," that if he proposed "retreating to the 1967 lines, dividing Jerusalem, and ceding Israeli security" his prosecution would stop—but that he would never do this (Kozin, Hachmon, and Bender, 2019). He turned his personal legal problems into evidence of his loyalty to the right wing and presented himself its champion. In late February 2019, the Attorney General announced his decision to indict Netanyahu, subject to a hearing, on two counts of breach of trust (in Cases 1000 and 2000), and one of bribery (Case 4000). At another press conference, Netanyahu insisted that the left was engaged in political persecution in order to bring down the right-wing government and that the indictment was the product of inhuman pressure on the Attorney General. Netanyahu also emphasized that "for the first time in the history of the state" it had been decided to conduct a pre-indictment hearing before elections— and this was incompatible with democracy (Hoval, 2019).

Between December 2017 and May 2020, when the investigations of Netanyahu expanded, we conducted a series of surveys to examine the public's attitudes toward corruption.[1] The findings buttress the argument that the allegations against Netanyahu did not harm him politically and may even have helped him. In January 2019, before the Attorney General announced his decision to file an indictment, subject to a hearing, 51% of those who defined themselves as right wing or very right wing believed that some Israeli journalists and media outlets were active participants in an attempt to oust Netanyahu. After the Attorney General's announcement, that is, in February 2019, the figure skyrocketed: 87% of those who defined themselves as very right wing and 89% of those who defined themselves as right wing now believed this claim. Before the Attorney General's announcement, 65% of the far right wing agreed with Netanyahu that the investigation against him was biased, and 62% of the right wing, but none of those who defined themselves as being on the left. A month later, after the Attorney General's announcement, 73% of those who defined themselves as very right wing agreed with Netanyahu that the investigation was biased (an increase of seven percentage points), and 70% of those who defined themselves as right wing, an increase of eight percentage points; once again none of those who defined themselves as left, and only 5% of those who leaned left agreed. These results indicate that the allegations against Netanyahu may have augmented his potential voters' antipathy to the judicial system, not only his own critical attitude. In the election for the 21st Knesset on April 9, the Likud won 35 seats, 5 more than it won in the 2015 election.

6.4.2 Toward the September 2019 Election

In a survey of a representative sample of the Jewish population of Israel, conducted on April 11, 2019, two days after the election, more people expressed confidence in Netanyahu (48.5%) than in the judicial system (47.2%). Despite the success of Netanyahu and the Likud in the election, due to the demand of Avigdor Lieberman, the leader of Yisrael Beiteinu, to form a government without the ultra-Orthodox (and the Arab) parties, Netanyahu was unable to form a government, and the Knesset was doomed. The date for the early elections for the 22nd Knesset was set for September 17, 2019. On May 8, 2019, State Attorney Shai Nitzan was interviewed by *Makor Rishon*. In response to the claim that what Netanayhu did was never considered as a bribe, he answered that "any legal precedent needs to start from a certain point" (Bandel and Yifrah, 2019). Netanyahu was quick to exploit the inter-view to argue that the system was persecuting him. A month later, Netanyahu appointed his loyalist Amir Ohana as justice minister. Soon, Ohana will take

130 *Doron Navot and Yair Goldshmidt*

steps that reflect Netanyahu's intention to make major changes in the judicial system.

In the September 2019 election, the Likud dropped to 32 seats. But at this stage, too, the dynamics that Netanyahu's opponents had hoped to see in the wake of the announcement of an indictment (subject to a hearing) did not take place. The right-wing religious parties maintained their united front. Moreover, Netanyahu's confrontations with the prosecution and judicial system encouraged some right-wing leaders to criticize them, rather than Netanyahu. For example, before the expiration of the mandate that the President had given Netanyahu to form a coalition, the head of The New Right party in the Knesset, Naftali Bennett, wrote:

> if the judicial system is successful in bringing down Netanyahu because of cigars and articles on *Walla!*, it will be a critical blow to the entire national camp. Any leader of the right who follows him will be afraid of the media and of the courts… Friends, I'm not defending only Netanyahu, but the entire national camp and our State of Israel against the unfair legal and media persecution of Netanyahu, the leader of the right wing-religious camp and the Prime Minister of Israel.
>
> (Berger, 2019)

On September 18, 2019, a day after the second election, Netanyahu initiated a meeting with the heads of the right-wing parties—Shas, United Torah Judaism, and Yemina—in which it was unanimously agreed to establish the "right-wing-religious bloc," led by Netanyahu that would work to form the next government. It was decided to establish a joint negotiating team of the parties in the bloc (Shemesh, 2019). All parties pledged not to conduct separate coalition negotiations with Benny Gantz, while Netanyahu promised that all of them would be included in a new government. It seems that the intimate link between the allegations against Netanyahu and the repeated election campaigns meant that Netanyahu's partners perceived that joining Gantz was illegitimate. The allegations strengthened the feeling of "us" against "them" and paved the way for this unprecedented pledge. From this time on the rightwing parties' relations with Netanyahu became even closer.

6.4.3 *Toward the March 2020 Election*

On November 21, 2019, the Attorney General announced his decision to indict Netanyahu for fraud and breach of trust (in Cases 1000 and 2000) and for bribery (Case 4000). About an hour after the decision was published, Netanyahu convened a news conference and repeated the harsh charges he had made in the past. Netanyahu classified the accusations as "false," "politically motivated," and an "attempted coup" (Ha'aretz, 2019). After the Attorney General's decision, Transport Minister Bezalel Smotrich tweeted that people should "go out to the streets" in order to prevent a "judicial dictatorship."

Netanyahu and the Very Short History of the "Right-Wing Bloc" 131

Ex-Minister of Justice, chair of The Jewish Home party, and MK, Ayelet Shaked added that "in the event of elections, only the public decides, and not the court" (Barsky, 2019).

About a week later, Netanyahu met with the heads of the Judea-Samaria Council and announced that at its next session the government would approve a budgetary allocation of 40 million shekels to fund security and rescue units in Judea, Samaria, and the Jordan Valley. At the end of the meeting, the Council Chair said, "You are again proving your loyalty, your determination, and your perseverance in developing Jewish settlement in Judea and Samaria and the Jordan Valley… We… support you" (Prime Minister's Office, 2019).

In December 2019, Justice Minister Ohana, appointed Dan Eldad to replace the State Attorney and managed to sow dissension among the senior echelons of that office. In addition to the attempt to weaken this office, Ohana helped Netanyahu signal the seriousness of his intentions to reform the law enforcement apparatus. On the eve of the Likud primaries, in which only Gideon Sa'ar ran against Netanyahu, the justice minister said, "my worldview in regard to the judicial system is clear… After the era of judicial activism and legal advisor activism, the time has come for governance activism" (Zerahia, 2019). At the end of the month, Netanyahu defeated Sa'ar in a landslide victory. The moment the primary results were published, the leaders of the right-wing-religious bloc parties declared their commitment to it and their trust in Netanyahu. Shas leader Deri, "as a partner to the cause," proclaimed that he "was delighted by the great expression of trust that [Netanyahu] received this evening from so many people. We will maintain the right wing bloc…" The chair of The Jewish Home party, Rafi Peretz, came with a similar massage, and so did Ayelet Shaked (Azoulay, Somfalvi, Rubinstein, Tvizer, Rabad, and Janko, 2019).

On January 1, 2020, Netanyahu announced that he was going to ask the Knesset to grant him immunity. Netanyahu also argued that he enjoyed substantive immunity for his negotiations with Moses, the *Yedioth Ahronot* publisher, because he had acted by virtue of his position as an MK in order to thwart the *Israel Hayom* bill (Lis, 2020a). The very next day, the High Court of Justice rejected the petition to bar Netanyahu from receiving the mandate to form a government, on the grounds that it was hypothetical. It did note that "factual developments of some nature could affect the relevance of the decision and the extent to which it corresponds to reality" (HCJ 19/8145). These petitions and judicial decisions made it easier for Netanyahu to base the campaign on the question of who is qualified to decide who is appropriate to serve as prime minister—the courts or the public (Yakobson, 2020).

At the end of January 2020, Netanyahu announced that he would not request immunity (Lis, 2020b). Leaving the legal threat in place made his claims more reliable and helped him to continue running a campaign based on the question of "do the people have the right to choose their leaders as they wish?" About two weeks before the election, the acting State Attorney Eldad announced that he had instructed the police to open an investigation

132 *Doron Navot and Yair Goldshmidt*

against Fifth Dimension, a company that had been headed by Gantz, even though he made it clear that Gantz was not a suspect in the case (*Calcalist*, 2020). Despite the substantial imbalance between the cases, the semblance of equivalence played into Netanyahu's hands at the electoral level, allowing him to argue selective enforcement against him.

About two weeks before the March 2, 2020 election for the 23rd Knesset, the leaders of the right-wing parties signed a letter of fidelity to Netanyahu and thus gave formal substance to the "right-wing bloc." They stated that "we will not support and will not join any government other than a government formed by the Likud and with Benjamin Netanyahu as its head. We emphasize that we will not conduct any separate negotiations to establish another government" (Azoulay, 2020). In the election, Likud won 29.46% of the valid votes and increased its Knesset representation to 36 seats. In close proximity to the beginning of the prime minister's trial, this was the party's best result since 2003. The bloc maintained its unity. Subsequently, under cover of the Covid-19 pandemic, Netanyahu managed to split the Blue and White (Kahol-Lavan) alliance and set up a rotation government with Gantz and his party.

6.4.4 The Netanyahu–Gantz Government and the March 2021 Election

Netanyahu's trial opened on May 24, 2020, a week after the 35th government passed a vote of investiture in the Knesset. Beyond the opening of the trial, the central issue before the government was the Covid-19 virus pandemic. The Israeli public remained split about the functioning of Netanyahu during the pandemic, and its influence on the electoral success of the Likud is unclear.

In December 2020, Sa'ar—who failed to challenge Netanyahu in the Likud primaries—announced that he is leaving the Likud and is forming a new right-wing party, New Hope. According to Sa'ar, the Likud "had become a tool for the personal interests of the person in charge, including matters relating to his criminal trial" (Staff and Wootliff, 2020). Two weeks later, another senior Likud member, Ze'ev Elkin, left the Likud and joined Sa'ar's new party. He stated that:

> As someone who is closely watching this dangerous process, I see how your [Netanyahu's] personal considerations are getting mixed up with national considerations, and even triumphing … we're going to elections because you want to influence [the appointment of the] State Attorney and the Attorney General, and because of your hope for a French law [to stop your corruption trial].
>
> (Staff, 2020)

Elkin's announcement came one day after the 23rd Knesset was dissolved, after the government did not approve the national budget as the law requires. According to Sa'ar, Elkin, and other Likud defectors, Netanyahu failed because of his trial and his attempts to thwart it. As for the Likud, it

Netanyahu and the Very Short History of the "Right-Wing Bloc" 133

presented the leaders of New Hope as opportunistic politicians who left the party because of their marginal position.

The fourth election in two years took place on March 23, 2021. New Hope won six seats in the Knesset, exactly the number of seats the Likud lost. To compensate for this loss, Netanyahu tried to achieve the support of the Islamic party, Ra'am, headed by Mansur Abbas, for the coalition that he attempted to form. However, Bezalel Smotrich, the chair of The Religious Zionism, vetoed it, and by so doing he sealed Netanyahu's fate. At least for the time being, after a dozen years in power, Netanyahu became (again) the leader of the opposition.

6.5 Discussion and Conclusions

In this chapter we argued that the legal proceedings against Netanyahu were a major factor in the consolidation of his position as the leader of the right-wing-religious bloc, and tried to explain how and why this happened. Our assertion is that in Israel, like in other countries (most prominently Hungary, Poland, Turkey, Venezuela, and India), there is tension between populism and the rule of law. In Israel this tension has two additional facets. First, the populist regime Netanyahu introduced in Israel is characterized by the selective and sectorial allocation of resources, which contravenes the activist liberal agenda of the judicial system. In other words, not only does Israeli populism criticize the courts as elitist; the conflict that pits the populists and their supporters against the courts has an economic basis as well. This is why for more than two decades, and especially over the last decade, the Israeli right is motivated to modify and weaken the court system, including the composition of the Judicial Appointments Committee, judicial doctrine, the powers of the High Court of Justice, the role of the Attorney General, and the status of ministries' legal advisors. The second facet is Netanyahu's personal legal troubles, whose impact exceeded the criminal charges against him, in part because many in the right and religious parties and publics perceived the proceedings as directed against them as a collective. That is, Netanyahu's claims about his unjustified prosecution fit in with the Israeli right's hostility to the judicial system. This even intensified it. The situation redoubled his commitment to remake the judicial system—even if only to escape the fury of the law—and also helped consolidate his image as the leader of the entire camp; it allowed him to personify the idea that the legal system is attacking and persecuting the right wing through one person. Right-wing media commentator Avishay Ben-Haim claimed that the case against Netanyahu was also a case against him: "The trial is not of Netanyahu but is the battle of the elite against second Israel [A code name for the relatively poor traditional Mizrchi Jews]" (Ezra, 2020).

Ultimately, the case against Netanyahu turned him into a person who is willing, interested, and able to do battle with the judicial system—unlike other politicians, who are either not interested or not able to do so, whether out of

134 *Doron Navot and Yair Goldshmidt*

fear, belief in the system, or other reasons. If we recall that some past justice ministers—who were perceived as hostile to the State Attorney's Office and the Supreme Court—had failed political careers, it is clear that only a man with the personal motivation and abilities of Netanyahu was able and willing to take on such a complex and dangerous mission. In the words of Haggai Segal, a prominent spokesperson for the settlers' cause: "These cases merely generated a rare opportunity to finally put an end to the protracted dictatorship of the High Court of Justice" (Segal, 2019).

For those who would like to reform the judicial system—the settlers, the ultra-Orthodox, local authorities that benefited from the sectorial arrangements, and others who view the courts with a jaundiced eye—this made Netanyahu the ideal candidate.

Note

1 We conducted ten surveys of representative samples of the Israeli population during this period. The interviews were conducted by phone by the Smith Institute. We acknowledge the Israel Science Foundation (ISF) support for most of these surveys through ISF grant 1609/17 to the first author.

References

Adamker, Yaki. 2016. "Among the Natural Partners: The Evening Netanyahu Spoke 'Ultra-Orthodox'." *Walla!*, November 21 [Hebrew].

Arato, Andrew. 2016. *Post Sovereign Constitutional Making*. Oxford: Oxford University Press.

Azoulay, Moran. 2018. "Coalition Leaders Decided: Elections on April 9." *Ynet*, December 24 [Hebrew].

Azoulay, Moran. 2020. "15 Days before Election: Deri Got Rightwing Bloc to Sign Loyalty to Netanyahu." *Ynet*, February 16 [Hebrew].

Azoulay, Moran and Aviad Glickman. 2011. "Netanyahu: I'm Against Limiting High Court Petitions." *Ynet*, November 26 [Hebrew].

Azoulay, Moran, Attila Somfalvi, Ro'i Rubinstein, Inbar Tvizer, Ahiya Rabad, and Adir Janko. 2019. "He Owns the Likud: Netanyahu Routs Sa'ar in Primary." *Ynet*, December 27, 2019 [Hebrew].

Bandel, Netanel and Yehuda Yifrah. 2019. "Voters Don't Decide if a Man Is Guilty." *Makor Rishon*, May 8 [Hebrew].

Barsky, Anna Rayva. 2019. "'Smutrich: if the People of Israel Do Not Go to the Streets They Will Awake for a Dangerous Judicial Tyranny'." *Ma'ariv*, November 22 [Hebrew].

Barsky, Anna Rayva. 2020. "Pledging Loyalty: Leaders of Rightwing Bloc Sign Joint Letter Supporting PM." *Maariv*, February 16 [Hebrew].

Barzilai, Gad. 1998. "Judicial Hegemony, Partisan Polarization, and Social Change." *Politika* 2: 31–51. [Hebrew].

Bender, Arik, Dana Somberg, and Karni Eldad. 2015. "Tempest on the Left: Send a Bulldozer to Raze the Supreme Court." *Maariv*, July 29 [Hebrew].

Netanyahu and the Very Short History of the "Right-Wing Bloc" 135

Benn, Alouph. 2018. "Netanyahu's Last Day in Power." *Ha'aretz*, February 21 [Hebrew].

Berger, Binyamin. 2019. "Bennett Protects Netanyahu against Investigations." *JDN News*, October 20 [Hebrew].

Bizportal. 2017. "Netanyahu Attacks: Posted on Facebook about Investigations—with Personal Message for Drucker." *Bizportal*, January 3 [Hebrew].

Blokker, Paul. 2019. "Populist Counter-Constitutionalism, Conservatism, and Legal Fundamentalism." *European Constitutional Law Review* 15: 519–543.

Calcalist. 2020. "Acting State Attorney: Fifth Dimension Case Sent for Police Investigation: Gantz Not a Suspect." *Calcalist*, February 20 [Hebrew].

Dolev, Daniel, Yaki Adamker, and Maya Horodniceanu 2020. "HCJ Strikes Down Regularization Law as Unconstitutional." *Walla!*, June 9 [Hebrew].

Ezra, Guy. 2020. "Avishai Ben-Haim: My Trial Begins on Sunday." *Serugim*, May 22 [Hebrew].

Filc, Dani. 2010. *The Political Right in Israel.* New York: Routledge.

Filc, Dani. 2018. "Political Radicalization in Israel: From a Populist Habitus to Radical Right Populism in Government." In *Expressions of Radicalization*, Steiner, Kristian and Andreas Önnerfors (eds.), 121–145. Cham: Palgrave Macmillan.Finchelstein, Federico. 2017. *From Fascism to Populism in History.* Oakland: University of California Press.

Friedmann, Daniel. 2019. *The End of Innocence.* Rishon Leziyyon: Yedioth Ahronoth. [Hebrew].

Galnoor, Yitzhak and Dana Blander. 2013. *The Political System in Israel.* Tel Aviv, Jerusalem, and Rishon Leziyyon: Sapir College, Am Oved, and the Israel Democracy Institute [Hebrew].

Gorali, Moshe. 2020. "High Court's Goodbye Present to Regev: Abolishing Bonus for Appearances in Judea-Samaria." *Calcalist*, May 14 [Hebrew].

Gur-Arye, Miriam. 2014. "Ethical Panic and Government Corruption." *Law and Business* 17: 447–467 [Hebrew].

Gutwein, Danny. 2016. "The Rule of Loyalty." *Theory and Criticism* 47: 225–247 [Hebrew].

Gutwein, Danny. 2019. "Bibi's Thatcherism Serves the Left—So It Will Keep Losing." *The Hottest Place in Hell*, April 19 [Hebrew].

Ha'artez. 2015. "The Likud Get Used to Their New Status." *Ha'aretz*, March 18 [Hebrew].

Ha'aret'z. 2018. "Police Recommendations in Netanyahu Cases: Full Document." *Ha'aretz*, February 13 [Hebrew].

Ha'aret'z. 2019. "Netanyahu Decries 'Attempted Coup' Against Him After Corruption Charges." *Haaret'z* November 21. www.haaretz.com/israel-news/netanyahu-decries-corruption-charges-an-attempted-coup-against-him-1.8161747

HCJ 19/8145. Orna Berry et al. v. the Attorney General et al., January 2, 2020 (not yet published) [Hebrew].

Hermann, Tamar, Ella Heller, Hanan Cohen, Dana Bublil, and Fadi Omar. 2016. *Israel Democracy Index 2016.* Jerusalem: Israel Democracy Institute [Hebrew].

Hoffmann-Dishon, Yaron. 2019. "Elections for 22nd Knesset: Analysis of Voting by Socioeconomic Cluster." Adva Center, September 25 [Hebrew].

Hoval, Revital. 2018. "Police Recommend Indicting Netanyahus for Bribery in Case 4000." *Haaret'z*, December 2 [Hebrew].

136   *Doron Navot and Yair Goldshmidt*

Hoval, Revital. 2019. "Two Articles and a Half? Ha'aretz Checked Netanyahu's Claims against the Facts." *Ha'aretz*, March 3 [Hebrew].

Ilan, Shahar. 2019a. "Netanyahu's Petty Cashbox: Big Money for Ultra-Orthodox." *Calcalist*, March 24 [Hebrew].

Ilan, Shahar. 2019b. "Budget of Religious Services Ministry Doubled in Netanyahu Government." *Calcalist*, April 4 [Hebrew].

Israel Hayom. 2018. "The Complete Version: Netanyahu's Response to Police Recommendations." *Israel Hayom*, February 13 [Hebrew].

Kamm, Zev and Yael Freidson. 2015. "Netanyahu Defends Supreme Court: We Are a Law-Abiding Country." *nrg*, July 29 [Hebrew].

Knesset Channel. 2017. "Question Time with Prime Minister Benjamin Netanyahu." *YouTube*, January 25 [Hebrew].

Knesset News. 2014. "Finance Committee to HCJ: Don't Remove 5 Localities from National Priorities List." *Knesset website*, February 17 [Hebrew].

Knesset News. 2018. "Ban on Coalition Funds Voted Down on Preliminary Reading." *Knesset website*, June 13 [Hebrew].

Kozin, Yaniv, Alon Hachmon, and Arik Bender. 2019. "Netanyahu Asks to Confront State's Witnesses." *Maariv*, January 7 [Hebrew].

Kremnitzer, Yuval. 2020. "The Emperor's New Nudity: The Media, the Masses, and the Unwritten Law." *Theory and Criticism* 52: 19–48. [Hebrew].

Leshem, Baruch. 2017. *The Netanyahu School for Political Marketing*. Tel Aviv: Matar. [Hebrew].

Levi, Eyal. 2019. "From the Victory over Netanyahu to Resignation from Politics: The Lost Decade of Tzipi Livni." *Ma'ariv*, February 9 [Hebrew].

Levitsky, Naomi. 2001. *His Honor*. Tel Aviv: Keter. [Hebrew].

Lis, Jonathan. 2020a. "Netanyahu Claims Immunity Is Always Temporary, But His Request to the Knesset Tells a Different Story." *Ha'aretz*, January 2 [Hebrew].

Lis, Jonathan. 2020b. "Netanyahu Officially Indicted in Court After Withdrawing Immunity Bid." *Haaretz*, January 28. www.haaretz.com/israel-news/elections/ .premium-indictments-against-netanyahu-officially-filed-in-court-1.8464667

Lis, Jonathan. 2021. "Israel Election Results: President Rivlin Tasks Netanyahu with Trying to Form Government." *Ha'aretz*, April 6. www.haaretz.com/israel-news/ elections/.premium-israel-election-results-rivlin-set-to-announce-nominee-to-form-government-1.9685860

Magid, Jacob. 2020. "High Court Orders Razing of Outpost Homes, But Okays Legalization of Others." *The Times of Israel*, August 27. www.timesofisrael.com/ high-court-orders-razing-of-outpost-homes-but-okays-legalization-of-others/

Mautner, Menachem. 2020. *Liberalism in Israel: Its Past, Problems, and Futures*. Tel Aviv: Tel Aviv University Press. [Hebrew].

Milman, Omri and Zvi Zerahia. 2020. "Despite COVID-19: Government Hands Out Almost a Billion Shekels in Coalition Money." *Calcalist*, September 10 [Hebrew].

Navot, Doron. 2012. *Political Corruption in Israel*. Jerusalem: Israel Democracy Institute.

Nir, Shai. 2017. "Confrontation at the Top." *Davar Rishon*, July 14 [Hebrew].

Peleg, Guy. 2017. "Revealed: Noni Moses at Center of PM Affair." *Channel 12 News*, January 8 [Hebrew].

Peleg, Guy. 2019. "Mandelblit to Former Senior Jurists: Obligation to Public Decision in Netanyahu Files before the Election." *Channel 12 News*, January 1 [Hebrew].

Prime Minister's Office. 2018. "Netanyahu's Speech in Knesset on the 69th Anniversary of its Establishment." Prime Minister's Office, January 30 [Hebrew].

Prime Minister's Office. 2019. "PM Meets with Heads of YESHA Council." Prime Minister's Office, November 28 [Hebrew].

Pulver, Sharon. 2016. "Chief Justice Naor: Government's Criticism of Court Should Not Be Heard in a Democratic Country." *Ha'aretz*, March 29 [Hebrew].

Ravid, Barak. 2016. "Netanyahu Backs Shaked: Everyone has the Right to Criticize the Supreme Court." *Ha'aretz*, April 5 [Hebrew].

Rogenhofer, Julius Maximilian and Ayala Panievsky. 2020. "Antidemocratic Populism in Power: Comparing Erdoğan's Turkey with Modi's India and Netanyahu's Israel." *Democratization* 27 (8): 1394–1412.

Roznai, Yaniv and Tamar Hostovsky-Brandes. 2020. "Democratic Erosion, Populist Constitutionalism, and the Unconstitutional Constitutional Amendments Doctrine." *Law & Ethics of Human Rights* 14 (1): 19–48.

Sadeh, Shuki. 2020. "They're Marketing a Pitiless Economy." *TheMarker*, "One Hundred Influences" (n.d.) [Hebrew].

Segal, Haggai. 2019. "The End of Innocence: The Story of High Court's Dictatorship is Many Times Larger than Netanyahu." *Makor Rishon*, May 23 [Hebrew].

Segal, Ze'evi. 2020. "Olmert: No Chance Netanyahu will Form Next Government." *Kol Hazman*, February 28 [Hebrew].

Shemesh, Michael. 2019. "Netanyahu Agreed with Leaders of Rightwing Parties on Bloc Led by Him." *Kan*, September 18 [Hebrew].

Sprinzak, Ehud. 1986. *Every Man Whatsoever Is Right in His Own Eyes: Illegalism in Israeli Society.* Tel Aviv: Sifriat Poalim. [Hebrew].

Staff, Toi. 2020. "Quitting Likud to Join Sa'ar, Ze'ev Elkin Says Netanyahu Forced These Elections." *Times of Israel*, December 23. www.timesofisrael.com/zeev-elkin-quits-likud-to-join-saar-accuses-netanyahu-of-destroying-party/

Staff, Toi and Raoul Wootliff. 2020. "Gideon Sa'ar Quits Likud, 'a Tool for Netanyahu's Interests,' to Lead 'New Hope'." *Times of Israel*, December 8. www.timesofisrael.com/likuds-gideon-saar-expected-to-form-his-own-party-in-challenge-to-netanyahu/

Tadmor, Erez. 2017. "How Kahlon become the Body Armor for the Destroyers of Israeli Democracy." *Mida*, September 30 [Hebrew].

The Economist. 2015. "Netanyahu v the Supreme Court." *The Economist*, May 2. www.economist.com/middle-east-and-africa/2015/05/02/netanyahu-v-the-supreme-court

Tsfati, Yariv. 2017. "Attitudes toward Media, Perceived Media Influence, and Changes in Voting Intentions in the 2015 Elections." In *The Elections in Israel 2015*, Michal Shamir, and Gideon Rahat (eds.), 225–251. London: Routledge.

Tuchfeld, Mati. 2019. "Netanyahu's Campaign Revealed." *Israel Hayom*, January 9 [Hebrew].

Weissman, Lilach. 2009. "Netanyahu Government Begins to Take Shape." *Globes*, March 23 [Hebrew].

Weissman, Lilach. 2011. "Netanyahu Shelves Bill for Hearings for Supreme Court Nominees." *Globes*, November 15 [Hebrew].

Wootliff, Raoul. 2018. "Police Recommend Bribery Charges against Netanyahu in Telecom-media Case 4000." *The Times of Israel*, December 2. www.timesofisrael.com/police-recommend-bribery-charges-for-netanyahu-in-case-4000/

Yakobson, Alex. 2020. "Let the People Choose and the Judges Judge." *Ha'aretz*, January 15 [Hebrew].

Yoez, Yuval. 2014. "HCJ: State Will Stop Providing Guaranteed Income to Kollel Students as of 2015." *Globes*, May 25 [Hebrew].

Zerahia, Zvika. 2019. "Netanyahu Launches Aggressive Campaign against Courts and Media." *Calcalist*, December 28 [Hebrew].

7 Public and Legal Responsibility of Senior Elected Representatives in the Executive Branch

Benjamin Netanyahu as a Case Study

Mordechai Kremnitzer and Dana Blander

> *For just as man is the best of the animals when perfected, so he is the worst of all when sundered from law and justice.*
>
> (Aristotle, *Politics*)

7.1 Background

Benjamin Netanyahu was the first incumbent prime minister in Israel who was simultaneously a criminal defendant accused of bribery, fraud, and breach of trust.[1] The charges relate to acts during his tenure as prime minister, and the offenses in question are ostensibly crimes of moral turpitude.[2] A criminal investigation of an incumbent prime minister is not unprecedented in Israel. In the past, Ariel Sharon and Ehud Olmert were investigated while serving as prime ministers; however, in the case of Sharon, it was decided not to bring an indictment against him, while Olmert stepped down before an indictment was filed against him.[3] The precedent, then, lies in the combination of being an incumbent prime minister (or candidate) and facing criminal proceedings at the same time. Moreover, the open attack on judicial and legal entities by a prime minister under indictment—accusing them of "concocting cases," "attempting to overthrow the government," "a bizarre and baseless indictment"—and even resorting to personal insults, was also unparalleled in both its fury and content.[4] Although Netanyahu was unable to form a government after the March 2021 elections, and at the time this chapter is written, no longer prime minister, his case allows us to shed light on public responsibility of elected office holders, as well as to offer ways to prevent a recurring situation.

This dangerous precedent of a prime minister who is a criminal defendant calls for a comprehensive discussion of the relationship between public responsibility and legal responsibility, between fitness and discretion, and between ethics and law. First, we will address public responsibility as expected of an elected official. Next, we will explore the Israeli legal doctrine that exists in cases where a public figure commits an act that is "not done." Subsequently, we will endeavor to understand why the constitutions of other countries

DOI: 10.4324/9781003267911-9

140   *Mordechai Kremnitzer and Dana Blander*

generally do not include special provisions for such cases, and will review the existing parliamentary mechanisms for preventing situations of this type. And finally, we will explore the dangers inherent in having a prime minister under indictment while in office, and propose a suspension provision for such cases.

Our argument is that, in the absence of established norms of public responsibility at the individual or parliamentary level, it is necessary to enshrine in law a mechanism for suspending a prime minister in the event that an indictment has been filed against him for severe offenses involving moral turpitude. It is important to emphasize that our point of departure in this chapter is the existing judicial doctrines concerning the appointment and removal of high-ranking officials in the executive branch, as recently reaffirmed by the High Court of Justice (HCJ *Netanyahu, 2020*).[5] The legislature has either adopted these doctrines in part or avoided explicitly altering them through legislation; and, as shown below, the political system has (even if unwillingly) internalized them to a great extent. A deeper exploration of these doctrines as they relate to the origins of the debate over the nature and scope of judicial review is beyond the scope of this paper.[6]

7.2 Public Responsibility

It is customary in the literature to focus on the "public responsibility" of elected and appointed officials—a notion that is one of the pillars of democracy. In the words of Gad Barzilai: "The concept of public responsibility is a meta-narrative for the existence of a democracy, since without a government's responsibility to its citizenry, the state in fact loses the raison d'être of democratic representation" (2014: 341). Yitzhak Zamir (2012) emphasizes that

> public responsibility is not stipulated by a legal principle, nor is it enshrined in law. Its underlying notion is of public trust from which all elected officials derive their standing, their role, and their powers by virtue of their status as trustees of the public...; this implies that a public figure...must utilize his office solely to serve the public.

Further, he states, public responsibility is reflected in three principles: personal responsibility; accountability; and transparency. Personal responsibility implies that a public figure bears individual responsibility for what he has done and what he has accomplished or achieved in office. This includes: criminal responsibility (for illegal actions); civil and/or administrative responsibility (compensating another for unlawful harm, subject to immunity);[7] and social responsibility, which can take the form of criticism or condemnation or harm to one's career. Resigning from public office is the accepted way of demonstrating personal responsibility by a prime minister, and the political sanction in such a case is generally a vote of no confidence in the government (in a parliamentary system), or impeachment (in a presidential system).

Public and Legal Responsibility of Senior Elected Representatives 141

Moreover, given Netanyahu's personal and public conduct since the start of the investigations against him, and all the more so since the filing of the indictment and the onset of his trial, there is a need to delineate an additional layer of public responsibility, namely, *public responsibility in cases of investigative and legal proceedings*. Thus, a public official is responsible for his conduct *vis-à-vis* the investigation and the trial. He is also responsible for the repercussions of the actions that he takes (attacking legal or judicial bodies) or neglect to take (not stepping down or suspending himself from office)—in light of the impact of these charges on the ethical standards of the public and the other branches of government. Granted, when a person is suspected of illegal behavior, he is liable to react with anger and complaints against the investigating and accusing entities; but even in such a case, there are red lines that a public figure is prohibited from crossing, even if he believes himself to be innocent.

Public responsibility encompasses, then, all of the actions that are "not done" in our society. There is an inverse relationship between the need for legal intervention and the accepted (and respected) public norms embedded in Israeli political culture. Stated otherwise, if certain norms of public behavior were entrenched in the political culture of Israel, there would be no need for the courts to intervene.[8]

7.3 From Ginossar to Deri-Pinhasi, Rochberger-Gapso, and Netanyahu: Supreme Court Decisions on Holding Public Office under Criminal Indictment

The relevant background for a discussion of tenure as prime minister while under indictment are the decisions of the Supreme Court in the cases of senior elected or appointed officials at various stages of criminal proceedings against them.

7.3.1 High Court of Justice (HCJ) Case – Ginossar (1993)

The origins of the Deri-Pinhasi doctrine, that will be introduced later, on the irreconcilability between a pending indictment and service as a senior public official, can be found in the principle established in the matter of Yossi Ginossar's appointment to the position of director general of the Ministry of Construction and Housing.[9] The name of Ginossar, who had served in high-level positions at the General Security Services (GSS), had been tied to two serious criminal cases related to his role in the organization: the Nafsu affair and the Bus 300 affair.[10] Under these circumstances, the Court determined that the appointment of an individual who had committed crimes involving moral turpitude in the past causes grave harm to the image, prestige, and role of the government as public trustee in a democratic society. This, in addition to its negative impact on the rule of law, integrity of government, and credibility of the officeholder.[11]

7.3.2 Deri-Pinhasi Doctrine (1993)

The ruling that was handed down in the matter of Ginossar paved the way for the Supreme Court decision by which then-Prime Minister Yitzhak Rabin was forced to dismiss Interior Minister Aryeh Deri when an indictment was drawn up against him for offenses involving moral turpitude, including bribery (HCJ *Deri*, 1993).[12] Although the Basic Law: The Government empowered the prime minister to dismiss a minister, there was no provision at the time regarding the suspension or removal of a minister for committing criminal offenses.

The Court insisted that, unlike the case of other public officeholders, appointing (or removing) an individual as minister is an explicitly political matter that is often based on party or coalition interests and is not necessarily a reflection of the skills, qualities, or personal characteristics of the candidate. Consequently, the prime minister has broad discretionary powers concerning appointment or removal, and the courts do not hasten to intervene except in cases where these are exercised in a patently unreasonable manner. In this context, it is necessary to consider the severity of the offenses and the nature of the actions that the official is charged with in the indictment, which itself is based on administrative evidence of the crimes committed. The court ruled that the nature and severity of the offences are irreconcilable with carrying on as a minister. Therefore, the minister has to resign or be dismissed by the prime minister. It is important to recall that this ruling was arrived at against the backdrop of a political situation in which the dismissal of Minister Deri was liable to cause the Shas party to leave the coalition (which in fact occurred) and to have far-reaching ramifications for government policy (approval of the Oslo Accords, the peace agreement between Israel and the Palestinians) (Koren and Shapira, 1997: 346–347). The Court made a similar decision in the matter of Deputy Minister and Member of the Knesset (MK) Rafael Pinhasi (HCJ *Pinhasi*, 1993).[13] The Court underscored that, as an elected official, an individual who holds the office of deputy minister is expected to meet a higher, more ethical standard of behavior than that of appointed public servants.

Since the Deri and Pinhasi cases, several provisions in Basic Law: The Government were put in place that directly address the possibility of a government minister being convicted of an offense involving moral turpitude. Para. 6 of the basic law stipulates that a person convicted of such an offense and sentenced to prison shall not be appointed as a minister for seven years from the end of his incarceration or the date of sentencing (the later of the two). Para. 23(b) states further that the tenure of a minister convicted of an offense involving moral turpitude shall be terminated as of the date of sentencing.

7.3.3 HCJ Case – Mayors Rochberger and Gapso (2013)

The case law arising from the Deri and Pinhasi affairs guided the Court in addressing the question of mayors accused of offenses involving moral turpitude during their tenure, in situations where the city councils on which they served decided not to utilize their power to remove them from office.[14] Much like the legal basis for the Deri-Pinhasi doctrine, the Local Authorities (Election and Tenure of Heads and Deputy Heads) Law, 5735-1975 stipulates that conviction on offenses involving moral turpitude leads to termination of a mayor's tenure. However, in keeping with the ruling discussed above, the Court determined that even prior to a conviction, the city council must consider exercising its powers to remove the mayor from office on grounds of conduct unbecoming his status, based on administrative evidence.

The Court noted that when an individual achieves a position via elections, the right to elect and be elected takes on added importance, but this consideration does not nullify other weighty concerns of public trust, moral integrity, and ensuring the honesty of public officials. The Court added that the city council is an elected body whose decisions are often political; however, in this case, they center on an assessment of the conduct of the mayor, and potential damage to the values that the law is intended to safeguard. The court ruled that the mayors should be removed from office.

As a result of these cases, the Law was amended to incorporate a mechanism whereby a public committee headed by a retired District Court judge can suspend the head of a municipality if an indictment is filed against him while in office, or there is a pending indictment filed prior to his tenure.[15]

It is true that there has been criticism over the years regarding the Deri, Pinhasi, and Gapso/Rochberger decisions. The argument being made is that they represent an extreme example of judicial activism without constraints.[16] Underlying this claim is the fact that according to the laws on which these decisions were based on only the conviction of an official for crimes involving moral turpitude leads to his removal from office, but no similar determination was made with respect to the filing of an indictment. Dotan (2018) holds that these rulings are akin to "judicial impeachment" based on standard judicial review without a constitutional foundation, indicating that this is a practice unique to Israel, and one that has a significant impact on the relations between the branches of government. In any event, even the most vehement of critics, who believe that the Court, in handing down these rulings, took upon itself the role of "moral watchdog" (Friedman, 2016), do not argue that these decisions stemmed from political bias. More importantly, looking at the outcome, the Court decisions led in certain cases to changes in legislation that incorporated these principles and helped establish a norm of public responsibility. As Dotan (2018) also notes, it is difficult to say that excessive use was made of this power, since, in most of the appeals concerning the appointment and removal from office of politicians and high-ranking officials, the Court refrained from intervening, while reiterating the high moral standards expected from senior officials and the principle of public responsibility. He also describes the evolution of this doctrine in the context of a political culture characterized by a tenuous awareness of public responsibility, as a result of which elected officials and public servants are slow to reach the conclusion that they should step down (Dotan, 2018: 726, 743). In his opinion as well, this principle is seen by the public as desirable and necessary, and can strengthen the standing of the Court vis-à-vis the other branches of government. We share the view that norms of public responsibility should not require the imprimatur of a Supreme Court decision but should be entrenched at the political level. However, since this is not the case in Israel, the Court's role is to fill the void.

7.3.4 Existing Law and HCJ Netanyahu (2020)

In the original Basic Law: The Government (1968), there was no mention of a situation in which a prime minister is investigated, much less charged with criminal acts. Basic Law: The Government (Direct Election of the Prime Minister), enacted in 1992, included sections relating to such circumstances and these sections were also adopted in Basic Law: The Government of 2001, and other new sections were added.[17] According to section 18 of this basic law, if the prime minister is convicted of an offense involving moral turpitude, the matter will be brought before the Knesset Plenum, which can remove him from office by a majority vote, a situation deemed as if the entire government had resigned. If the Knesset does not exercise this authority, the prime minister's tenure will be terminated if and when the Court's decision becomes final.

The Government Law, 5761-2001 sets forth provisions in section 4 regarding the future handling of an indictment filed against a prime minister or other minister prior to their taking up the position. It can therefore be inferred that, even in the event of an ongoing indictment or criminal proceedings, they may be permitted to assume office. Yet, the law does not include specific provisions in the case of an incumbent prime minister and/or an MK tasked of forming the government in the case that he is under indictment (before conviction).

The scenario of a prime minister that an indictment had been filed against him became a reality when Benjamin Netanyahu ran in the 23rd Knesset elections as head of the Likud list. Yet, in these elections the Likud garnered the largest number of votes (see Table 7.1). The voter's support for Netanyahu, regardless of the legal proceedings against him, might prove, as other research shows, that other considerations of party loyalty, ideological identification, and group affiliation may supersede concerns of ethical conduct by the candidate in the voters' decision-making process (De Vries and Solaz, 2017.) In a broader sense, the fact that the legal proceedings did not have a significant negative impact on voting patterns can also be seen as a reflection of the populist mood, characterized by resentment toward elites in general and the judiciary in particular (Friedman, 2019; Müller, 2016).

Following the elections for the 23rd Knesset, when a majority of 72 MKs recommended to the President to entrust Netanyahu to form a government, the HCJ consented to address the matter of his disqualification.[18] The central

Public and Legal Responsibility of Senior Elected Representatives 145

Table 7.1 Progress of criminal proceedings, and support for the Likud led by Benjamin Netanyahu in elections for the 20th–24th Knesset (2015–2021)

Stage of criminal proceedings	Elections and date	No. of voters for Likud	Share of voters for Likud (%)	No. of seats for Likud
Earlier investigations[a]	20th Knesset March 17, 2015	985,408	23.4	30
February 2019— Attorney General decides to file indictment, subject to hearing[b]	21st Knesset April 9, 2019	1,140,370	26.46	35
	22nd Knesset Sept. 17, 2019	1,113,617	25.1	32
Jan. 24, 2020— Indictment filed at Jerusalem District Court[c]	23rd Knesset March 2, 2020	1,352,449	29.46	36
Ongoing Trial	24th Knesset March 23, 2021	1,066,892	24.19	30

Source: Central Elections Committee of each Knesset.

Notes:
a For early investigations of Netanyahu see Note 3.
b This was preceded by police investigations (beginning in January 2017); police recommendations to file charges in Cases 1000 and 2000 (February 2018); and a recommendation to bring charges in Case 4000 (December 2018).
c This was preceded by a hearing in October 2019; the Attorney General's decision to file an indictment against Netanyahu (November 21, 2019); the filing of a request for immunity from prosecution, and its subsequent withdrawal, in January 2020.

question placed before the Court was whether MK Netanyahu could be tasked with forming a government, given the serious criminal charges he was facing. An expanded panel of judges heard the case, rejecting the petitions unanimously (HCJ *Netanyahu*, 2020; HCJ *Netanyahu*, supplementary decision, 2020).

Addressing the arguments of the petitioners on assigning the task of forming a government to MK Benjamin Netanyahu, who is under indictment, the Court considered four possible entities that have discretion in the formation of a government, in accordance with section 10(a) of Basic Law: The Government, namely, the President of Israel; the Knesset Speaker; an MK charged with the task; and a majority of MKs, who wish to assign him the task. With regard to the President, which is a symbolic authority in Israel, the Court noted that according to section 10(b) of the Basic Law, the President has to assign the task to an MK, according to a request of a majority of MKs, and has no discretion in the matter. The same holds true with respect to the Speaker of the Knesset, whose authority in this proceeding is limited to convening a session to establish a government. Concerning the discretion of

146   *Mordechai Kremnitzer and Dana Blander*

the MK appointed to form a government, the Court issued a majority ruling that the existing case law in the matter has not addressed the discretion of the nominee (as contrasted with that of the appointing entity).

In the case of a majority of MKs who wish to assign the task of forming a government to an MK under indictment for serious offenses, a majority of the Justices determined that the absence of a limitation in the law concerning the fitness of the nominee does not abrogate the discretion entailed in such a decision. The Court may intervene in the discretion of the MKs in highly exceptional circumstances, which did not exist here.[19] The Court found that the decision on assigning the task of forming the government lies at the very heart of the democratic process, as it is a direct exercise of the mandate granted to the MKs to constitute the executive arm of government in accord with the will of the voters.

With the exception of its final conclusion, the Court's decision reaffirmed the Deri-Pinhasi doctrine. A majority of the Justices held that this ruling applied *a fortiori* in the matter of the prime minister, in light of his unique status as head of the government empowered to remove ministers from office, and his ultimate seniority within the executive branch.[20]

The Court emphasized that its ruling was made solely on the judicial level; in other words, the decision of the MKs does not contravene the law. For a majority of the Justices, the situation that prompted the petitions represents "a moral failing of Israel's society and political system" (HCJ *Netanyahu*, supplementary decision, 2020: 54). Most of the Justices called upon the Knesset to amend the Basic Law for the future in such a way as to prevent assigning the formation of the government to an individual charged with serious criminal offenses. Accordingly, the remedy for this challenging situation, in the eyes of the Justices, lies not with the Court but in the public and political arena.[21]

7.4 Parliamentary Oversight

In a democracy, the parliament has the power to remove the head of the executive branch from office, either by a vote of no confidence (in a parliamentary system) or by impeachment (in a Presidential system). The same applies if criminal proceedings are being conducted against the head of the executive branch, at any stage of the process. The parliamentary tools are political, and are not a substitute for the criminal proceeding. Their role is to reflect desirable public norms, beyond the simple letter of the law.

A study of the constitutions of democratic countries indicates, somewhat surprisingly, that in most cases, there is no explicit or detailed reference to a situation in which the head of the executive branch is accused of criminal acts. Consequently, in most democratic nations, the head of the executive branch can stand trial like any citizen, and the launching of an investigation, or even the filing of an indictment, is not an automatic ground for ending his term of office, suspending him, or formally limiting his powers. One exception is

France, where the President (but not the prime minister or cabinet ministers) enjoys immunity from criminal prosecution while in office.[22] As a rule, in all legal systems based on the rule of law, the members of the executive branch, including its head, are subject to the law, and bear legal responsibility if they violate it. In some of the countries (Sweden, Denmark, Iceland, Ukraine, France, and Poland), specific offenses by elected officials—primarily abuse of government power—are defined as criminal in nature. For the most part, there are either special courts in these countries for deliberating the impeachment of members of the executive branch, or the case is trialed at the highest instance (European Commission, 2013).

In any event, the disparity between countries and the lack of detailed legal provisions regarding criminal proceedings against members of the executive branch might be explained by the view that members of the executive branch being suspected or accused of criminal activity is an implausible scenario. However, the rising number of cases involving prime ministers, presidents, and cabinet ministers shows that no country is immune from such an event (Warf, 2019). Yet a situation where the head of the executive branch continues to serve while on trial for severe criminal offenses is still a rare occurrence.[23] Apparently, there is an ingrained assumption in a democratic political culture, that in the event of an indictment, the head of the executive branch will voluntarily step down (or pushed to do it by his colleagues) or be removed from office through parliamentary proceedings.

Parliamentary oversight is intended to serve as a checkpoint prior to criminal proceedings. In some countries, the consent of parliament is required to open criminal proceedings against elected officials, or at a certain stage in the process.[24] Under a presidential system, the parliament has the authority to impeach the President in a special proceeding generally reserved for extreme situations. In the United States, where no incumbent President has ever been tried for criminal offenses, the prevailing approach is that a President should not stand trial while in office; in extreme and exceptional cases, he is to be impeached by a decision of both houses of Congress, and only then put on trial (U.S. Department of Justice, 2000). Nevertheless, parliamentary procedures require the existence of a majority. The expectation of parliamentary oversight in the event that it becomes necessary to sanction members of the executive branch or its head for violating public responsibility is usually politically unrealistic, given the majority coalition's support of the government. However, in countries where the political culture and tradition of public responsibility is more firmly entrenched, political loyalty can be set aside in favor of protecting public norms.

7.5 The Dangers of a Sitting Prime Minister under Criminal Indictment

The fact that the person being investigated or accused of criminal acts is a prime minister can be a crucial stumbling block in uncovering the truth. The

148 *Mordechai Kremnitzer and Dana Blander*

unique status of the accused sparks concerns that the principle of equality before the law will be undermined by the prime minister's advantage over other defendants. Such a situation places an unnecessary weight on the Justices hearing his case. Though they are presumed to be capable of disregarding the special standing of the accused and the symbolic and political significance of his conviction and to judge him as they would an ordinary citizen, the task is a daunting one that is best forestalled from the outset. The witnesses face an even greater difficulty, as they are compelled to stand before individuals of vast influence and power who are liable to abuse the government powers at their disposal to "settle scores" with them. This is an onerous burden that can deter witnesses from speaking the truth.

The ability to arrive at the truth is liable to be hampered already at the fact-finding stage, when the special status of the prime minister can stand in the way of the investigation. This can occur even without the prime minister or someone acting on his behalf attempting to abuse their position to stymie the investigation, all the more so if the prime minister refuses to cooperate. Already at the Olmert case, the Court noted that "if it later emerges that the Prime Minister's conduct does not permit the criminal investigations against him to be carried out properly, the Attorney General may have reason to declare the Prime Minister temporarily incapacitated."[25]

Moreover, the prime minister's need to be present in investigation rooms as well as courtrooms makes it extremely difficult for him to function. The emotional burden faced by any such defendant, coupled with the effort he must expend on his defense, are hardly compatible with the demands of higher office. The situation may reach the point where he becomes incapable of performing his duties.

Another issue is the profound conflict of interest of a prime minister who is accused of criminal acts. It should be recalled that the prime minister, by virtue of his position, oversees the ministers, who are in charge of the investigative authorities and the prosecution. Even if he avoids being involved directly in issues related specifically to him, or indirectly in matters of law and justice in general, his seniority may influence the functioning of his subordinates regarding the accusations against him.

Furthermore, the concern that a prime minister under indictment might make use of his powers to disrupt the proceedings against him is not limited to attempting to influence the legal authorities directly. As noted by Netanyahu himself when he was leader of the opposition, with regard to then-Prime Minister Olmert:

> A Prime Minister who is up to his neck in investigations has no moral or public mandate to determine matters so crucial to the State of Israel, since there is a genuine, and not unfounded, concern that he will make decisions based on his personal interest in his political survival, and not on the basis of the nation's interests.[26]

Public and Legal Responsibility of Senior Elected Representatives   149

Thus, legal proceedings against a prime minister, in and of themselves, raise suspicions that his conduct and decisions at the public level may be motivated not only by concern for the public good but also by an effort to influence the legal process. Even in decisions of the utmost importance—on war and peace, or, as it was in the present case of Netanyahu, the handling of the Covid-19 pandemic—there is the ever-present concern that the motivations underpinning them are less than pure and proper, thereby causing catastrophic damage to the proper functioning of the state and to the public trust in the government. In addressing the problems stemming from this conflict of interest, the Court limited itself to adopting the position of the Attorney General whereby Prime Minister Netanyahu will sign a statement of conflict of interest. However, it is unclear if an agreement of this type can serve as a genuine solution to a conflict as severe and pervasive as this one which involves the prime minister.

For all these reasons taken together, the prime minister should be barred from continuing to serve after an indictment has been filed against him for serious offenses involving moral turpitude. Below, we propose an outline for a legal mechanism that should be utilized to avoid such a situation.

7.6 The Ideal Law

As the Court has reiterated, the ability of a government to govern is based on the public's trust in that government, its integrity, and its concern for the public interest. The filing of an indictment centered on offenses involving moral integrity by nature detracts from the public's faith in those who serve it.[27] Our opinion, similar to the one expressed repeatedly by the Court, is that the optimal situation would be if the launching of significant criminal proceedings against a public official led to his removal from office or to his being barred from office at the outset, in accordance with a public norm internalized by elected representatives and senior public servants that would dictate such a result. If the accepted norm does not in itself lead to ending or preventing the officeholder's tenure, his political party should steer him in this direction. These measures, it must be clarified, do not constitute a full or partial admission of guilt by the elected official with regard to the allegations or charges against him. It is rather an acknowledgment of both his obligation not to serve in a senior public position while under suspicion, and the need to devote all his time and energy to dealing with the investigation and trial. For these reasons, Justice Barak-Erez, for example, stated that there is a normative obligation, even if not legally enforced, for the candidate to refrain from taking on such a position when he is under a cloud of suspicion.[28]

Before we describe the desirable law, we wish to make clear that we are opposed to arrangements whose purpose is to grant special immunity from criminal prosecution to the prime minister at any stage of the process be it an investigation, indictment, trial, or ruling (Kremnitzer et al., 2019, 2020; Lurie and Fuchs, 2017). Any attempt to enact into law special immunity from criminal prosecution renders grave harm to the principles of the rule of law and equality before the law. And as public opinion polls prove, a substantial majority of the Israeli public do not wish to see the prime minister evade justice (via immunity, "the French Law"), and instead hold that he should stand trial as any other citizen.[29]

We suggest that The Basic Law: The Government should be amended in such a way as to extend the approach outlined in the Deri-Pinhasi doctrine to the case of a prime minister. It is beyond the purview of this chapter to discuss this proposal in detail; thus, we will confine ourselves to presenting it in a concise, preliminary form.

Our focus is the suspension of an incumbent prime minister when charged with a severe crime involving moral turpitude. We propose that a mechanism be stipulated in the Basic Law: The Government by which the Attorney General can render a reasoned legal opinion regarding the suspension of the prime minister from the moment that an indictment is filed until the (final) judgment has been handed down.[30] For this reason, we hold that a suspension provision must be clearly enshrined in law. Since the term of office of the accused would thus be curtailed before a final judgment has been handed down, the impact of the indictment on his tenure should be temporary in nature, in a manner that takes into account the possibility of an acquittal, which would justify his return to office.[31] Such a conclusion is also called for by the presumption of innocence and the requirement of a fair trial for all. The advantage of such an arrangement is that it forestalls the possibility of a (direct or indirect) change of government caused by the (not temporary) removal of a prime minister from office.

Discretion in determining the gravity of the crimes, and the presence or absence of moral turpitude, should lie with the Attorney General as a professional, apolitical figure and by virtue of his role as the authorized interpreter of law—subject to the court's approval of his legal opinion and its reasoning to ensure the factual, nonpartisan nature of his decision. A decision based on discretion seems preferable to a dry legal principle by which the very accusation of certain crimes leads to an automatic suspension. Without examining the circumstances of the offenses, such a principle is liable to be too expansive and to bring about a result that is not justified. We would propose that the court's approval be applied also to preliminary arguments regarding absence of good faith, political persecution, or discrimination by legal authorities.

It would obviously be preferable if a suspension provision were not necessary, and if there were no need to involve the law, the Attorney General, or the Court in this matter. But, as stated, without a show of public responsibility on the part of officeholders, and given the paralysis of the political and parliamentary mechanisms, there is reason for the Knesset to enshrine such an arrangement in law in order to prevent such cases from recurring.[32]

7.7 Conclusions

The point of departure of this chapter is the recognition of the importance of public responsibility at all levels. If norms of public responsibility were ingrained in our elected representatives, there would be no need at all for this paper. The legal principles that we reviewed, and the proposal raised in the previous section for amending Israel's legislation, are an example of what Zamir terms "the migration of principles from the field of ethics into the field of law. Ethical principles that did not stand the test of reality become legal principles" (2012: 13). The detailed provisions in Israeli law concerning the possibility of a criminal conviction of a prime minister, still do not cover all the scenarios in which a prime minister accused of criminal offenses might continue to serve—attest to the weakness of public norms.[33]

We witness in this case a phenomenon that threatens the very existence of Israeli democracy, namely, employing the law against itself; in other words, adhering to the letter of the law, to justify actions that undermine norms that are essential to fulfilling the spirit of the law (Sadurski, 2019: 254–255). While it is true that Prime Minister Netanyahu was legally permitted to serve in office, the law is not the crux of the matter. Instead of demonstrating public responsibility by resigning from office or not submitting his candidacy (although the law does not require it), Netanyahu was using the "stamp of approval" that the law ostensibly granted him to continue in office until a final ruling, even as he chips away at every layer of public responsibility in both the actions of which he stands accused and in his verbal attacks against the law enforcement agencies and the courts.

As we have shown in the present case, the possible barriers along the way— the legislators, have also not demonstrated awareness of the vital meaning of public responsibility, which goes beyond the question of criminal guilt or innocence and beyond coalition loyalties.

It should be noted in this context that the political parties, which should have played a role in establishing suitable public norms and blocking the tenure of an individual who is not fit to serve, also failed in this task. The prime minister's party (which voted for him unquestioningly, time and again, to lead them and to form a government) as well as the other parties (which forged an alliance with the Likud based on the faulty perception that, since the prime minister enjoys a presumption of innocence, this makes him fit to hold office) all had a hand in nullifying the gap—highlighted repeatedly by the Court—between formal eligibility to serve and discretion regarding what constitutes a suitable appointment. Yet, at the end of the day what brought Netanyahu's term to its end was a political pact between parties, proving the important role these institutions can still play in guarding democracy.[34]

Our concern is that the situation of an accused prime minister staying in office is liable to turn the clock back to the days before the Deri-Pinhasi precedent. This runs the risk of implying that charges of government corruption can be overlooked, as if they are inconsequential, sending a negative message

152 *Mordechai Kremnitzer and Dana Blander*

on the importance of these offenses, and the gravity of violating them. Without doubt, a nod in this direction would strike a critical blow to the ability to promote moral integrity in public service—a value that is the life breath of a democracy.

The one bright spot in the process we have described here is that the principles established by the Court in the realm of moral integrity and norms of good government have become to a large extent entrenched in the political culture. And the decisions of the Court (forcing Deri and Pinhasi to step down, and removing the mayors from office) may be able to influence voters in general to attach more weight to the integrity of candidates, thereby furthering the desired outcome of popular oversight of elected representatives and the consolidation of public norms regarding the people's expectations of its officials (Yair et al., 2020). Such expectations may have a positive impact on the conduct of public officials. Thus, in the absence of a manifestation of responsibility on the part of public figures themselves, there is a growing need for the court to act as a "responsible adult" in order to steer the ship of state toward a place of law and order, inculcating norms of moral integrity and an ethos of public responsibility.

In conclusion, let us reiterate that the public has a crucial role to play in enshrining norms of good government. Elected officials act according to their discretion; courts render judgments to the best of their; the law says its piece. But ultimately, as stated by the philosopher Jean-Jacques Rousseau, "the most important [law] of all is engraved not on marble nor on bronze, but in the hearts of the citizens; a law which creates the real constitution of the State" ([1762] 2018).

Notes

1 MK (Member of Knesset) Benjamin Netanyahu was also the first MK tasked with forming the government while he was under criminal procedures. He had been tasked with forming a government following the elections to the 21st and 22nd Knessets when the Attorney General decided to bring an indictment against him pending a hearing. The indictment had already been filed with the court, and the trial date set, not long before the elections for the 23rd Knesset. When the elections to the 24th Knesset were held his trial was already on its way. Nevertheless, he was given the role of forming the government but was unable to form it. On June 2021 the Bennett–Lapid government was formed, and Netanyahu became the leader of the opposition.

2 Indictment against Benjamin Netanyahu et al., Jerusalem District Court, January 28, 2020.

3 It should be noted that the first prime minister involved in a suspected criminal offense was Yitzhak Rabin. Yet, finally, only his wife was accused of illegally possessing foreign currency in the Dollar Account affair of 1977 (Meltzer, 2019). Ariel Sharon was investigated during his tenure, but with regard to acts committed before he took office. While Ehud Barak was also investigated under advisement, it was only after he had concluded his term as prime minister. Netanyahu was in

Public and Legal Responsibility of Senior Elected Representatives 153

fact investigated during his first term as prime minister (1996–1999) in the Bar-On–Hevron affair, in which no indictment was filed, and was investigated again when he was no longer in office in what became known as the "Amedi affair" and the "Illegal Gifts affair"; he was not brought to trial in those cases (Navot, 2012). Olmert finally stood for trial on several allegations and on May 2014, he was found guilty and sentenced to serve time in prison.

4 For examples of Prime Minister Benjamin Netanyahu's attacks, and the public atmosphere surrounding his trial, see inter alia: Aschkenasy (2020); Azoulay and Karni (2020); Bandel (2020); *Ha'aretz* (2021).

5 HCJ 2592/20 *Movement for Quality Government in Israel v. Attorney General* (unpublished; decided May 6, 2020) (hereafter: *HCJ Netanyahu, 2020*).

6 For a review of various positions in this debate, see for example: Roznai (2021); Gavison, Kremnitzer, and Dotan (2000).

7 Elected officials are protected by material and procedural immunity that is intended to allow them to perform their duties without fear (Tuttnauer, 2011).

8 Opinion of Justice M. Cheshin in HCJ 1993/03 *Movement for Quality Government in Israel v. The Prime Minister*, IsrSC 57(6) 817, 917–918 (2003).

9 See HCJ 6163/92 *Eisenberg v. Minister of Construction and Housing*, IsrSC 47(2) 229 (1993) (hereafter: HCJ *Ginossar*, 1993). For a broader discussion of the Court's attitude toward appointments of senior civil servants accused of criminal offenses, see Bendor and Tamir (2014).

10 In the Nafsu affair, the Chief Military Prosecutor determined that in the course of Nafsu's interrogation by the GSS on suspicion of espionage and weapons smuggling, illegal methods of interrogation were used against him. This was denied by the investigators, among them Ginossar. In the Bus 300 affair, Ginossar was appointed a member of the Zorea Commission, which investigated the circumstances surrounding the death of two arrested terrorists who were handed over to the GSS; in reality, he served as a "Trojan horse" on behalf of the head of the GSS to prevent the truth from being exposed. Before criminal proceedings were launched in the case, the President of Israel granted pardons to all parties involved, including Ginossar.

11 Accordingly, the Court insisted on a substantial as opposed to a mechanical test; in other words, the possibility should not be ruled out that the appointment of a candidate to a public position will be deemed unreasonable, even in the absence of an indictment or a criminal investigation, and even when it involves serious actions that do not reach the level of criminal offenses.

12 HCJ 3094/93 *Movement for Quality Government in Israel v. Government of Israel*, IsrSC 47(5) 404 (1993) (hereafter: HCJ *Deri*, 1993).

13 HCJ 4267/93 *Amitai – Citizens for Sound Administration and Moral Integrity v. Yitzhak Rabin, Prime Minister of Israel*, IsrSC 47(5) 441 (1993) (hereafter: HCJ *Pinhasi*, 1993).

14 *OMETZ – Citizens for Proper Administration and Social Justice in Israel v. Yitzhak Rochberger, Mayor of Ramat Hasharon*, IsrSC 66(3) 135, 236–67 (2013) (hereafter: HCJ *Mayors*, 2013).

15 Local Authorities Law (Suspension of Local Authority Head Due to Indictment) (amendments), 5774-2013.

16 For a review of these rulings from a critical perspective, see Dotan (2018); Friedmann (2016).

154 *Mordechai Kremnitzer and Dana Blander*

17 In the amended version of the Basic Law: The Government from 1992 (Direct Elections), three sections were incorporated that address it: 16(b), 25, and 26. In the present Basic Law: The Government from 2001, there are six different sections that relate to this possibility: 6(c), 17, 18, 23, 27, and 30(c).

18 Petitions submitted to the HCJ aiming to bar Netanyahu in advance from forming the government were rejected by the Court as premature and theoretical. See, for example: HCJ 2848/19, *Adv. Shachar Ben Meir v. Benjamin Netanyahu, Member of the 21st Knesset* (April 23, 2019); HCJ 7928/19 *Adv. Shafik Rafoul v. Benjamin Netanyahu, Prime Minister* (December 12, 2019); HCJ 8145/19 *Dr. Orna Beri v. Attorney General* (January 2, 2020).

19 Specifically, the Court determined that intervention in the discretion of the Knesset shall be permitted, as a rule, only in cases of harm to human rights or principles of democratic government. See para. 16 of Justice Barak-Erez's opinion, para. 8 of Justice Baron's opinion, and para. 16 of Justice Amit's opinion (HCJ *Netanyahu*, supplementary decision, 2020).

20 For a different view see Weill (2020). She holds that the legislature wished to distinguish between the case of a minister accused of criminal offenses and the prime minister, whose ending his tenure is akin to dissolving the government. In contrast, Benoliel (2020) holds that the doctrine of defensive democracy can be applied in the case of a prime minister accused of serious crimes in order to defend democracy from being eroded by corruption.

21 Similarly, in other cases brought before the Court, it refrained from intervening when the Knesset or alternative oversight mechanisms could act. See: HCJ 5261/04 *Adv. Yossi Fuchs v. Prime Minister of Israel, Ariel Sharon*, IsrSC 59(2) 446 (2004)); HCJ 9223/10 *Movement for Quality Government in Israel v. Prime Minister of Israel* (unpublished; decided November 19, 2012); HCJ 3095/15 *Movement for Quality Government in Israel v. Prime Minister of Israel* (unpublished; decided August 13, 2015).

22 The system of government in France is semi-presidential. The President is directly elected by the public. According to Section 68 of the French Constitution, the President, for as long as he is in office, is not called to account for acts committed during or prior to his tenure, and is immune from investigation and criminal as well as civil prosecution, except in cases of treason or war crimes, genocide, or crimes against humanity. For the legal provisions in France and other states see: European Commission (2013); Ben-David (2009); Unger (2018); Blander (2020).

23 Italy's Prime Minister Silvio Berlusconi, who stood trial on various charges while serving in office, is an exceptional case (Blander, 2020). According to Section 96 of the Italian Constitution, the prime minister and other ministers are subject to "normal justice," and bear criminal responsibility for offenses committed while in office. In 2004 and 2009, during the term of Silvio Berlusconi, attempts were made to grant immunity to the prime minister and other high-ranking officials (the president, presidents of both houses of parliament, and the president of the Constitutional Court) during their term in office, for acts committed before or during their tenure, including suspension of pending criminal proceedings. These efforts failed after the Constitutional Court declared the law to be unconstitutional on the grounds that it harmed the principle of equality before the law. Ultimately, a law was passed in 2011 allowing the prime minister and members of government to postpone proceedings against them, since this would disrupt the performance of their duties (Quigley, 2011).

Public and Legal Responsibility of Senior Elected Representatives 155

24 In a parliamentary democracy, members of the executive branch are usually also members of parliament, and therefore parliamentary immunity is relevant in their case.

25 HCJ 6231/08 *Yoav Yitzhak v. Prime Minister Ehud Olmert* (unpublished; decided August 4, 2008).

26 Quotation from the arguments of the petitioners, as cited in the opinion of Justice Amit, section 12 (HCJ *Netanyahu*, supplementary decision, 2020). These remarks were made by Netanyahu in the context of negotiations with Syria.

27 Opinion of Justice Daphne Barak-Erez (HCJ *Netanyahu*, supplementary decision, 2020).

28 Compare with the opinion of Justice Melcer, who holds that this should not be required of a candidate, since it would be tantamount to an admission of guilt and a person does not incriminate himself (HCJ *Netanyahu*, supplementary decision, 2020).

29 The public is consistent in its opposition to such solutions. When asked in 2008, in the context of the investigations of then-Prime Minister Ehud Olmert, if they held that a sitting prime minister should not be investigated for the duration of his term, 55% were opposed to such a notion and 40% supported it (*Peace Index*, October 2008). When asked a similar question in 2017 with regard to Prime Minister Benjamin Netanyahu, 70% were opposed to a law that would exempt him from criminal proceedings for as long as he served in office (the so-called French Law), and 26% were in favor (*Peace Index*, October 2017).

30 Note that section 16(b) of the existing Basic Law refers to the possibility that "the Prime Minister is unable to fulfill his duties" temporarily, and not solely for health reasons; this situation is considered permanent after 100 days have passed. But the arrangement is not explained in detail. The Court recognized in principle the possibility that the Attorney General could declare the prime minister to be incapacitated not only for health reasons and also at the stage of criminal investigations (HCJ 6231/08 *Yoav Yitzhak v. Prime Minister Ehud Olmert*, para. 4 of the opinion of Justice Asher Grunis (published in *Reshumot* [official government gazette], August 4, 2008). Regarding the "incapacitation doctrine" in the existing legal circumstances, see Medina and Saban (2020).

31 In keeping with the rationale for suspension of the prime minister, we would propose further that ministers be suspended from office when an indictment is filed against them until a final judgment has been handed down. (See also Navot et al., 2015: 21).

32 Concurrently, it is advisable that the government completes the process of formulating and adopting a code of ethics, which was initiated with a report by the Public Committee on Formulating a Code of Ethics for Members of Government, 5768-2008, headed by Supreme Court President (Emeritus) Meir Shamgar.

33 Justice Mazuz quotes the statement that "good laws originate in bad moral practices." In his view, legal provisions and court decisions relating to moral integrity and good governance came into being in response to undesirable occurrences; were it not for them, we would have no need for these "good laws" (HCJ *Netanyahu*, supplementary decision, 2020).

34 Levitsky and Ziblatt (2018: 11) see the political parties as a barrier to electing unsuitable candidates, enabling the former to serve as defenders of democracy.

References

Aschkenasy, Bini. 2020. "Mandelblit: 'The Challenge in Netanyahu's Trial: The Campaign of Lies and Distortions'." *The Marker*, September 3 [Hebrew].

Azoulay, Moran, and Yuval Karni. 2020. "Netanyahu Attacks: 'Mandelblit's Plot to Overthrow Government Has Been Exposed'." *Ynet*, June 6 [Hebrew].

Bandel, Netael. 2020. "'Baseless and Stacked Against Him': Full Text of Netanyahu's Speech at Opening of His Trial." *Ha'aretz*, May 24. [Hebrew].

Barzilai, Gad. 2014. "What Is Responsibility?: Law and the Public Space. Thoughts on *Public Responsibility in Israel*, edited by Raphael Cohen-Almagor, Ori Arbel-Ganz, and Asa Kasher." *Law and Government* 16: 341–348. [Hebrew].

Ben-David, Lior. 2009. *Investigation and Criminal Trial of a Sitting Prime Minister (or President)*. Knesset Research and Information Center [Hebrew].

Bendor, Ariel, and Michal Tamir. 2014. "The Reciprocal Engulfment of Law and Ethics in Israel: The Case of Appointments to Senior Positions." *Transnational Law and Contemporary Problems* 23: 229–260.

Benoliel, Daniel. 2020. "Removal from Office of a Prime Minister Under Indictment." *Law and Government* 21: 7–48 [Hebrew].

Blander, Dana. 2020. "Is Prime Minister Netanyahu Setting a Global Precedent?" Jerusalem Post, January 7. www.jpost.com/israel-news/is-prime-minister-netany ahu-setting-a-global-precedent-613375

De Vries, Catherine Eunice, and Hector Solaz. 2017. "The Electoral Consequences of Corruption." *Annual Review of Political Science* 20 (1): 391–408.

Dotan, Yoav. 2018. "Impeachment by Judicial Review: Israel's Odd System of Checks and Balances." *Theoretical Inquiries in Law* 19 (2): 705–744.

European Commission for Democracy through Law (Venice Commission). 2013. *Report on The Relationship between Political and Criminal Ministerial Responsibility.* 8–9 March.

Friedman, Nick. 2019. *The Impact of Populism on Courts: Institutional Legitimacy and the Popular Will*. Oxford: The Foundation for Law, Justice and Society.

Friedmann, Daniel. 2016. *The Purse and the Sword: The Trials of Israel's Legal Revolution*. Translated by Haim Watzman. New York: Oxford University Press.

Gavison, Ruth, Mordechai Kremnitzer, and Yoav Dotan, eds. 2000. *Judicial Activism: For and Against*. Jerusalem: Magnes Press. [Hebrew].

Ha'aretz. 2021. "Netanyahu attacked the public prosecution." *Ha'aretz*, April 5 [Hebrew].

Koren, Dani, and Boaz Shapira, eds. 1997. Coalitions. Tel Aviv: Zmora-Bitan. [Hebrew].

Kremnitzer, Mordechai, Amir Fuchs, and Assaf Shapira. 2019. "Proposed Immunity Bill—Contempt for the Rule of Law: Press Release." Israel Democracy Institute, May 6. https://en.idi.org.il/articles/26682

Kremnitzer, Mordechai, Yuval Shany, Guy Lurie, Amir Fuchs, and Nadiv Mordechay. 2020. "Addressing the Prime Minister's Request for Immunity: An Opinion." Israel Democracy Institute, January 26 [Hebrew] www.idi.org.il/articles/29643

Levitsky, Steven, and Daniel Ziblatt. 2018. *How Democracies Die*. New York: Penguin Random House.

Lurie, Guy, and Amir Fuchs. 2017. "Law Prohibiting the Investigation of a Prime Minister: An Opinion." Israel Democracy Institute, October 19 [Hebrew]. www.idi. org.il/ministerial-committee/12355

Public and Legal Responsibility of Senior Elected Representatives 157

Medina, Barak, and Ilan Saban. 2020. "Conflict of Interest on the Part of a Prime Minister, Defensive Democracy, and the Power to Declare Incapacitation." *ICON-S-IL Blog*, October 11 [Hebrew].

Meltzer Roberts, Sharon. 2019. "'Listen, There's a Problem Here': The Dollar Account Affair." Ministry of Justice, April 1 [Hebrew]. www.gov.il/he/Departme nts/publications/reports/roots_1977

Müller, Jan Werner. 2016. *What Is Populism?* Philadelphia: University of Pennsylvania Press.

Navot, Doron. 2012. *Political Corruption in Israel.* Jerusalem: Israel Democracy Institute.

Navot, Doron, Yuval Feldman, Mordechai Kremnitzer, Lina Saba, Tehilla Schwartz Altshuler, and Amir Fuchs, eds. 2015. "Program to Fight Government Corruption in Israel." Israel Democracy Institute. [Hebrew]. Quigley, Brendan. 2011. "Immunity, Italian Style: Silvio Berlusconi versus the Italian Legal System." *Hastings International and Comparative Law Review* 34 (2): 435–464.

Rousseau, Jean-Jacques. [1762] 2018. *Rousseau: The Social Contract and Other Early Political Writings.* In *Cambridge Texts in the History of Political Thought*, edited and translated by Victor Gourevitch. 2nd ed. Cambridge: Cambridge University Press.

Roznai, Yaniv. 2021. *Constitutional Oversight.* Jerusalem: Israel Democracy Institute. [Hebrew].

Sadurski, Wojciech. 2019. *Poland's Constitutional Breakdown.* Oxford: Oxford University Press.

Tuttnauer, Or. 2011. "The Two Faces of Parliamentary Immunity." *Parliament* 70. [Hebrew].

Unger, Yaron. 2018. "The Status of a Prime Minister Under Criminal Proceedings." Knesset Legal Department [Hebrew].

U.S. Department of Justice. 2000. *A Sitting President's Amenability to Indictment and Criminal Prosecution.* www.justice.gov/olc/opinion/sitting-President%E2%80%99s-amenability-indictment-and-criminal-prosecution

Warf, Barney. 2019. *Global Corruption from a Geographic Perspective.* New York: Springer.

Weill, Rivka. 2020. "Is Judicial Impeachment of an Israeli Prime Minister Constitutional?" *Law and Government* 21: 49–67. [Hebrew].

Yair, Omer, Raanan Sulitzeanu-Kenan, and Yoav Dotan. 2020. "Can Institutions Make Voters Care about Corruption?" *The Journal of Politics* 82 (4): 1430–1442.

Zamir, Yitzhak. 2012. "Introduction." In *Public Responsibility in Israel*, edited by Raphael Cohen-Almagor, Ori Arbel-Ganz, and Asa Kasher, 7–18. Jerusalem: Hakibbutz Hameuchad and the Jerusalem Center for Ethics. [Hebrew].

Israeli Supreme Court Cases Cited

HCJ 1993/03 *Movement for Quality Government in Israel v. Prime Minister*, IsrSC 57(6) 817 (2003) [Hebrew].

HCJ 2592/20 *Movement for Quality Government in Israel v. Attorney General* (unpublished; decided May 6, 2020) [Hebrew].

HCJ 2592/20 *Movement for Quality Government in Israel v. Attorney General* (unpublished; supplementary ruling on May 27, 2020) [Hebrew].

158   *Mordechai Kremnitzer and Dana Blander*

HCJ 2848/19 *Adv. Shachar Ben Meir v. Binyamin Netanyahu, Member of 21st Knesset* (unpublished; decided April 23, 2019) [Hebrew].

HCJ 3094/93 *Movement for Quality Government in Israel v. Government of Israel*, IsrSC 47(5) 404 (1993) [Hebrew].

HCJ 3095/15 *Movement for Quality Government in Israel v. Prime Minister of Israel* (unpublished; decided August 13, 2015) [Hebrew].

HCJ 4267/93 *Amitai – Citizens for Sound Administration and Moral Integrity v. Yitzhak Rabin, Prime Minister of Israel*, IsrSC 47(5) 441 (1993) [Hebrew].

HCJ 4921/13 *OMETZ – Citizens for Proper Administration and Social Justice in Israel v. Mayor of Ramat Hasharon Yitzhak Rochberger*, IsrSC 66(3) 135 (2013) [Hebrew].

HCJ 5261/04 *Adv. Yossi Fuchs v. Ariel Sharon, Prime Minister of Israel*, IsrSC 59(2) 446 (2004) [Hebrew].

HCJ 6163/92 *Eisenberg v. Minister of Construction and Housing*, IsrSC 47(2) 229 (1993) [Hebrew].

HCJ 6231/08 *Yoav Yitzhak v. Prime Minister of Israel Ehud Olmert* (unpublished; decided August 4, 2008). [Hebrew].

HCJ 7928/19 *Adv. Shafik Rafoul v. Binyamin Netanyahu, Prime Minister of Israel* (unpublished; decided December 12, 2019) [Hebrew].

HCJ 8145/19 *Dr. Orna Beri v. Attorney General* (unpublished; decided January 2, 2020) [Hebrew].

HCJ 9223/10 *Movement for Quality Government in Israel v. Prime Minister of Israel* (unpublished; decided November 19, 2012) [Hebrew].

Indictment

State of Israel v. Benjamin Netanyahu et al., filed in Jerusalem District Court, January 28, 2020. [Hebrew].

Response

Response from Attorney General, HCJ 2592/20 *Movement for Quality Government in Israel v. Attorney General* (unpublished; summation of arguments May 6, 2020) [Hebrew].

Reports

Report of Public Committee to Formulate Code of Ethics for Members of Government, 5768-2008. [Hebrew].

Legislation

Government Law, 5761-2001 [Hebrew].

Local Authorities Law (Suspension of Local Authority Head due to Filing of Indictment) (amendments), 5774-2013 [Hebrew].

Basic Law: The Government (1968) [Hebrew].

Basic Law: The Government (1992) [Hebrew].

Basic Law: The Government (2001) [Hebrew].

Constitutions

Constitution of 4 October 1958, France
Constitution of the Italian Republic

Public Opinion Surveys (Located in the DataIsrael Data Base of the Israel Democracy Institute)

Peace Index, May 2008 [Hebrew].
Peace Index, October 2017 [Hebrew].

Part 2
Voters, Parties, and the Media

8 Persistent Optimism under Political Uncertainty

The Evolution of Citizens' Election Projections During a Protracted Political Crisis[1]

Keren Tenenboim-Weinblatt, Christian Baden, Tali Aharoni, and Maximilian Overbeck

Uncertainty is inherent to democratic elections. Even when a candidate or a party is the clear favorite to win, the final outcome depends on citizens' free choice – both whether to vote and to whom – and on the various developments in the run-up to the elections, possibly until the very last minute (see Fuchs, 2017). This uncertainty is even larger in a multiparty system, such as Israel, where the outcome is not binary (as in the United States, for instance) and the eventual composition of the government depends on coalition negotiations. However, the 2019–2021 elections in Israel have taken this uncertainty to a new level. Repeated failures to form a government led to three rounds of elections within less than one year (between April 2019 and March 2020), followed by the establishment of a short-lived government and another, fourth election (in March 2021). In that, the 2019–2021 Israeli elections link to global trends of political turmoil that challenge liberal democracies, and fit observations that we live in an age of radical uncertainty about the future (e.g., Harari, 2018; Mounk, 2018).

One of the central human mechanisms for coping with uncertainty – both individually and collectively – is the construction of future scenarios (Gilbert & Wilson, 2007; Kay & King, 2020; Neiger, 2007). Accordingly, before elections, the public sphere is filled with projections about the outcomes and implications of the upcoming elections, made by pollsters, commentators, politicians, and other actors (see Tenenboim-Weinblatt, 2018; Weimann, 1990). The citizens, in turn, formulate their own expectations vis-à-vis the various projections they are exposed to, reflecting their political identities and desires (Babad, 1997; Tenenboim-Weinblatt, Baden, Aharoni, & Overbeck, 2020). The case study of the successive Israeli elections offers a unique opportunity to examine how such expectations evolve over time, under increasing political uncertainty: How do the predicted outcomes change, if at all, and on what grounds? Do people become less certain about their predictions? Do they lose or maintain hope that the desired outcomes will be achieved, and how does it affect their motivation to vote?

DOI: 10.4324/9781003267911-11

164   *Keren Tenenboim-Weinblatt et al.*

This chapter thus sets out to answer the following broad question: How did Israeli citizens' election projections – as set against the backdrop of a deepening political crisis – evolve over the course of the successive elections, and with what consequences? For this investigation, we introduce a conceptual framework that understands projections as complex dynamic discursive constructs with social implications. Focusing on the 2019–2020 elections, we examine the evolving projections of Israeli citizens, using data from a panel survey and focus groups. We show that despite the growing conditions of uncertainty, Israeli citizens' overall optimism about the elections' outcomes and implications did not decrease over the three successive elections, and argue that this persistent optimism may explain the higher voter turnout in each round. In the epilogue we consider additional insights from the 2021 election, which saw a reversal in voters' growing optimism and turnout, but which eventually redeemed the opposition's hopes for political change.

8.1 Political Projections: A Conceptual Framework

Political projections are scenarios about the expected outcomes and implications of political events, such as elections, referenda, crises, and wars. Much previous work has focused on the challenges and cognitive biases associated with the attempt to accurately predict the future (e.g., Silver, 2012; Tetlock & Gardner, 2015; Kahneman, 2011). However, getting it right is not the only motivation for projections. For instance, future scenarios encapsulated in campaign slogans such as "Bibi or Tibi" (a Likud slogan juxtaposing Netanyahu and an Arab-Israeli politician)[2] or "Kahol-Lavan or Erdoğan" (a Blue and White slogan likening Netanyahu to the Turkish president)[3] portray binary future outcomes that play to the fears of the respective parties' constituencies for mobilization purposes. Moreover, projections can affect political reality regardless of whether they are accurate: they can propel political action aimed at bringing about desirable futures or avoid undesirable scenarios, and sometimes trigger self-fulfilling and self-defeating dynamics (Merton, 1948; Tenenboim-Weinblatt, 2018).

Based on theoretical and empirical work of the PROFECI project (http://profeci.net/), we suggest a conceptual framework of projections (see Figure 8.1) that centers upon the expected outcome (Predicted State), qualified by its estimated likelihood (Probability), as well as its desirability (Evaluation). Furthermore, expectations may be warranted by specific considerations (Anchors) and imply suitable responses (Implications).

The **predicted state** refers to the expected outcomes of future events – for example, who will win the elections, or how will the elections affect the economic situation in the years to come. From a discursive perspective, the predicted state can be viewed as an assertive speech act that expresses a belief in a future state of the world. As such, it differs from other future-oriented speech acts (e.g., promises, calls for action), which express a desire for specific future states (Searle, 1979; see also Kampf, 2013; Stalpouskaya,

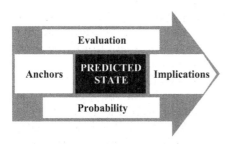

Figure 8.1 Projections.

2020). Predicted states may refer to specific outcomes within a prestructured set of possibilities (e.g., the winning candidates, allocation of seats in parliament), or lay forth open-ended scenarios (e.g., about the security situation in Israel); they may pertain to fixed points in time (e.g., election day), or to an indefinite future (Neiger & Tenenboim-Weinblatt, 2016). In Israel, the composition of the government, as well as the identity of the prime minister, are determined by coalition negotiations rather than the popular vote alone, elevating the relevance of narrative projections beyond the immediate election results.

Next, projections can incorporate an assessment about the **probability** of the predicted state. Besides estimates of low to high chances, such assessments may also eschew specified probabilities and concentrate on whether a proposed outcome is possible and relevant. Specified probabilities can be expressed numerically (e.g., one-in-ten, 95% chance), graphically (see Pentzold & Fechner, 2020), or verbally (e.g., unlikely, certain), whereas possibilities are usually expressed in verbal, narrative forms (e.g., there is a chance, not impossible). Specific probability estimates have been considered key to professional forecasting and have largely dominated the literature on political predictions (Silver, 2012; Tetlock, 2005; Tetlock & Gardner, 2015). Nevertheless, numerical probabilities appear relatively alien to laypeople's thinking about the future (Kahneman, 2011; Westwood, Messing, & Lelkes, 2020) – especially under radical uncertainty (Kay & King, 2020), when projections might lend themselves better to possibilistic rather than probabilistic reasoning.

Projections frequently include **evaluations** of the predicted state. People can evaluate future scenarios as positive (desirable) or negative (undesirable) for themselves, their communities (their family, political camp, country, the human race), or for others (e.g., opposing parties, specific political actors). In addition, evaluations can foreground normative considerations (i.e., whether the predicted state satisfies specific values), interest-based assessments (e.g., whether it serves an actor's aspirations), or affective evaluations (i.e., how a person expects to feel about the predicted future; "affective forecasting"; see Wilson & Gilbert, 2003; Tenenboim-Weinblatt et al., 2022).

166 *Keren Tenenboim-Weinblatt et al.*

While probability and evaluation are attributes of predicted states, **anchors** capture any reasoning used to justify the projection. People infer likely future events or developments from presently available knowledge, following two main strategies: First, they can rely on projections made by other people, such as political commentators, pollsters, politicians, or trusted friends. Second, they can make their own inferences, extrapolating future developments from present or past states of the world (e.g., predicting the identity of the next prime minister based on a contender's character and believed intentions, observable behavior, track record, poll performance, or historical analogies).

Finally, projections can also raise behavioral **implications**. If a predicted state is viewed as undesirable, it may trigger attempts to avert it or dodge its impact (e.g., adjust voting intentions, protest, migrate to another country). Conversely, a desirable predicted state may motivate people to work toward achieving it (e.g., turn out to vote, donate to a campaign, help mobilizing voters). In political and communication science, scholars have examined the relationship between electoral expectations and behavior in contexts such as the bandwagon and underdog effects, focusing mostly on the influence of public opinion polls (e.g., Mutz, 1998; Rothschild & Malhotra, 2014; Stolwijk, Schuck, & de Vreese, 2017). The ways in which political projections – in their complex, multifaceted form – play into political participation are still to be delineated.

The meaning and social significance of projections arise from the interplay between predicted states, their probability and desirability assessments, as well as linked anchors and planned responses. While projections can be constructed bottom-up, reviewing possible anchors to derive likely future states and then appraising these, other paths are also possible. For instance, behavioral implications can be the starting point for constructing and evaluating predicted states, as in politicians' dire or rosy scenarios strategically aimed at mobilizing voters. In voters' own projections, the evaluation component sometimes domineers, as manifested in wishful thinking, where expectations are being shaped by political preferences (Babad, 1997; Krizan, Miller, & Johar, 2010), or optimism bias, that is, people's tendency to "overestimate the likelihood of positive events, and underestimate the likelihood of negative events" (Sharot, 2011, p. 941; see also Kahneman, 2011). Estimations of desirability and likelihood may also be on more equal footing, as in the case of hope, constituting a combination of expectations and wishes (Leshem & Halperin, 2020). Anchors can attenuate the impact of voters' evaluations on their expectations, as shown in studies that document the combination of preferences and available information (e.g., poll results or knowledge about previous elections) in peoples' expectations about parties' electoral success (Blais & Bodet, 2006; Meffert & Gschwend, 2011).

In this chapter, we examine the development of projections related to the 2019–2020 Israeli elections and the interplay of their constitutive elements, with a focus on the optimistic trends that emerge from this analysis.

8.2 Methods

The investigation draws upon two data sets – a panel survey and a series of focus groups – that have been collected as part of the ERC-funded project PROFECI at the Hebrew University of Jerusalem.

For the panel survey, we recruited 1,191 Israeli voters, using a stratified sampling procedure to represent the composition of the electorate. The survey, which was administered online, underrepresents ultra-Orthodox voters (who do not normally participate in online surveys), and to a lesser extent also Arab citizens of Israel and older voters (see the Methodological Appendix). There were ten survey waves altogether – seven full waves prior to the elections, aimed to capture respondents' expectations, as well as three brief postelection waves (see Figure 8.2). In each of the seven pre-electoral waves, participants were asked to predict the identity of the next prime minister and the largest party, as well as the composition of the future government coalition. Furthermore, the survey recorded respondents' estimated probability and affective evaluation of the predicted outcomes, as well as a range of control variables. For the present study, we focus on those 442 participants that participated in all seven full survey waves.

The focus groups comprised five groups of 10–12 Israeli voters (four groups of Jewish voters and one of Arab voters). Each group was convened five times over the duration of the first two election rounds. In each meeting, participants were asked to predict what would happen in the forthcoming elections and coalition talks, and what might be the future implications of these events. Each meeting also included a discussion of current election-related media discourse. All meetings were transcribed and qualitatively analyzed, focusing on participants' strategies for constructing and negotiating projections. For additional methodological details, see the Appendix.

In the following sections, we first present key findings in relation to each aspect of projections separately. Next, we consider the interplay of elements in connection with people's political identities, which reveals an overall pattern of persistent optimism among Israeli voters.

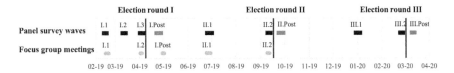

Figure 8.2 Timeline of data collection.

Note: I–III: election rounds; 1–3: survey waves/focus group meetings relevant to each round.

8.3 Evolution of the Elements of Political Projections Across the 2019–2020 Elections

8.3.1 Predicted State

Over the seven pre-electoral waves (see Figure 8.2 for the index), survey participants expressed their predictions regarding the identity of the future prime minister (Figure 8.3), the party expected to win the largest number of seats in parliament (Figure 8.4), and the parties expected to join the next government coalition (Figure 8.5).

Throughout the three election rounds, a majority of respondents predicted the incumbent Netanyahu to remain prime minister. However, this majority decreased from 79% in February 2019, following the announcement of election round I, to 57% prior to round III, one year later. Inversely, the percentage of respondents who expected Gantz to become prime minister grew from 18% to 35%.[4] The beginning of the third election campaign (III.1) was the highest point for Gantz (39%) – and correspondingly, the lowest point for Netanyahu (52%).

Likewise, a majority of respondents expected Netanyahu's Likud to win the largest number of seats in the Knesset (Israeli parliament) throughout the first two election rounds. However, their percentage dropped sharply from 80% (I.1) to 51%–54% (I.2–I.3) following the establishment of the challenger list Blue and White. The two parties eventually tied in election round I, while in round II, Blue and White emerged as largest party. Subsequently, a majority of respondents (56%) initially expected Blue and White to hold on to its lead in the third round (III.1). Toward the end of the campaign, which

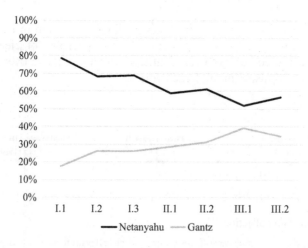

Figure 8.3 Expected prime minister (percentage of respondents).

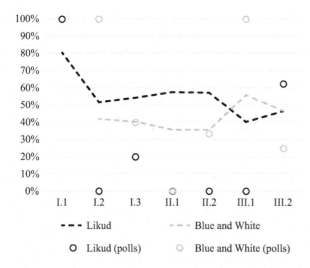

Figure 8.4 Expected largest party (percentage of respondents and opinion polls).

Note: Circles represent the share of polls in the three main TV channels (Kan 11, Channel 12, and Channel 13) that predicted either party to win most seats during the survey wave and the week before; the remaining polls predicted a tie.

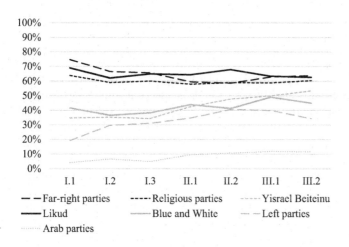

Figure 8.5 Expected parties in the coalition (percentage of respondents).

resulted in a Likud win, both parties almost tied in people's expectations. All trend reversals in voters' expectations cohered with the projections published in election polls – in direction if not in magnitude.

Concerning the coalition composition, a persistent majority of respondents expected the Likud, the parties to its right, and the ultra-Orthodox parties to

170 *Keren Tenenboim-Weinblatt et al.*

comprise the future government.[5] All other parties and lists were projected to join the coalition by a lesser, albeit overall rising share of respondents. Generally, participants tended to expect increasingly inclusive coalitions.

The same patterns were also reflected in the focus group discussions. Before Blue and White was established, the dominant projection was that Netanyahu would be the next prime minister, Likud would be the largest party, and the government would be similar to the outgoing, right-wing religious government. Few participants cautiously projected possible changes, while most agreed that, in the words of one participant, "What has been is what will be" (Or, M, 49, I.1).[6] However, scenarios grew in diversity and complexity during the subsequent meetings. While many still expected Netanyahu to remain prime minister, participants also developed projections regarding other possible outcomes (e.g., rotation, another prime minister). The following interaction, recorded in June 2019, anticipated what would materialize 11 months later:

GIL (M, 35, II.1): Blue and White will split. There are guys there who will say 'we are not going to be in the opposition again. And we are not having another election'

HANI (F, 49): They won't have a problem being martyrs and sacrifice themselves for the Israeli nation.

GIL: And people will understand this. Ten of them will leave and there will be a big government.

8.3.2 Probability

Survey respondents reported an overall high level of certainty about their projections (on a scale of "very low chance" – 0 to "very high chance" – 100), which decreased only slightly over the three election rounds (see Figure 8.6). On average, participants predicted the largest party with higher probability (86%–80%) than the future prime minister (83%–77%), and the coalition composition with lower probability (77%–71%). Considering the complexity of coalition talks, however, this level of certainty still appears unrealistic.

Yet, the responses also suggest some rational adjustment of probabilities, concerning both the higher certainty for the less contingent predictions of the largest party and prime minister, and the diminishing confidence following the repeated failure to form a government. The same awareness of increased uncertainty is reflected in the declining share of people that expressed absolute certainty (100%) in their projections (37%–21%, 32%–19%, and 17%–11% regarding the largest party, prime minister, and coalition, respectively).

The focus groups showed some similar trends, with several participants expressing a small decline in certainty through decreasing probabilities. For instance, Tzeela (F, 26) initially estimated "80%" chance for a Netanyahu government (I.1), but later gave her unity government prediction only "70%" chance (II.1). More commonly, however, people shifted from high certainty to confusion. For example, before the first election, Natan (M, 43) claimed to be

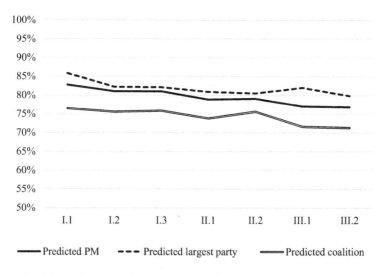

Figure 8.6 Mean chance attributed to expected outcome.

"100% (sure) that Bibi is going to be elected" (I.1), but conceded that "everything is possible" afterwards (II.1). The open structure of the focus groups generally opened more opportunities for possibilistic rather than probabilistic discourse, as will be demonstrated below.

8.3.3 Evaluation

Asked to assess how they would feel if their predictions were to materialize, on average, voters expected to be happy – the political crisis and radical uncertainty notwithstanding. Expected affect was least positive in wave I.1 (largest party: M=56.7; prime minister: 56.2; coalition: 56.4), and well above 60 in all later waves (see Figure 8.7). Across all waves and all projections, 18% to 28% of respondents marked their expected happiness at the positive endpoint (100). This high degree of optimism contrasts against participants' slightly negative affect experienced following the actual election results, which averaged below the neutral starting point for all three postelection waves (round I: M= 49.6; round II: 47.8; round III: 43.5). Yet, respondents expected to feel happy again when the second and third elections were called, with a small over-time increase in expected happiness.

Beyond expected election outcomes, survey respondents were also asked to evaluate their implications for the overall state of the country in three years (see Figure 8.8). In all waves, respondents expressed, on average, a slightly positive outlook (3.32–3.62 on a five-point scale), with a plurality of respondents (40%–45%) rating Israel's future state as "good". Over-time changes were small (mostly, a slight, temporary rise toward Election Day). Envisaging

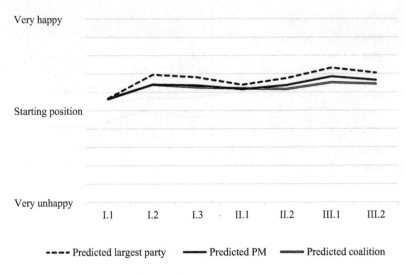

Figure 8.7 Mean expected affect toward projected outcome.

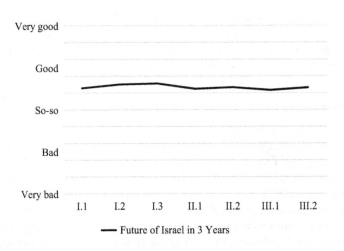

Figure 8.8 Mean expected future of Israel in three years.

neither doom nor a bright future, the political crisis barely affected Israelis' general confidence that things will be okay – a finding echoed also in the focus groups, as expressed for instance by Hani (II.1): "We will survive".

8.3.4 Anchors

To anchor their projections, voters relied on a variety of sources, as well as on their own experiences, logics, and worldviews. The survey shows respondents' stable reliance on central news outlets for political information – mostly, the popular website *Ynet* and the main TV channels (Channel 12, followed by Channel 13 and Kan 11), and to a lesser extent, the leading newspapers (*Israel Hayom*, *Yedioth-Ahronot*), other news sites (*Walla!*, *Mako*) and radio stations (Galei-Tzahal, Kan). Mainstream Arabic-language television channels and news sites likewise dominated among Arabic-speakers. A majority (54%–57%) reported that they follow polls to a large or very large extent. Over time, we recorded a slight increase in respondents' tendency to follow key political and media actors on social media (e.g., the share of respondents following political analyst Amit Segal rose from 7% to 10%).

Focus group participants' media exposure patterns resembled those identified in the survey. Interestingly, however, other than a few instances – for example, Gil (I.Post) humorously quoting Amit Segal's saying that "in Israel you go to elections every four years and eventually Bibi wins, it's sort of a ritual" – people rarely mentioned specific media outlets, actors, or texts in relation to their projections, even when asked directly about their sources. Polls were more commonly mentioned, and some participants relied heavily on these ("You can't ignore the polls!" [Benny, M, 60, I.1]), while others dismissed them as unreliable. In most cases, participants presented their projections as informed by their own observations, omitting any sources that might have informed these conclusions.

8.3.5 Behavioral Implications

Political participation, and particularly voting turnout, is one of the key potential behavioral implications of election-related projections. In the three rounds of elections, turnout increased from 68.5% in round I, to 69.8% and 71.5% in rounds II and III, respectively, with a more dramatic increase in Arab towns (from 49.2%, through 59.2%, to 64.7%). Our survey findings match these trends: The share of participants determined to vote rose from 76.4% in wave I.3 to 79.2% in wave III.2, especially among native Arabic-speakers (from 46% to 66.7%).

In the focus groups, many participants predicted that turnout would decrease for the second and third elections, owing to people's growing frustration. Nevertheless, an overwhelming majority of participants continued to express strong commitment to voting themselves. When one participant admitted being unsure whether to vote, others united to persuade him to turn out – one even offered him his gift card (received for his participation in the study) for voting (II.1). In the Arab group meetings, participants were divided on whether to vote from the outset, with passionate opinions both for and against. Following the failure to form a government in the first election and the (re)unification of the Joint List, calls for voting gained in traction, accompanied by scenarios regarding the Arab parties' possible role in enabling a center-left coalition: "I want to go back to ninety-three [when the Arab

174 *Keren Tenenboim-Weinblatt et al.*

parties supported Rabin's coalition] [...] You are betraying your homeland when you are not voting" (Sami, M, 34, II.2).

Participants furthermore discussed who to vote for so as to best make their votes count. They engaged in heated debates about the merits of ideological and value-based voting, as opposed to strategic voting informed by current polls and election projections. The dilemma was vividly presented by Denis (M, 34, I.1):

> I am very confused, every election, every time once again. If I see a poll going here or there [...] I say 'walla', maybe I will vote this or that, because whoever I wanted to vote for has no chance [...[but maybe [...] the values that are the reason I vote should determine [...], whether I think it will be successful or not.

Toward the second election, participants increasingly focused on the competition between the two largest parties, invoking pragmatic motives. Hoping to secure the mandate for government formation for the party leading their preferred camp, fewer participants advocated in favor of supporting third parties, especially those who might not pass the electoral threshold.

8.4 The Interplay of Projection Elements: Optimistic Expectations

In the following, we examine how the different projection elements work together to give shape to an overall pattern of optimism.

8.4.1 Expectations and Evaluations: Wishful Thinking

Throughout our analysis, several patterns emerge that suggest a strong connection between predicted and preferred outcomes. This is evident in the shares of survey respondents who expected to feel good (above 55 on the 0–100 slider), bad (below 45) or neutral (45–55) about their respective predicted election outcomes (see Figures 8.9 and 8.10).

First, in line with the overall prevalence of positive evaluations (see Figure 8.7), both Figures 8.9 and 8.10 show a dominance of respondents who expect to feel good about their predicted outcomes.

Second, in both figures, we see a third major group of respondents who predicted a Netanyahu/Likud victory and expected to be unhappy about this outcome. All other combinations (unhappy about a predicted Gantz/Blue and White victory; neutral regarding either outcome) are marginal. While both supporters and opponents predicted an electoral victory for Netanyahu and the Likud, those who predicted Gantz to become prime minister and Blue and White the largest party on the whole preferred this outcome (for further elaboration on this asymmetry, see Tenenboim-Weinblatt et al., 2022). The

Persistent Optimism under Political Uncertainty 175

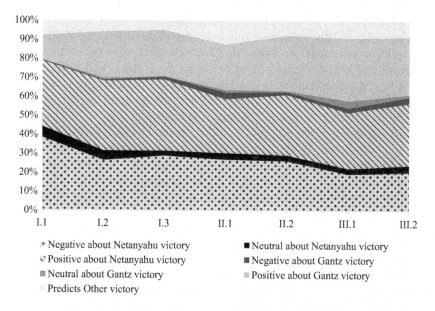

Figure 8.9 Expected affect by projected next prime minister (percentage of respondents).

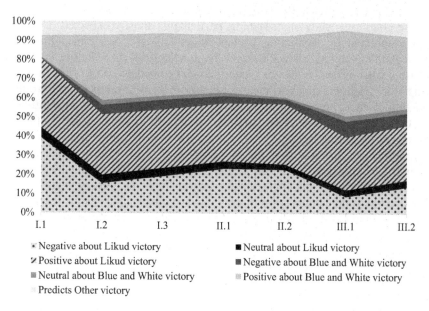

Figure 8.10 Expected affect by projected largest party (percentage of respondents).

176　*Keren Tenenboim-Weinblatt et al.*

same pattern was also found in the focus groups, with Netanyahu as the focal point of almost all evaluations. Even participants who saw Gantz as future prime minister mostly welcomed this outcome as an alternative to another Netanyahu government. As Yoel (M, 62, I.1), a right-wing anti-Netanyahu participant explained: "I prefer that he [Gantz] will run a bad government than to have a corrupted leader [...] That's the worst thing that can happen". The three groups can thus be characterized as *Pro-Netanyahu Optimists*, *Anti-Netanyahu Optimists*, and *Anti-Netanyahu Pessimists*.

Third, we find that the group of Pro-Netanyahu Optimists remained relatively stable over time (about one third of the respondents in all waves). By comparison, many participants in the Anti-Netanyahu camp turned from pessimists into optimists, changing their initial projection of an undesired Likud/Netanyahu victory to predict a desired victory of Blue and White/ Gantz. The first major transition occurred following the establishment of Blue and White prior to wave I.2, with another major shift following the second election (III.1), in which Blue and White emerged as the largest party. The observed optimistic trend thus reflects partly Netanyahu supporters' persistent belief in their victory, and partly the growing belief among their opponents that a change in government could be achieved.

The connection between wishes and expectations is also reflected in respondents' projected coalition composition. Specifically, projections strongly correlate with political leaning: Left-leaning participants were more likely to project that the center-left parties (including the Arab parties) would be part of the coalition, while right-leaning participants mostly expected a coalition dominated by right-wing parties. Most tellingly, over time, different participants expected Yisrael Beiteinu to join the coalition: Before the first election, when its leader Avigor Lieberman was considered part of the "right-wing bloc", right-leaning participants were more likely to predict that it would join the coalition; however, after Lieberman's refusal to rejoin a Netanyahu-led right-wing religious government and the subsequent failure of coalition talks, the same expectation became positively associated with leaning to the left.

In the focus groups, too, the scenario of a secular unity government including Netanyahu, Gantz, and Lieberman was proposed mainly by center-left participants toward the second election, and resisted by Netanyahu supporters. In many instances, participants freely admitted to wishful thinking. They answered questions about predicted states with a wish rather than a prediction, tied their predictions directly to their wishes ("I think the Likud will get stronger, I hope the Likud gets stronger" [Zohar, F, 38, II.1]), and even acknowledged the possible causal relation: "Maybe I believe it because I want to believe in it" (Peleg, F, 24, II.1).

8.4.2 Probabilities and Anchors: The Bases for Optimism

To understand the reasoning underlying contrasting optimistic projections, we examined how pro-Netanyahu and anti-Netanyahu focus group participants justified their optimistic predictions and presented the likelihood of desired outcomes.

One key difference between the two optimist groups concerns anti-Netanyahu participants' greater tendency to avoid probabilistic discourse. Especially toward round I, Pro-Netanyahu Optimists presented the scenario of another Netanyahu government as highly probable, using expressions such as "95%" (Zohar, I.1), "I am certain" (Vered, F, 36, I.1), "closed deal" (Dvir, M, 52, I.1), or "a very good chance" (Gil, I.2). Anti-Netanyahu Optimists resisted such high probability estimates, with one participant referring to them as "wrong thinking" (Tal, M, 44, I.1). Instead, they foregrounded possibilities: "either status-quo or a changeover [...] all scenarios are possible" (Bar, M, 44, I.2), "it's not certain that Bibi will easily win" (Yoel, I.1); "There is also chance that maybe there will be surprises" (Harel, M, 52, I.1).

One explanation for this caution is that Anti-Netanyahu Optimists foresaw no sweeping victory for the center-left camp, but relied on gradual processes that would eventually tip the scale (Or [I.1]: "Even a journey of a thousand miles begins in one step") or more indirect mechanisms. For instance, participants considered the possibility that some parties might not pass the electoral threshold, shifting the balance of power (Dalal [F, 36, I.2]: "there are some small right wing parties that are in risk of not passing the needed percentage. [...] It risks Netanyahu's potential government"). Likewise, they referred to Netanyahu's pending corruption cases, which might lead to his demise (Kobi [M, 23, I.1]: "even if he is elected, it is possible that [...] an indictment will be filed, and then he will have to retire").

Pro-Netanyahu Optimists vehemently dismissed such scenarios, suggesting instead backlash narratives. For instance, Aliza (F, 58, I.1) was confident that the corruption cases would strengthen Netanyahu:

> The Likud will rise big time, and it's going to rise only because everything that happened with Netanyahu [...] what the media did was to raise Bibi [...] Someone told me: "I will take my wife and I will take my children [...] to vote Likud, precisely because of everything they did to Bibi".

Furthermore, Pro-Netanyahu Optimists regularly referred to Netanyahu's unmatched capabilities and experience: "I don't see anyone equaling him [...] in his power, in his charisma, in his ability to run a country under so many threats" (Vered, I.1); "There is no one who communicates like him. Everyone looks small next to him" (Carmela, F, 55, I.1).

After Netanyahu's failure to form a government, Pro-Netanyahu Optimists no longer expressed absolute or extremely high certainty in his success, either. Continuing to predict a Likud victory, they nevertheless hedged their predictions and more frequently provided justifications based on complex political scenarios. Accounts ranged from detailed explanations of how a Netanyahu-led unity government would be established to descriptions of how

178   *Keren Tenenboim-Weinblatt et al.*

right-wing voters would finally come around to vote for the Likud or to pro-Netanyahu parties:

> I'm not sure [...] I don't believe so much in the polls, it doesn't seem to me that there will be another tie. In my opinion, whoever supports Lieberman will think twice (and) [...] vote for the Likud or one of the parties that will go with Bibi.
>
> (Zohar, II.1)

While distrust in the polls was more common among right-wing participants, also some left-wing optimists resisted their predictions. "Anybody in this room sees a possibility that Gantz will form a government in two weeks?", asked Benny, a right-winger, in wave II.2. "Why not?" queried Gloria (F, 51). "Because he doesn't have 61 (seats)!" replied Benny, anchoring his response in recent polls. "It's a possibility", insisted Yasmin (F, 47), a left-wing optimist, "it can still happen! [...] there are surprises coming in my opinion!"

Notably, for Anti-Netanyahu Optimists, the failure to form a government and the call of new elections were often the very basis for increased optimism, leading to further intensification of the discourse on open possibilities for change:

> I felt hope (when new elections were called). "Walla", there might be an opportunity here for a correction. My hope is that more seculars will vote, more Arabs will vote [...] and maybe there will be an opportunity to really make a change here.
>
> (Harel, II.1)

The mobilization of Arab voters played a key role in scenarios advanced by the Anti-Netanyahu Optimists, including those among the Arab participants. Ahmad (M, 30, II.1), who would have liked to see Arab parties join the coalition, explained: "I expect there will be an awakening, that [...] the dissolution of the Knesset will give a push [...] The Arab parties will come together, consolidate, and get more (seats)". While a majority of focus group participants predicted that the Arab parties would not join the government, the "blocking bloc" scenario was recurrently invoked to anchor the possibility of change: Bar (II.1): "I think they (the Arabs) will not recommend Bibi and then there will be a blocking bloc for Gantz. I don't know, anything can happen".

Alongside explanations based on possible behaviors of voters and politicians, Anti-Netanyahu Optimists also started to challenge Netanyahu's stamina, basing their observations on visuals ("You can see on his face that he's taking it very hard" [Or, II.1]) and psychological analysis:

> I think that with all the pressure there is and the failure to form a government, that was the beginning of the end. [...] I think he will not last and there is really going to be a revolution
>
> (Yasmin, II.1)

Pro-Netanyahu Optimists, of course, fiercely rejected such claims. Continuing to believe in Netanyahu's superior capabilities, they invoked both precedent and the possibility of surprises: "the magician always succeeds in the end somehow" (Gil, II.2).

8.4.3 Implications of Positive Expectations for Political Participation

Finally, we find an important link between optimistic expectations and political participation, and in particular voting. As shown in Table 8.1, people were more likely to vote the happier they expected to feel about the projected outcome in all survey waves but the first (before the establishment of Blue and White). This association is even more intense in the small subsample of Arab participants.

In the focus groups, too, while most participants were determined to vote (least so in the Arab group), enthusiasm was notably reduced among the more pessimistic participants. The following interaction between an Anti-Netanyahu Optimist (Yoel) and an Anti-Netanyahu Pessimist (Ksenia, F, 52, II.2) illustrates the point:

KSENIA: I will go (to vote). But I'm much more indifferent [...] And if there will be a huge queue then maybe I will not return.
YOEL: It's really your chance that something will happen! [...] how do you allow yourself to be so passive and not fight? [...]
KSENIA: I'll tell you why, because I'm in despair. [...] I think we're deteriorating on some slope without seeing its end, and I'm desperate.

Table 8.1 Spearman's rho correlations between intention to vote and expected happiness about the election outcomes

Survey wave	Correlation between expected happiness about predicted largest party and intention to vote		Correlation between expected happiness about predicted prime minister and intention to vote	
	Entire sample (N=442)	Arabic native speakers (N=51)	Entire sample (N=442)	Arabic native speakers (N=51)
I.1	.065	.083	.096*	.164
I.2	.201**	.302*	.172**	.281*
I.3	.192**	.293*	.140**	.312*
II.1	.150**	.355*	.122*	.371*
II.2	.174**	.217	.200**	.339*
III.1	.242**	.341*	.177**	.392**
III.2	.147**	.334*	.118*	.361*

Note: Intention to vote was measured on a four-point scale (will surely not vote, will probably not vote, will probably vote, will surely vote); Expected happiness was measured on a scale of 1–100 (0 = I will feel very bad; 100 = I will feel very good).

$* p<.05 ** p<.01.$

180　*Keren Tenenboim-Weinblatt et al.*

Among the persistent optimists, the failed government formation not only did not diminish, but actually reinforced their commitment to political participation:

> I was very happy. I think it [the new election] gives some hope that something can be done, and so I joined the Labor party [...] I think that we should fight and that it was a decisive proof that it ain't over 'til it's over.
> (Yasmin, II.1)

8.5 Summary and Discussion

In this chapter, we have explored Israeli citizens' evolving projections regarding the outcomes of the 2019–2020 elections. Based on an integrative conceptualization of political projections, and using a combination of panel survey and focus groups, we have examined both the aggregate evolution and social-discursive dynamics of prospective public opinion (Price, 1992; Shamir & Shamir, 2000).

We show how voters' expectations of a Netanyahu and Likud victory declined over time, and how this decrease was matched by a growing belief that Gantz's Blue and White might stand a chance to form a center-left coalition. Nevertheless, Netanyahu held on to a solid majority that believed him to be the most likely future prime minister throughout all three rounds of election. We show that people rarely attributed their expectations directly to specific sources, such as media reports, political commentators, or politicians, but rather presented them as personal extrapolations from available indicators, ranging from polls to personal impressions of the candidates' psychological states. We furthermore document voters' high, barely declining certainty about their projections, as well as their persistent expected happiness about the outcomes, reinforcing their commitment to voting.

The analysis also shows important interrelations between these elements: First, voters' expectations (predicted states) were linked to their desired outcomes (evaluations), forming three main groups that reflect the polarized and personalized Israeli political climate (Rahat & Sheafer, 2007; Shamir, Dvir-Gvirsman, & Ventura, 2017): Pro-Netanyahu Optimists, Anti-Netanyahu Optimists, and Anti-Netanyahu Pessimists. Over the three rounds of elections, these groups developed along different trajectories: While Pro-Netanyahu Optimists continued to believe in Netanyahu's desired victory, Anti-Netanyahu Pessimists gradually became Optimists, leading to an overall increase of optimist citizens. Besides people's dispositional optimism – "the generalized, relatively stable tendency to expect good outcomes" (Scheier & Carver, 2018, p. 1082) – part of political optimism thus appears to adapt to circumstances and new information. As these findings show, such new information is not only an antidote to wishful thinking (Babad, 1997; Blais & Bodet, 2006) but sometimes its catalyst. Somewhat paradoxically, the failure

Persistent Optimism under Political Uncertainty   181

to form a government only reinforced such thinking, particularly among supporters of the two big parties.

Second, different groups relied on somewhat different strategies to anchor their optimistic projections and estimate their probabilities. For Anti-Netanyahu Optimists, hoping for a change in government, specific likelihoods were cast aside in favor of a belief that change is possible – owing to the complexity of hard-to-predict interdependencies (e.g., electoral thresholds, coalition arithmetic, possible indictments) and some irreducible role played by luck. By contrast, Pro-Netanyahu Optimists were initially able to derive confident, desirable projections by extrapolating from the present situation and past elections. However, following Netanyahu's initial failure to form a government, also Pro-Netanyahu Optimists had to use increasingly contingent explanatory strategies to justify positive expectations. In line with the approach that sees optimism as an explanatory style (Seligman, 1991; Peterson & Steen, 2002), negative events were thus viewed as caused by transient conditions, which can change in the next elections.

Finally, our findings emphasize optimism's motivational aspects, which propel voters to invest efforts in goals that are believed to be attainable (Carver, Scheier, & Segerstrom, 2010; Peterson, 2000). Voters' belief in positive election outcomes correlated with their intention to vote throughout all three rounds of elections. Together with the persistent and growing optimism identified in this study, this stable association may explain the counterintuitive increase in turnout from election to election, despite all sides' repeated failure to achieve their desired outcomes.

Conceptually, the analysis presented in this chapter thus shows the usefulness of the conceptual framework of projections in accounting for the interplay of cognitive, emotional, motivational, and discursive aspects of optimism in politics. By combining surveys and focus groups in a longitudinal perspective, the study enabled a nuanced identification of key dynamic processes in future-oriented political thinking. Yet, the extraordinary setting of the case study, its reliance on self-reports and its not-fully-representative sample limit its generalizability and call for additional research.

Normatively, our findings raise the question what to make of the documented, persistent optimism. The benefits of optimism, most notably its motivational force and potential for facilitating positive self-fulfilling prophecies, contrast against the perils of hubris, planning fallacies, unhealthy delusions, and dangerous risk-taking (for useful discussions of optimism's benefits and costs, see Kahneman, 2011; Peterson, 2000).

In politics, optimism's capacity to foster participation and persistence in the face of obstacles is crucial to healthy democracies, arguably outweighing its costs. Yet, one cannot avoid wondering whether persistent optimism in the face of failure was not also part of what led Israel into three election rounds in less than one year, with major economic and various other repercussions. Society and democracy might be better served if optimistic impulses were directed more toward addressing pressing social issues, rather than the

182 *Keren Tenenboim-Weinblatt et al.*

persistent expectation that the outcomes of new elections will eventually favor one's side.

Finally, in the present study, optimism was mostly not enthusiasm, but more an expectation that "things will be okay" (Hani, II.1), somewhere between "so-so" and "good" in the survey's measure of participants' expected future of Israel. Given the ongoing crises and conflicts structuring politics, our persistent hope that, despite all, positive outcomes are possible may be exactly what is needed to move forward toward an uncertain future.

8.6 Epilogue: The 2021 Election

The government formed following the third election in spring 2020 turned out to be short-lived. Instead of the agreed rotation between Netanyahu and Gantz, the coalition collapsed within half a year, prolonging the political crisis. To assess Israeli citizens' electoral expectations toward this fourth round of elections in less than two years, we ran another wave of the survey in the week before the election.[7]

Projections concerning the largest party were relatively uncomplicated. With the disintegration of the Blue and White alliance, following Gantz's decision to join Netanyahu's government, no center-left list could challenge the Likud's status as the largest party in parliament. Accordingly, a large share of respondents (80%) predicted Likud to be the largest party, matching the responses from wave I.1, before the establishment of Blue and White (see Figure 8.4), as well as the eventual election results.

However, the prevalent projections concerning the prime minister's identity and the composition of the government were far off from the eventual outcome: a rotation government headed by Naftali Bennett (leader of the right-wing party Yemina with seven seats) and Yair Lapid (leader of the center-left party Yesh Atid, the second largest party, with seventeen seats), based on a broad coalition of eight parties (including the Arab party Ra'am). In the pre-electoral survey, not only was Netanyahu most often projected as the next prime minister, but the share of respondents making this projection (73%) significantly increased compared to the previous six pre-electoral survey waves (I.2–III.2; Figure 8.3). Lapid was expected to become prime minister by no more than 13% of the respondents, and a mere 3% correctly predicted that Bennett would assume the prime minister position. Only 14 respondents (1.4%) rightly projected a government that included both Yemina and the left-wing party Meretz and that excluded the Likud and the ultra-Orthodox parties. While 10% of respondents imagined a coalition that included Ra'am, none of them anticipated the eventual constellation of this coalition. And yet, as in previous elections, people expressed high certainty about their various projections (averaging 74–86, on a 0–100 scale).

Despite this high degree of certainty, participants' overall optimism declined. On average, people still expected to feel good about the electoral

Persistent Optimism under Political Uncertainty 183

outcomes (mean values of 54–58 for the different projections, on a 0–100 happiness scale), but less so than before previous elections (see Figure 8.7). Respondents also expressed a slightly diminished positive outlook about the overall state of the country in three years (3.42 on a five-point scale). While still on the positive side, it was the first wave in which participants selected "so-so" more often than "good". As in previous waves, there was a significant association between optimistic expectations and intention to vote, particularly concerning projections about the prime minister's identity and most intensely among Arab respondents. These findings tally with the substantially lower turnout in the March 2021 election (67.2% overall; 45.6% in Arab towns) in comparison to the three previous rounds, and further underscore the important role of optimism in political participation.

In line with the dynamics detected in the previous elections, the change in optimism was driven primarily by the Anti-Netanyahu camp. Whereas the group of Netanyahu supporters maintained its stable optimism (Pro-Netanyahu Optimists were 35% of the sample, alongside a negligible share of pessimistic Netanyahu supporters), the group of Anti-Netanyahu Pessimists (33%) grew in size in relation to Anti-Netanyahu Optimists (22%). The trend that developed over the second and third rounds, where many Anti-Netanyahu voters abandoned their pessimistic outlook, was thus reversed toward the fourth election. Although the Anti-Netanyahu camp did not manage to form a government following both the first and second elections, it seems that as long as Netanyahu also failed, the realm of possibility grew wider from the perspective of his opponents, and their hopes rose. Once Netanyahu succeeded in forming a government after the third election and Gantz agreed to join his coalition, it became more difficult to envision change in the fourth round.

And yet, this was precisely the election where such a change came about – less as a consequence of citizens' optimism, which declined toward the fourth round, and more due to realignments among Israel's political elites. The successive four elections, along with the growing discontentment among Netanyahu's former allies (from Lieberman's resignation in 2018 to Sa'ar's formation of the New Hope [Tikva Hadasha] party in 2020), eventually prepared the ground to the formation of an initially-unlikely government. The politicians' own persistent optimism in their ability to unseat Netanyahu – despite the extreme obstacles on the way – has likely played a crucial role in this process. "I am an optimist by nature", said Lapid following the third election (when he remained in the opposition), "otherwise I would probably be in a different profession" (Lapid, 2020). Within a polarized political climate and with the next crisis always around the corner, both Israeli politicians and citizens would do well to cultivate those aspects of optimism that sustain democratic societies: belief in the possibility of winning in the next elections, but also in the ability of societies and governments to move toward better futures between elections.

184 *Keren Tenenboim-Weinblatt et al.*

Notes

1 This study is funded by ERC Starting Grant 802990 (PROFECI).
  We are indebted to Sharon Ben-Arie and Bat-Sheva Hass for the coordination of the project, to Nidaa Nassar, Aysha Agbarya, Moran Avital, Naama Weiss-Yaniv, Yaara Abado, Dvora Newman, and Hila Yerushalmi for their research assistance, and to Ohad Ufaz and the staff at IPSOS and iPanel for their contribution to the administration of the focus groups and surveys.
2 www.jpost.com/israel-news/netanyahu-stump-speech-to-be-aired-with-10-minute-delay-judge-rules-582433
3 www.jpost.com/israel-news/gantz-warns-netanyahu-becoming-israeli-erdogan-618803
4 Sums in Figures 8.3 and 8.4 do not add up to 100%, as some respondents predicted third actors/parties to emerge as prime minister/largest party.
5 Figure 8.5 accounts for the changing party configurations: "Far-right parties" include the Jewish Home/Yemina/The New Right and Otzma Yehudit/Union of Right-Wing Parties; "Religious parties" include Shas and United Torah Judaism; Before Blue and White was formed, its line refers to its constituent parties; "Left parties" include Labor/Labor–Gesher–Meretz and Meretz/Democratic Camp; and "Arab parties" include either the Joint List or its constituent parties. Kulanu, Zehut, Hatnua'h, and Gesher (when it ran separately) are not included in this figure.
6 All names are pseudonyms; participants' gender (F/M) and age are marked at first appearance; focus group meeting numbers are as introduced in Figure 8.2.
7 The survey was completed by 329 of the 442 respondents who participated in all previous waves. Additionally, 697 new participants were recruited as a refreshment sample, resulting in a total of 1,026 respondents.
8 The Arab groups were recruited and moderated by Nidaa Nassar (Baladna Director, MA Hebrew University of Jerusalem) and Aysha Agbarya (PhD Candidate, Hebrew University of Jerusalem).

References

Babad, Elisha. 1997. "Wishful Thinking Among Voters: Motivational and Cognitive Influences." *International Journal of Public Opinion Research* 9 (2): 105–125.

Blais, André, and Marc André Bodet. 2006. "How Do Voters Form Expectations about the Parties' Chances of Winning the Election?" *Social Science Quarterly* 87 (3): 477–493.

Carver, Charles S., Michael F. Scheier, and Suzanne C. Segerstrom. 2010. "Optimism." *Clinical Psychology Review* 30 (7): 879–889.

Fuchs, Camil. 2017. "Surveys and Election Forecasts in a World of Social Media and Party Dealignment." In *The Elections in Israel 2015*, edited by Michal Shamir and Gideon Rahat, 213–236. New York: Routledge.

Gilbert, Daniel T., and Timothy D. Wilson. 2007. "Prospection: Experiencing the Future." *Science* 317 (5843): 1351–1354.

Harari, Yuval Noah. 2018. *21 Lessons for the 21st Century*. New York: Random House.

Kahneman, Daniel. 2011. *Thinking, Fast and Slow*. New York: Farrar, Straus and Giroux.

Kampf, Zohar. 2013. "Mediated Performatives." In *Handbook of Pragmatics*, edited by Jef Verschueren and Jan-Ola Östman, 1–24. Amsterdam: John Benjamins.

Kay, John, and Mervyn King. 2020. *Radical Uncertainty: Decision-Making Beyond the Numbers*. New York: W. W. Norton & Company.

Krizan, Zlatan, Jeffrey C. Miller, and Omesh Johar. 2010. "Wishful Thinking in the 2008 US Presidential Election." *Psychological Science* 21 (1): 140–146.

Lapid, Yair (Speaker). 2020. "Yair Lapid: I Did Not Understand What Happened to Him, Ganz Collapsed Under Pressure." Haaretz [Audio podcast]. June 23. www.haaretz.co.il/digital/podcast/weekly/.premium-PODCAST-1.8941742 [Hebrew].

Leshem, Oded Adomi, and Eran Halperin. 2020. "Hoping for Peace during Protracted Conflict: Citizens' Hope Is Based on Inaccurate Appraisals of Their Adversary's Hope for Peace." *Journal of Conflict Resolution* 64 (7–8), 1390–1417.

Meffert, Michael F., and Thomas Gschwend. 2011. "Polls, Coalition Signals and Strategic Voting: An Experimental Investigation of Perceptions and Effects." *European Journal of Political Research* 50 (5): 636–667.

Merton, Robert K. 1948. "The Self-Fulfilling Prophecy." *The Antioch Review* 8 (2): 193–210.

Mounk, Yascha. 2018. *The People Vs. Democracy: Why Our Freedom Is in Danger and How to Save It*. Cambridge: Harvard University Press.

Mutz, Diana C. 1998. *Impersonal Influence: How Perceptions of Mass Collectives Affect Political Attitudes*. Cambridge: Cambridge University Press.

Neiger, Motti. 2007. "Media Oracles: The Political Import and Cultural Significance of News Referring to the Future." *Journalism: Theory, Practice & Criticism* 8 (3): 326–338.

Neiger, Motti, and Keren Tenenboim-Weinblatt. 2016. "Understanding Journalism Through a Nuanced Deconstruction of Temporal Layers in News Narratives." *Journal of Communication* 66 (1): 139–160.

Pentzold, Christian, and Denise Fechner. 2020. "Data Journalism's Many Futures: Diagrammatic Displays and Prospective Probabilities in Data-Driven News Predictions." *Convergence* 26 (4): 732–750.

Peterson, Christopher. 2000. "The Future of Optimism." *American Psychologist* 55 (1): 44–55.

Peterson, Christopher, and Tracy A. Steen. 2009. "Optimistic Explanatory Style." In *The Oxford Handbook of Positive Psychology*, edited by Shane J. Lopez, and Charles R. Snyder, 313–321. New York: Oxford University Press.

Price, Vincent. 1992. *Public Opinion*. London: Sage.

Rahat, Gideon, and Tamir Sheafer. 2007. "The Personalization(s) of Politics: Israel, 1949–2003." *Political Communication* 24 (1): 65–80.

Rothschild, David, and Neil Malhotra. 2014. "Are Public Opinion Polls Self-Fulfilling Prophecies?" *Research & Politics* 1 (2): 1–10. doi:10.1177/2053168014547667

Scheier, Michael F., and Charles S. Carver. 2018. "Dispositional Optimism and Physical Health: A Long Look Back, a Quick Look Forward." *American Psychologist* 73 (9): 1082–1094.

Searle, John R. 1979. *Expression and Meaning: Studies in the Theory of Speech Acts*. Cambridge: Cambridge University Press.

Seligman, Martin E.P. 1991. *Learned Optimism*. NY: Knopf.

Shamir, Jacob, and Michal Shamir. 2000. *The Anatomy of Public Opinion*. Ann Arbor: University of Michigan Press.

186 *Keren Tenenboim-Weinblatt et al.*

Shamir, Michal, Shira Dvir-Gvirsman, and Raphael Ventura. 2017. "Taken Captive by the Collective Identity Cleavage: Left and Right in 2015 Elections." *The Elections in Israel 2015*, edited by Michal Shamir and Gideon Rahat, 139–164. New York: Routledge.

Sharot, Tali. 2011. "The Optimism Bias." *Current Biology* 21 (23): 941–945.

Silver, Nate. 2012. *The Signal and the Noise: Why So Many Predictions Fail-But Some Don't*. New York: Penguin.

Stalpouskaya, Katsiaryna. 2020. *Automatic Extraction of Agendas for Action from News Coverage of Violent Conflict*. PhD Dissertation. Munich: LMU Munich. https://edoc.ub.uni-muenchen.de/25807/1/Stalpouskaya_Katsiaryna.pdf

Stolwijk, Sjoerd B., Andreas R.T Schuck, and Claes H. de Vreese. 2017. "How Anxiety and Enthusiasm Help Explain the Bandwagon Effect." *International Journal of Public Opinion Research* 29 (4): 554–574.

Tenenboim-Weinblatt, Keren. 2018. "Media Projections and Trump's Election: A Self-Defeating Prophecy?" In *Trump and the Media*, edited by Pablo J. Boczkowski and Zizi Papacharissi, 111–118. Cambridge: MIT Press.

Tenenboim-Weinblatt, Keren, Christian Baden, Tali Aharoni, and Max Overbeck. 2022. "Affective Forecasting in Elections: A Socio-Communicative Perspective." *Human Communication Research*. https://doi.org/10.1093/hcr/hqac007

Tetlock, Philip E. 2005. *Expert Political Judgment: How Good Is It? How Can We Know?* Princeton: Princeton University Press.

Tetlock, Philip E., and Dan Gardner. 2015. *Superforecasting: The Art and Science of Prediction*. New York: Crown.

Weimann, Gabriel. 1990. "The Obsession to Forecast: Pre-Election Polls in the Israeli Press." *Public Opinion Quarterly* 54 (3): 396–408.

Westwood, Sean Jeremy, Solomon Messing, and Yphtach Lelkes. 2020. "Projecting Confidence: How the Probabilistic Horse Race Confuses and Demobilizes the Public." *Journal of Politics* 82 (4): 1530–1544. https://doi.org/10.1086/708682

Wilson, Timothy D., and Daniel T. Gilbert. 2003. "Affective Forecasting." *Advances in Experimental Social Psychology* 35 (35): 345–411.

Methodological Appendix

Panel Survey

Participants

1,191 participants were recruited by the Israeli survey company iPanel, using a stratified sample (response rate according to AAPOR RR3 code: 0.71). Figure 8.11 represents the target quotas set to represent the Israeli population eligible to vote, as well as the composition of both the initial survey wave (I.1) and of those 442 participants who completed all seven full waves and whose responses are analyzed in this chapter (excluding the epilogue). Compared to the actual election results, survey responses suggest a persistent overrepresentation of center-left and, to a lesser extent, far-right voters. However, over-time shifts in recorded voting intentions tally with those observed in the elections.

Procedure

All survey waves were administered online, in Hebrew or Arabic. The survey contained four main question blocks: (1) Predictions about the future prime minister, largest party, coalition composition (multi-choice), and the future of the country (1: very bad – 5: very good). The believed probability of predicted outcomes and their desirability were measured using continuous sliders (0: very low chance/will feel very bad – 100: very high chance/will feel very good; starting position at 50); (2) news and social media usage; (3) political participation and voting intention; and (4) demographics. In the brief postelection waves, only participants' vote choice and satisfaction with the electoral results were recorded.

Data Processing and Analysis

Participants were assigned anonymous identifiers to match responses across waves. Analyses were performed using SPSS software.

Focus Groups

Participants

A total of 55 Israeli voters participated in five focus groups (one of young Jewish voters; three of Jewish voters above the age of 29; one of Arab voters), each of which were convened five times. Each group was designed to ensure an even gender representation and varied religious identifications and education levels. The Jewish groups were recruited by IPSOS to include at least three voters each who would self-identify as right-wing, centrist, or left-wing voters respectively, and at least five undecided voters. Meetings were convened in Hebrew by the first and third author, at the IPSOS premises in Ramat Gan. For the Arab group, participants were recruited to vary political leaning, considering the different political cleavages in the Arab sector. Meetings were convened in Arabic by a native speaker in the Haifa area.[8] Each meeting lasted 90 minutes and was recorded in audio and video. Each group retained between six and nine participants in the final wave. Participants received remuneration in the form of gift vouchers.

Procedure

Each meeting commenced with instructing participants to respect different viewpoints and engage in an open-ended discussion. The meetings comprised four phases: (1) collection of participants' projections and expectations regarding the forthcoming elections (or, in the postelection meetings, the coalition talks) and their wider implications for the country; (2) in-depth discussion of selected scenarios, wherein participants were prompted to explain their reasoning; (3) engagement with election-related media coverage;

188 *Keren Tenenboim-Weinblatt et al.*

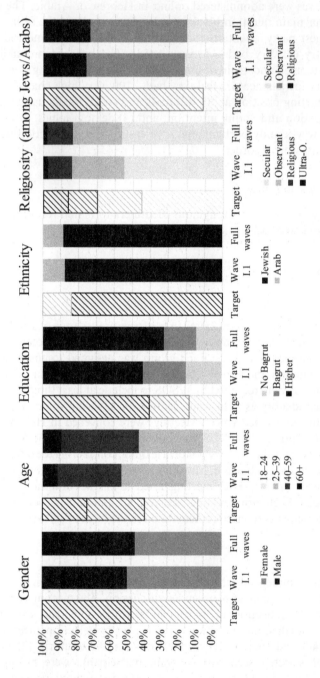

Figure 8.11 Sample composition and sampling biases.

Note: Population values obtained from cbs.gov.il, Agudat HaGalil (for the Arab population), iPanel, and Wikipedia.

and (4) discussion of what, in view of the participants, should be done with regard to the elections. Throughout all discussions, moderators kept their interventions to a minimum, encouraging an interactive discussion between participants. Following each meeting, participants filled out a short questionnaire, addressing their media exposure and voting intentions.

Data Processing and Analysis

All analyses were conducted based on fully anonymized transcripts, using MAXQDA software. The qualitative analytic strategy departed from an initial deductive coding based on the broad conceptualization of projections and their elements, which was further refined through the inductive identification of recurrent patterns. Finally, findings were contextualized against the results of the panel survey for integrative analysis.

All procedures for the collection and analysis of data used in this study were approved by the IRB (Institutional Review Board) of the Hebrew University of Jerusalem, the PROFECI project's ethics advisory board, and the panel of ERC ethics review

9 Ethnic Demons and Class Specters
Ethnic and Class Voting in Israel Revisited[1]

Gal Levy, Maoz Rosenthal, and Ishak Saporta

Since the publication of Michal Shamir and Asher Arian's 1982 article "The Ethnic Vote in Israel's 1981 Elections," the question of whether ethnic voting exists in Israeli Jewish society[2] has been an integral part of research on Israeli politics. We revisit this issue to determine the extent to which ethnic voting is a coherent phenomenon that explains Israeli voters' electoral behavior. Two issues underlie this study. The first centers on the widespread perception that voting tendencies in Israel are "tribal" and hence derive from ethnic identities. The second concerns the extent to which ethnic identity influences voting patterns in comparison to economic status, on one hand, and religiosity, collective identity, and policy positions on the other.

The discussion of ethnic politics, class relations, and voting patterns is not unique to Israel (e.g., Roemer, Woojin, and Van der Straeten, 2007). In recent years, the subject of political and electoral behavior has focused on the rise of populism, which in the eyes of many expresses the intersection of identity and class interests (Gandesha, 2018). However, research still tends to emphasize and presuppose the existence of antagonism between material and identity concerns in voting. Thus, while the tendencies of middle-class voters are regarded as consistent with their lifestyle, similar choices among the lower class are seen as an expression of its seemingly static ethnic characteristics (Anthias, 2013: 124). One testimony to this disparity comes from the French sociologist Didier Eribon, who describes his journey to his hometown and the working-class society from which he broke away. Eribon (2019) explores why the workers who used to identify with the Communist Party ended up supporting the xenophobic right of Jean-Marie Le Pen. But first he wonders:

> if we wish to explain why at this or that moment the popular classes vote for the right ... we need to ask if we are correct to assume, without questioning our assumption, that it is somehow more natural that those classes should vote for the left, especially given that it is not always the case that they do. And indeed, it has never absolutely been the case that they do.
>
> (p. 135)

DOI: 10.4324/9781003267911-12

Based on this assumption, there is a tendency to see the lower class as if it is driven by a "false consciousness," motivated by identity, and votes against its (class) interests. In contrast, the middle class, supposedly devoid of any discourse regarding identity, is understood to vote rationally. Thus, not only are we overlooking the ethnic-identity aspect of the middle-class vote, but we are also making the mistake of giving an empirical basis to a seemingly theoretical assumption, one that is wrong in our view, that dichotomously separates ethnic (identity) and class (interests) voting (Anthias, 2013; Hashash, 2017). These issues, which are also related to the discussion of ethnic voting in Israel, reiterate the extent to which the question of the relationship between class and ethnic voting remains unresolved.

If the theoretical debate about ethnic voting confronted critical structural approaches with approaches based on an analysis of political preferences and an ideological interpretation of reality, it seems that the social protest of summer 2011 shook things up (Levy, 2017a). At the sociopolitical level, the protest proposed a new agenda based on a demand for political solutions to economic hardships, especially those of the middle class (Ram and Filk, 2013; Rosenhek and Shalev, 2014; Levy 2017a). The success of the Yesh Atid party, led by Yair Lapid, in 2013 reflected this claim (Talshir, 2015). However, in the three elections in 2019–2020, the centrist alliance of Yesh Atid, Telem, and Hosen Yisrael that formed Blue and White (Kahol-Lavan), had left the Israeli parliament in a political deadlock. In May 2020, this stalemate resulted in the breakup of Blue and White, with Hosen Yisrael (keeping the party label of Blue and White), led by Benny Gantz, joining Benjamin Netanyahu and the Likud to form what has been termed as a *rotation government*. That government lasted less than a year, and in March 2021, following breaches of the coalition agreement by Netanyahu, Israel went to another election, which led to the formation of another rotation government led by Yair Lapid and Naftali Bennett from Yemina, with Blue and White part of this broad and unique coalition. The 2019–2020 electoral rounds up until Blue and White broke up provided us with an almost "natural experiment" whereby Likud was facing a political party that moved beyond the Israeli left and right identifications. Thus, Israeli voters could potentially step out of their tribal identity marked by these political labels. Hence, we ask whether Israeli (Jewish) voters used this opportunity to break out of the political choices that their ethnic identity supposedly dictates.

This question has an additional purpose. The 2011 Tent Protest prompted a rethinking of the validity of existing explanations regarding ethnic politics and these claims' correspondence with reality (e.g., Mizrachi, 2016; Levy, 2017b). Thus, we also aim to reevaluate the extant understandings of ethnic voting, particularly the tendency to attribute to Mizrahim (Jews from Asia and Africa) a static, identity-based voting behavior. We aim to show that, while the various approaches point to factors that are essential in understanding Israeli political behavior, each in itself does not provide an exhaustive explanation of the phenomenon. Particularly, we highlight

192   *Gal Levy, Maoz Rosenthal, and Ishak Saporta*

the importance of an approach that takes into account the positioning, the intersections, and the entirety of the identity, class and political contexts in which voters are situated. In our view, whether it points to structural-demographic factors such as class and ethnic origin or focuses on ideologies and political preferences – the extant literature fails to provide comprehensive empirical and theoretical answers to the connections between all of these factors and voting tendencies.

9.1 Ethnic Class or Ideological Voting

Studies of Israeli electoral behavior maintain that the collective identity schism overshadows any other rift, creating two distinct camps: the right and the left (Shamir and Arian, 1999; Shamir, Dvir-Gvirsman, and Ventura, 2017: 146). Consequently, there is a strong overlap between political ideology, concrete policy positions, and religious identity. Moreover, the dimensions of ethnicity and class do not constitute significant categories of identity in the political context (Shamir et al., 2017: 158–159). Critics of this approach have focused on social and class structures and on the entirety of the interactions between class and identity groups and the state. Thus, studies that examine how a hierarchical incorporation regime limits the access of ethnic groups to material and symbolic resources used the multiple citizenship model (Shafir and Peled, 2002). Following the 2011 social protest, Mizrachi (2016) offered an alternative explanation to the question of why Mizrahim vote for right-wing parties. This explanation centered on the existence of distinct worlds of meaning and interpretation and on the liberal blindness to its own identity traits. Aiming to bridge the gap between these approaches, Grinberg (2019) suggested thinking about these voting patterns in tribal terms, emphasizing both underlying identity and material interests.

Grinberg also argued that the Blue and White party was, in fact, the representative of the secular Ashkenazi tribe. Hence, the elections illustrated that it is not policy positions that determine the pattern of interbloc politics, but the quasi-Pavlovian position taken by Jewish voters in an intertribal campaign, which was manifested this time in the struggle for Netanyahu's political survival (Grinberg, 2019). Thus, in contrast to the hypothesis that right and left denote a combination of social identity that is consistent with policy positions and voting (Arian and Shamir, 2008), Grinberg sees these identities as tribal and not representing particular policy demands. Jewish society is divided into two tribes, their markers being Ashkenazi (Jews of European origins) versus Mizrahi, secular versus traditional, and upper-middle class versus lower class. Correspondingly, voting is organized according to myths created in tribal discourse. Thus, it reflects electoral conduct that seems irrational from the outside, whose purpose is to define and establish the boundaries between "us" and "them" (Grinberg, 2019: 119–125). Electoral behavior, therefore, is nothing but a contest for positions of power between rival tribes, particularly between politicians who exploit this tribal rivalry.

Ethnic Demons and Class Specters 193

Despite its intuitive appeal, this explanation leaves a methodological and analytical lacuna. In particular, the use of the term tribe leaves many questions open, such as the relationship between the ethnic and class components (Hashash, 2017). The explanation remains focused on the current interests of the political elite that the tribal vote protects, and does not examine the role of social mobility and intergenerational changes, or, alternatively, barriers to mobility. Indeed, the scholarship on stratification and social mobility in Israel shows that over the years there have been shifts in the economic and social status of Mizrahim, expressed in their identification with symbols and perceptions that indicate differences between generations and between Mizrahim from different socioeconomic backgrounds (Cohen, Lewin-Epstein, and Lazarus, 2019; Lewin-Epstein and Cohen, 2019). And while we stand with Grinberg in his desire to understand the full range of interconnections between ethnicity, class, and political interests, we also learn from feminist research the importance of understanding intersection as a factor influencing electoral behavior (Anthias, 2013; Hashash, 2017). Equipped with this perspective, we sought to examine how ethnic politics were reflected in the support for the two main parties which according to Grinberg were representing the opposing tribes during the 2019–2020 elections: Likud and Blue and White (Grinberg, 2019, 2021).

9.2 Ethnic Voting in Israel: Review and Hypotheses

Ethnic politics has been part of the Israeli political grammar since its inception in Mandatory Palestine (Herzog, 1986). Following the establishment of the state, the ethnic parties failed, not least due to the Zionist parties' efforts to delegitimize Mizrahi interests, co-opt the Mizrahi leadership and recruit Mizrahim as ordinary members, while preventing their promotion to leadership positions (Cohen and Leon, 2011; Levy and Emmerich, 2001; Shafir and Peled, 2002). During the dramatic election campaign of 1981, ethnicity became a political weapon of great symbolic value. Since then, Mizrahim have been pitted against Ashkenazim and Likud voters against the Labor/Alignment (Ma'arach) voters, and the "ethnic demon" has become an integral part of the Israeli political landscape (Levy, 2015). Consequently, researchers into the so-called "ethnic problem" have pondered the gap between its prominence in the political discourse and the perpetuation of the social and economic disparities between Mizrahim and Ashkenazim. In electoral research, questions about the political behavior of Mizrahim have often obscured the fact that the voting patterns of the middle class, who are mostly Ashkenazi, also have an identity aspect. Given the research approach that viewed the Mizrahi vote as an anomaly, one can understand the surprise with which the Jewish public received the emergence of the Shas party and its inclusion in the government (Peled, 2001). If until the 1977 political upheaval (the *mahapach*) ethnic sectarianism was regarded as a temporary side effect stemming from cultural differences in the process of nation-building (Lissak,

194   *Gal Levy, Maoz Rosenthal, and Ishak Saporta*

1999), in the early 1980s explanations arose that saw the ethnic issue as a structural problem intertwined with power relations within Jewish Israeli society (Swirski, 1981; Smooha, 1984). They also regarded ethnic politics as interest-driven, expressing the power struggles prevalent in society (Ram, 2017). Shafir and Peled (2002) proposed examining ethnic politics in the context of what they called "the citizenship regime."

The citizenship regime, or incorporation regime, is a conceptual tool that links social structures such as identity, class, and political behavior to the discursive mechanisms that legitimize them. According to Shafir and Peled (2002), citizenship discourses are a mechanism that explains how institutions (parties and other organizations) and political mobilization set the competition for power and hegemony, establishing a differential pattern of conferring rights and status. Via its institutions, the Labor movement established a republican citizenship discourse (*mamlachtiut*) that privileged veteran Israeli Ashkenazim and was used to recruit new immigrants from the Middle East and North Africa to the young country. Since the 1970s, this discourse competed with two other distinct discourses: the liberal and the ethno-national. The former was espoused by the Ashkenazi middle class. This class clung to the institutions of the capitalist market in the wake of the political demise of the ethos of mamlachtiut. The latter became prominent with the rise of the Mizrahi working class, alongside the ultra-Orthodox and national-religious Zionists, who challenged the secular state. At the same time, the political consolidation of the Palestinian citizens of Israel required the state to strengthen its civic foundations as opposed to its national ones (Jamal, 2017; Levy, 2005; Shafir and Peled, 2002). The incorporation regime, therefore, is hierarchical and fragmentary, with political voting being an expression of class and the status of the ethnic group vis-à-vis the government.

At the turn of the millennium, the processes of neoliberalization intensified and the vision of liberal peace waned (Shalev and Levy, 2005); poverty increased and the middle class shrank (Rosenhek and Shalev, 2014); the ideological differences between political parties blurred, and social unrest grew, even among the middle class (Grinberg, 2013). The 2011 protest revealed the interpretive limits of the multiple citizenship model. In the wake of the protest and the political discourse's focus on economic issues, the Yesh Atid party emerged. A new political alliance was forged among the Ashkenazi middle class, between Yesh Atid and the rebranded National Religious Party (NRP), The Jewish Home. However, Benjamin Netanyahu's attempt to renew a republican order centered around the Ashkenazi middle class (Levy, 2015) failed, and the coalition that supposedly reflected a cross-partisan response to the protest's demands (Talshir, 2015) did not survive. The gap between the parties and the public widened, as evident in the limited success of the two parties with the highest seats share in Knesset in the 2015 elections: the Likud and the Zionist Camp (Kenig and Tuttnauer, 2017). The multiple citizenship model

Ethnic Demons and Class Specters 195

and the focus on citizenship discourses ignore these upheavals, especially the changes in the patterns of civic participation (Levy, 2017b).

In the first three elections of this election cycle Likud and Blue and White were the major parties and won the majority of votes. Nevertheless, unlike in 2015, due to the absence of a decisive victory and the stubborn refusal to see the Arab-Palestinian party, the Joint List, as a legitimate coalition partner, the September 2019 election resulted in a political stalemate (Rosenthal, *Ynet*, February 6, 2020a). Toward the March 2020 election, the public's attention turned to the Covid-19 virus, reducing the focus on Netanyahu and increasing the focus on the virus's health risks (Greenwald and Rosenthal, 2021). Consequently, immediately after the election, the political agenda's focus shifted away from Netanyahu's leadership, and calls for the creation of a government that should focus on the health crisis and its consequent economic perils grew (Cavari, Rosenthal, and Shpaizman, 2021). This shift in attention resulted in cooperation between Benny Gantz and Netanyahu. They formed a new political entity they called the *rotation government*, which in essence was a mutual veto government where both Gantz's faction and Likud were able to veto each other's initiatives. The formation of the Netanyahu–Gantz government led to a split within Blue and White where Gantz's faction retained that name, and the rest of Blue and White (Yesh Atid and Telem) became part of the opposition.

As the population vaccination rate increased, Netanyahu sought a new election. This fourth election in March 2021 resumed the focus on Netanyahu and his leadership as prime minister. In the post-electoral bargaining process, Netanyahu was unable to form a coalition. Yair Lapid formed a diverse coalition that renewed his previous alliance with The Jewish Home (now rebranded as Yemina) and Gantz's Blue and White. This coalition also included an Arab Islamist party (Ra'am) alongside right-wing parties led by Gideon Sa'ar and Avigdor Lieberman, joined by the Labor party and the left-wing Meretz. The new government's policy agenda, reflected in the coalition agreements, signed between the parties joining the coalition and the coalition's formateur, and the government's guidelines signed jointly by all coalition partners, is different in terms of diversity and content of the public policies it related to in comparison to the previous government. However, it avoided two core issues of Israeli politics: state and religion, and the occupation of the Palestinian territories (Cavari et al., 2021). At the time of writing this coalition has come to its end and the political future of some of its parties remains bleak.

Grinberg regarded the 2019–2021 irresolution and the focus on Netanyahu's political fate as a reflection of the existence of an ethnically, religiously, and economically distinct tribal system that manifests itself at the ballot box (Grinberg, 2021). The 2021 Bennett–Lapid coalition reflects this claim because the representatives of "Second Israel," namely Likud and Shas, were left out of the coalition. His analysis also underscored that the struggle revolves around the material and symbolic privileges conferred by virtue of belonging to a particular social tribe. The tribal thesis in fact reinforces Peled's

196 *Gal Levy, Maoz Rosenthal, and Ishak Saporta*

structural-class thesis as well as Mizrachi's proposal to see right- and left-wing voters as fixed in their worlds of meaning. Our first hypothesis reflects these approaches:

> Hypothesis 1: in this election cycle, party and ethnic identity coincided, with more Mizrahim voting for Likud and fewer for Blue and White.

Viewing voting as tribal and detached from social needs at the individual level produces a static picture of voting behavior and overlooks the connection between concrete interests and collective electoral behavior. It also ignores how social mobility affects personal interests and voting behavior (Rosenthal, Zubida, and Nachmias, 2018; Rosenthal, 2019). After several decades in which Mizrahim were seen as a homogeneous category, and especially since the publication of Shlomo Swirski's *Not Backward but Held Back* (1981), there have been voices proposing a reevaluation of this view. Cohen and Leon (2008) held that, following Likud's rise to power,

> as a result of the rise of the Mizrahi middle class at the beginning of the 21st century, the Mizrahim have ceased being a homogenous, marginal weak socio-economic group. Instead, we are required to discuss [...] their new capacities to collaborate autonomously in setting the political, social, and cultural agenda.
>
> (p. 87)

Other studies reexamined the categories of Mizrahim and Ashkenazim, suggesting that while both are dynamic, they still play part in maintaining the ethno-class order (Sagiv, 2014; Sasson-Levy and Shoshana, 2014; Schwartz, 2014). For our purposes, the very formation of a new class horizon for Mizrahim, which motivates their political and social conduct, is significant.

Research indicates mixed trends of social inequality between Ashkenazim and Mizrahim. Despite the socioeconomic inequality between them that has persisted into the third generation, the gap between the groups is narrowing due to the increase in the number of Mizrahim pursuing higher education (Cohen et al., 2019). However, there is still a disparity between the two groups, limiting the social mobility of Mizrahim (Yaish and Gabay-Egozi, 2019). In addition, there is an economic disparity between Mizrahi subgroups (Lewin-Epstein and Raviv, 2016; Plaut and Plaut, 2016) and between Mizrahim born outside of Israel and those born in Israel (Cohen et al., 2019). Furthermore, there have also been noticeable changes in the variety of cultural identities prevalent in the Mizrahi public, and in varying patterns of self-definition as Israeli, Jewish, and Mizrahi (Lewin-Epstein and Cohen, 2019). These trends raise the question of whether, despite widespread claims about tribal behavior, class differences as reflected in educational levels would not also suggest differences in patterns of ethnic voting. Thus:

Hypothesis 2: voters' economic status moderates the connection between ethnic origin and voting.

Steadily and over time, religiosity has been a strong predictor of policy positions and voting patterns in Israel (Shamir and Arian, 1999; Arian and Shamir, 2008; Hirsch-Hoefler, Canetti, and Pedahzur, 2010). Sociological research shows that Mizrahim tend to be more religious than other ethnic groups in Israeli Jewish society (Katz-Gerro, Raz, and Yaish, 2009). Hence, the intersection between ethnicity and religiosity raises the question of how and whether each of these factors influences voting patterns, individually and in combination. Thus, the influence of societal groups' level of religiosity on their voting patterns should also be examined. We therefore propose that:

Hypothesis 3: voters' religiosity moderates the connection between ethnic origin and voting.

A final argument stems from the rational voter approach. According to this view, voters' social backgrounds have a relatively small impact compared to that of their positions on the policy issues at stake, whether or not these positions overlap with their social identity (Bargsted and Kedar, 2009; Getmansky and Zeitzoff, 2014). Generally, studies that emphasize the impact of policy issues on voters also point out the social background associations with these stances. However, these studies emphasize that while voters' social background is important in understanding their behavior, the more explicit factor is their policy positions. Thus, we posit a hypothesis that contests those we have presented so far:

Hypothesis 4: voting is influenced by voters' policy positions on the key issues at stake.

9.3 Data and Method

We rely on data from the Israel National Election Studies from the April 2019 pre-electoral wave.[3] The next rounds of elections during the 2019–2021 cycle added policy issues (Greenwald and Rosenthal, 2021) and affected electoral volatility between the various parties to some extent (Rosenthal, *Globes*, March 7, 2020b). However, the first electoral round allowed us to examine our hypotheses as the competition between Blue and White and Likud had provided us with a "natural experiment" whereby voters were able to step out of their habitual behavior that connects party attachments and ethnic identity. We used the Jewish respondents only, as voting considerations within the Jewish population are different from those of the Arab population (Rosenthal et al., 2018).

We measured the vote using two variables – voting for Likud and voting for Blue and White, based on self-reported voting intentions in the pre-electoral

198 *Gal Levy, Maoz Rosenthal, and Ishak Saporta*

poll. The question asked: "If the elections were held today, which party would you vote for?" The answers to the question included the various parties that participated in the election, as well as the option of submitting a blank ballot and the answers "I do not intend to vote," I don't know," and "I refuse to respond." In order to focus the analysis on Likud and Blue and White, we created two dummy variables: "voting for Likud" (24.43% who reported their intention to vote for Likud rather than any other party) and "voting for Blue and White" (24.78% who intended to vote for Blue and White rather than anyone else).

Ethnicity. Based on respondents' *self-report of country of birth*, we created a dummy variable of *natives of Asia or Africa* versus the rest. Of the respondents, 70.9% said that they were born in Israel, 9% were born in Asia or Africa, 10.2% were born in Europe or America, and 9.7% were born in the former Soviet Union. Based on *self-reports of father's and mother's country of birth*, in keeping with the same categories above, we classified Israeli-born respondents as follows: Those who reported that both their father's and their mother's country of origin was in Asia or Africa were classified as Mizrahim (23.91%), those who reported that their father's or their mother's (but not both) origin was Mizrahi were classified as mixed Mizrahim (9.56%), and the rest were included in the remaining group. Based on these distinctions, we created one dummy variable of Mizrahim born in Israel (15.95%) versus the rest, and another dummy variable of native Israelis who had only one parent of Mizrahi descent, to whom we refer as "mixed" (7.89%), versus the rest.[4]

Level of Religiosity – Secularism. In accordance with previous studies (Arian and Shamir, 1999), we created three categories: religious (18.45%), traditional (31.67%), and secular (49.88%).[5]

Policy Positions. We selected questions on positions that similar studies have used and that deal with issues that are at the core of the political agenda.[6]

Position toward the establishment of a Palestinian state: The question was "Do you think Israel should consent or not consent to the establishment of a Palestinian state in Judea, Samaria and the Gaza Strip as part of a final status agreement?" The answers ranged from fully agree (16.41%), agree (29.10%), agree under certain conditions (13.02%), and disagree (41.45%).

Opposition to the influence of Jewish religion on the Israeli public sphere: The question read "Do you think the Israeli government should or should not ensure that public life in the country is conducted according to Jewish religious tradition?" The possible answers were full agreement with the government's involvement in making the Israeli public sphere accord with Jewish tradition (24.76%), partial agreement (15.17%), opposition (25.31%), and full opposition (34.75%).

Class Background. To measure socioeconomic background, we used *level of education*. We created a dichotomous variable to distinguish between those having received an academic education (at any level) and those with no academic education. We did so assuming that an academic education in Israel is related to income level, affects the chances of social mobility (Semyonov

Ethnic Demons and Class Specters 199

and Lewin-Epstein, 2011), and has a decisive impact on both social and political perceptions (Lewin-Epstein and Cohen, 2019). In the survey, 44.82% of respondents reported having an academic education compared to 55.17% who did not.[7]

9.4 Analysis and Findings

Table 9.1 presents the relationships between the variables.[8] The correlations show that education, secularism, and ethnic origin are interrelated but in intricate ways. As a matter of fact, of the three categories of Mizrahim we defined, only those born in Asia or Africa are significantly less educated and more religious than the rest of the population, whereas Israeli-born Mizrahim and "mixed" Mizrahim born in Israel are not statistically different on education and secularism. Furthermore, only those born in Asia or Africa tend to vote for Likud, while the two other groups of Israeli-born Mizrahim do not tend to vote differently from others, neither for Likud nor for Blue and White. Moreover, even foreign born Mizrahim are not statistically different from others in terms of support for Blue and White. The relationship of the three categories of Mizrahim with the two policy positions we explored are low, and except for one (Israeli-born Mizrahim with support for separation of state and religion), not different from other population groups – just like in their vote. On the other hand, the relationships between religiosity and education with the vote and issue variables are consistently significant and high: Secular and educated people support a two-state solution, oppose the influence of religion on the state, and vote less for Likud and more for Blue and White. Opponents of a two-state solution oppose the separation of state and religion, and vote for Likud rather than Blue and White.

According to Hypothesis 1, voting supposedly reflects a tribal pattern of behavior, which creates behavioral clusters that combine socioeconomic, ethnic, and political characteristics into a single identity. In the basic analysis of correlations, we would expect to find, along with Mizrahi ethnicity, religiosity (low levels of secularism), nonacademic education, opposition to the two-state solution and opposition to the separation of state and religion that would lead to supporting Likud. However, the correlations show that most of these phenomena are true for Mizrahim born abroad, but not for Mizrahim born in Israel, whether or not they are "mixed." The correlations also seem to confirm Hypothesis 4 that policy positions are a strong and significant predictor of which party one will vote for. However, these policy positions do not stand on their own, isolated from structural variables. The connection between policy positions and vote relates to respondents' level of secularism (Shamir and Arian, 1999; Arian and Shamir, 2008).

Being religious is associated with lower socioeconomic status and being born abroad of Mizrahi descent. But in the spirit of Hypotheses 2 and 3, the effect of these factors on voting is conditional and complex, and therefore requires a closer analysis. Recall that Hypotheses 2 and 3 refer to socioeconomic

Table 9.1 The relationships between the variables

	Academic education	Born in Asia/Africa	Israeli-born Mizrahi	Israeli-born "mixed" Mizrahi	Level of secularism	Against the two-state solution	Support for separation of state and religion	Vote for Likud	Vote for Blue and White
Academic education	1.000								
Born in Asia/Africa	−0.540***	1.000							
Israeli-born Mizrahi	−0.123	−1.00***	1.000						
Israeli-born "mixed" Mizrahi	−0.024	−1.00***	−1.00***	1.000					
Level of secularism	0.322***	−0.295***	−0.096	−0.013	1.000				
Against the two-state solution	−0.342***	−0.039	0.098	0.0726	−0.568***	1.000			
Support for separation of state and religion	0.220***	−0.125	−0.116*	−0.078	0.741***	−0.451***	1.000		
Vote for Likud	−0.434***	0.525***	0.052	0.000	−0.269***	0.604***	−0.294***	1.000	
Vote for Blue and White	0.311***	−0.089	−0.010	−0.106	0.571***	−0.551***	0.512***	−1.00***	1.000

Note: *** $p \leq 0.001$; ** $p \leq 0.01$; * $p \leq 0.05$.

Ethnic Demons and Class Specters   201

background and religiosity as moderating Mizrahi voting. To evaluate these relationships we estimate multivariate, three-way interaction models, where each model includes policy positions, ethnic background, religiosity, and socio-economic level factors as independent variables, and all of their two- and three-way interactions.[9] The models and their results are presented in Table 9A.2 in the Appendix; Figures 9.1 and 9.2 illustrate visually the interactions and their effect on the vote of Mizrahim born outside of Israel and Israeli natives of Mizrahi or mixed origin for Likud and for Blue and White.

The two figures are divided into three sub-diagrams, each of which reflects a distinct category: Mizrahim born outside of Israel, Israeli-born Mizrahim, and Israeli-born "mixed" Mizrahim. Each sub-diagram has an additional division denoting (from left to right) subgroups of religious, traditional, and secular voters. Each of these internal diagrams is designed so that the x-axis shows those with an academic education relative to those without an academic education, and the y-axis shows the probability of voting for Likud (Figure 9.1) and Blue and White (Figure 9.2). Within each diagram, a vertical line denotes the connection between education and the probability of voting for the party in question given the level of religiosity (religious, traditional, or secular) represented in that sub-diagram. Within each level of religiosity, a change in level of education generates a change in the probability of voting for Likud in Table 9.1 (and for Blue and White in Table 9A.2) over the alternatives. The probability is represented by the point in the middle of the line and by the range of the estimate (the length of the line). In general, when the line is longer and contains a higher value range, the result is less significant. In contrast, a shorter vertical line denotes a lower probability value range, making the mean (denoted by the point in the middle of the line) more significant.

Figure 9.1 shows that for traditional Mizrahim born abroad, without an academic education, the probability of voting for Likud is almost 60% (with a range of 40%–70%). This group is the most likely to vote for Likud, closely followed by religious Mizrahim born abroad, with no academic education. Israeli-born Mizrahim who are traditional and do not have an academic education have a 40% likelihood to vote for Likud. In contrast, secular and educated Mizrahim born in Israel are consistently less likely to vote for Likud. Although the broad range makes it difficult to determine a clear trend of Likud voting among most of the subgroups of Mizrahim born in Israel, the difference between them and Mizrahim born abroad is clear. Among the "mixed" respondents, there are minimal differences between the subgroups in their likelihood of voting for Likud with overall low probabilities and wide probability ranges. Thus, for the Likud voting interaction models, the probability of a tribal vote is high among Mizrahim born abroad but fades when it comes to the other groups. Hence, socioeconomic background and level of religiosity are factors that influence the likelihood of voting for Likud, demonstrating the diverse voting behavior among Mizrahim. This finding contrasts with the tribal argument assumed by Hypothesis 1 that most Mizrahi groups are consistently likely to vote for Likud.

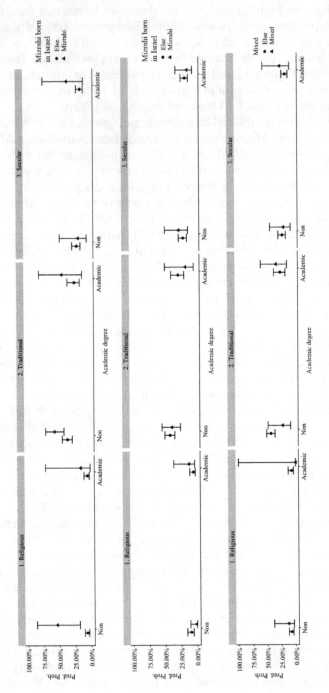

Figure 9.1 Vote for Likud in three categories of Mizrahim (Mizrahim born abroad, born in Israel, and "Mixed" Mizrahim born in Israel) by education and religiosity.

Ethnic Demons and Class Specters 203

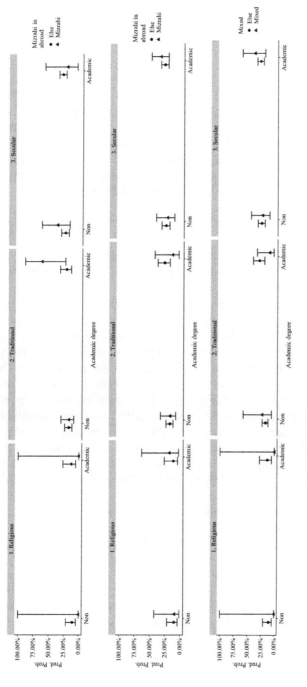

Figure 9.2 Vote for Blue and White in three categories of Mizrahim (Mizrahim born abroad, born in Israel, and "Mixed" Mizrahim born in Israel) by education and religiosity.

In Figure 9.2, as in the previous figure, we find a contrast between the characteristics of the groups. Increased levels of education and secularism change the voting patterns and increase the Mizrahi tendency to vote for Blue and White, especially for Israeli-born and mixed Mizrahim. The picture with regard to Mizrahim born outside of Israel is more blurred, and the group with the highest probability of voting for Blue and White (over 60% but with a wide range) is that of the educated traditional voters.

Thus, the effect of Mizrahi origin on voting depends on the voters' class and level of religiosity, refuting Hypothesis 1, while confirming Hypotheses 2 and 3. Mizrahim who have higher economic status and who are secular are more inclined to vote for Blue and White than Mizrahim with lower economic status who are likely to vote for Likud. Hence, differences in Mizrahi respondents' socioeconomic backgrounds lead to voting patterns inconsistent with the tribal explanation, at least in the April 2019 election.

9.5 Conclusion

The goal of this chapter is both simple and complex. It is simple in that we sought to ascertain the existence and nature of ethnic voting in Israel in this election cycle. It is complex because we probed into the causal mechanism behind these voting patterns. To this end, we included a discussion of Grinberg's (2019) thesis, according to which the last rounds of elections revealed the tribal nature of the political breakdown of Israeli Jewish society. Due to the diverse material and cultural explanations attempting to shed light on the so-called ethnic problem, Grinberg claimed that the two-bloc alignment in the 2019–2021 election rounds was an expression of tribal voting (Grinberg, 2021).

Grinberg's explanation differs from the prevailing narratives regarding the effect of ethnic background on voting patterns. These narratives include the "four tribes" account presented by then President Reuven Rivlin in 2015. Rivlin claimed that Israeli society is based on the existence of four tribes – secular, national-religious, ultra-Orthodox, and Arab – that must strive for a common social "structure of ownership."[10] This argument ignores the social conflict inherent in this tribal division, and fails to see the ethnic groups within Jewish society, despite the political implications of the phenomenon of ethnicity (Levy, 2015; Mintz, 2017: 16). Another common explanation sees ethnicity as the foundation of all dimensions of Israeli political conflict, interwoven with the "Second Israel" argument, which is based on overlapping cleavages between Mizrahim and Ashkenazim. This explanation, which is based in part on an analysis that accurately reflects the history of this relationship, sees the Mizrahi vote for Likud and Shas as the fitting political solution to the struggle against Ashkenazi cultural hegemony (Stern, *Ha'aretz,* September 26, 2020). Leaving aside the ideological aspect of this explanation, it is also inconsistent with the findings of recent sociological research, which shows how overlapping schisms in Israeli society (such as the ethnic and socioeconomic schisms) have to a certain extent become crosscutting.

Ethnic Demons and Class Specters   205

In contrast to these two arguments, Grinberg maintains that electoral behavior is underpinned by clear political interests, chief among them the desire to obtain or retain privileges. From this perspective, the claim that Mizrahim are right wing in their positions and the Ashkenazim left wing, or any reduction of the political struggle to a simplistic concept of identity politics, is unsatisfactory. Previous research has tended to choose between explanations emphasizing the class factor in understanding ethnic voting (e.g., Peled, 2001; Shalev and Levy, 2005; Levy, 2015) and those that underscore identity and culture (e.g., Mizrahi, 2016). Thus, unintentionally, they have left the study of ethnic politics captive to a rigid conception of social (ethnic) categories. Whereas political behavior research continues to view the variables of ethnicity and class as assimilated into the political cleavage of collective identity (e.g., Shamir et al., 2017), critical research has drawn static boundaries between the different categories of identity (e.g., Levy, 2017b).

The literature has therefore been blind to social dynamics and the ways in which the intersection of class, ethnicity, space, and gender frequently shapes these categories and their boundaries (Anthias, 2013). Due to its empirical limitations, this study does not purport to offer answers to all of these aspects. We merely point out that when it comes to Mizrahim as a category in sociopolitical analysis, one should take note both of the multiple marginalities to which Mizrahim belong (Hashash, 2017) and their patterns of mobility as a group falling in between the Ashkenazim and the Palestinian citizens of Israel under one, Zionist incorporation regime (Shafir and Peled, 2002; Cohen and Leon, 2008). Our hypotheses examine the interactions between ethnic identity, class background, level of religiosity, and policy positions. Our findings indicate that, while all of these factors are relevant, none of them stands on its own.

Our most striking finding concerns the first two hypotheses, indicating that ethnicity is a factor that affects voting by way of class (Shalev and Levy, 2005). This is evident in the voting pattern for Blue and White, where an increase in Mizrahi voters' level of education was directly proportionate to their preference for that party. Hence, the recent educational mobility of Mizrahim, which implies social class mobility, corroborates the explanation that a lack of academic education increases the tendency of Mizrahim to vote for Likud (or for the political right in general). Of course, this finding requires further research that delves deeper into this relationship with more comprehensive data on education and class.

While the connection between ethnicity and class lies at the core of critical research, the role of cultural factors, reflected in religiosity levels and perceptions of collective identity, also needs to be clarified. In research on political behavior the prevailing explanation is that religiosity trumps ethnicity. Accordingly, the left-right continuum reflects the meanings that voters give to their political identity, which is based on policy preferences (once identified as dove-hawk), rather than the ethnic ties that constitute their collective identity (Shamir et al., 2017, p. 169). Another explanation claims that there are different and distinct worlds of meaning and interpretation that dictate

206 *Gal Levy, Maoz Rosenthal, and Ishak Saporta*

Mizrahi and Ashkenazi political behavior (Mizrachi, 2016). This thesis is consistent with the current widespread tendency to see the inclination toward traditionalism as an inherent feature of Mizrahi identity. However, it ignores the fact that religious belief takes many varied forms in people's self-definition, including among the middle class (Kaplan and Werczberger, 2015: 579).

We demonstrated that the connection between religiosity and social status has led to different voting patterns among one ethnic group. Therefore, the tendency to see one ethnic group as religiously homogeneous and in a way that determines its voting patterns needs to be reexamined. Consequently, any investigation of the connection between ethnicity, religiosity, class, and voting patterns among any social group in Israel requires an examination that accounts for the intersection of religious identity with other identities. We are left, then, with our important finding, which also requires further research. The vote for the two parties, which represented the axis of the political battle in Israel in three of the 2019–2021 election campaigns, shows that ethnic politics are part of Israeli politics and reveals the need to understand them from a perspective that examines the variety of intersections involved. The frequent 2019–2021 campaigns were fertile ground for voters to reassess their party preferences and attachments. It may well be that a close examination of each of these rounds' results will provide a better assessment of the voting patterns' volatility. However, it would appear that the ubiquitous statements deeming the Mizrahim or Ashkenazim as social categories, and therefore coherently partisan, need to be refined and updated.

Notes

1 We thank Michal Mor-Millerman and Yuval Bartov for their assistance in preparing this chapter. We are also grateful to Dana Kaplan, Amnon Cavari and Sivan Hirsch-Heffler for fruitful discussions, and to the editors of this volume and the two anonymous referees for helpful comments. We are solely responsible for any mistakes and errors.
2 We use the phrase "ethnic identity" to refer to the phenomenon of the political presence of differences in the country of origin and cultural identity among Jews in Israel.
3 www.tau.ac.il/~ines/2019.html
4 As a control, we used another variable based on the respondents' subjective definition of self-identity. This variable included four categories: Ashkenazi, Mizrahi, Mixed, and others. The gamma correlation between the subjective identity variable and the variable we constructed to define ethnicities by place of birth was 0.544 and significant. Due to the high correlation between the two variables, we saw no point in measuring them separately and focus on the structural place of birth variable.
5 We also tested our models using the original variable that included five levels of religiosity. This variable showed minor differences between the traditional groups included in it. Therefore, for simplicity we used the three-level variable of religiosity.
6 Support for socialism versus for capitalism had weak correlations that were for the most part not significant vis-à-vis the other variables.
7 As a robustness test, we also used expenditures, which led to results very similar to those of education (the correlation between the two variables is 0.245 and statistically significant).

Ethnic Demons and Class Specters   207

8 Since most of the variables are nominal and ordinal, we use Goodman Kruskal's gamma index using R software's DescTools package.
9 We estimated the models using the mfx package in R; the diagrams were created using the R sjPlot package.
10 See the Institute for Policy and Strategy website: www.idc.ac.il/he/research/ips/pages/4tribes.aspx

References

Anthias, Floya. 2013. "Hierarchies of Social Location, Class and Intersectionality: Towards Translocational Frame." *International Sociology* 28 (1):121–138.

Arian, Asher and Michal Shamir. 2008. "A Decade Later, the World Had Changed, the Cleavage Structure Remained: Israel 1996—2006." *Party Politics* 14 (6): 685–705.

Bargsted, Mathew A. and Orit Kedar. 2009. "Coalition-Targeted Duvergerian Voting: How Expectations Affect Voter Choice under Proportional Representation." *American Journal of Political Science* 53 (2): 307–323.

Cavari, Amnon, Maoz Rosenthal and Ilana Shpaizman. June 2021. "The Government of Change: Not Only Personal." The Israeli Policy Agendas Project, Interdisciplinary Center (IDC), Herzliya. www.idc.ac.il/he/research/cap/pages/not-just-personal.aspx [Hebrew].

Cohen, Uri and Nissim Leon. 2008. "The Question of the Mizrahi Middle Class in Israel." *Alpayim* 32: 83–101 [Hebrew].

Cohen, Uri and Nissim Leon. 2011. *The Herut Movement's Central Committee and the Mizrahim, 1965–1977: From Patronizing Partnership to Competitive Partnership.* Jerusalem: The Israel Democracy Institute [Hebrew].

Cohen, Yinon, Noah Lewin-Epstein, and Amit Lazarus. 2019. "Mizrahi-Ashkenazi Educational Gaps in the Third Generation." *Research in Social Stratification and Mobility* 59: 25–33.

Eribon, Didier. 2019. *Returning to Reims*. Tel Aviv: Am Oved (translation: M. Ben-Naftali).Gandesha, Samir. 2018. "Understanding Right and Left Populism." In *Critical Theory and Authoritarian Populism*, edited by J. Morelock, 49–70. London: University of Westminster Press.

Getmansky, Anna and Thomas Zeitzoff. 2014. "Terrorism and Voting: The Effect of Rocket Threat on Voting in Israeli Elections." *American Political Science Review* 108 (3): 588–604.

Greenwald, Gilad and Maoz Rosenthal. 2021. "Stability, Diversity, and Ideology in Media Agenda Setting of Public Policy Issues in Israel's 2019–20 Election Period." *Misgarot Media* 20: 8–34 [Hebrew].

Grinberg, Lev Luis. 2013. "The J14 Resistance Mo(ve)ment: The Israeli Mix of Tahrir Square and Puerta Del So." *Current Sociology* 61 (4): 491–509.

Grinberg, Lev Luis. 2019. "Settler Disunity: Examining Israel's Political Stalemate." *Catalyst* 3 (3): 115–131.

Grinberg, Lev Luis. 2021. "Tribalism is a Perverse Type of Identity Politics." *Haaretz* June 4. www.haaretz.co.il/opinions/.premium-1.9736645 [Hebrew].

Hashash, Yali. 2017. "We Are All Jews: On 'White Trash,' Mizrahim and Multiple Marginalities within the Hegemony." *Theory and Criticism* 48: 249–264. [Hebrew].

Herzog, Hanna. 1986. *Political Ethnicity – The Image and the Reality*. Tel Aviv: Hakibbutz Hameuchad. [Hebrew].

208   Gal Levy, Maoz Rosenthal, and Ishak Saporta

Hirsch-Hoefler, Sivan, Daphna Canetti, and Ami Pedahzur. 2010. "Two of a Kind? Voting Motivations for Populist Radical Right and Religious Fundamentalist Parties." *Electoral Studies* 29 (4): 678–690.

Jamal, Amal. 2017. *Arab Civil Society in Israel*. Tel Aviv: Hakibbutz Hameuchad [Hebrew].

Kaplan, Dana, and Rachel Werczberger. 2015. "Jewish New Age and the Middle Class: Jewish Identity Politics in Israel under Neoliberalism" *Sociology* 51 (3): 575–591.

Katz-Gerro, Tally, Sharon Raz, and Meir Yaish, 2009. "How do Class, Status, Ethnicity, and Religiosity Shape Cultural Omnivorousness in Israel?" *Journal of Cultural Economics* 33 (1): 1–17.

Kenig, Ofer and Or Tuttnauer. 2017. "The decline of the large mainstream parties." In *The Elections in Israel 2015*, edited by Michal Shamir and Gideon Rahat, 21–46. New Brunswick: Transaction Publishers.

Levy, Gal, 2005. "From subjects to citizens: On educational reforms and the demarcation of the 'Israeli-Arabs'." *Citizenship Studies* 9 (3): 271–291.

Levy, Gal. 2015. "Shas, the Ethnic Demon and Mizrahi Politics." In *The Elections in Israel 2013*, edited by Michal Shamir, 157–179. New Brunswick: Transaction Publishers.

Levy, Gal. 2017a. "Shake the Tree or Rock the Boat: The Not Nice Protest and Radical Democracy in Israel." *World Political Science* 13 (2): 303–31.

Levy, Gal. 2017b. "Mizrahi Politics and the Question of Religion: The Multiple Citizenship Paradigm Revisited." *The Public Sphere* 13: 197–225. [Hebrew].

Levy, Gal and Ze'ev Emmerich. 2001. "Shas and the 'Ethnic Phantom'." In *Shas: The Challenge of Israeliness*, edited by Yoav Peled, 126–158. Tel Aviv: Miskal – Yediot Aharonot & Hemed Books [Hebrew].

Lewin-Epstein, Noah and Yinon Cohen. 2019. "Ethnic Origin and Identity in the Jewish Population of Israel." *Journal of Ethnic and Migration Studies* 45 (11): 2118–2137.

Lewin-Epstein, Noah and Or Raviv. 2016. "The Correlates of Household Debt in Late Life." In *Socioeconomic Inequality in Israel* edited by Nabil Khattab, Sami Miaari, and Haya Stier. 13–40. New York: Palgrave Macmillan.

Lissak, Moshe. 1999. *The Mass Immigration in the Fifties: The Failure of the Melting Pot Policy*. Jerusalem: Bialik Institute [Hebrew].

Mintz, Alex. 2017. "A New National Order for Israel: Opportunities and Risks in a Complex and Changing Reality." In *The Shared Israeliness Initiative*, edited by Alex Mintz, 15–20. Herzliya: IDC [Hebrew].

Mizrachi, Nissim. 2016. "Sociology in the Garden: Beyond the Liberal Grammar of Contemporary Sociology." *Israel Studies Review* 31 (1): 36–65.

Peled, Yoav. 2001. "A Puzzle Called Shas." In *Shas: The Challenge of Israeliness*, edited by Yoav Peled. 52–74. Tel Aviv: Miskal – Yediot Aharonot & Hemed Books. [Hebrew].

Plaut, Pnina. O., and Steven E. Plaut, 2016. "Household Inequality and the Contribution of Spousal Correlations." In *Socioeconomic Inequality in Israel*, edited by Nabil Khattab, Sami Miaari, and Haya Stier. 41–57. New York: Palgrave Macmillan.

Ram, Uri. 2017. "Sociology in the Age of Netanyahu: Critical Trends in Israeli Sociology at the Beginning of the 21st Century." *Megamot* 2: 13–68 [Hebrew].

Ram, Uri and Dani Filk. 2013. "The 14th of July of Daphni Leef: The Rise and Fall of the Social Protest." *Theory and Criticism* 41: 17–43. [Hebrew].

Roemer, John. E., Lee Woojin and Karine Van der Straeten. 2007. *Racism, Xenophobia, and Distribution: Multi-Issue Politics in Advanced Democracies*. Cambridge: Harvard University Press.

Rosenhek, Zeev and Michael Shalev. 2014. "The Political Economy of Israel's 'Social Justice' Protests: A Class and Generational Analysis." *Contemporary Social Science* 9 (1): 31–48.

Rosenthal, Maoz. 2019. "When Does Descriptive Representation Become Substantive? Systematic Luck, Social Power and the Allocation of Resources." *Ethnicities* 19 (6): 1015–1037.

Rosenthal, Maoz. 2020a. "Only External Intervention Would Yield Government Formation." *Ynet* February 6. www.ynet.co.il/articles/0,7340,L-5673123,00.html [Hebrew].Rosenthal, Maoz. 2020b. "The Power and Importance of the Political Campaign." *Globes*, March 7. www.globes.co.il/news/article.aspx?did=1001320489 [Hebrew].

Rosenthal, Maoz, Hani Zubida and David Nachmias. 2018. "Voting Locally Abstaining Nationally: Descriptive Representation, Substantive Representation and Minority Voters' Turnout." *Ethnic and Racial Studies* 41 (9): 1632–1650.

Sagiv, Talia. 2014. *On the Fault Line: Israelis of Mixed Ethnicity*, Tel Aviv: Hakibbutz Hameuchad [Hebrew].

Sasson-Levy, Orna and Avi Shoshana. 2014. "Hishtaknezut: Ethnic Performance and Its Failure." *Theory and Criticism* 42: 71–97 [Hebrew].

Schwartz, Ori. 2014. "'Very Ashkenazi Iraqis': On Authenticity, Class Boundaries, and the Metaphoricity of Ethnic Language in Israel." *Theory and Criticism* 43: 103–130 [Hebrew].

Semyonov, Moshe and Noah Lewin-Epstein. 2011. "Wealth Inequality: Ethnic Disparities in Israeli Society." *Social Forces*, 89 (3): 935–959.

Shafir, Gershon and Yoav Peled. 2002. *Being Israeli: The Dynamics of Multiple Citizenship*. Cambridge: Cambridge University Press.

Shalev, Michael and Gal Levy. 2005. "The Winners and Losers of 2003: Ideology, Social Structure and Political Change." In *The Elections in Israel 2003*, edited by Asher Arian and Michal Shamir, 167–186. New Brunswick: Transaction Publishers.

Shamir, Michal and Asher Arian. 1982. "The Ethnic Vote in Israel's 1981 Elections." *Electoral Studies* 1 (3): 315–331.

Shamir, Michal and Asher Arian. 1999. "Collective Identity and Electoral Competition in Israel." *American Political Science Review* 93 (2): 265–277.

Shamir, Michal, Shira Dvir-Gvirsman and Raphael Ventura. 2017. "Taken Captive by the Collective Identity Cleavage: Left and Right in the 2015 Elections." In *The Elections in Israel 2015*, edited by Michal Shamir and Gideon Rahat, 139–164. New Brunswick: Transaction Publishers.

Smooha, Sammy. 1984. "Three Approaches to the Sociology of Ethnic Relations in Israel." *Megamot* 28, 2–3, 169–206 [Hebrew].

Stern, Itay. 2020. "Avishai Ben-Haim: 'Netanyahu Is a Symbol, Harming Him Is Harming Religious and National Sentiment.'" *Ha'aretz*, September 26. www.haar etz.co.il/gallery/media/.premium-MAGAZINE-1.9183342 Viewed January 26, 2021 [Hebrew].

Swirski, Shlomo. 1981. *Not Backward but Held Back*. Haifa: Mahvarot LeBikoret [Hebrew].

Talshir, Gayil. 2015. "The New Israelis: From Social Protest to Political Parties." In *The Elections in Israel 2013*, edited by: Michal Shamir, 31–58. New Brunswick: Transaction Publishers.

Yaish, Meir and Limor Gabay-Egozi. 2019. "Intracohort Trends in Ethnic Earnings Gaps: The Role of Education." *Socius* 5: 1–14.

Appendix

Table 9A.2 Multivariate models

Variables	Mizrahi born abroad voting Likud	Mizrahi born in Israel voting Likud	"Mixed" Mizrahi voting Likud	Mizrahi born abroad voting Blue and White	Mizrahi born in Israel voting Blue and White	"Mixed" Mizrahi voting Blue and White
(Intercept)	−4.52***	−4.44***	−4.21***	−1.54**	−1.68**	−1.45*
	(−0.54)	(−0.56)	(−0.52)	(−0.57)	(−0.61)	(−0.57)
Opposition to a two-state solution	0.85***	0.80***	0.81***	−0.47***	−0.47***	−0.48***
	(−0.1)	(−0.1)	(−0.1)	(−0.08)	(−0.07)	(−0.08)
Opposition to the influence of religion on the state	−0.24**	−0.23**	−0.24**	0.33***	0.35***	0.34***
	(−0.09)	(−0.09)	(−0.09)	(−0.1)	(−0.09)	(−0.09)
Mizrahi born abroad	1.15			−13.02***		
	(−1.27)			(−0.83)		
Traditional	1.70***	1.89***	1.52***	0.65	1.05	0.96
	(−0.46)	(−0.48)	(−0.46)	(−0.54)	(−0.58)	(−0.53)
Secular	1.04*	1.20*	0.91*	1.01	1.05	0.9
	(−0.47)	(−0.49)	(−0.45)	(−0.52)	(−0.57)	(−0.51)
No academic education	0.06	0.59	0.08	−0.21	−0.17	−0.28
	(−0.43)	(−0.45)	(−0.42)	(−0.62)	(−0.69)	(−0.62)
Mizrahi born abroad traditional	−0.28			14.79***		
	(−1.51)			(−1.19)		
Mizrahi born abroad secular	0.01			12.61***		
	(−1.43)			(−1.17)		
Mizrahi born abroad with no academic education	1.73			−0.02		
	(−1.72)			(−1.02)		
Traditional with no academic education	0.47	0.02	0.69	−0.06	−0.38	−0.38
	(−0.53)	(−0.55)	(−0.52)	(−0.71)	(−0.76)	(−0.7)
Secular with no academic education	0.35	−0.35	0.29	−0.03	0.05	0.15
	(−0.51)	(−0.53)	(−0.5)	(−0.65)	(−0.72)	(−0.65)
Traditional Mizrahi born abroad with no academic education	−1.77			−1.76		
	(−1.94)			(−1.4)		

Table 9A.2 Cont.

Variables	Mizrahi born abroad voting Likud	Mizrahi born in Israel voting Likud	"Mixed" Mizrahi voting Likud	Mizrahi born abroad voting Blue and White	Mizrahi born in Israel voting Blue and White	"Mixed" Mizrahi voting Blue and White
Secular Mizrahi born abroad with no academic education	−3.03 (−1.98)			1.05 (−1.41)		
Mizrahi born in Israel		0.88 (−0.83)			0.53 (−1.12)	
Traditional Mizrahi born in Israel		−1.53 (−1.15)			−1.37 (−1.44)	
Secular Mizrahi born in Israel		−1.14 (−0.99)			−0.21 (−1.17)	
Mizrahi born in Israel with no academic education		−2.77* (−1.34)			−0.62 (−1.58)	
Traditional Mizrahi born in Israel with no academic education		3.30* (−1.6)			1.43 (−1.9)	
Secular Mizrahi born in Israel with no academic education		3.42* (−1.52)			0.16 (−1.69)	
"Mixed" Mizrahi			−13.88*** (−0.6)			−13.19*** (−0.76)
Traditional mixed			14.25*** (−0.86)			11.86*** (−1.11)
Secular mixed			14.46*** (−0.87)			13.67*** (−0.91)
Mixed with no academic education			14.49*** (−1.01)			0.65 (−0.93)
Traditional mixed with no academic education			−15.83*** (−1.32)			1.04 (−1.42)
Secular mixed with no academic education			−15.18*** (−1.32)			−1.24 (−1.2)

(*continued*)

Table 9A.2 Cont.

Variables	Mizrahi born abroad voting Likud	Mizrahi born in Israel voting Likud	"Mixed" Mizrahi voting Likud	Mizrahi born abroad voting Blue and White	Mizrahi born in Israel voting Blue and White	"Mixed" Mizrahi voting Blue and White
Model indices						
AIC	942.82	959.92	961.89	1010.24	1016.61	1012.64
BIC	1011.94	1029.05	1031.03	1079.37	1085.75	1081.78
Log likelihood	−457.41	−465.96	−466.95	−491.12	−494.31	−492.32
Deviance	914.82	931.92	933.89	982.24	988.61	984.64
N	1030	1031	1031	1030	1031	1031

Note: The regression table distinguishes between six models: three models of different ethnic groups (Mizrahim born abroad, Mizrahim born in Israel, and "mixed" Mizrahim born in Israel) and their vote for Likud, and three other models of their vote for Blue and White. Within each model we examine the impact of the independent variables on their own (policy positions, ethnicity, level of secularity relative to religious people, and lack of academic education compared to those with an academic education), interactions between two independent social variables, and interactions between the three social variables. Due to the relationships between the ethnic groups and the relatively small number of respondents in some of the groups (mainly the mixed Mizrahim), we use robust standard errors.

10 Joint Lists in Israeli Politics

Assaf Shapira

In Knesset elections, citizens vote for a list of candidates. A list can represent a single party, but it can also represent two parties or more – such a list is called "joint list." The 2019–2020 elections (less so in 2021) were characterized by a multitude of joint lists: in the 2020 elections six of the eight lists elected to the Knesset were joint lists. Thus, unsurprisingly, issues relating to such lists gained much public and political attention – both before the election, including the dramatic formation of joint lists hours before the deadline for their submission to the Central Elections Committee, and after, when these lists subsequently split.

Joint lists have accompanied the Israeli political system since its inception. They are also not unique to Israel. Theoretical and comparative studies have noted the mainly (albeit not exclusively) positive effects of these lists on the political system. Accordingly, the current chapter offers a thorough review and analysis of joint lists in Israel over the years, seeking to understand their political role. It begins with theoretical and comparative background information. Thereafter, it reviews the legal background required to understand the phenomenon of joint lists in Israel, subsequently presenting the research questions and hypotheses. In the following section, I present an empirical analysis of the joint lists represented in the Knesset over the years, identifying the main trends. A separate discussion is dedicated to the 2019–2021 elections. The final section examines the broad implications of joint lists for Israel's political system and this study's contribution to the general literature.

Based on the findings of this study, joint lists in Israel have changed significantly since the 1990s, both quantitatively, with more joint lists elected to the Knesset, and qualitatively, with more parties joining such lists in order to pass the electoral threshold (and not for other reasons), and with increasing numbers of parties that previously failed to pass the threshold elected as part of joint lists. In addition, cooperation between parties that are part of the same joint list no longer leads to actual unification, and there has been a moderate decline in the stability of joint lists during a Knesset term and their continuity between two sequential elections. These changes stem from a variety of institutional and cultural characteristics, such as the raising of the electoral threshold, the method of allocating Knesset seats, and rules regarding

DOI: 10.4324/9781003267911-13

214   *Assaf Shapira*

party finance and party splits, as well as the broad phenomenon known as "the crisis of political parties," in particular political personalization and the direct election of the prime minister. Consequently, many of the advantages that the comparative politics literature attributes to joint lists are not evident in Israel today.

10.1 Theoretical and Comparative Background

10.1.1 Pre-electoral Coalitions

Scholars generally regard joint lists as a specific type of pre-electoral coalition. Pre-electoral coalitions are defined as various types of cooperation between two or more independent parties in parliamentary elections, provided that cooperation is public and exceeds one constituency (Golder, 2006). This is quite a widespread phenomenon. Indeed, a study of 233 elections in 19 developed democracies between 1970 and 2011 found that in 47% of cases, pre-electoral coalitions were elected to parliament (Tillman, 2015). In recent years, research concerning this issue has gained momentum, especially in the context of Eastern European democracies (Marek and Powell, 2011; Ibenskas and Sikk, 2017).

There are several distinct types of pre-electoral coalitions (Golder, 2006). For example, parties can cooperate by supporting common candidates: in democracies that use single-member districts, two parties, x and y, may decide in advance not to run against each other in all or some constituencies. In constituencies where party x is not running, it publicly supports party y's candidate and vice versa.

The specific type of pre-electoral coalition known as a joint candidate list is relevant to party-list electoral systems. In this format, two or more parties compete together using a single joint list of candidates; if the list is elected to parliament, its candidates become a single parliamentary party group – known in Israel as a Knesset faction. Koren and Shapira (1997) distinguish between two subtypes of joint lists, using the term "electoral alignment" to describe the subtype to which I refer in this study: the parties on the joint list maintain separate formal status, distinct institutions, independent budgets, and choose their candidates separately.

10.1.2 Factors Contributing to the Formation of Joint Lists

Besides the almost-obvious factors of ideological proximity (Golder, 2006), and, in the era of personal politics, the nature of personal relations between party leaders, the main factor motivating the formation of joint lists is an electoral system that makes it difficult for small parties to be elected to parliament or favors large lists (Golder, 2006; Tillman, 2015). Notable examples for this are a high electoral threshold, small constituencies (in terms of the number of MPs elected in each constituency), formula for allocating seats that benefit large lists (e.g., the D'Hondt method), the granting of "bonus" seats to the largest list (e.g., the Italian parliamentary elections in 2006–2013), and granting the initial right to form a government to the head of this list (e.g., in Greece and Bulgaria).

Various models try to predict when parties have an electoral interest in joining or creating a joint list. Most are based on Downs' (1957) spatial model. Some claim that this is especially worthwhile in "saturated" systems, wherein many parties compete for a relatively small number of seats in parliament, making it difficult for each party to gain additional votes (Van De Wardt and Van Witteloostuijn, 2019). In such a situation, each party usually occupies a specific "niche," and any attempt to deviate from that niche requires a "battle" against parties from the same political bloc, which may be mutually harmful (due to a mutually negative campaign) and affect postelection cooperation.

In addition, scholars argue that joint lists can attract more voters (beyond the voters of the separate parties), perhaps due to voters' tendency to choose larger lists (Kaminski, 2001). An official union between parties may also facilitate a "rebranding" of the new party, making it easier to appeal to wider publics (Bélanger and Godbout, 2010). Joining or creating a joint list also helps parties save financial resources by operating only one large campaign organization (Van De Wardt and Van Witteloostuijn, 2019). Yet researchers also note the electoral risk involved in joining a pre-electoral coalition. For instance, supporters of the separate parties may not support the pre-electoral coalition and the ideological compromises it entails (Blais and Indridason, 2007).

Other explanations focus on the relationship between pre-electoral coalitions and government formation. Indeed, some claim that parties join pre-electoral coalitions in order to provide the public with a clear indication of their preferences regarding the future government's composition (Tillman, 2015), and that parties running in such a framework are more likely to join the ruling coalition after the elections (Golder, 2006).

Parties that are part of the same joint list and parliamentary party(ies) group face the dilemma of whether to unite into a single party. The rules in some countries, such as a higher electoral threshold for joint lists compared to lists representing only one party (e.g., the Czech Republic, Italy, Lithuania, Poland, Romania, and Slovakia), encourage full unification. In addition, certain democracies do not allow joint lists to compete as such in elections. In Norway, only a single party or a nonpartisan body can submit a list of candidates. Yet, parties may prefer to continue running on a joint list – rather than uniting – in order to maintain independent ideologies, institutions, budgets, and processes of candidate and leader selection.

10.1.3 Implications for the Political System

The literature focuses on the advantages of joint lists. One such advantage is that they reduce fragmentation in parliament and the government, which may in turn increase government stability (Taagepera and Sikk, 2010) and

216 *Assaf Shapira*

governability (Tuttnauer and Philipov, 2013). Others highlight that a government based on a pre-electoral coalition will enjoy better governance capacity thanks to the ideological proximity between the parties that comprise it (Goodin, Güth, and Sausgruber, 2008). According to another claim, the formation of a joint list made up of independent parties, especially if they represent different sectors, can potentially promote an aggregation of interests and mitigate social rifts and rigid ideological positions. This, because each party must compromise and exercise flexibility in order to achieve cooperation (Sartori, 2005; Reilly, 2006). Joint lists also reduce the risk of harming representation that may result from a full union between parties: the independent parties (that may represent distinct sectors and ideologies) continue to exist and operate within a broader framework.

Pre-electoral coalitions may also increase voters' ability to identify clear pre-electoral alternatives ("pre-electoral identifiability") and limit the alternatives. This may in turn, reduce voter confusion (Marinova, 2015) and increase turnout (Tillman, 2015). Furthermore, a party that is part of a pre-electoral coalition only rarely breaks a pre-electoral promise to support a particular postelection government (Golder, 2006; Martin and Stevenson, 2001).

In addition, joint lists can stabilize the political system by creating a small number of durable lists that compete in each election (Kreuzer and Pettai, 2009). Likewise, joint lists may facilitate future unification between the partner parties: the joint contest helps to reduce the ideological disparity between the parties and to create trust and working relationships between their institutions (Ibenskas, 2016). Such stability is also a condition for politicians' responsiveness and accountability. Indeed, they must contend with the voters, who can reward or punish the list again in the next elections.

Alongside these advantages, the literature also highlights the drawbacks of joint lists, mainly arguing that in some cases the frequency of their formation and disintegration may undermine stability and "confuse" voters (Cox, 1997; Marinova, 2015). In this context, scholars have discerned that the instability of joint lists in Eastern European democracies is an important factor contributing to the more general political uncertainty in these countries (Marinova, 2015; Marek and Powell, 2011).

10.2 Joint Lists in Israel – Legal, Institutional, and Historical Background

10.2.1 Legal Background

Currently, Israeli law distinguishes between a party, a list, and a (Knesset) faction. A party is an extra-parliamentary institution that is regulated according to rules that appear in the Parties Law, 1992. In the run-up to elections, one or more parties can submit a list of candidates to the Central Elections Committee. According to the Knesset Elections Law, 1969, a list submitted by two or more parties is called a "joint list of candidates." Such a list is submitted by representatives of all relevant parties, and the party affiliation of each candidate is specified (Sections 57(b)–57(c) of the Knesset Elections Law). Joint lists also submit a general agreement concerning their joint association (Section 59(2) of the Knesset Law, 1994) and agreements relating to party funding (Party Finance Law, 1973).

Once a list is elected to the Knesset, it becomes a faction (what is called in research literature "the parliamentary party"). Just like a list, a faction can consist of Members of Knesset (MKs) who represent more than one party. During the Knesset's term, factions can split (see below) and merge.

The Parties Law, which determines the fundamental aspects of political parties, was enacted in 1992. Prior to this, there was no formal definition of a party. Only thereafter could a body be officially registered at the Parties Registrar as a "party." This new law also affected the submission of candidate lists: previously, lists were submitted either by factions represented in the outgoing Knesset or by a certain number of voters. In 1992, the Knesset Elections Law was also amended, dictating that only parties can submit a list of candidates. Nevertheless, the term "party" appeared in legislation prior to 1992 – including the Elections Law (Propaganda Methods), 1959, and the Party Finance Law, 1973.

Beyond the additional information and agreements submitted by joint lists, there are relatively few legal differences between joint lists/factions and other lists/factions. Notably, unlike several other democracies, Israel does not have a higher threshold for joint lists. The existing differences relate mainly to two aspects, which are discussed in the next section: funding and splits.

10.2.2 Institutional Rules

Increased Electoral Threshold. According to the literature, a high threshold encourages smaller parties to join or create joint lists. This is particularly pronounced in saturated political systems, such as the one that developed in Israel in the 1990s (see below). The threshold in Israel significantly increased since the 1990s – in the first Knesset elections (1949) it stood at 0.83%, before the 1951 elections it was increased to 1%, and later to 1.5% (before the 1992 elections), 2% (2006), and 3.25% (2015). There are examples of joint lists created ahead of the elections in which the threshold increased – Meretz and United Torah Judaism in 1992 and The Joint List in 2015.

Formulae for the Allocation of Surplus Seats. Since amendment no. 4 to the Knesset Elections Law was instituted in 1973 (the "Bader-Ofer law"), larger lists possess an advantage in terms of the distribution of Knesset seats. Until then (apart from the 1949 elections), seats were distributed according to the Hare quota formula, which "ignores" the size of the list. Since then, the D'Hondt method has been used to distribute surplus seats, in a way that favors large lists.

Party Finance Rules. The rules outlined in the Party Finance Law of 1973, entitle parties to get both ongoing public funding and public funding for elections. They give small parties a clear financial incentive to join or create joint lists that are expected to pass the electoral threshold: Only parties represented in the Knesset are entitled to ongoing funding, and only parties that won seats in elections are entitled to election funding (in 1994 it was determined that a list which received at least 1% of the vote but did not pass the threshold would also receive funding). Subsequently, the raising of the threshold increased the incentive for smaller parties to join or create joint lists that are expected to pass the new, higher threshold.

With regard to party funding, since the enactment of the Party Finance Law in 1973, every party represented in the Knesset has received ongoing funding. However, between 1973 and 1994, the monthly funding depended solely on the number of seats the party held in the Knesset (it was equal to the number of seats × 5% of one funding unit).[1] Therefore, if two parties that were members of a joint faction united into one party, the funding of the united party would simply be equal to the funding of the two separate parties together. However, an amendment to the Party Finance Law in 1994 supplied separate parties that are part of a joint faction a financial incentive not to unite: this amendment stipulates that each party receives an additional monthly funding, equal to 5% of one funding unit (today 6%), beyond the amount each party receives based on its number of seats. As of June 2021, the supplement given to each separate party, equal to 6% of a funding unit, is 83,316 NIS per month. Therefore, if two parties that are members of a joint faction unite, they "lose" this amount. Indeed, in the 24th Knesset, the two parties that make up United Torah Judaism, Agudat Yisrael and Degel HaTorah, receive total monthly funding of 749,844 NIS; if the parties were to unify, their funding would be reduced to 666,528 NIS.

In the past, joint lists enjoyed a similar advantage over single parties regarding the expenditure ceiling in the elections (the maximum amount that the list is allowed to spend during the elections period or for election purposes). However, this advantage was abolished in 2018 as part of amendment to the Party Finance Law.

Party Splitting Rules. In many established democracies, "soft" sanctions are imposed on MPs who leave their faction in the middle of a parliamentary term (this phenomenon has various names, among them party splitting, defection, party-switching, and floor-crossing). "Rigid" sanctions, that is, ousting those who split from parliament, are rare in established democracies (Janda, 2009). Soft sanctions include a ban on joining an existing faction or forming a new faction, meaning that the defector remains an independent/ single MP; and restrictions on his/her ability to fulfill various parliamentary positions, especially in committees. In some cases, defectors are exempt from some or all of the restrictions if they meet various conditions, such as a minimum number of defectors (Council of Europe, 2014).

Similarly, Israel also imposes sanctions on defectors unless they meet various conditions (see below). In this respect, there is a striking difference between a faction representing one party and a joint faction: independent parties that are members of a joint faction can split at any time without incurring any sanctions. This rule has two effects. First, parties have an incentive to run in elections as a joint list instead of uniting into a single party. As such, they can later split if they so desire (they can also plan to do so in advance). Second, the possibility of splitting without sanctions can undermine the stability of joint lists.

Until 1991, there were no explicit formal rules regarding the splitting of factions. MKs could submit a request to split and form a new faction (or join another faction), and the decision on this matter – whether to approve the request or not – was (and still is) in the remit of the Knesset's House Committee. If it did not authorize a defector to form a new faction or join an existing faction, s/he was considered a "single MK" and was denied rights such as membership in committees, and, from 1973, ongoing party funding. A historical survey reveals that all requests to split from a joint faction were approved; other requests were also generally approved, yet not always. Thus, even before 1991, it was easier for joint factions to split compared to factions that did not represent several parties.

In 1991, the Knesset adopted amendments that defined rules and sanctions regarding the splitting of factions. The Knesset Law distinguishes between "segmentation" (*hitpalgut*) and "defection" (*prisha*). Severe sanctions are imposed on defectors: if they do not resign from the Knesset near the date of their defection, they are not entitled to serve as ministers or deputy ministers during that Knesset term and are not entitled to run in the next elections as part of a list that includes a party represented in the current Knesset. Defectors are also not entitled to form a faction or join a faction during the entire term.

As a rule, if at least a third of a faction's members split or if the split occurs in a joint faction, initiated by one of its constituent parties, this constitutes segmentation rather than defection (Section 59 of the Knesset Law; in 2021, it was determined that a split of a group of four faction members also constitutes segmentation). Moreover, the segmentation of at least one-third (and since 2021 – of four) of a faction's members carries one sanction: if it is carried out in the first two years of the Knesset term, the defectors are not entitled to get ongoing funding during the same term. However, segmentation of a joint faction carries no sanctions whatsoever.

10.2.3 Joint Lists and the Crisis of Political Parties

As in many democracies, for several decades the parties in Israel – mainly the large, aggregative (as opposed to niche, radical, or sectorial) parties – have found themselves in the midst of a severe crisis (e.g., Kenig and Tuttnauer, 2017; Dalton and Wattenberg, 2000; Rahat and Kenig, 2018). Albeit with some exceptions, especially the ultra-Orthodox parties, parties have lost their ability to maintain power and stability over time. The result, mainly from the mid-1990s onwards, is an extremely fragmented and unstable party system,

220 *Assaf Shapira*

with high levels of electoral volatility, an increase in the number and power of new parties and lists, and the disappearance of others. The party system, which was previously stable – apart from a short transition period in the mid-1970s, when the dominance of the left bloc was replaced by a balanced two-bloc system – disintegrated during this period and failed to crystallize and stabilize once again. This is a clear case of dealignment (Hazan, 2021).

Two developments that are linked to this crisis demonstrate how it affects joint lists: political personalization and the direct elections for prime minister.

Political Personalization. The significance attributed to politicians increased – both in their own eyes and in the perception of the media and the public – while that of the parties decreased (Rahat and Kenig, 2018). One of the main expressions of it in Israel is the growth in number and power of personal parties: "Parties whose leader founded the party – he 'chooses' himself for the leadership, he selects the party's candidates for elected public offices and determines its policy" (Rahat, 2019: 20; author's translation).

While such parties existed in Israeli politics in the past (e.g., Moshe Dayan's Telem in 1981 elections), over the past decade this phenomenon has expanded considerably. Instead of joining – or remaining in – existing parties, politicians form their own personal parties. Almost all the new parties[2] elected to the Knesset since the 2013 elections were personal parties: Yesh Atid (Yair Lapid), Hatnu'a (Tzipi Livni),[3] Kulanu (Moshe Kahlon), The New Right (Naftali Bennett and Ayelet Shaked), Gesher (Orly Levy-Abekasis), Telem (Moshe Ya'alon), Hosen Yisrael (Benny Gantz), The Green Movement (Stav Shafir), Democratic Israel (Ehud Barak), Derech Eretz (Yoaz Hendel and Zvi Hauser). Even Otzma Yehudit (Itamar Ben-Gvir) and Noam (Avi Ma'oz) possess elements that are typical to personal parties.

The multiplicity of personal parties increased the number of parties that contested for a place in the political arena. This arena became more fragmented and saturated – thus further encouraging the establishment of joint lists. In particular, many personal parties are small, so they tend to compete in the framework of joint lists. However, it is unlikely that they will unite with other parties because consequently the leader will lose his/her position.

Direct Elections for Prime Minister. In 1996–2001, Israel used a unique hybrid government system: the prime minister was directly elected by the public, while the Knesset was elected separately. It affected joint lists in at least three ways. First, this phenomenon greatly reinforced the personalization of politics (Rahat and Kenig, 2018). Second, in the Knesset elections of 1996 and 1999, it motivated the major parties that had nominated candidates for the position of prime minister, Labor, and Likud, to establish joint lists with small parties, thus gaining their support in the race for prime minister (Gesher, Tzomet, and Meimad).

Third, it contributed to the success of small parties (that were not part of a joint list), including new parties (Haderech Hashlishit and Yisrael Be'aliyah in 1996 and Yisrael Beiteinu, the Center Party, and Am Ehad in 1999) and parties that had previously competed on joint lists (Balad and Shinuy in 1999). Indeed, the new system allowed and even encouraged voters to split their vote: to vote in one ballot for their preferred candidate for prime minister, a Labor or Likud candidate, and with the second vote for a small list reflecting a specific ideological position or sectoral identity. As a result, the power of the two largest electoral lists decreased from 76 seats (out of 120) in 1992 to 46 seats in 1999; and the effective number of parliamentary parties, a measure that weighs the number of parties represented in parliament with their size, increased from 4.39 to a peak of 8.69 (Kenig, 2020).

The influence of the direct elections did not fade after this system was abolished in 2001. While the power of the major lists increased again and political fragmentation decreased, the major parties never regained the number of seats they won in previous elections (1965–1992). The direct elections therefore had a long-term effect on the formation and maintenance of a fragmented and saturated political system (thus encouraging the establishment of joint lists).

10.3 Research Questions and Hypotheses

The theoretical and comparative literature on joint lists claims that they can significantly impact the political system. The magnitude of this influence depends mainly on three factors, as tackled by the research questions:

How widespread is the phenomenon of joint lists?
Which parties join or create joint lists?
What is the fate of the joint lists after the elections – do they maintain stability and continuity, and even unite into a single party?

The initial hypotheses, based on the above-mentioned institutional and cultural characteristics of Israel's political system, are: (a) There has been an increase in the scope of the phenomenon over the years, mainly from the 1990s onwards; (b) This increase was mainly caused by small parties that joined joint lists in order to pass the threshold; (c) Since the 1990s, joint lists maintain less stability and continuity than they previously did.

10.4 An Empirical Study of Joint Lists in Israel

The study examined all lists elected to the Knesset from the foundation of the state to the 2021 elections and the parties they represented. A list is a list of candidates submitted to the Central Elections Committee that competed as such in Knesset elections. The formal definition of a party is a little more problematic, because parties, as formal bodies, officially existed in Israel only since the enactment of the Parties Law in 1992. However, parties certainly existed prior to this, and the term "party" appears, as noted, in earlier legislation. Where necessary, I also relied on other characteristics of a party: the name of

222 *Assaf Shapira*

the party and its self-determination (as a party or not), its institutions, and candidate selection procedures.

I identified a total of 73 joint lists composed of 179 parties. Joint lists were elected in all elections except those of 1951 and 1961, each representing two to four parties. The full list appears on the website of the Israel Democracy Institute (Shapira, 2021).

10.4.1 The Scope of the Phenomenon

The data indicates that the number of joint lists has increased over the years: the share of joint lists and of parties competing as part of joint lists that were elected to the Knesset has increased (Figure 10.1), and the lists elected to the Knesset represented more parties (Figure 10.2).

We can discern a moderate increase in the scope of the phenomenon in the 1973 elections through the 1984 elections. In 1973, for the first time, three joint lists were elected to the Knesset, most of the parties were elected as part of joint lists, and the average number of parties per list reached 1.5. Another increase occurred in the 1990s – especially in the elections between 1996 and 2003. This is not surprising: almost all the factors that are expected to lead to an increase in the volume of joint lists – a higher threshold, amendments to the rules on party splitting and party finance, increased political personalization, and direct elections – appeared or strengthened during or shortly before this period. After a decline in the scope of the phenomenon during the first decade of the 2000s, it expanded again and reached a peak in the 2019–2020 elections (see below more on these elections).

There is a strong correlation between the election year and each of the examined variables: the percentage of joint lists elected to the Knesset (Spearman correlation $r = 0.85$, $p<0.05$), the percentage of parties elected to the Knesset in joint lists (Spearman correlation $r = 0.85$, $p<0.05$), and the average number of parties per list (Spearman correlation $r = 0.82$, $p<0.05$).

Figure 10.3 shows the percentage of MKs elected in joint lists. Here, too, we find a clear (albeit lower) correlation between the election year and this variable (Spearman correlation $r = 0.43$, $p<0.05$). During two periods most MKs were elected through joint lists – 1965–1984 and 2019–2020. Indeed, during these periods all the major lists were joint lists, and they were also, relatively speaking, large. This contrasts with the 1996–2006 elections. In these elections joint lists were also a notable phenomenon, but in each election only one large list was a joint one, and in addition the large lists were smaller, due to the influence of the direct elections for prime minister.

10.4.2 Which Parties Join or Create Joint Lists?

I examined two main motivations for joining or creating a joint list: (a) Joining a list that is a governing alternative. I defined a list as a governing alternative if it (or one of the parties within it) were (or were a dominant part of) one of

Joint Lists in Israeli Politics 223

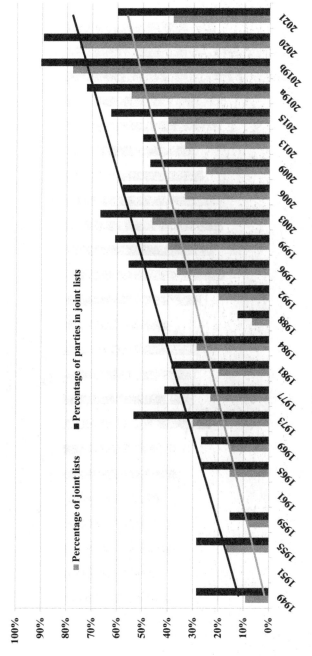

Figure 10.1 Percentage of joint lists elected to the Knesset out of all lists elected; Percentage of parties elected to the Knesset through joint lists out of all parties elected.

224 *Assaf Shapira*

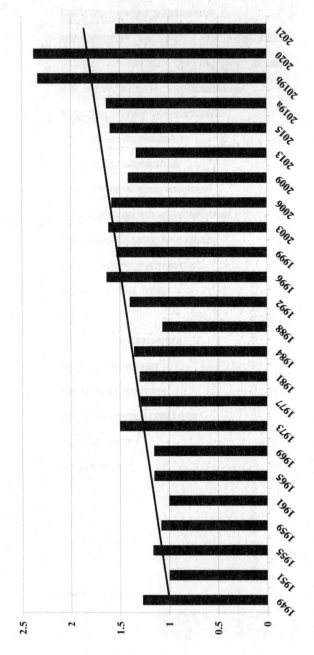

Figure 10.2 Average number of parties in a list elected to the Knesset.

Joint Lists in Israeli Politics 225

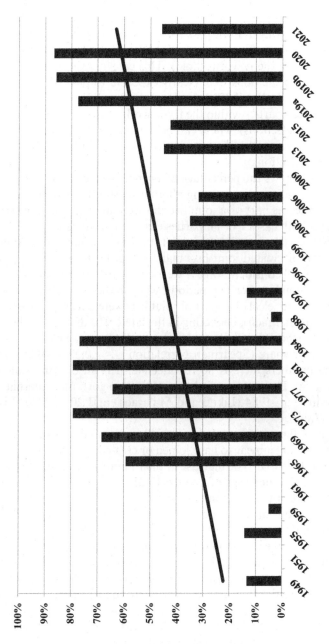

Figure 10.3 Percentage of MKs elected through joint lists.

226   *Assaf Shapira*

the two largest lists in the previous elections or if the list became one of the two largest lists in the election under examination; (b) Fear or danger of not passing the threshold. I included parties that had never before been elected to the Knesset independently (i.e., not as part of a joint list); parties that in the previous elections did not pass (or were part of a list that did not pass) the threshold; and parties that passed it by less than 1% (if the threshold was raised, I looked at the new threshold). This category did not include parties that according to the polls were clearly expected to pass the threshold (e.g., Hosen Yisrael in the April 2019 elections). It also did not include established alliances between parties within the framework of the same joint list (starting with their third elections). These can be seen as "institutionalized" joint lists that survive because of different motivations (e.g., United Torah Judaism since the 1999 elections).

Figure 10.4 shows the percentage of parties elected to the Knesset as part of a joint list that was a governing alternative and the percentage of parties that were elected as part of a joint list and were in danger of not passing the threshold (in both cases – of all parties elected in joint lists).

Before 1965, the few elected joint lists were not governing alternatives; parties joined or created joint lists mainly in order to pass the threshold or out of ideological considerations. If we focus on the period since 1965, there is a clear distinction between two periods: while in the years 1965–1984 the vast majority of parties elected as part of joint lists were part of a governing alternative (Likud/Ma'arach), beginning in the late 1980s they are in the minority. There is a statistically significant correlation between the election year (from 1965) and their share (Spearman correlation r = −0.53, p<0.05). However, in absolute numbers there is no real decline: it is an old phenomenon that continues today. During several elections, the two governing alternatives were joint lists: in 1965–1984 (Likud and Ma'arach) and 2019–2020 (Likud and Blue and White).

In contrast, there has been a significant increase in the number and proportion of parties that appear to have joined or created joint lists in order to pass the electoral threshold. The increase in their number since the 1990s is unsurprising, given the increases of the electoral threshold.[4] A clear correlation is evident between the election year (beginning in 1965) and the percentage of such parties out of all parties elected in joint lists (Spearman correlation r = 0.48, p<0.05).

A noteworthy phenomenon is the increase in the number of parties elected to the Knesset on joint lists that were not previously elected to the Knesset independently – that is, without "proving" their real electoral support. This refers to both parties that did not previously run independently and parties that did so but failed to pass the threshold. Figure 10.5 shows the proportion of these parties out of all parties elected as part of joint lists.[5] It indicates that this is a relatively new phenomenon. It first appeared in the 1984 elections, when two such parties were elected to the Knesset – Tzomet (as part of the Hathi'ya-Tzomet list) and Metzad (as part of the Morasha list). It culminated

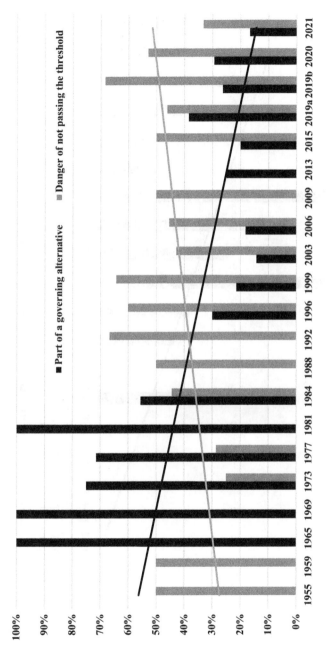

Figure 10.4 Percentage of parties elected as part of a joint list that was a governing alternative, out of all parties elected as part of joint lists; percentage of parties that were in danger of not passing the threshold and were elected as part of a joint list, out of all parties elected as part of joint lists.

Note: The 1949 elections were not included since there was no clear indication which parties were expected to have difficulty passing the threshold and which lists would be a governing alternative; the 1951 and 1961 elections were not included since no joint lists were elected.

228 *Assaf Shapira*

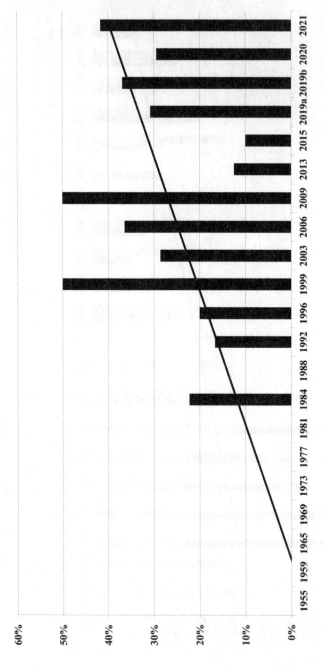

Figure 10.5 Percentage of parties elected through joint lists that were not previously elected to the Knesset independently, out of all parties elected in joint lists.

Note: The 1949 elections were not included since they were the first Knesset elections; the 1951 and 1961 elections were not included since no joint lists were elected.

in the 1999 and 2009 elections and was also notable in the 2019–2021 elections. Ta'al (a personalized Arab party whose leader is Ahmad Tibi) undoubtedly holds the record in this regard: it has been elected to the Knesset continuously since 1999, always as part of a joint list. The Spearman correlation between election year and this variable is 0.78 ($p<0.05$).

10.4.3 Stability and Continuity of Joint Lists

Did joint lists last throughout the Knesset term (until its dissolution or the beginning of the elections period – whichever occurred first)? The question was examined in two ways: (a) How many parties left joint factions based on joint lists during the term, out of the total number of parties elected to the Knesset through joint lists? If all the parties left a certain faction except one party, I also considered this party as leaving the faction (after all, the joint faction no longer exists); (b) How many joint factions based on joint lists fell apart during the term, out of the total number of these factions? The departure of a single party from the joint faction is considered as its disintegration.

No correlations were found between the election year and the number or percentage of parties that left joint factions, nor with the number and percentage of joint factions that disintegrated during the term. In general, Knesset factions based on joint lists do not tend to fall apart at mid-term (although in 2020 this phenomenon was more prominent, see below). Only 14 out of 73 (19.2%) joint lists elected to the Knesset fell apart, with only 25 out of 179 (14%) parties elected as part of joint lists leaving them at mid-term.

However, even if the lists do not fall apart frequently, today, they no longer lead to unification. This is contrary to the past, and also to the claim advanced in the literature that competing in a joint list makes it easier to unite the parties. Four prominent parties in Israeli politics were initially established as joint lists – the Labor, Likud, the National Religious Party (NRP), and Meretz. Since the establishment of Meretz as a joint list in 1992, not a single party was established based on a joint list, though there have been long-term collaborations between parties in the framework of joint lists – most notably Agudat Yisrael and Degel Hatorah, that ran together continuously since the 1992 elections.

Figure 10.6 examines whether joint lists maintain continuity between consecutive elections. For each joint list, I examined whether it ran with the same composition at the next election. On some occasions, it appeared that one party joining or leaving did not de facto affect the stability of the list: the departing/joining party ran as part of the joint list only once; only one MK was elected on its behalf; and it was not represented at all in the following Knesset terms. Thus, I treated the list as stable despite such changes. A joint list whose all components united before the next election was also considered stable.

230 *Assaf Shapira*

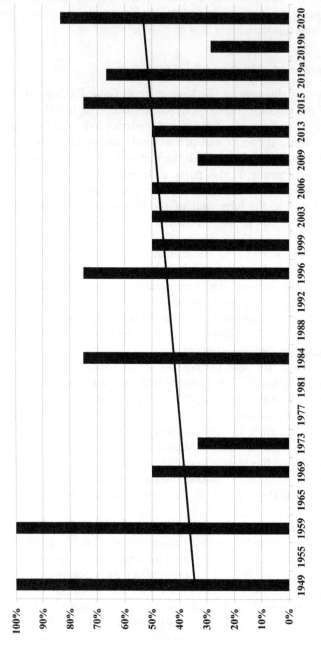

Figure 10.6 Percentage of joint lists elected to the Knesset that did not compete in the same party composition in the next election, out of all joint lists elected to the Knesset.

Note: The 1951 and 1961 elections were not included since no joint lists were elected.

No correlation was found between election year and the share of joint lists that did not maintain continuity at the next election. However, there are signs that continuity has decreased. First, when comparing periods, one-third of all joint lists elected up to 1988 did not continue in the same lineup in the following term, compared with 54% of the joint lists elected since 1992.[6] Second, until the early 1990s, there were several elections in which all joint lists maintained continuity in the next round – something that has not happened since 1992. In addition, the number of joint lists that did not continue in the same composition for the next election peaked after the 2020 elections – five out of six lists.[7]

10.5 Summary of Findings

10.5.1 Summary

As expected, the scope of joint lists has increased significantly: at first in the early 1970s, and more intensively in the mid-1990s and later in the 2019–2020 election cycle. As hypothesized, this increase is mainly due to small parties joining or creating joint lists, apparently in order to pass the threshold. At the same time, in the past and today, joint lists are also formed as a governing alternative. Another finding is that since the 1990s there has been a significant increase in the number and proportion of parties elected through joint lists that had not previously been elected to the Knesset independently. Finally, the degree of stability and continuity of joint lists has moderately declined: cooperation between parties in the same joint list no longer leads to a full union between them, and there has also been a moderate decline in the continuity of joint lists between subsequent elections. This has become a more pronounced phenomenon after the 2020 elections; nevertheless, even today the vast majority of joint lists do not fall apart during the Knesset term.

These changes stem from the combination of a wide range of factors. While the direct election of the prime minister and political personalization contributed to an increase in the number of new, smaller parties seeking election to the Knesset, raising of the threshold forced many of them to join or create joint lists. The advantages that joint lists and factions (also medium and large) offer in terms of party funding, party splitting, and the electoral formula also encourage parties to join or create joint lists. Yet, at the same time, these factors also motivate parties not to unite but to pursue independence. Likewise, they make it easier for them to split during the term. Political personalization, for its part, also makes it difficult for personal parties to relinquish their independent status, sometimes encouraging them to split up and join a new framework. Of course, these factors explain general trends; to understand each case, additional explanations, such as ideological proximity between parties and considerations related to resource-saving or a desire to attract additional publics, are necessary.

232 *Assaf Shapira*

10.5.2 *Spotlight on the 2019–2021 Elections*

In the first three of the four elections of 2019–2021, the increase in the number and proportion of joint lists reached a peak: in terms of the percentage of parties elected through joint lists (90% in the September 2019 elections), the percentage of MKs elected to the Knesset through joint lists (87% in the 2020 elections), and the average number of parties per list (2.375 in the 2020 elections). We may even say that joint lists became the default in these Knesset elections.

The 2021 elections did not continue this trend. It may mark a "return to normality": all indices examining the scope of joint lists marked a decline compared to the previous three elections (see Figures 10.1–10.3). Alongside specific circumstances (such as a split in The Joint List, which stemmed, among other things, from disagreements over its political strategy and ideology), this can be attributed to a "learning curve," especially considering the large number of parties that left joint factions (Blue and White, Labor–Gesher–Meretz, and Yemina) during the 23rd Knesset in order to join the government. Parties that experienced such defections refused to run again in a joint list. For example, Yesh Atid refused to run in these elections together with parties such as Telem, Ha'yisraelim, and Hosen Yisrael (now known as the Blue and White party).

Other trends, however, continued through the 2021 elections, in particular, the instability of joint lists (see Figure 10.6). In the second election in this cycle (September 2019), apart from United Torah Judaism and Blue and White, all other joint lists had new party composition; and in March 2021, all joint lists except United Torah Judaism had new party composition. As noted, the splits after the 2020 elections were particularly unusual, since three joint lists fell apart shortly after the elections. Some of the splits violated promises made before the elections regarding joining or not joining the government – a fairly rare phenomenon, according to the comparative politics literature. However, it is difficult to know if this is the beginning of a new trend – as of August 2021, similar splits did not occur with the establishment of the government after the 2021 elections.

The parties that joined or created joint lists before the 2019–2021 elections were characterized by a multiplicity of personal parties, of parties that had not previously been elected to the Knesset independently (see Figure 10.5), and of parties that were in danger of not passing the threshold (see Figure 10.4). In fact, there is a much overlap between these three characteristics. They all characterize, at least to some extent, Ta'al, The Green Movement, Israel Democratic, Gesher, Telem, The New Right, Derech Eretz, Noam, and Otzma Ye'hudit.

Moreover, a significant portion of these parties apparently did not intend to run independently (Gesher, The New Right, and Otzma Ye'hudit are the exceptions). It seems that these parties served only as a platform via which their leaders could join or create joint lists. Other parties likewise served only as platforms, albeit in a different manner. Kulanu was elected independently twice, but in the run-up to the September 2019 elections it ceased to exist de facto and was "swallowed" by the Likud. The main reason that it continued to maintain its official independence in the September 2019 and 2020 elections, as part of a joint list with the Likud, was financial: the supplement to the ongoing public funding that each separate party receives. Ahi and One Future parties, which competed in joint lists with Likud in the April 2019 and 2021 elections (respectively), were inactive parties that joined the joint list only to serve a complex political agreement. Their representatives were in fact members of other parties (The Jewish Home and The National Union-Tkuma, respectively). It was agreed in advance that after the elections they would split and join their original parties. This, in exchange for these parties agreeing to form joint lists with other parties in the elections, what served the Likud, that feared that small right-wing parties, that were not expected to pass the threshold, would run independently and hurt it chances to form a coalition.

10.6 Discussion

The literature attributes many potential advantages to joint lists. However, a sobering view of the role they play in Israel today reveals that most of these advantages do not materialize. The reasons for this relate to distinctions between different types of joint lists and party systems.

Some of the positive implications of joint lists – especially the stabilization of the political system and their contribution to the responsiveness and accountability of politicians – can only be realized if cooperation within the framework of joint lists is stable over time, especially if it leads to full unification between the parties; This is not the case in Israel, as was evident in the 2019–2021 election cycle. The use of the term "technical bloc" (*block techni*) in these elections expresses it: it refers to joint lists established only for the purpose of elections, knowing that future cooperation between the parties is questionable, at best. If the scenario of the 2020 elections – after which many of the joint lists disintegrate and even violated promises given to voters regarding the formation of a government – is repeated, it may be possible to argue that the damage caused by joint lists outweighs their advantages, as has also been argued regarding Eastern Europe. Such a claim has a broader significance for understanding Israel's political system. Indeed, it may be more appropriate to compare the Israeli political system to new, unstable democracies rather than to veteran established democracies.

However, we cannot deny that joint lists may offer advantages even if the collaborations are unstable. A study examining the rhetoric of joint lists in the 2015, 2019, and 2020 election campaigns in Israel found that they were more pragmatic and less ideological than the rhetoric characterizing the separate parties in the same elections (Akirav, 2020) – in accordance with the

234   *Assaf Shapira*

conventional argument that joint lists contribute to the softening of rigid ideological positions.

The systematic study of joint lists in Israel suggests that it may be valuable to distinguish their role within different types of party systems. From the mid-1960s to the end of the 1970s, when Israel had a stable party system, these were characterized by parties that join stable joint lists in a way that reduced fragmentation in the political system – for example, the cases of National Religious Party, Ma'arach, and Likud. In such a system, new parties/lists that successfully enter the political system are largely the product of a union between existing parties or at least their stable cooperation in the same joint list. Indeed, along with the increase in the number of joint lists from the mid-1960s to the early 1980s, the effective number of parliamentary parties has declined (Kenig, 2020).

In contrast, the second type is characterized by an expansion of political fragmentation, as occurred in Israel since the 1990s. This may be part of the dealignment or "disintegration" of the party system, with growing numbers of new parties joining the political system, some of them join or create joint lists and then split from them. Long-term collaborations between parties, let alone actual unifications, are rare. This is reflected in the (higher) effective number of parliamentary parties since the mid-1990s and the party system's instability (dealignment). In such a situation, not only that joint lists do not help in reducing fragmentation and instability but they escalate them.

Notably, many of the joint lists that ran in Israeli elections during the second period are not the product of actual cooperation between two independent parties and therefore do not contribute to an aggregation of publics and worldviews or the formation of clearer, distinct governing alternatives. Some of the parties elected as part of joint lists do not represent publics and worldviews but are pure personal parties. Some of them were never elected to – or even ran for – the Knesset independently, so the extent of their actual electoral and public support is unclear. In some cases, it even seems that they only serve as platforms for leaders, or that they are "fictitious parties" that continue to exist formally only because of economic or political interests (on "diminished" subtypes of political parties, see Luna et al., 2021). By contrast, an example of a joint list that is composed of independent parties representing different publics and therefore contributes to aggregation is The Joint List. Its member-parties represented at least three distinct publics and worldviews – the Islamist Ra'am, the nationalistic Balad, and the Jewish-Arab Communist Hadash (however, Ra'am left it before the 2021 elections).

Thus, the study suggests that it may be useful to distinguish between a legal-formal definition of cooperation between parties in the framework of a joint list and a substantive definition of such cooperation. Substantive cooperation is public cooperation between at least two parties that have an independent existence, for example in terms of institutions and activists. If a party does not have an actual independent existence, it is difficult to see the list – even if it is formally a joint one – as a substantive pre-electoral coalition, with all the implications attributed to it and its influences on the political system.

Notes

1 A funding unit is an amount on which public party funding is based. As of June 2021, it stands at 1,388,600 NIS.
2 There are different criteria for defining new parties (Barnea and Rahat, 2011). Here I adopt a minimalist definition, which combines two criteria: the name of the party and the formal definition of the party. For example, Hatnu'a and The New Right split from Kadima and The Jewish Home (respectively), but since they began to use a different name and officially (according to the Parties Registrar) represented different bodies, I define them as new.
3 Hatnu'a, like other parties mentioned in this paper, was not the party's official name when it was first elected, but rather the name it was identified with.
4 Though we saw such cases much earlier: even a low threshold can incentivize certain small parties to join or create joint lists, and beyond that there are other motivations, such as ideology, to join or create joint lists.
5 Two parties that were never fully independently elected were not included in this category because they were the dominant part of a list that had previously been elected to the Knesset – Ra'am because since the 1999 elections it "took over" the Ra'am-Mada list; Tkuma/National Union-Tkuma because it was the dominant member of The National Union list in 2009. Until the end of 2012, the party was called Tkuma, and subsequently The National Union-Tkuma.
6 The rationale behind this division is that the lists elected in 1992 have been already influenced from the instability caused by the direct election in 1996.
7 In previous elections their share was higher, but their number was considerably lower: two lists did not continue in the same composition after the 1949 election, one list after 1959, three lists after 1984.

References

Akirav, Osnat. 2020. "The Role of Joint Lists and the New Political Rhetoric in Israel, 2015–2020." *Israel Studies Review* 35 (3): 111–136.

Barnea, Shlomit, and Gideon Rahat. 2011. "'Out with the Old, in with the 'New': What Constitutes a New Party?" *Party Politics* 17 (3): 303–320.

Bélanger, Éric, and Jean-François Godbout. 2010. "Why Do Parties Merge? The Case of the Conservative Party of Canada." *Parliamentary Affairs* 63 (1): 41–65.

Blais, André, and Indridi H. Indridason. 2007. "Making Candidates Count: The Logic of Electoral Alliances in Two-Round Legislative Elections." *The Journal of Politics* 69 (1): 193–205.

Council of Europe. 2014. *Post-Electoral Shifting in Members' Political Affiliation and its Repercussions on the Composition of National Delegations*. Parliamentary Assembly, Committee on Rules of Procedure, Immunities and Institutional Affairs.

Cox, Gary W. 1997. *Making Votes Count: Strategic Coordination in the World's Electoral Systems*. Cambridge: Cambridge University Press.

236 *Assaf Shapira*

Dalton, Russell J., and Martin P. Wattenberg (eds.). 2000. *Parties without Partisans: Political Change in Advanced Industrial Democracies.* Oxford: Oxford University Press.

Downs, Anthony. 1957. "An Economic Theory of Political Action in a Democracy." *Journal of Political Economy* 65 (2): 135–150.

Golder, Sona N. 2006. *The Logic of Pre-Electoral Coalition Formation.* Columbus: Ohio State University Press.

Goodin, Robert E., Werner Güth, and Rupert Sausgruber. 2008. "When to Coalesce: Early Versus Late Coalition Announcement in an Experimental Democracy." *British Journal of Political Science* 38 (1): 181–191.

Hazan, Reuven Y. 2021. "Parties and the Party System of Israel." In *The Oxford Handbook of Israeli Politics and Society*, Reuven Y. Hazan, Alan Dowty, Menachem Hofnung, and Gideon Rahat (eds.), 351–366. New York: Oxford University Press.

Ibenskas, Raimondas. 2016. "Marriages of Convenience: Explaining Party Mergers in Europe." *The Journal of Politics* 78 (2): 343–356.

Ibenskas, Raimondas, and Allan Sikk. 2017. "Patterns of Party Change in Central and Eastern Europe, 1990–2015." *Party Politics* 23 (1): 43–54.

Janda, Kenneth. 2009. "Laws against Party Switching, Defecting, or Floor-Crossing in National Parliaments." *World Congress of the International Political Science Association.* Santiago, Chile.

Kaminski, Marek M. 2001. "Coalitional Stability of Multi-Party Systems: Evidence from Poland." *American Journal of Political Science* 45 (2): 294–312.

Kenig, Ofer. 2020. "2020 Elections – Analysis of Results." Israel Democracy Institute, February 8. www.idi.org.il/articles/30934 [Hebrew].

Kenig, Ofer, and Or Tuttnauer. 2017. "The Decline of the Large Mainstream Parties." In *The Elections in Israel 2015*, Michal Shamir and Gideon Rahat (eds.), 21–46. New York: Routledge.

Koren, Danny, and Boaz Shapira. 1997. *Coalitions: Israeli Politics: 50 Years – 100 Events.* Tel-Aviv: Zmora-Bitan [Hebrew].

Kreuzer, Marcus, and Vello Pettai. 2009. "Party Switching, Party Systems, and Political Representation." In *Political Parties and Legislative Party Switching*, William B. Heller and Carol Mershon (eds.), 265–285. New York: Palgrave Macmillan.

Luna, Juan P., Rafael P. Rodríguez, Fernando Rosenblatt, and Gabriel Vommaro. 2021. "Political Parties, Diminished Subtypes, and Democracy." *Party Politics* 27 (2): 294–307.

Marek, Paulina, and G. Bingham Powell. 2011. "Pre-Election Coalitions and Party System Development: Central European Variations." *APSA 2011 Annual Meeting paper.* available at SSRN https://papers.ssrn.com/sol3/papers.cfm?abstract_id=1903444.

Marinova, Dani. 2015. "A New Approach to Estimating Electoral Instability in Parties." *Political Science Research and Methods* 3 (2): 265–280.

Martin, Lanny W., and Randolph T. Stevenson. 2001. "Government Formation in Parliamentary Democracies." *American Journal of Political Science* 45 (1): 33–50.

Rahat, Gideon. 2019. *The Decline of the Group and the Rise of the Star(s): From Party Politics to Personal Politics.* Jerusalem: The Israel Democracy Institute [Hebrew].

Rahat, Gideon, and Ofer Kenig. 2018. *From Party Politics to Personalized Politics? Party Change and Political Personalization in Democracies.* Oxford: Oxford University Press.

Reilly, Benjamin. 2006. "Political Engineering and Party Politics in Conflict-Prone Societies." *Democratization* 13 (5): 811–827.

Sartori, Giovanni. 2005. *Parties and Party Systems: A Framework for Analysis.* Colchester: ECPR press.

Shapira, Assaf. 2021. "All the Joint Lists in One Place." Israel Democracy Institute, April 28. www.idi.org.il/articles/32955 [Hebrew].

Taagepera, Rein, and Allan Sikk. 2010. "Parsimonious Model for Predicting Mean Cabinet Duration on the Basis of Electoral System." *Party Politics* 16 (2): 261–281.

Tillman, Erik R. 2015. "Pre-Electoral Coalitions and Voter Turnout." *Party Politics* 21 (5): 726–737.

Tuttnauer, Or, and Michael Philipov. 2013. "Government Maintenance: How to Rule Together?" In *Reforming Israel's Political System*, Gideon Rahat, Shlomit Barnea, Chen Friedberg, and Ofer Kenig (eds.), 447–470. Jerusalem: The Israel Democracy Institute [Hebrew].

Van De Wardt, Marc, and Arjen Van Witteloostuijn. 2019. "Adapt or Perish? How Parties Respond to Party System Saturation in 21 Western Democracies, 1945–2011." *British Journal of Political Science* 51 (1): 1–23.

11 The Arab Electorate and Parties, 2019–2021

Toward a Non-Zionist Israeli Identity?

Doron Navot, Samer Swaid, and Muhammed Khalaily

During the period between December 2018, when early elections for the 21st Knesset were announced, and until the 36th government was sworn in in May 2021, the citizens of Israel found themselves on a roller coaster, most notably the Arab citizens. Their participation rate in the March 2020 elections was relatively high compared to the past two decades, and the Arab parties won a record number of Knesset seats. However, a year later, Arab turnout reached an all-time low since the establishment of the State. In few years their political parties joined, split, rejoined, and split again. The prominence of Ayman Odeh, the leader of the Joint List, who had been a hero for many in the Arab electorate, has been waning, while Mansour Abbas, the head of a Muslim party, became one of the most central politicians, not only among the Arab public, but also among the general Israeli public. The present chapter seeks to explain the instability of Israeli Arabs' political participation patterns, including the shifting status of the parties representing them.

Our thesis is that this instability is connected to the way in which the parties and politicians are constructing a new Israeli identity among the Arabs. At least some of the leaders of the parties that make up the Joint List support an Israeli identity for their society; but they want to give it a non-Zionist content, whether for nationalist reasons or to keep their constituents from switching their support to Jewish parties. Clearly the Arab leadership's success in creating a non-Zionist Israeli identity is incomplete. This is because most Jewish politicians are not willing to establish a coalition that depends on avowed Palestinians; but no less, because of the strategy that the leadership employed in appealing to the public in the 2019–2021 election campaigns. The result is a fragile identity, that is reflected in the vacillating public moods, the Joint List's volatile status, and the steps taken by the Arab leaders. As we finalize this chapter in the summer of 2021, there is a new Arab politics in Israel, but no politician or party has developed a discourse and agenda that bridge between the Israeli and Palestinian identities.

DOI: 10.4324/9781003267911-14

11.1 Conceptual Framework

Most studies of Israeli Arab politics have been from an integrated perspective that takes account of the Jewish character of the state, on the one hand, and the Arab society's preferences, on the other. The dominant assumption in the literature is that Arab politics is totally subservient to the issue of Palestinian nationalism, to the extent allowed by the restrictions imposed by the Jewish state (Jamal, 2019; Haidar, 2018; Shaked, 2018). Accordingly, the starting point of research is the complexity of Palestinian identity (Ghanem and Ozacky-Lazar, 2002; Ghanem, 2001; Jamal, 2019; Smooha, 2018). In other words, it is the logic of majority-minority relations that underpins Arab politicians' behavioral patterns (Kaufman and Israeli, 1997; Ghanem and Ozacky-Lazar, 2002; Jamal, 2002; Rouhana, Shihadeh, and Sabbagh-Khoury, 2011; Zucker, 2017). These theoretical assumptions are found even among scholars who for normative reasons emphasize the Palestinians' agency, and adopt an anticolonialist epistemology as a conceptual framework (Jamal, 2020). In this chapter we will look at the politics of the Arabs in Israel as a phenomenon that includes a struggle for power within parties, between parties, and in the hearts of the Arab public, waged chiefly by the politicians. The emphasis here is on the dynamics that prevail between the Arab public at large and the politicians and parties that aspire to represent it.

To describe and analyze these relations we will use a new concept we have coined – "non-Zionist Israeli identity."[1] This concept denotes a deliberate process in which the political Arab subject becomes more Israeli, but remains a vigorous opponent of Zionism and especially of the country's Jewish identity, with the many implications this has for the nature of society, the status of the Arabs, and their ability to at least try to shape the public space as they wish. This position sees the category of "Israeli" as having a positive potential for the Arab citizens of Israel. It includes support for the two-state solution alongside a desire to turn Israel into the state of all its citizens, and a desire to influence Israeli politics. This ideological project is also marked by less attention to issues that were prominent in the "politics of identity" phase. Thus, to understand this identity better, we briefly consider the politics of identity that preceded it.

The politics of identity in the Palestinian case was devised and led by Azmi Bishara (Jamal, 2006) and was the hallmark of Arab politics in Israel from 1993 until the last few years (Rekhess, 2014). In this view, "Palestinian" is by far the primary identity of Arabs who hold Israeli citizenship. The Palestinians are not merely a national minority but are also an indigenous people and as such are entitled to special collective rights. Membership in the Palestinian nationality must be expressed in the struggle to liberate the Palestinians from Israeli occupation, and, consequently, the distinction between the Palestinians in the territories and the citizens of Israel must be blurred (Haidar, 2018). Israeli identity is a legal datum and their affiliation

240 *Doron Navot, Samer Swaid, and Muhammed Khalaily*

with Israel should be merely formal. Nevertheless, according to Bishara, their Israelization is not a matter of choice (Bishara, 1996). Their status as "Israeli Arabs" and their Israeli identity are problematic and a flawed ideal, because in essence they establish the Arabs' acceptance of their status as second-class citizens and incomplete human beings. Consequently, Israelization must be actively opposed by adopting a national-civic-democratic discourse (Bishara, 1996; Jamal, 2020).

Non-Zionist Israeli identity as we conceive it is to be distinguished not only from the politics of identity but also from Israelization. Israelization refers to a process, which is not necessarily conscious or deliberate, in which the Arab subject effectively becomes more Israeli in diverse ways – notably language (for example, frequent use of the Hebrew words in Arabic conversation), consumption of culture (for example, watching Hebrew-language Israeli series), and, in more extreme cases, in political behavior (flying the Israeli flag on Independence Day or voting for Jewish parties). Israelization involves the adoption of an Israeli identity that is the same as that of the Jewish majority (Smooha, 2018, 69). Non-Zionist Israeli identity, by contrast, is a self-conscious and deliberate project, given that it takes place in a country where the majority's Israeli identity is deeply rooted in Zionism. Not only is the Arabs' Israeli identity not that of Zionism, but to a great extent it is an intentional and deliberate rejection thereof and accordingly demands constant effort.

What is triggering the transition, albeit dynamics, toward a non-Zionist Israeli identity? Kabha sees it as "sobering up by the Palestinians and understanding of the balance of power" vis-à-vis the Jewish majority, including "internalization of the protracted struggle in which they have come out the loser" (2019, 243). We do not see it necessarily as a response to the balance of power, nor surrender or regrouping to prepare for the renewal of the struggle. We suggest that, in the wake of the Arab Spring, Israel's luster has increased for its Arab citizens, while the notion of Palestinian identity as a component of Pan-Arabism was weakened (Hazran and Khalaily, 2018). Another factor that has fostered Israeli identity is Resolution 922 adopted by the government in December 2015.[2] The resolution has improved the economic situation of the Arabs (Maron, 2020) and consequently made Israeli identity a more significant economic asset. 922 also created a stratum of those involved in its implementation, such as "resource mobilizers" employed by the local authorities.[3] Harvesting the fruits of 922 requires acquaintance with the patterns of Jewish government and a willingness to display their Israeli identity more prominently than in the past, while expressing their commitment to the Palestinian people in ways that Jews find less threatening. The frequent interactions with Jews in the labor market are another reason for the rise of this identity (Arraf, 2020). The actions by political parties and politicians are still another major influence. Here the establishment of the Joint List and Ayman Odeh's leadership were important factors in the development of the non-Zionist Israeli identity. Odeh sought to consolidate his leadership in part

The Arab Electorate and Parties, 2019–2021 241

by setting himself apart from the positions of Mohammad Barakeh, the previous head of Hadash, who would have been the chair of the Joint List had Odeh not insisted on running against him (Abu Elnaser, 2015).

We do not claim that the politics of identity and the politics of non-Zionist Israeli identity are totally incompatible. Nevertheless, there has been a change in the political emphases, and one can point to a shift, even if only partial and perhaps temporary, from one type of politics to another.

11.2 The Establishment of the Joint List

In the January 22, 2013 election for the 19th Knesset, before the Joint List was established, there were three main Arab lists (Hadash, Ra'am-Ta'al, and Balad). Hadash received 113,439 votes and four Knesset seats (slightly more than 3% of valid ballots), Ra'am-Ta'al received 138,450 votes and four seats (close to 4% of valid ballots), and Balad received 97,030 votes and three seats (slightly less than 3% of valid ballots). Thus, the parties representing the Arab sector placed a total of 11 representatives in the Knesset.

In 2014, the Knesset passed the Governance Law, in which one provision raised the threshold to 3.25%. This pushed the Arab parties to regroup, and the Joint List was created on January 23, 2015, shortly before the election for the 20th Knesset, held on March 17. The Joint List received most of the votes cast by Arabs (83.2%; the rest went to Jewish lists) and emerged as the third-largest faction in the Knesset, with 13 seats (10.61% of all valid ballots). Turnout in the Arab society, which had been dropping since the 16th Knesset election, rose from 54% to 63.7% (Rudnitzky, 2020a).

11.3 The Breakup of the Joint List and the April 2019 Election

Throughout the term of the 20th Knesset, however, the Joint List was plagued by organizational problems, disagreements, and crises among its components. Some of these disagreements stemmed from internal quarrels in Hadash, the leading faction in the Joint List, between Odeh and Barakeh; others derived from the rivalry between Ahmad Tibi and Ayman Odeh on leadership of the Joint List.

On September 2018, Ra'am chose Mansour Abbas as party chairman, replacing former Member of Knesset (MK) Masoud Ghnaim, in an open vote by the delegates to the 20th convention of the southern wing of the Islamic Movement. Abbas is a religious and yet democratic politician, who sees his own and the party's primary role as dealing with concrete internal problems, such as violence in the Arab society. Abbas will move to the front stage as the two-year election cycle further unfolds, as the change in Ra'am corresponds with the changes and shifts within the Arab society.

On January 8, 2019, MK Tibi, a politician who keeps a close eye on public opinion polls, announced the dissolution of the Joint List. Tibi is a fierce opponent of Zionism (Hecht, 2020; Rappaport, 2019). Thus, his decision to secede from the Joint List suggests that the non-Zionist Israeli identity can have different guises. Also, his final decision before the April 2019 election not to run alone but to join forces with Hadash (and still later to return to the Joint List) reflects the problems that the political leadership has in molding its Israeli identity. As a preparation for the April 2019 election, Hadash chose the same list as for the previous election (2015), except for the replacement of the Jewish representative, Dov Khenin, by Ofer Kasif. Balad, by contrast, revamped its list, with the new elected candidates being more pragmatic than previous lists.

The results of the internal elections in the Arab parties reflect the attempts to respond to their public's growing Israeli identity and help shape it. Hadash may seem to have become more nationalist, after selecting Kassif, whose main interest is the occupation and conflict, to replace the more pragmatic Khenin. But it stuck with Odeh, the unofficial flag bearer of the new Israeli identity of the Arabs in Israel, as its leader. Balad, identified with radical national conflict, selected less controversial (from the Jewish perspective) candidates.

When the internal candidate selection processes were complete, the parties began negotiations with the hope to rebuild the Joint List. However, all the attempts to bridge among the four parties failed (Almasar, 2019). Balad and Ra'am announced that they would run together, and at the very last moment, Hadash and Ta'al decided to run together, so two Arab lists competed in the April 2019 election, rather than a single united list or three as in the past.

The public had expected that ultimately all the parties would form a single list, and its disappointment brought about a decline in turnout from 63.5% in 2015 to 49.2% in April 2019 (Rudnitzky, 2020b). The Arab turnout of 2019 was the lowest since these parties ran to the Israeli Knesset (see Figure 11.1). Hadash and Ta'al won six seats. Ra'am and Balad pulled in only four, clearing the threshold by slightly more than 3,000 votes. The Arabs' representation fell from 13 to 10.[4]

At the same time, the percentage of Arabs who voted for Zionist parties increased from 16.8% in 2015 to 28.4%, an indication of the growth of the Israelization process and the tenuous nature of the line separating it from a non-Zionist Israeli identity (see Figure 11.2).

In fact, weighting the turnout of Arab voters and the percentage of those who voted for Zionist parties reveals that only about a third of the Arab citizens of Israel voted for one of the two lists that claimed to represent them (Hadash–Ta'al and Ra'am–Balad) (see Figures 11.1, 11.2, and 11.3).

Given these results, the party leaders resolved to reconstitute the Joint List. When the prospect of early elections in September 2019 became real, they immediately declared that they preferred a Joint List and would announce its official establishment without delay. That same night the factions sat down together and decided to support the bill to dissolve the Knesset; their main argument was the opportunity to reestablish the Joint List (Azam, 2019).

The Arab Electorate and Parties, 2019–2021   243

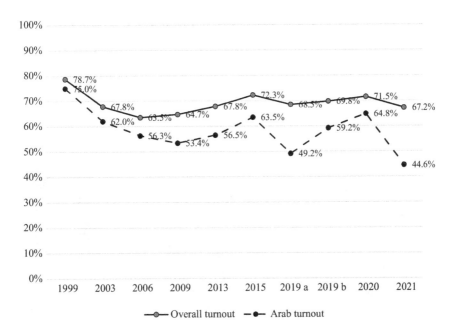

Figure 11.1 Arab turnout vs. overall turnout between the years 1999–2021.
Source: Rudnitzky, 2020b.

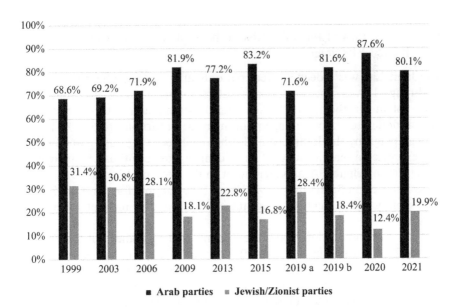

Figure 11.2 Breakdown of the Arab vote in Knesset elections between Arab and Zionist parties between the years 1999–2021.
Source: Rudnitzky, 2020b.

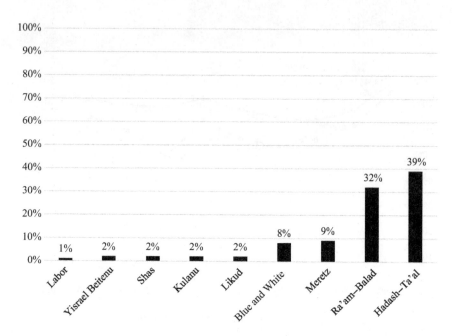

Figure 11.3 Breakdown of the Arab vote in the April 2019, 21st Knesset election.
Source: Rudnitzky, 2020b.

11.4 The Return of the Joint List in the September 2019 and March 2020 Elections

The Joint List was indeed revived, but only after a stormy fight about slots 11 through 14 and other birth pangs that left bitterness in the electorate. This may explain why the first poll taken after the submission of the list predicted only a moderate 3.5 percentage-point increase in turnout, to 52.5%. But as the campaign by the Joint List and other civil society groups gained steam and expressed a sense of a new Israeli identity, public enthusiasm increased. Some 59% of eligible Arab voters went to the polls on Election Day of the 22nd Knesset on September 17, 2019, and the support for the Arab Parties was slightly more than 10 percentage points higher in September than in April.

There were no disputes about the makeup of the list ahead of the election for the 23rd Knesset in March 2020. Turnout rose again, by nearly six percentage points, and support for the Joint List increased by a similar amount. In addition, there was a sharp drop in Arab voters' support for Meretz. Meretz had received close to 9% of the Arab vote in the April 2019 election: more than 40,000 votes, equivalent to 1.2 mandates; without them, or even half of them, the party would not have passed the electoral threshold. Its share of

The Arab Electorate and Parties, 2019–2021 245

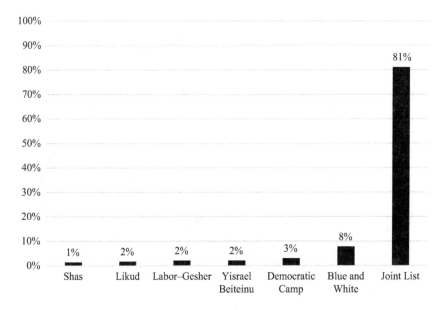

Figure 11.4 Breakdown of the Arab vote in the September 2019, 22nd Knesset election.
Source: Rudnitzky, 2020b.

the Arab vote fell to 3% in the September 2019 election, when it ran as part of the Democratic Camp, and declined again in March 2020 when it ran as part of Labor–Gesher–Meretz (see Figures 11.4 and 11.5). By contrast, Blue and White maintained its total of about 8% – the equivalent of approximately one seat in the April and September elections, and then 5% in the March 2020 election (see Figure 11.5).

11.5 Public Opinion, Voter Turnout, The Campaign and the Formation of the Rotation Government of Netanyahu and Gantz

Survey data we collected toward the election for the 22nd Knesset (September 2019), indicate that the first priority of Arabs were local problems, consistent with our thesis of a predominant Israeli identity.[5] We can see in Table 11.1, that violence and crime headed the list of issues deemed important – with over a quarter of the respondents choosing this issue. At the same time, the Palestinian issue (the occupation) was secondary.

In addition, we tried to understand the low turnout, and examined why so many Arabs did not vote. As we conjectured, abstention is not necessarily an act against Israel, nor is it a sign of contentious politics. Rather, it is a manifestation of mistrust in the democratic process and in the Arab parties (see Table 11.2).

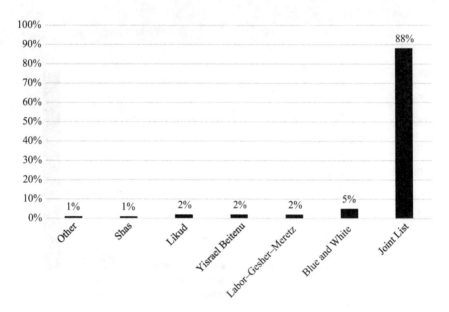

Figure 11.5 Breakdown of the Arab vote in the March 2020, 23rd Knesset election.
Source: Rudnitzky, 2020b.

Table 11.1 Issues of concern to Arab voters (August–September 2019)

	Survey 1 (%)	Survey 2 (%)	Survey 3 (%)	Survey 4 (%)	Average (%)
Violence and crime in Arab society	24.9	25.7	28.4	29.8	27.2
The Nation-State Law	10.4	16.6	14.5	18.5	15
Unequal budgets	13.6	16.6	13.6	14	14.4
The housing problem in the Arab sector	11.6	12.1	15.5	15.3	13.6
Ending the occupation	13.8	5.7	15.2	13.1	11.9
Recognition of the unrecognized villages in the Negev	12.3	11.3	8.4	5.1	9.3
Other	13.4	12	4.4	4.2	8.6
Total	100	100	100	100	100

Source: Four election polls, conducted by Statnet. The samples are representative of the Arab adult population; Survey 1, N=1,231, August 5–August 10, 2019; Survey 2, N=1,312, August 17–August 21, 2019; Survey 3, N=1,245, August 31–September 3, 2019; Survey 4, N=1,265, September 8–September 10, 2019.

The Joint List's main slogans in the campaigns for the 22nd and 23rd elections were – "More Joint List – More Influence," and – "More Joint List – Less Right Wing." The most important civic project to encourage voting (toward the September 2019 election), the September 17 Coalition, followed a similar line:[6] "This Time We're Going to Vote" (referring back to

The Arab Electorate and Parties, 2019–2021   247

Table 11.2 Reasons for not voting, Arab voters, closed question (August–September 2019)

	Survey 1 (%)	Survey 2 (%)	Survey 3 (%)	Survey 4 (%)	Average (%)
Total number of nonvoters among respondents	408	395	269	244	329
Percentage of nonvoters among respondents	33.2	30.1	21.5	19.3	26
I don't trust the Arab parties	26.9	27.7	22	20.3	24.2
My vote won't change my standard of living in any way	22.2	15.4	25.3	21.5	21.1
The Arab parties' discourse isn't for me	4.6	7	3.2	10	6.2
My vote legitimizes Israeli democracy	3.2	4.5	5.7	4.6	4.5
There is no chance for political change in Israel	15.4	15.8	15.1	17.8	16
I have no confidence in the Knesset	8.2	11.5	4.9	10	8.6
I have no confidence in the Israeli Government	8.3	4.5	11.2	8.5	8.1
Other	11.2	13.6	12.6	7.3	11.1
Total	100	100	100	100	100

Source: Four election polls, conducted by Statnet. The samples are representative of the Arab adult population; Survey 1, N=1,231, August 5–August 10, 2019; Survey 2, N=1,312, August 17–August 21, 2019; Survey 3, N=1,245, August 31–September 3, 2019; Survey 4, N=1,265, September 8–September 10, 2019.

the April 2019 election), and "This time We'll Decide," with reference to the impact on the Israeli political system as a whole.

The leaders of the Joint List, and especially Odeh, repeated these slogans at parlor meetings, election rallies, and in the media, both in Hebrew and Arabic. Moreover, Odeh declared that the Joint List intended to be a key player and to influence the composition of the new Government. In a lengthy interview with Nahum Barnea on August 22, 2019, he said that he was "willing to join a center-left government" (Barnea, 2019). He enumerated the conditions for joining the coalition or supporting from the outside, along the lines of the second Rabin government, when Mada and Hadash supported the coalition without joining it. The conditions, which were essentially the realization of the Arabs' national and civic aspirations, expressed full recognition of the category of "Israeli Arab." The interview, which ran on the paper's front page, triggered a lively discussion in both the general political community and the Arab public. According to surveys[7] and the social media, the Arab public supported Odeh. Many of those who said they were planning to vote (77.8% stated they intend to vote) favored the inclusion of an Arab party or Arab Knesset members in the coalition, or at least support for the government from the outside (a blocking majority).

After the September 17, 2019 election, 10 of the 13 Joint List MKs advised the president to ask Gantz to form the government. The Balad MKs did not recommend anyone (Bender, 2019). A survey conducted on September 20–21, 2019 indicated that 75% of the Arabs supported recommending Gantz for prime minister; 79% of those who had voted for the Joint List favored this; only 2% supported a recommendation for Netanyahu and 19% preferred that their MKs not recommend any candidate.[8]

In early October 2019, the Arab society was shocked by a triple murder in Majd al-Krum (Gadban, 2019). The Joint List MKs were swift to sponsor a fierce protest against violence in the Arab society and played an important role in recruiting people to take part in it. The protest included unusual actions, such as blocking major traffic arteries. In this way the protest was moved from the Arab street to the general Israeli arena and placed the violence among the Arabs in Israel at the top of the public agenda. Israeli society as a whole was exposed to the most acute problem of the Arab society; it became a topic that all politicians had to talk about, including the two candidates for prime minister, Netanyahu and Gantz. A campaign against violence and crime in the Arab society became the Joint List's main demand in its negotiations with Gantz before recommending him to the president, and a milestone for any cooperation between Jews and Arabs.

When the Knesset decided to hold another election for the third time within a year, the Joint List organized rapidly. It decided to freeze its candidate slate so as to avoid personal or interparty arguments and immediately set to work on its campaign. The Joint List's main slogan was "With the Joint List You have a Voice"; that of the Coalition to encourage voting was "All of Us Are Going to Vote." The campaigns focused again on the power that the Arabs could wield. The leaders of the Joint List spoke about winning 15 or 16 Knesset seats and reached Election Day with a sense that this time the Arabs would fully realize their electoral potential. The results of the March 2, 2020 election showed an increase of six percentage points in Arab turnout (65%) and a gain of two Knesset seats, to 15. This filled the Arab citizens with a sense of power and confidence, especially because the two additional seats denied the right wing a majority of 61 Knesset seats.

Another poll held immediately after the election[9] found that the Arab public was pleased with the electoral results. More than 71% responded that they were satisfied or very satisfied; more than 74% said that they were satisfied or very satisfied with Odeh's performance. He even managed to overtake Tibi on the popularity index, with 33.3% saying that he represented them best, as against 27.6% who opted for Tibi. This was the first time in the past decade that Tibi failed to outpoll his rivals on this question.[10] At this point, the Arabs entertained real hopes that their representatives would be part of the next Israeli government, or at least support it from the outside and help bring down Netanyahu. They certainly supported this idea: 83% said that they wanted (to a great or very great extent) the party they had voted for be part of the government now. If one deducts the 12% who had voted for parties other than the Joint List, the figure remains above 70%. At this juncture, the mainstream media reported that Blue and White had agreed to some of the demands presented by Odeh and the Joint List, including a war on crime, housing solutions, and legalization of homes erected without building permits (Magid, 2020).

Odeh persuaded Balad's representatives to deviate from their custom and recommend that the President ask a Jewish MK to form the next government. Balad's leader, Shihadeh, explained the decision to recommend Gantz, a former chief of the general staff, as meant to preserve the unity of the Joint List: "Balad's decision shows that the party wants to change the condition of Arab society and to influence decision-making, and that it, like the other components of the Joint List, wants to depose Netanyahu" (Shihadeh, 2020). Odeh explained that "we want a center-left government, and all 15 members of the Joint List are recommending this. But this is less from love of Mordecai than from hatred of Haman" (Eichner and Shalan, 2020).

But the adulation for Odeh declined after Gantz decided to join forces with Netanyahu. The Arab public identified Odeh, more than anyone else, with the decision to recommend Gantz for prime minister. When Gantz and Netanyahu established their rotation government, Odeh's standing took a sharp blow. A poll we conducted in June 2020[11] found that Tibi had regained his status as the most popular Arab MK who best represented the Arab public (37%), leading over Odeh (21%) by a significant margin.

In the same June 2020 poll, 83% of the respondents said that they wanted to vote in the next Knesset election.[12] This indicates that their disappointment at the Joint List's failure to influence the composition of the Government did not change their desire to vote and have an impact, and, more generally, to be an active and significant player in Israeli politics. Moreover, the Arabs emerged from the three successive elections between April 2019 and March 2020 encouraged, even though Netanyahu remained in office. A majority said that the year of elections had given them confidence in their ability to influence Israeli politics; only 15% fully disagreed, as against a majority that agreed strongly or very strongly. The question about the political power of the Arab citizens produced similar results. Even more interesting, the Arab parties' standing changed during the year, with most of the public reporting that the elections had increased their confidence in the Arab parties, enhanced their standing, and made them a legitimate and significant player in the Israeli arena. This, it must be remembered, was despite Odeh's failure to keep his election promise of helping to depose Netanyahu. Although the Joint List was unable to influence the formation of the government, the aforementioned June 2020 survey indicated that the electorate's faith in the influence of the parties and their representatives had increased (see Table 11.3). This also indicates that joining the coalition is not the only indicator of political success, as the mere increase in political representation is viewed as such.

Table 11.3 Positions on various political issues, Arab voters (June 2020)

	Agree very strongly (%)	Agree strongly (%)	Agree moderately (%)	Agree somewhat (%)	Absolutely disagree (%)	Don't know/ declined to answer (%)
The past year of elections gave me confidence that the Arab citizens can influence Israeli politics.	36.8	21.1	17.7	8.0	14.6	1.9
The past year of elections gave me confidence in the political power of the Arab citizens of Israel.	37.5	24.0	16.5	7.1	14.1	0.8
The past year of elections gave me confidence in the Arab parties.	32.5	24.9	17.5	6.6	17.1	1.4
The past year of elections changes the status of the Arab parties in Israel and they became part of the political game.	30	26.2	20.0	8.5	12.7	2.5
During the past year of elections, the representatives of the Joint List dealt too much with the Palestinian issue at the expense of the daily problems of the Arab citizens.	23.4	17.4	25.3	11.2	19.1	3.6
The two-state solution is the just and most feasible solution.	32.9	15.6	16.3	8.2	23.6	3.5
The solution to the Israeli–Palestinian conflict is a unitary state on the entire territory.	20.5	13.8	10.5	9.7	41.0	4.6
The Palestinian national affiliation is an important element in my identity.	44.7	11.1	16.1	5.7	19.8	2.6
The Israeli civic affiliation is an important element in my identity.	35.8	15.6	20.0	10.2	15.6	2.8

Source: Post-election poll conducted by Statnet, June 15–June 23, 2020. The sample is representative of the Arab adult population (N=595).

11.6 The Breakup of the Joint List and the March 2021 Election

Odeh led the Joint List to a historic accomplishment at the polls and to a joint recommendation of Benny Gantz as the most suitable candidate to form a coalition. When Gantz decided to join a rotation government headed by Netanyahu, Odeh's position and the line he led suffered a severe blow. In actuality, Gatz's move led to the end of the Joint List as a union of four parties. Thereafter, two different political lines were created – the Israeli-Palestinian democratic line led by Odeh, and the Arab Muslim conservative line led by Abbas.

Moreover, following these developments, Abbas claimed that there is no difference between the right and left in Israel. Hence, there is no point in disqualifying the right and Netanyahu, since this only weakens the bargaining power of the Arabs. From now on what must be done is to take a stand of "neither right nor left" and join one of the blocs, as long as it agrees to advance the civic interests of Arab citizens. This is necessary, even at the cost of disregarding the occupation and the need to resolve the condition of the Palestinians in the West Bank and elsewhere, since the issue is not on the agenda of Israeli politics anyway, and even if it were, the Arabs have little influence over it. According to Abbas, Arab MKs should address crime and violence, the housing crisis, and the economic and health crisis (Azulay and Lukash, 2020).

An additional controversy emerged regarding the LGBTQ community's rights. The backdrop to the controversy was a donation that Al-Arz tahini factory made to the Association for LGBTQ Equality in Israel. The same tahini factory insisted on going public. As a result, some Arab citizens called for a boycott of the factory. Odeh, for his part, did not take a clear stand on the merits of the matter, expressing support indirectly, stating it was hypocritical to boycott Al-Arz and at the same time strengthen Israeli companies that support the military and settlements. The post he published caused an outrage on the Arab street. The public outrage was exacerbated by Odeh's vote in favor of the *anti*-conversion therapy law. The law prohibits from performing conversion therapies aimed at altering sexual orientation. Ra'am and Abbas led a campaign against Odeh and the other MKs who supported the *anti*-conversion law, arguing that it contradicts the religious values of the Arab society (Zinger, 2020). These disagreements over social issues paved the way for the dissolution of the Joint List. Given the different goals and different worldviews – Odeh, the avowed and proud Palestinian with progressive positions and pretensions to enhance Israeli democracy, and Abbas, a pure pragmatist, the Arab with a conservative agenda – a separate candidacy was inevitable.

Despite the negotiations between Ra'am and the rest of the Joint List components, Ra'am decided to run separately, claiming there is a large gap between the parties' approaches toward the Israeli political system and social issues. The remaining components of the Joint List – Hadash, Ta'al, and Balad – reached agreement and ran jointly.

252 Doron Navot, Samer Swaid, and Muhammed Khalaily

Ultimately, the March 2021 electoral results were influenced by events and developments both in the general Israeli political system and in the Arab interparty level. First, the election came after a year of dealing with the Covid-19 pandemic, which particularly hurt the Arab society and thus the relevance of the agenda previously presented by Odeh. Second, Ra'am split from the Joint List, and ran separately with a new agenda – emphasizing conservativism and pragmatism and glossing over the Palestinian identity and issues that are related to the conflict. Third, Netanyahu changed his approach toward Arab voters and the politicians who represent them, emphasizing the Arab Israeli identity, and highlighting the prime minister's commitment to their welfare.

Still, more than anything, the competition between Hadash and Ra'am approaches stood out on both the political and social level. That is, between an approach that sees an unbreakable link between Palestinian and Arab identities and the political issue of civil rights, and an approach that seeks to advance the status of the Arab population disengaged from the Israeli–Palestinian conflict and the humbling of the Palestinian identity. On the one hand, an approach that seeks to connect with the center-left and completely precludes the right, and on the other hand, an entirely pragmatic approach that calls for integration into the decision-making hubs and advancing the interests of the Arab population even at the cost of completely disregarding the conflict.

These approaches were reflected in the campaigns of the two lists. The Joint List continued to attack the right and Netanyahu, warning against Netanyahu's false statements, his attempts at illuding the Arab voters, stating that the embrace he offers is for electoral purposes. In contrast, Ra'am led a campaign that questioned the paradigm of the Joint List and highlighted its inability to influence the political system.

Ultimately, voter turnout decreased to 44.6%. While the Joint List received 6 seats (Hadash, 3; Ta'al, 2; and Balad, 1), Ra'am managed to pass the electoral threshold and received 4 seats. Compared to the previous election, there was a 20 percentage points drop in turnout (65% in March 2020), and political representation dropped from 15 seats to 10 (see the breakdown of the Arab vote in Figure 11.6). But in other important respects, Arab representation did not decline as much as it changed, as Ra'am became the first Arab party to sign coalition agreements and become part of a government in Israel.

The campaign for the 24th Knesset election focused on two main issues: First, the status of Arab politics in the Israeli political system and the relationship to the polarization between the two main blocs – right and left. Ra'am stressed that it is not part of the bloc map and is not allied either with the right or the left, and that all it cares about is the civil status of Arab citizens and solving the problems that keep the average citizen awake at night. The Joint List blamed Ra'am for negotiating with the Likud and Netanyahu, who sabotaged the political legitimacy of the Arab electorate and of the parties representing it, and was unwilling to cooperate with them. The second

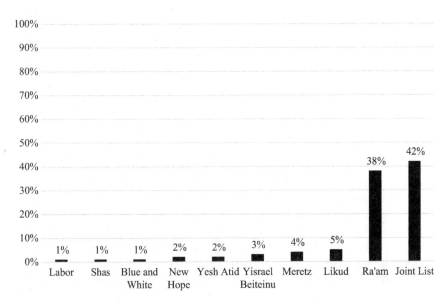

Figure 11.6 Breakdown of the Arab vote in the March 2021, 24th Knesset election.
Source: Rudnitzky, 2020b.

issue was social values: While Ra'am stressed its commitment to the traditional values of Arab society and Muslim religion and its firm opposition to the rights of the LGBTQ community. The Joint List tried to hide the issue, stating there are more important issues to address since it is not on the agenda and not of interest to the Arab public. In fact, Ra'am represented the conservative approach while the Joint List represented the more liberal and progressive approach. The Joint List received 6 electoral seats, while Ra'am received 4. The representation of the Arab parties decreased from 15 MKs in the 23rd Knesset to 10 in the 24th Knesset. Although there was a decline, the image of the blocs and polarization in the political arena gave great power to Ra'am, which expressed its willingness to join the government to advance the interests of the Arab public. Although there were negotiations between the Likud and Ra'am as well as between Yesh Atid and Ra'am, it did not recommend any of the candidates to the president and left the door open for both candidates (Zoabi, 2021). Ultimately, a historical agreement was signed between Ra'am and the parties forming the anti-Netanyahu coalition, making it the first Arab party in the coalition.

11.7 Discussion and Summary

There has been a profound change in Arab politics in Israel in recent years. In the period of the Oslo Accords and the two decades that followed, the emphasis was on the indigenous identity. Now the focus is on a new type of Israeli identity. We label it a "non-Zionist Israeli identity." The change we have noted is fragile, reversible and far from total. The 2019–2021 four-election cycle provides various manifestations of this non-Zionist Israeli identity, as well as of its fragility and complexity, from the changing turnout rates, through Ra'am's joining the Bennett–Lapid government coalition following the election for the 24th Knesset.

The desire expressed by the majority of the public to see their representatives sitting at the government table is an expression of the Israeli identity of the Arab public. At the same time, it is important for its leaders that this identity be non-Zionist (and not, for example, merely post-Zionist). There are five intersecting reasons for this: ideology, a desire to avoid losing voters to Zionist Jewish left-wing parties, a response to the national aspirations of their constituency, intraparty politics, and interparty dynamics. In practice, the national aspirations and ideology receive only lip service, whereas the new Israeli identity set the tone in the campaign and during coalition negotiations. Still, the commitment to the national issue has not gone away and will influence Arab politics in the future as well, if only on the rhetorical level and in the relations among politicians and parties.

The disappointment in Gantz has undermined the status of Odeh and of the entire Joint List. Thus, we are witnessing two opposing reactions – increasing pragmatism on the part of Ra'am and its voters, which involves blurring the Palestinian national identity, alongside a sharpening of the nationalist positions of all the Joint List components. Regardless, we expect that the Joint List will have difficulty surviving. It has become an arena for wrestling politicians who are fighting for political power and seeking to convince the public of the righteousness of their path. Now, in light of Abbas' pragmatic line, it is doubtful whether the other three components will remain together for long.

For now, the non-Zionist Israeli politics of Odeh and the Joint List reached a dead end. It did not offer a feasible plan to improve the situation of the Palestinians in the Occupied Territories, and it has not been able to formulate a persuasive vision of the status of Arab citizens in Israel, one that is not soon shattered by reality, as happened following the March 2020 election for the 23rd Knesset. Worse, it led to a massive disappointment.

Abbas offered the Arab citizens a different vision, and while clearly not a Zionist, the politics he leads in the name of Arab identity and Muslim identity is less Israeli when compared to Odeh. With the establishment of the Bennett–Lapid–Abbas coalition, it would seem that Abbas's conservative and pragmatic emphasis provides a way out of the impasse that the more Israeli politics of The Joint List has led to.

In fact, Abbas is nothing less than a revolution in the politics of the Arabs in Israel, since at the moment he dismisses the Palestinian component. The extent to which non-Palestinian Arab politics can provide a sustainable

The Arab Electorate and Parties, 2019–2021   255

solution for Arabs in Israel, and how it will affect the more nationalist parties, is a subject for a separate article.

Notes

1 To the best of our knowledge, no scholar has ever used this term or conceptualized this option. Recently Sammy Smooha (2018) referred to a limited and bounded Israeli identity. One of the two factors he sees behind this limitation is the Arab rejection of Zionism. As we understand him, Smooha does not attach any significance to a non-Zionist Israeli identity and sees it as only a very incomplete and narrow form of Israeli identity, owing to two normative factors that are almost mirror images. One is the rejection in principle of the possibility that an Israeli identity can be non-Zionist, because of the commitment to Zionism. The other is the rejection in principle of the possibility of a non-Zionist Israeli identity by the "resistance," which rejects out of hand the very category of "Israeli Arab."

2 Government decision No. 922, for the years 2016–2020, budgeted at approximately NIS 15 billion. The rationale behind the approval of the plan was the general recognition of the importance of the economic integration of the Arab society as a key component for economic growth. The plan includes a number of areas: employment, infrastructure and transportation, housing, education, and the empowerment of Arab local authorities.

3 Some graduates of the cadet program have already found positions in Arab local authorities. Their job is to mobilize resources for the Arab local authorities and to help them make full use of the budgets available under Resolution 922. For information on the various cadet programs, see www.gov.il/he/Departments/Guides/rese rve-local-government. For more on the resource-mobilizer program, see www.gov. il/he/departments/news/moard_project

4 See the Central Elections Committee website for the 21st Knesset: https://votes21. bechirot.gov.il/

5 The first poll, conducted between August 5 and August 10, 2019, involved a representative sample of 1,231 Arab adults. The turnout predicted by this poll was 52.5%. The second poll, conducted between August 17 and August 21, 2019, involved a representative sample of 1,312 Arab adults. It predicted a turnout of 56%. The third poll, conducted between August 31 and September 3, 2019, involved a representative sample of 1,245 Arab adults. It predicted a turnout of 53.5%. The fourth and last poll, conducted between September 8 and September 10, 2019, a week before the election, involved a representative sample of 1,265 persons and predicted a turnout of 57.2%. The actual figure on Election Day was 59.5%. All the polls were conducted by Statnet.

6 The September 17 coalition consisted of civil society organizations that ran a get-out-the-vote campaign. It included media advertisements and field activity in Arab population centers.

7 The survey was conducted for the Konrad Adenauer Program for Jewish-Arab Cooperation at Tel Aviv University on a representative sample of 506 Israeli Arabs. See https://bit.ly/39sP5gg

8 According to a public opinion poll conducted by the Master Institute of a representative sample of 307 Arab adults. It included questions about the Arabs' preferences and what they wanted Arab MKs to do in the 22nd Knesset. Some 73% wanted the

MKs to focus on socioeconomic issues; 22% wanted them to concentrate on the Palestinian problem. See www.alarab.com/Article/916894

9 This survey was conducted on March 8–March 10, 2020, immediately after the election for the 23rd Knesset, before Gantz joined forces with Netanyahu and before the Covid-19 pandemic took off. The data were collected by Statnet and involved a representative sample of 371 Arab adults.

10 According to a survey conducted in 2010, Ahmed Tibi was the most popular MK for 25% of the Arabs, followed by Mohammad Barakeh, the then-chairman of Hadash, with 10%. Since then, Tibi has remained the most popular Arab parliamentarian in all the polls conducted. For more, see www.ynet.co.il/articles/0,7340,L-3828456,00.html

11 The poll of a representative sample of 595 Arab adults, was conducted by Statnet from June 15– June23, 2020.

12 Of course, this 83% figure does not mean that they will indeed get out and vote; according to the formula employed by Statnet, the prediction was for a 67% turnout.

References

Abu Elnaser, Zaher. 2015. "Odeh official winner of first place on the Hadash list." *PANet*, January 17 [Arabic].

Almasar. 2019. "After failure of negotiations, Abbas accuses Ta'al and Dahamshe warns of burning up votes." *Almasar*, February 21 [Arabic].

Arraf, Suha. 2020. "Arab physicians not excited by Netanyahu. Impossible to ignore us." *Siḥah mekomit,* March 19 [Hebrew].

Azam, Shehadeh. 2019. "After dissolution of Knesset: Will the components of the Joint List reunite?" *PANet,* May 30 [Arabic].

Azulay, Moran, and Alexandra Lukash. 2020. "Abbas: 'I have not given up on the Joint List, I am not in anyone's pocket'." *Ynet*, March 15 [Hebrew].

Barnea, Nahum. 2019. "Ayman Odeh surprises: 'I'm ready to join a center-left coalition'." *Yedioth Ahronoth*, August 22 [Hebrew].

Bender, Arik. 2019. "The Joint List recommends Gantz: To put an end to Netanyahu's rule." *Maariv,* September 22 [Hebrew].

Bishara, Azmi. 1996. "The Israeli Arab: A study of a divided political discourse." In *Zionism: A Contemporary Controversy*, edited by Pinhas Ginosar and Avi Bareli, 312–399. Sede Boker: The Ben-Gurion Heritage Center. [Hebrew].

Eichner, Itamar, and Shalan Hassan. 2020. "Joint List unanimously recommends Gantz." *Ynet*, March 15.

Gadban, Imad. 2019. "Double murder in Majd al-Krum. Declaration of a state of emergency and a strike. Anger and shock in the streets." *PANet*, October 1 [Arabic].

Ghanem, As'ad. 2001. "Parties and ideological currents of the Palestinian-Arab minority in Israel." *State and Society* 1 (1): 89–114 [Hebrew].

Ghanem As'ad, and Sarah Ozacky-Lazar. 2002. "Israel as an ethnic state: The Arab vote." In *The Elections in Israel 1999*, edited by Asher Arian and Michal Shamir, 121–140. Albany: SUNY Press.

Haidar, Aziz. 2018 (ed.). *Political Aspects in the Lives of the Arab Citizens of Israel.* Jerusalem: The Van Leer Jerusalem Institute and Hakibbutz Hameuchad [Hebrew].

Hazran, Yusri, and Muhammed Khalaily. 2018. "Arab society in Israel and the 'Arab Spring'." *Hamerhav ha-tzibburi* 14: 9–46 [Hebrew].

The Arab Electorate and Parties, 2019–2021   257

Hecht, Ravit. 2020. "Tibi accuses 'the Left' of the occupation and shatters the utopia of Jewish-Arab political cooperation." *Ha'aretz*, July 10 [Hebrew].

Jamal, Amal. 2002. "Abstention as participation: On the illusions of Arab politics in Israel." In *The Elections in Israel 2001*, edited by Asher Arian and Michal Shamir, 57–100. Jerusalem: The Israel Democracy Institute [Hebrew].

Jamal, Amal. 2006. "The political vision of the people and the challenge of a state for all its citizens: A study of the writings of Azmi Bishara." *Alpayim* 30: 71–113 [Hebrew].

Jamal, Amal. 2019. "Emerging elites and new political ideas amongst Palestinians in Israel." In *Understanding Israel: Political, Societal and Security Challenges*, edited by Joel Peters and Rob Geist Pinfold, 149–166. London: Routledge.

Jamal, Amal. 2020. "An introduction to the study of Palestinian Arab society in Israel." In *The Contradictions of Control: State Policies Towards Arab Citizens*, edited by Amal Jamal, 9–34. Tel Aviv: The Walter Lebach Institute for the Study of Jewish-Arab Coexistence [Hebrew].

Kabha, Mustafa. 2019. "The Arabs in Israel: The influences of the establishment of a Palestinian state on their identity and aspirations to realize their national desires." In *25 Years of the Oslo Process*, edited by Ephraim Lavie, Yael Ronen, and Henry Fishman, 237–254. Jerusalem: Carmel.

Kaufman, Ilana, and Rachel Israeli. 1997. "The Odd Group Out: The Arab-Palestinian Vote in the 1996 Elections." In *The Elections in Israel 1996*, edited by Michal Shamir and Asher Arian, 107–148. Albany: SUNY Press.

Lustick, Ian. 1980. *Arabs in the Jewish State: Israel's Control of a National Minority*. Austin: University of Texas Press.

Magid, Jacob. 2020. "Joint List negotiating with Blue and White." *Times of Israel,* March 11.

Maron, Asa. 2020. "Translating social investment ideas in Israel: Economized social policy's competing agendas." *Global Social Policy* 20 (1): 97–116.

Nasr, Muhasan. 2019. "Balad joins joint list and Mazen Ghnayim resigns and drops his candidacy." *Al-Arab,* July 28 [Arabic].

Rappaport, Miron. 2019. "Tibi after dramatic split with the Joint List: 'I will lead the formation of the blocking majority'." *Sihah mekomit,* January 15 [Hebrew].

Rekhess, Elie. 2014. "The Arab minority in Israel: Reconsidering the '1948 paradigm'." *Israel Studies* 19 (2): 187–217.

Rouhana, Nadim, Mtanis Shihadeh, and Areej Sabbagh-Khoury. 2011. "Turning points in Palestinian politics in Israel: The 2009 elections." In *The Elections in Israel 2009*, edited by Asher Arian and Michal Shamir, 93–122. New Brunswick: Transaction.

Rudnitzky, Arik. 2020a. "Analysis of the Arab vote in the 2020 elections." Israel Democracy Institute, March 17 [Hebrew].

Rudnitzky, Arik. 2020b. *Voter Turnout in Knesset Elections: The Real, the Ideal and the Hope for Change*. Jerusalem: The Israel Democracy Institute [Hebrew].

Shaked, Ronni. 2018. "From al Ard to Balad: The search for a national identity." In *Political Aspects in the Lives of the Arab Citizens of Israel*, edited by Aziz Haider, 167–195. Jerusalem. The Van Leer Jerusalem Institute and Hakibbutz Hameuchad [Hebrew].

Shihadeh, Mtanis. 2020. "The Joint List's recommendation: what has changed." *Arab 48,* March 21 [Arabic].

Smooha, Sammy. 2018. "Shared and limited Israeli identity." *Alpayim+* 1: 62–89 [Hebrew].

Zinger, Eran. 2020. "The crisis in the Joint List, following the support of Hadash MKs of the anti conversion therapy law" *Kan* 11, July 25 [Hebrew].

Zoabi, Baker. 2021. "The Joint List and Ra'am have not recommended anyone, but it is still possible that everything depends on them." *Siḥah mekomit*, April 6 [Hebrew].

Zucker, Daniel. 2017. "Joint but excluded? The Joint List in the 2015 elections." In *The Elections in Israel 2015*, edited by Michal Shamir and Gideon Rahat, 103–122. London: Routledge.

12 Three in a (Right-Wing) Boat

Media, Politicians, and the Public in the Age of Digital Communication[1]

Alon Zoizner, Keren Tsuriel, Dror K. Markus, Vered Porzycki, Guy Mor-Lan, Avishai Green, Effi Levi, Yariv Tsfati, Israel Waismel-Manor, Tamir Sheafer, and Shaul R. Shenhav

"Any understanding of power must involve an examination of the relationship between social actors, but less obviously, it must also encompass the relationship between social actors and technologies," wrote Andrew Chadwick (2017, p. 19). This, in a nutshell, is the issue presented in this chapter. In the modern political landscape, the massive use of digital networked technologies such as websites and social media, has dramatically changed the relationship among the three dominant social actors, namely the media, politicians, and citizens.

According to the classical agenda-setting theory, the media heavily influence what the public perceives as important, which can, in turn, affect vote choices (McCombs & Shaw, 1972; Sheafer & Weimann, 2005). Politicians also try to impact citizens' agenda using direct means of communication such as public speeches, and to integrate their agenda into media coverage (Davis, 2007). Whether by competition or cooperation, it has been traditionally assumed that both politicians and the media are powerful actors.

This may be no longer the case. As Chadwick (2017) asserted, new online mediated technologies are now the arena where agendas are being set and communicated. The unique affordances of each digital platform, be it traffic and comments on news websites or likes and shares on social media, emphasize the audiences' increasing control over content and the ability to choose the kind of news they consume and how (Bruns, 2008; Napoli, 2012). Thus, new media technologies may restore the capacity of citizens to actively shape the political arena in which they live (Cover, 2006).

While there has been increased scholarly attention to the rising power of audiences in shaping journalistic reports (McGregor, 2019) as well as politicians' priorities and rhetoric (Dassonneville et al., 2020; Mueller & Saeltzer, 2020), others continue to emphasize the enduring power of traditional media (Djerf-Pierre & Shehata, 2017), and, in particular, of political elites in setting the public agenda. As politicians have adapted to social media (Zamir & Rahat, 2017), they can now cut out the media as a middleman and

DOI: 10.4324/9781003267911-15

260 *Alon Zoizner et al.*

directly communicate with the public (Loosen et al., 2020). Moreover, since more powerful politicians (e.g., government members) enjoy greater media visibility (Hopmann et al., 2012), this enables them to maintain their traditional power in affecting the media and public agenda (Wolfsfeld, 2011).

Owing to these competing expectations of the relationship among the three actors, the current chapter examines *issue congruence*, or *agenda congruence* among the media, politicians, and the public, that is, the extent to which each actor discusses the same topics and considers them important (Barberá et al., 2019; Sheafer & Weimann, 2005). By focusing on four election campaigns that took place in 2019–2021, this chapter identifies the actors whose agendas overlap the most, and specifically which part of the political spectrum – right, center, or left – dominates the Israeli political agenda.

12.1 The Citizens: Voicing Their Priorities

Citizens are no longer "a mass of isolated individuals who are inherently susceptible to manipulation" (Webster, 1998, p. 191). They are not large anonymous audiences comprising passive and muted receivers whose tastes, views, and preferences are quite unknown (Livingstone, 2003). The introduction of the Internet and digital media armed audiences with new tools that marked a shift in power.

First, the information environment of citizens is now characterized by an abundance of information, where multiple actors distribute information through various channels. Sources of information like websites and social media platforms are now competing with traditional media for audience attention. Social media platforms, for example, have become a dominant tool for citizens to consume political information, which is not necessarily mediated by traditional media outlets (Gottfried & Shearer, 2017). This may pose a threat to the traditional media's power, for instance by reducing their ability to set the public agenda.

The second reason for the possible shift in power is the audiences' new powerful tool: their attention to information, pronounced by (1) the number of visits to and comments on news websites; or (2) their footprints on social media, such as likes and shares. This activity is constantly measured and used to match content to users' agenda (Lameiras et al., 2018).

Taken together, these changes mark a power shift toward the citizens, who now play an active role in shaping not only their media diet but also its content, produced by the media themselves and politicians (Napoli, 2012).

12.2 The Media: Tuned to the Citizens

The new digital era has tremendous effects on traditional journalism (Bell et al., 2017), specifically its infrastructure, roles, work practices, and content (Turow, 2011). Adding novel platforms to the traditional modes of news production and consumption created a new hybrid media system that obeys new

Three in a (Right-Wing) Boat   261

rules (Chadwick, 2017). Most media organizations have added two platforms to their arsenal: online websites that serve as new interactive means to engage the audience with their content (Tsuriel et al., 2019; Turow, 2011), and social media pages that allow for more reciprocal and dialogical relationships.

Audience matrices serve as the media's mobilizer. These matrices can show, for example, that a specific topic or angle gained interest among a large section of the audience (Lamot & Paulussen, 2020). These data points also serve as future guidelines, helping the media decide what and how to cover issues in order to keep the audience engaged (Tandoc, 2019).

Being able to gauge citizens' preferences is a powerful incentive to the media to flex their agenda, so that it will better match those of the audience. Therefore, it is reasonable to expect high congruence between the media's agenda and citizens' issue priorities – especially with those of the majority in a particular society. In the Israeli context, opinion polls during the 2019–2021 elections constantly showed that the majority leaned toward a right-wing ideology.[2] Thus, we expect that, overall, the Israeli media's agenda will be more congruent with the issue priorities of right-wing citizens. In other words, the issues considered important among right-wing citizens will be also more prominent in media coverage, compared to the issues emphasized by center-aligned or left-leaning citizens.

> **H1**: There will be higher congruence between the agendas of the Israeli media in general and right-wing citizens, compared to center-aligned and left-leaning citizens.

Nonetheless, one must take into account that certain news outlets can have explicit political ideologies that shape their reporting style and content (e.g., Tenenboim-Weinblatt et al., 2016). Thus, by focusing on specific news outlets we can expect higher congruence between the agenda of a given news outlet and the segment of citizens that share its political views. Specifically, we expect to find that the left-leaning *Ha'aretz* will embrace the left-wing agenda, the mainstream *Ynet* will be more congruent with the agenda of the center-aligned public, and the right-wing *Israel Hayom*, which is known for its support for Prime Minister Benjamin Netanyahu and his policies, will be more congruent with the priorities of right-wing citizens.

> **H2**: There will be higher congruence between the agenda of a given news outlet and of citizens who share its political inclinations, compared to other citizens.

Due to the increased ability of journalists and news editors to gauge what the public prefers, we examine the extent to which the media are dependent on information coming from politicians, compared to citizens. On the one hand, traditional approaches consider the media highly dependent on political elites, who control the flow of information on many issues and know how the media operate (Wolfsfeld, 2011). Government actors enjoy a higher degree of influence compared to opposition members (Hopmann et al., 2012). On the other hand, recent studies have pointed to politicians' limited power. For example, they can shape the news agenda mostly by addressing issues that are already important to the media (Meyer et al., 2020). Others have argued that the digital era enables journalists to "push back against politicians' attempts to control political narratives" (McGregor, 2019, p. 1074) and to rely more on public inputs on social media platforms (Barberá et al., 2019). Moreover, social media enable politicians to have direct communication with the public (Stier et al., 2018). This allows them to cut out the media as a middleman (Loosen et al., 2020). Due to these parallel processes, we expect that:

> **H3**: The agenda of the Israeli media in general will be more congruent with that of the citizens, compared to the politicians' agenda.

12.3 Politicians: Even More Tuned to the Citizens

Due to the affordances provided by new technologies such as social media matrices, politicians know who their audiences are in terms of demographics and political interest (Diaz et al., 2016), and shape their messages according to their priorities (Stier et al., 2018).

While politicians may have an incentive to be attentive to issues that are important to the general public in order to appeal to larger parts of the electorate (Wagner & Meyer, 2014), studies have found that politicians' agenda mainly reflects the priorities of their supporters (e.g., Barberá et al., 2019; Dassonneville et al., 2020; Neundorf & Adams, 2018). This is especially the case in polarized political systems, as in Israel, where voters have more consistent preferences than in less polarized systems, and they are motivated to publicly express these preferences (Spoon & Klüver, 2015).

> **H4**: The agenda of left, right-wing and center-aligned politicians will be more congruent with their own supporters, compared to the agenda of rival bloc supporters.

The 2019–2021 elections offer a unique opportunity not only to examine congruence among actors' issue priorities, but to also explore what these priorities comprise and how they may have changed during a short period of four meaningful political events, including the widescale Covid-19 pandemic.

12.4 Issue Agendas in Israeli Politics

To test our hypotheses, we examine the congruence of issue agendas among the media, politicians, and the public. We focus on four dominant issues in Israeli politics: security and peace, socioeconomic issues, state-religion, and political corruption. The first three have traditionally been high-profile topics

Three in a (Right-Wing) Boat 263

in Israel (Tsfati et al., 2011), and are considered dominant dimensions for understanding the Israeli cleavage structure that divides the left and right (Arian & Shamir, 2008; Shamir & Arian, 1999).

The fourth issue, political corruption, has made intermittent appearances over the years, especially when specific cases of corruption emerged (Tsfati et al., 2011). This was also the case during the four 2019–2021 election cycles, as Prime Minister Benjamin Netanyahu was indicted on three counts of bribery, fraud, and breach of trust.

12.5 Method

To examine issue congruence among the three actors (media, politicians, and the public), we combined three different data sets containing the agenda of each actor to measure the attention (or priority) they give to the four policy issues.

12.5.1 Media Agenda

To measure the attention given by the media to each issue, we scraped the contents of 36 Israeli news websites.[3] We analyzed the content of every news item published on each website on a daily basis during the period in which we collected the politicians' Facebook posts (see below). We utilized a computational content analysis (described in the Appendix) to analyze the level of attention to the four main policy issues across 642,048 news items. Although we collected news articles on a daily basis, we calculated the *weekly* attention per news outlet for each of the four issues to allow more time points for comparison with the public opinion data, as described below.

12.5.2 Public Agenda

We gauged the public's issue priorities through large N panel data ($N = 8,106$) that comprised 12 waves that were uniquely positioned to seize the unusual case of three consecutive elections within one year (10 waves in total), and an additional fourth election after a single year (2 waves). Respondents were recruited via iPanel, an online research company that operates a large panel of survey participants (Israeli Arabs were not included in the data collection[4]). Tables 12A.1 and 12A.2 in the Appendix report additional information on the panel participants. Panelists were rewarded for taking part in the surveys. Data collection for the first three elections began in January 2019, before the first election, and continued until March 2020, after the third election. Data collection for the fourth election began in January 2021, and continued until March 2021.

To measure the public's issue priorities, we used the widely known "most important problem" question (MIP; e.g., Spoon & Klüver, 2015; Sheafer & Weimann, 2005). In each of the 12 waves, respondents were asked: "What do you think is the most important problem the government should address? Please mention just one." Answers were coded by human coders according to a codebook containing seven categories – security, peace, socioeconomic issues, religion and state, political corruption, unity and hatred, and "other" (Krippendorff's α was not lower than .7). Of these categories, we focused on four: corruption, security and peace (a joint category comprising the original two separate categories), socioeconomic, and state-religion issues.

To identify the importance that citizens gave the issues in each wave, we counted the number of times each issue was raised by the respondents, and divided it by the total number of answers. To illustrate, a score of 0.12 indicates that 12% of the respondents in a given time point believed that a given issue was the most important problem. We also divided the respondents into three ideological blocs by asking them to place themselves on a scale ranging from 1 (right) to 7 (left). We coded responses of 1–3 as right-wing voters, 4 as center-aligned voters, and 5–7 as left-wing voters.[5]

Unlike the media and politicians' Facebook data, which were collected on a daily basis, the panel data included only 12 waves throughout the entire period. Since the recruitment of respondents per wave usually lasted more than a week, we split each wave to a weekly timespan to allow more time points for comparison, resulting in 31 weekly time points.

12.5.3 Politicians' Agenda

The agenda of Israeli politicians was examined through a computational content analysis (described in the Appendix) of the Facebook posts in their public pages. We focused on the pages of individual politicians rather than on parties because of increased political personalization in Israel and the rising impact of politicians, compared to parties, in affecting voting behavior (Balmas et al., 2014). Moreover, Israeli citizens engage more with the Facebook pages of individual politicians than of parties (Zamir & Rahat, 2017). We collected 36,169 Facebook posts by 205 politicians from 27 parties. Data collection for the first three elections took place between January 9, 2019, and March 14, 2020 (three months before the first elections up to one week after the third election). For the fourth election, we collected data between December 23, 2021, and March 28, 2021 (three months before and one week after Election Day).[6]

We defined the ideological bloc – center-aligned, left, and right wing – of each politician according to her party affiliation. The right-wing group included The Jewish Home, National Union-Tkuma, Likud, The New Right, Yisrael Beiteinu, Kulanu, Magen, Noam, Otzma Yehudit (Jewish Power), Shas, New Hope, Yahad, Yemina, and Zehut.[7] Center-bloc parties were Blue and White, Gesher, and Yesh Atid. The left-wing parties included Balad, Labor, Hadash, Meretz, Ra'am and Ta'al (see Table 12A.3 in the Appendix for descriptive statistics).[8]

12.6 Results

12.6.1 Issue Congruence Across the Three Actors

We first examined whether the agenda of the Israeli media in general was more congruent with that of right-wing citizens, compared to center-aligned and left-leaning citizens (H1). We present Pearson correlations in Figure 12.1, with higher scores indicating more similarities between the agendas of a pair of actors on a weekly basis (the unit of analysis is the weekly attention to a given issue among each actor). Looking at the media–citizens correlations, we found that media agenda is more congruent with that of right-wing citizens ($r = .83$), compared to left-wing and center-aligned citizens ($r = .64$ and $r = .66$, respectively). Thus, we can confirm H1. Examining the media–politicians relationship, media content was also the most congruent with the agenda of right-wing politicians ($r = .79$), followed by left-wing ($r = .61$), and center-aligned politicians ($r = .55$). We also examined these correlations separately for the period of election rounds 1–3 and the fourth election, which was conducted one year later. Results lead to the same conclusions. However, in the fourth election, which was accompanied by Covid-19, we observe stronger correlations between the media and citizens, compared to the three previous rounds. This may be due to citizens' increasing reliance on traditional media in times of crises (Van Aelst et al., 2021).

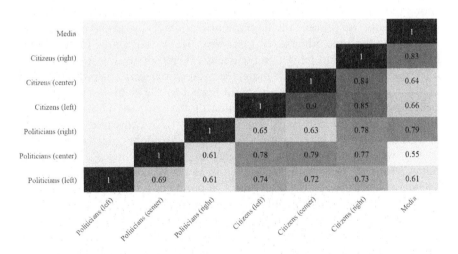

Figure 12.1 A heat map showing the Pearson correlations among the agendas of the media, politicians, and the public. The stronger the correlation between each pair, the darker the cell.

Notes: (1) All correlations are statistically significant. (2) The number of observations for the media–citizens correlations is lower ($N = 112$) than for media–politicians correlations ($N = 300$) due to the lower number of time points in the panel survey.

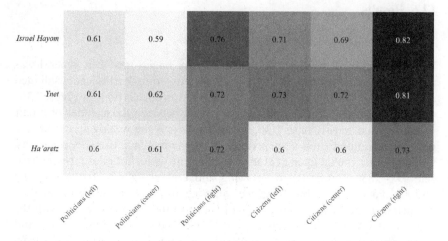

Figure 12.2 A heat map of Pearson correlations among the agendas of the three leading news outlets (*y*-axis), politicians, and the public (*x*-axis). The stronger the correlation between each pair, the darker the cell.

Note: All correlations are statistically significant.

The second hypothesis (H2) focused specifically on the agenda of three leading news outlets – *Ha'aretz*, *Israel Hayom*, and *Ynet* – each representing a distinct ideological perspective (Tenenboim-Weinblatt et al., 2016). Figure 12.2 shows the correlations between each news outlet and a given actor – citizens or politicians. We observe the highest correlations between the news outlets' agenda and the issue priorities of *right-wing citizens*, compared to the agenda of center-aligned and left-leaning citizens. Therefore, we reject H2. In parallel, the agenda of the three outlets is more congruent not only with that of the right-wing public but also with regard to the right-wing politicians' issue priorities. For example, the agenda of the left-wing *Ha'aretz* is more congruent with the agenda of right-wing ($r = .72$) compared to left-wing politicians ($r = .60$). When examining rounds 1–3 and the fourth election separately, we again observe the dominance of the right-wing agenda in each outlet. However, the fourth election led to increased congruence between the agenda of each news outlet and that of left-wing citizens (although the congruence with the right-wing public is still the highest).

We also tested whether the Israeli media agenda is generally more congruent with the public agenda, compared to the politicians' agenda (H3). We compared the correlations between each pair of actors in all four elections. The findings show that the media agenda was slightly more congruent with that of the public ($r = .78$) as opposed to the politicians' agenda ($r = .73$). Analyzing the first three election rounds yields similar patterns. However, focusing only on the fourth election, we observe that the correlations between the media and the politicians ($r = .93$) and citizens ($r = .92$) are similar and very high. In other words, the Israeli media agenda was overall not more congruent with citizens' compared to politicians' agenda. Specifically, in the fourth round, which was during Covid-19, all agendas were very congruent. Thus, H3 is only partially supported.

Finally, H4 posited that the agenda of left-wing, right-wing, and center-aligned politicians will be more congruent with their own supporters, compared with the agenda of their rival's supporters. As shown in Figure 12.1, the agenda of left-wing and center-aligned politicians is congruent with issue priorities expressed by all three groups somewhat equally, including those of right-wing citizens. Right-wing politicians are the only political bloc whose issue priorities were more in line with their own right-wing supporters ($r = .78$), compared to center-aligned ($r = .63$) or left-wing citizens ($r = .65$). Similar patterns arise when analyzing separately election rounds 1–3, but when focusing on the fourth election, we observe an increasing congruence between right-wing politicians and left-wing citizens. This may be due to the increasing attention of both sides to Covid-19, as we demonstrate below. Thus, H4 is rejected.

Taken together, these results point to the dominance of the right-wing agenda in Israel: the issue priorities of the media and politicians across the political spectrum tend to express a right-wing agenda, especially in the first three election rounds. The fourth election led to more agenda congruence among all actors, probably due to the increasing importance of socio-economic issues as a result from the Covid-19 crisis.

12.6.2 Trends in Issue Priorities Across the Four Elections

Thus far, we examined agenda congruence across different actors in Israeli politics. In this section, we turn to identifying what these agendas comprise, that is, which issues were considered more important than others by these actors and whether we observe temporal changes in the level of importance across the four campaigns. We note that one should not directly compare the raw numbers of issue attention (presented in Tables 12.1–12.3) among the three actors, because of the different approaches utilized to identify issue priorities: while the journalists' and politicians' discourse refers to a wide range of topics (e.g., security, racism, law and order, etc.; see Appendix for more details), the panel respondents were asked to mention only *one* issue they considered most important. Therefore, this section only compares the general trends in issue attention among the three actors.

First, a comparison of the important issues raised by *citizens* reveals that socioeconomic issues were considered the most important problem in Israel among all groups of citizens in all election campaigns (see Table 12.1).[9] Security and peace issues, which are traditionally one of the main pillars of Israeli politics (Shamir & Arian, 1999; Shamir et al., 2017), were considered far less important by the citizens. Corruption, which was highly relevant because of Prime Minister Netanyahu's legal issues, was mostly third in terms

268   *Alon Zoizner et al.*

Table 12.1 Percentage of citizens mentioning each of the four issues as Israel's most important problem during the 2019–2021 elections

Topic	Group	Round 1	Round 2	Round 3	Round 4
Corruption	Left	7.77	9.82	15.77	8.43
	Center	6.99	8	9.77	17.22
	Right	3.18	3.16	2.55	2.77
Security/peace	Left	23.35	16.12	16.51	14.08
	Center	19.96	18.35	11.51	7.19
	Right	37.68	32.32	34.47	11.17
Socioeconomic issues	Left	48.16	44.73	42.28	47.31
	Center	53.73	49.34	54.28	57.94
	Right	46.3	45.62	43.69	65.77
State-religion issues	Left	4.19	4.87	2.72	2.14
	Center	3.18	5.5	3.51	2.42
	Right	2.1	3.08	2.78	1.47

Note: The numbers in each cell represent the percentages of citizens who mentioned each topic as the most important problem in Israel out of the entire topics mentioned by each ideological group.

Table 12.2 Media attention (in percentage) to the four issues out of the total media coverage during the 2019–2021 elections

Topic	Round 1	Round 2	Round 3	Round 4
Corruption	2.94	2.03	2.72	2.22
Security/peace	8.69	9.79	8.27	6.48
Socioeconomic issues	7.6	8.16	9.25	12.71
State-religion issues	3.05	3.36	2.8	3.19

Note: The numbers in each cell are percentages and indicate the average weekly attention paid to each issue, aggregated per election. For example, a score of 8.69 for security and peace in the first elections suggests that on average, almost 9% of the weekly media coverage during the first election campaign referred to this topic out of the available topics. Other topics discussed in the media were municipal issues, law and order, foreign affairs, environment, culture, and so forth.

of importance across all public groups. The state-religion issue was considered least important.

Second, focusing on the media agenda, Table 12.2 shows that the socioeconomic issues and the security and peace issues received more attention, compared to other issues, across all four campaigns. However, as opposed to the public, the media paid more balanced attention to these two issues.[10] Corruption did not gain much media attention and received similar amount of coverage as did state-religion issues.

Table 12.3 shows that socioeconomic issues were also prominent among politicians' discourse on social media, especially among politicians from the center bloc, who emphasized these issues more than other issues (differences are significant for all election rounds). Right-wing politicians paid similar

Table 12.3 Politicians' attention (in percentage) to the four issues out of their total Facebook discourse during the 2019–2021 elections

Topic	Group	Round 1	Round 2	Round 3	Round 4
Corruption	Left	3.85	4.8	7.06	2.37
	Center	4.06	6.37	7.18	3.88
	Right	2.25	1.73	3.56	2.22
Security/peace	Left	6.97	8.04	9.89	4.65
	Center	7.21	7.73	5.79	2.93
	Right	9.17	9.89	8.62	5.66
Socioeconomic issues	Left	11.21	11.01	12.28	6.13
	Center	12.82	13.1	12.4	14.03
	Right	8.95	10.75	8.18	12.83
State-religion issues	Left	2.34	2.27	2.3	1.14
	Center	2.35	2.77	3.18	1.95
	Right	3.68	4.77	5.15	4.77

Note: The numbers in each cell are percentages and indicate the average weekly attention to each issue aggregated per election. For example, a score of 9.17 for security and peace among right-wing politicians in the first election suggests that on average, 9% of their weekly Facebook discourse referred to this topic out of the entire available topics. Other topics discussed by politicians on Facebook included civil rights and racism, interparty competition, mobilization efforts, and so forth.

degrees of attention to security and peace and socioeconomic issues in the first three rounds (nonsignificant differences), but more attention was given to the latter in the fourth round (significant difference). Corruption was again mostly left behind.

Finally, we examined how and whether issue priorities varied across the four election campaigns. Figures 12.3–12.5 facilitate the interpretation of possible time trends. Focusing on the socioeconomic issues, one can observe the relative stability in the degree of attention each actor gave to this issue during the first three election campaigns. However, the fourth election, which took place during Covid-19, clearly increased the attention to socioeconomic problems. Media attention to these issues was significantly higher during the fourth election compared to the previous rounds. Interestingly, right-wing politicians and citizens both gave significantly more attention to socioeconomic issues during the fourth election, compared to previous rounds. This may be due to the success of the right-wing government in vaccinating the general population before the fourth election.

As for media coverage of corruption, the raw numbers in Table 12.2 indicate a marginally significant decline[11] in their attention to corruption in the second election, compared to the first. This may be explained by the corruption issue becoming "old news" as the elections progressed. The decision of the State Attorney's Office in November 2019 to press charges against Prime Minister Netanyahu was mainly reflected in the issue priorities of politicians. According to Table 12.3 and Figure 12.5, in the third

270 Alon Zoizner et al.

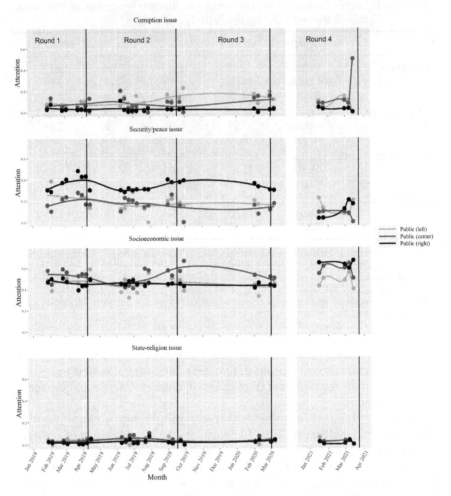

Figure 12.3 Issue importance among citizens during the 2019–2021 elections.

Notes: (1) The dots represent citizens' perceived importance of each issue on a weekly basis. (2) The *y*-axis indicates the percentage of answers mentioning a given issue as the most important problem out of the total answers for that week. (3) We added a trend line between the dots using Loess regression to capture nonlinear trends.

election there was a significant increase in the attention paid to corruption among left- (compared to the first election) and right-leaning politicians (compared to the second election). Attention to corruption among center-bloc politicians was relatively stable. Among citizens, left-wing supporters considered corruption more important in the third election compared to the first.

The first three election rounds were accompanied by various security challenges such as several rounds of missile attacks at the Gaza border.[12]

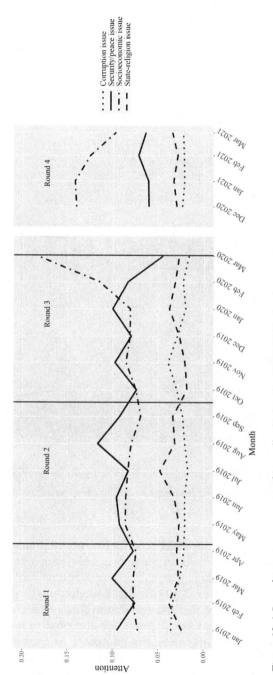

Figure 12.4 Issue importance among the media during the 2019–2021 elections.

Note: The *y*-axis represents a monthly aggregation of attention (percentage) for each issue.

272 Alon Zoizner et al.

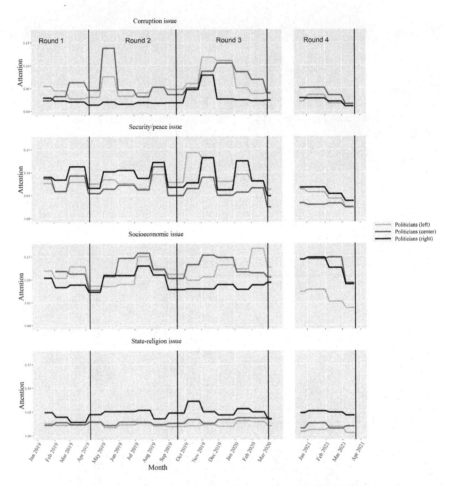

Figure 12.5 Issue importance among politicians during the 2019–2021 elections.

Note: The *y*-axis represents a monthly aggregation of attention (percentage) for each issue and ideological bloc.

However, these events did not make security the most dominant issue on the agenda of the media, politicians, or the public. This is apparent, for example, in Figure 12.3, which presents the public agenda over time: looking at the dots around April and September 2019 (the first two elections), one can see that the security threats did not increase the importance of security over socioeconomic issues for any ideological group. We also observe less attention by the media and the politicians to security and peace issues during the fourth election. Interestingly, while right-wing citizens perceived these issues significantly *less* important in the fourth election (compared to the previous rounds), no significant decline was observed among left-wing citizens.

Three in a (Right-Wing) Boat 273

Finally, the relatively low attention paid to the state-religion issue by most actors was stable in the initial three elections. The fourth election marked a significant decrease of attention among left-wing and center-aligned politicians.

12.7 Discussion

This chapter examined the relationships between the media, politicians, and the public in the context of the Israeli elections, in light of digital media technologies, whose affordances offer the three actors new ways to directly communicate with each other.

Our findings suggest that these affordances are mostly translated into the dominance of right-wing priorities in the Israeli political agenda. We find that overall, during the 2019–2021 elections, the issue priorities of Israeli online news outlets were more congruent with those of the right-wing bloc – both its supporters and politicians. Somewhat surprisingly, even the agendas of left-leaning (*Ha'aretz*) and mainstream news outlets (*Ynet*) were also more congruent with the issue priorities of right-leaning citizens (see also Eyal, 2019; Tsfati et al., 2011). These findings are against the common claim of citizens and politicians that the Israeli media are biased toward the political left (Gur, 2015).

Due to the increased feelings of media distrust among right-leaning citizens (Tsfati, 2017), we expect that this media–rightists' relationship is driven more by the news outlets' economic incentives to speak to the hearts and minds of the right-wing majority (Anderson & Gabszewicz, 2006) than vice-versa. At first glance, this right-leaning news agenda may gradually facilitate a reduction of media distrust among the right-wing public. However, since right-wing politicians have been criticizing the media as part of their campaign strategy over the last decades (Peri, 2004; Tsfati, 2017), we expect that the crisis of trust between right-leaning voters and the media will remain.

Our results also point to the dominance of politicians in shaping the media agenda. One would expect modern technologies to allow online news websites to gauge more easily the issue priorities of their own readers (Lamot & Paulussen, 2020). However, the fact that even left-leaning outlets, as *Ha'aretz*, emphasize a right-leaning agenda points to the great dependence of journalists on powerful political actors (Wolfsfeld, 2011), especially those from the right-wing government, which has been in power throughout the four election campaigns.

In other words, we do not find evidence for scholars' optimistic views of digital networked technologies that can empower citizens at the expense of political elites (e.g., Cover, 2006; McGregor, 2019) and allow for a more democratic direct connection between citizens and their representatives. If anything, our findings suggest that among politicians, the media are still considered an important actor that can shape the political discourse (Barberá et al., 2019; Djerf-Pierre & Shehata, 2017), and in parallel, that the digital

274 *Alon Zoizner et al.*

affordances available to journalists are not necessarily reflected in the news production process, which is still shaped by information that derives from political elites, especially those in the right bloc.

This chapter also examined what the Israeli political agenda comprised in the context of the 2019–2021 elections. Despite the right-wing dominance in the agenda of both journalists and politicians, the issues that were prioritized the most were not necessarily those that are traditionally "owned" by right-wing parties (Sheafer & Weimann, 2005): among the public, security and peace were only secondary to socioeconomic issues, and this was true even among right-wing citizens and across all four election periods. In parallel, journalists generally devoted equal levels of attention to each of these issues, even in times of security threats. The emphasis on socioeconomic issues may reflect the seeds of change ignited by the 2011 social justice protest, which has now matured (Rahat et al., 2016). Previous scholars argued that the Israeli society's constant preoccupation with national security threats and survival needs prevents its citizens from adopting more postmaterialistic values, that is, more emphasis on subjective well-being, self-expression, and quality of life (Yuchtman-Ya'ar, 2003). Our findings, however, suggest a gradual shift in citizens' priorities toward socioeconomic issues and postmaterialistic goals at the expense of security issues.

The importance of socioeconomic issues among citizens from all political blocs may be seen, at first glance, as an opportunity to bridge the gap between the Israeli left and right and to reduce affective polarization, that is, hostility and distrust between the opposing political sides. This may happen for two reasons. First, many parties in Israel, both from the left and right, publicly address socioeconomic issues in similar ways (Talshir, 2015). Second, the socioeconomic dimension is traditionally less central in the longstanding political cleavage between left-wing and right-wing supporters (Shamir et al., 2017).

However, interparty hostility across Western democracies is fueled not only by policy disagreements, but also by social identity explanations: citizens' political affiliations define them as unique social groups, which automatically promote positive sentiments toward the in-group (my party or bloc) and negative sentiments toward the out-group (the rival party or bloc; Huddy et al., 2018). In the Israeli context, identity-driven mechanisms for affective polarization are equally important as issue-based mechanisms (e.g., competing positions regarding the Israeli–Palestinian conflict): citizens' attachments to their political group (e.g., being a rightist or leftist) is a strong predictor for increased political hostility (Oshri et al., 2021). Therefore, even though socioeconomic issues dominate the public agenda, they are not expected to put out the flames between the rival political sides. This gap between the left and right may be reflected in the failed attempts to form a unity government in the first two elections, and in the instability of the Netanyahu–Gantz government after the third election. In the long run, however, the formation of the Bennett–Lapid government after the fourth election may facilitate reducing

Three in a (Right-Wing) Boat   275

affective polarization since cooperation between rival political actors results in less political hostility among citizens (Bassan-Nygate & Weiss, 2022).

Because of the dominance of the right-wing agenda, it is perhaps not surprising that corruption was less central in the eyes of the media and journalists throughout the four election campaigns. Its potential damage to the right-bloc leader, Benjamin Netanyahu, together with it becoming "old news" throughout the campaigns, may have made it less urgent in the minds of all actors. Another possibility is that in the heat of the intensive campaigns, corruption was framed as another "horse race" element rather than as an important substantive issue (Zoizner, 2021).

This chapter has some limitations. First, we did not address the question of who influences whom empirically: for instance, do right-wing politicians strategically influence the agenda of the media, or are they mostly responsive to it? While this is an important issue, the existing literature finds evidence for a reciprocal relationship among the agendas of the three actors (e.g., Neundorf & Adams, 2018).

Another limitation is the empirical focus of an unusual case study, namely three consecutive elections in less than a year, and an additional fourth election in the following year. This makes it is more difficult to generalize our conclusions to other political contexts. Nonetheless, this case study also allows us to examine whether trends in issue priorities, such as the dominance of right bloc, were unique to a single campaign or remained stable even during this turbulent time in Israeli politics. Our findings point to a relative stability in the issue priorities of the actors examined across the first three elections. This stability is also evident in other chapters in this volume (see the chapter by Lavi et al. on democratic values). Only the fourth election marked an increase in the dominance of socioeconomic issues (mostly among right-wing actors). In that sense, the uniqueness of this case study can be considered an advantage, as it points to the relatively stable relationships among the democratic actors, which are immune to external political shocks in a short time period.

Finally, this chapter focused more on prioritizing policy issues rather than their interpretation. We examined the *issues* that are prominent on the agendas of the media, politicians, and the public, not the *positions* expressed on these issues (for example, a Dovish or Hawkish point of view for security issues). We note, however, that issue priorities can affect public opinion (Barberá et al., 2019; Sheafer & Weimann, 2005) and decision makers (Zoizner et al., 2017), even without addressing competing policy positions. Despite these limitations, we believe that this chapter sheds light on the dynamics in Israeli politics, as expressed in the 2019–2021 elections, and specifically on the increasing dominance of the right-wing agenda in the Israeli political discourse.

Notes

1 This research was supported by the Israel Science Foundation (Grant No. 2315/18). The authors would like to thank Shira Dvir Gvirsman, Liron Lavi, Naama

276 *Alon Zoizner et al.*

Rivlin, Doron Ron, Nati Sror, Clareta Treger, the editors of this volume, and the anonymous reviewers for their valuable feedback on this project.

2 The Central Elections Committee collects opinion polls for each election. The ones of the 21st, 22nd, 23rd, and 24th Knesset can be found here: https://bec hirot21.bechirot.gov.il/election/Decisions/Pages/Surveys.aspx; https://bechirot22. bechirot.gov.il/election/Decisions/Pages/Surveys.aspx; https://bechirot23.bechi rot.gov.il/election/Decisions/Pages/Surveys.aspx; https://bechirot24.bechirot.gov. il/election/Decisions/Pages/Surveys.aspx

3 The full list contained mainstream Israeli news outlets (e.g., *Mako, Walla!, Ynet*), websites of print newspapers (e.g., *Ha'aretz, Israel Hayom, Maariv*), websites of TV channels (e.g., Channels 10, 12, 13, 20), and outlets representing different sectors (e.g., *Channel 7, Kikar Hashabat, Srugim*).

4 The exclusion of Israeli Arabs from the sample was conducted for two reasons: first, the issues that Israeli Arabs and Jews consider most important can be substantially different because of varying cultural, social, and political characteristics (Akirav, 2014). This requires a more fine-grained analysis that also considers factors such as ethnicity and religion. Second, Israeli Arabs consume more news in Arabic than in Hebrew (Ganayem, 2018). Since our computational content analysis was only conducted in Hebrew, we could not gauge for the majority of news content Israeli Arabs are exposed to.

5 Following Shamir et al. (2017), we identified only those answering the middle category in the 7-point ideological scale as part of the center bloc. The share of center-aligned respondents across waves was approximately 25%, similar to their share when measuring bloc membership according to vote intentions (Yair, 2021).

6 We used Facepager, a publicly available tool to extract content from politicians' public pages. However, this tool was denied access to Facebook content starting September 2019. We therefore shifted to CrowdTangle, a platform developed by Facebook, which allows access to public pages on the platform.

7 There were no posts by politicians from the Ashkenazi ultra-Orthodox party, United Torah Judaism.

8 When parties ran as part of a joint list with other parties (e.g., Gesher or Kulanu), we coded their ideological bloc according to the majority of politicians in the joint list.

9 We conducted ANOVA and Bonferroni post hoc tests among each group separately (left, center, and right) to examine whether the differences were statistically significant. Most differences were significant except for the state-religion vs. corruption among right-wing citizens. Socioeconomic issues encompass a greater variety of subtopics (e.g., unemployment, welfare, health system, housing), as opposed to security and peace (e.g., Gaza Strip, Iran's nuclear program), or the corruption issue (mainly Netanyahu's legal cases).

10 Security and peace issues were significantly more prominent than socioeconomic issues only in the second election. In the fourth election, held during the Covid-19 pandemic, socioeconomic issues were significantly more prominent than security and peace issues.

11 We examined whether there were significant differences in the extent of attention paid to each issue by each actor, using ANOVA and Bonferroni post hoc tests with the election round being the independent variable.

12 See the Israel Security Agency's ("Shin Bet") monthly reports, retrieved from: www. shabak.gov.il/publications/Pages/monthlyreports.aspx

References

Akirav, Osnat. 2014. "Catch-22: Arab members of the Israeli parliament." *Representation* 50 (4): 485–508.

Anderson, P. Simon, and Jean J. Gabszewicz. 2006. "The media and advertising: A tale of two-sided markets." In *Handbook of the Economics of Art and Culture 1*, edited by Victor A. Ginsburgh, and David Throsby, 567–614. Oxford: North-Holland.

Arian, Asher, and Michal Shamir. 2008. "A decade later, the world had changed, the cleavage structure remained: Israel 1996—2006." *Party Politics* 14 (6): 685–705.

Balmas, Mietal, Gideon Rahat, Tamir Sheafer, and Shaul R. Shenhav. 2014. "Two routes to personalized politics: Centralized and decentralized personalization." *Party Politics* 20 (1): 37–51.

Barberá, Pablo, Andreu Casas, Jonathan Nagler, Patrick J. Egan, Richard Bonneau, John T. Jost, and Joshua A. Tucker. 2019. "Who leads? Who follows? Measuring issue attention and agenda setting by legislators and the mass public using social media data." *American Political Science Review* 113 (4): 883–901.

Bassan-Nygate, Lotem, and Chagai M. Weiss. 2022. "Party competition and cooperation shape affective polarization: Evidence from natural and survey experiments in Israel." *Comparative Political Studies* 55 (2): 287–318.

Bell, Emily J., Taylor Owen, Peter D. Brown, Codi Hauka, and Nushin Rashidian. 2017. *The Platform Press: How Silicon Valley Reengineered Journalism*. New York: Tow Center for Digital Journalism.

Blei, David M., Andrew Y. Ng, and Michael I. Jordan. 2003. "Latent Dirichlet allocation." *Journal of Machine Learning Research* 3: 993–1022.

Bruns, Axel. 2008. *Blogs, Wikipedia, Second Life, and Beyond: From Production to Produsage*. New York: Peter Lang.

Chadwick, Andrew. 2017. *The Hybrid Media System: Politics and Power*. New York: Oxford University Press.

Cover, Rob. 2006. "Audience inter/active: Interactive media, narrative control and reconceiving audience history." *New Media & Society* 8 (1): 139–158.

Dassonneville, Ruth, Fernando Feitosa, Marc Hooghe, and Jennifer Oser. 2020. "Policy responsiveness to all citizens or only to voters? A longitudinal analysis of policy responsiveness in OECD countries." *European Journal of Political Research* 60 (3): 586–602.

Davis, Aeron. 2007. "Investigating journalist influences on political issue agendas at Westminster." *Political Communication* 24 (2): 181–199.

Diaz, Fernando, Michael Gamon, Jack M. Hofman, Emre Kıcıman, and David Rothschild. 2016. "Online and social media data as an imperfect continuous panel survey." *PLOS ONE* 11 (1): 1–21.

Djerf-Pierre, Monika, and Adam Shehata. 2017. "Still an agenda setter: Traditional news media and public opinion during the transition from low to high choice media environments." *Journal of Communication* 67 (5): 733–757.

Eyal, Nadav. 2019. "So, is the Israeli media biased in favor of the right?" *Ynet*, September 25. www.ynet.co.il/articles/0,7340,L-5596822,00.html [Hebrew].

Ganayem, Asmaa N. 2018. *The Internet among Arab Society in Israel*. Israel Internet Association (ISOC-IL). Retrieved from www.isoc.org.il/wp-content/uploads/2018/10/internet-arab-society.pdf [Hebrew].

Gottfried, Jeffrey, and Elisa Shearer. 2017. *Americans' Online News Use Is Closing in on TV News Use*. Pew Research Center.

278   *Alon Zoizner et al.*

Gur, Shahar. 2015. "Did you think that the Israeli media is biased in favor of the left? Think again." *Ifat Company for Media Studies*, December 16. ifat.co.il/-חשבתם שהתקשורת-שמאלנית-תחשבו-שוב [Hebrew].

Hopmann, David N., Peter Van Aelst, and Guido Legnante. 2012. "Political balance in the news: A review of concepts, operationalizations and key findings." *Journalism* 13 (2): 240–257.

Huddy, Leonie, Alexa Bankert, and Caitiin Davies. 2018. "Expressive versus instrumental partisanship in multiparty European systems." *Political Psychology* 39 (S1): 173–199.

Jagarlamudi, Jagadeesh, Hal Daumé III, and Raghavendra Udupa. 2012. "Incorporating lexical priors into topic models." In Proceedings of the 13th Conference of the European Chapter of the Association for Computational Linguistics: 204–213.

Lameiras, Mariana, Tiago Silva, and Antonio Tavares. 2018. "An empirical analysis of social media usage by local governments in Portugal." In Proceedings of the 11th International Conference on Theory and Practice of Electronic Governance: 257–268.

Lamot, Kenza, and Steve Paulussen. 2020. "Six uses of analytics: Digital editors' perceptions of audience analytics in the newsroom." *Journalism Practice* 14 (3): 358–373.

Livingstone, Sonia. 2003. "The changing nature and uses of media literacy." In *A Companion to Media Studies*, edited by Anghard N. Valdivia, 337–360. Malden, Oxford, and Carlton: Blackwell Publishing.

Loosen, Wiebke, Julius Reimer, and Fenja De Silva-Schmidt. 2020. "Data-driven reporting: An on-going (r) evolution? An analysis of projects nominated for the Data Journalism Awards 2013–2016." *Journalism* 21 (9): 1246–1263.

McCombs, Maxwell E., and Donald L. Shaw. 1972. "The agenda-setting function of mass media." *Public Opinion Quarterly* 36 (2): 176–187.

McGregor, Shannon C. 2019. "Social media as public opinion: How journalists use social media to represent public opinion." *Journalism* 20 (8): 1070–1086.

Meyer, Thomas M., Martin Haselmayer, and Markus Wagner. 2020. "Who gets into the papers? Party campaign messages and the media." *British Journal of Political Science* 50 (1): 281–302.

Mueller, Samuel David, and Marius Saeltzer. 2020. "Twitter made me do it! Twitter's tonal platform incentive and its effect on online campaigning." *Information, Communication & Society.* doi:10.1080/1369118X.2020.1850841

Napoli, Philip M. 2012. "Audience evolution and the future of audience research." *International Journal on Media Management* 14 (2): 79–97.

Neundorf, Anja, and James Adams. 2018. "The micro-foundations of party competition and issue ownership: The reciprocal effects of citizens' issue salience and party attachments." *British Journal of Political Science* 48 (2): 385–406.

Oshri, Oedelia, Omer Yair, and Leonie Huddy. 2021. "The importance of attachment to an ideological group in multi-party systems: Evidence from Israel." *Party Politics.* https://doi.org/10.1177/13540688211044475

Peri, Yoram. 2004. *Telepopulism: Media and Politics in Israel.* Stanford: Stanford University Press.

Rahat, Gideon, Reuven Y. Hazan, and Pzait Ben-Nun Bloom. 2016. "Stable blocs and multiple identities: The 2015 elections in Israel." *Representation* 52 (1): 99–117.

Shamir, Michal, and Asher Arian. 1999. "Collective identity and electoral competition in Israel." *American Political Science Review* 93 (2): 265–277.

Shamir, Michal, Shira Dvir-Gvirsman, and Rafael Ventura. 2017. "Taken captive by the collective identity cleavage: Left and right in the 2015 elections." In *The Elections in Israel 2015*, edited by Michal Shamir and Gideon Rahat, 139–164. New Brunswick: Transaction Publ.

Sheafer, Tamir, and Gabriel Weimann. 2005. "Agenda Building, Agenda Setting, Priming, Individual Voting Intentions, and the Aggregate Results: An Analysis of Four Israeli Elections." *Journal of Communication* 55 (2): 347–365.

Spoon, Jae Jae, and Heike Klüver. 2015. "Voter polarisation and party responsiveness: Why parties emphasise divided issues, but remain silent on unified issues." *European Journal of Political Research* 54 (2): 343–362.

Stier, Sebastian, Armin Bleier, Haiko Lietz, and Markus Strohmaier. 2018. "Election campaigning on social media: Politicians, audiences, and the mediation of political communication on Facebook and Twitter." *Political Communication* 35 (1): 50–74.

Talshir, Gayil. 2015. "'The new Israelis': From social protest to political parties." In *The Israeli Elections 2013*, edited by Michal Shamir, 31–58. New Brunswick and London: Transaction Publ.

Tandoc Jr, Edson C. 2019. "Tell me who your sources are: Perceptions of news credibility on social media." *Journalism Practice* 13 (2): 178–190.

Tenenboim-Weinblatt, Keren, Thomas Hanitzsch, and Rotem Nagar. 2016. "Beyond peace journalism: Reclassifying conflict narratives in the Israeli news media." *Journal of Peace Research* 53 (2): 151–165.

Tsfati, Yariv. 2017. "Attitudes toward media, perceived media influence, and changes in voting intentions in the 2015 elections." In *The Elections in Israel 2015*, edited by Michal Shamir and Gideon Rahat, 193–212. New Brunswick: Transaction Publ.

Tsfati, Yariv, Tamir Sheafer, and Gabriel Weimann. 2011. "War on the agenda: The Gaza conflict and communication in the 2009 elections." In *The Elections in Israel 2009*, edited by Asher Arian and Michal Shamir, 225–250. New Brunswick: Transaction Publ.

Tsuriel, Keren, Shira Dvir Gvirsman, Limor Ziv, Hagar Afriat-Aviv, and Lidor Ivan. 2019. "Servant of two masters: How social media editors balance between mass media logic and social media logic." *Journalism* 22 (8): 1983–2000. doi:10.1177/1464884919849417

Turow, Joseph. 2011. *Media Today: An Introduction to Mass Communication.* New York: Taylor & Francis.

Van Aelst, Peter, Fanni Toth, Laia Castro, Vaclav Štětka, Cales de Vreese, Toril Aalberg, . . . Yannis Theocharis. 2021. "Does a crisis change news habits? A comparative study of the effects of COVID-19 on news media use in 17 European countries." *Digital Journalism*, 9 (9): 1208–1238.

Wagner, Markus, and Thomas M. Meyer. 2014. "Which issues do parties emphasise? Salience strategies and party organisation in multiparty systems." *West European Politics* 37 (5): 1019–1045.

Webster, James G. 1998. "The audience." *Journal of Broadcasting & Electronic Media* 42 (2): 190–207.

Wolfsfeld, Gadi. 2011. *Making Sense of Media and Politics.* New York: Routledge.

Yair, Omer. 2021. "The hostile mediator phenomenon: When threatened, rival partisans perceive various mediators as biased against their group." *Public Opinion Quarterly* 85 (3): 864–866.

280 *Alon Zoizner et al.*

Yuchtman-Ya'ar, Ephraim. 2003. "Value priorities in Israeli society: An examination of Inglehart's theory of modernization and cultural variation." In *Human Values and Social Change: Findings from the Values Surveys*, edited by Ronald L. Inglehart, 117–133. Leiden: Brill.

Zamir, Shahaf, and Gideon Rahat. 2017. "Political personalization online: Parties and politicians in the 2015 elections." In *The Elections in Israel 2015*, edited by Michal Shamir and Gideon Rahat, 175–200. New York: Routledge.

Zoizner, Alon. 2021. "The consequences of strategic news coverage for democracy: A meta-analysis." *Communication Research* 48 (1): 3–25.

Zoizner, Alon, Tamir Sheafer, and Stefaan Walgrave. 2017. "How politicians' attitudes and goals moderate political agenda setting by the media." *The International Journal of Press/Politics* 22 (4): 431–449.

APPENDIX

Public Agenda

Table 12A.1 Descriptive statistics of respondents answering the MIP questions in all waves

Wave	N	Age (%)				Gender (%)		Bloc (%)		
		18–29	30–39	40–49	50+	Male	Female	Left	Center	Right
Wave 1	1,703	23.9	26.2	25.8	24.1	49.2	50.8	20.4	25.1	54.5
Wave 2	1,783	23	27.3	25.5	24.3	49.5	50.5	20.4	25.1	54.5
Wave 3	1,261	22.5	28.3	25.3	23.9	50.3	49.7	20.4	25.1	54.5
Wave 4	1,145	22.2	28.8	25.1	23.8	50.9	49.1	20.4	25.1	54.5
Wave 5	1,001	21.8	29	25.3	24	50.1	49.9	22.6	23	54.4
Wave 6	2,604	25.2	19.4	19.2	36.2	49	51	17.9	24.6	57.6
Wave 7	1,412	22.6	23.5	22	32	49	51	17.9	24.6	57.6
Wave 8	1,195	22.8	25.1	20.8	31.3	48.6	51.4	22.5	26.3	51.3
Wave 9	1,077	19.4	23.6	22.4	34.5	48.9	51.1	22.5	28.3	49.3
Wave 10	1,014	19.1	23.8	22.6	35.3	48.6	51.4	22.5	28.3	49.3
Wave 11	887	19.6	22.6	22.2	35.6	50.1	49.9	20.9	28.9	50.2
Wave 12	832	18.2	21.7	21.6	38.5	50	50	20.9	28.9	50.2

Note: As the ideological self-placement question was not asked in all waves, we assumed that it was relatively stable across the three consecutive elections, compared to vote choices (see Rahat et al., 2016). Therefore, for waves that did not include this question, we inferred the respondent's ideology based on the last wave in which this question was asked.

Three in a (Right-Wing) Boat 281

Table 12A.2 The panel sample compared to the Israeli population

		Panel sample (%)	Israeli population (%)
Gender	Females	50.4	51.5
	Males	49.6	48.5
Religiosity	Secular	51.4	43.4
	Traditional	27	35.1
	Religious	13.9	11.3
	Orthodox	7.6	10.2
Age	18–29	25.5	23.2
	30–39	19.8	19.5
	40–49	20.16	17.2
	50–59	15.5	13.8
	Above 60	18.9	26.2
Education	Up to high school/no diploma	13.8	28.8
	High school graduate	18.5	20.2
	Tertiary education	20.9	15.5
	Academic education	46.7	35.4

Notes: (1). Data on the Israeli population were collected from the Central Bureau of Statistics. (2) While recruiting respondents, we used quotas to increase representativeness. Naturally, along the 12 waves, some participants dropped, which harmed the sample's representativeness.

Source: We retrieved the Israeli population data from the following URLs: www.cbs.gov.il/he/publications/doclib/2018/2.%20shnatonpopulation/st02_03.pdf; www.cbs.gov.il/he/publications/DocLib/2020/seker_hevrati18_1788/h_print.pdf

Politicians' Agenda

Table 12A.3 Number of posts per political bloc over a period of three months before each election round

	Round 1	Round 2	Round 3	Round 4
Left-wing parties	2,276	2,255	876	1,937
Center-aligned parties	1,533	1,663	922	1,689
Right-wing parties	4,979	3,789	2,244	5,596

Notes: (1) The analysis included 62 politicians from the left bloc, 39 from the center bloc, and 104 from the right bloc. The average number of posts per politician across the four elections was 144.26, 194.38, and 188.88 for the left-, center-, and right-bloc politicians, respectively.

Computational Content Analysis

We classified the diverse issues discussed in the politicians' Facebook posts and news articles using topic modelling (Latent Dirichlet allocation – LDA; Blei et al., 2003), an approach that inductively learns how to identify topics in a large quantity of text. However, as our aim was to ensure the identification of specific topics of interest, we used a guided-LDA approach. This method

282   *Alon Zoizner et al.*

incorporates a set of predefined words that the researcher believes represent a certain topic in the texts to "nudge" the model to include such a topic (Jagarlamudi et al., 2012; Stier et al., 2018). For example, we determined that words like "allowance," "welfare," and, "poverty" represent the socioeconomic topic. That way, we facilitated the topic model by identifying the four policy issues as part of a wider set of inductive topics that the model automatically identifies within texts.

The predefined words used to guide the LDA model were based on the answers of the panel respondents to the open-ended MIP question. For each coding category (corruption, security and peace, socioeconomic issue, and state-religion issue), we used the most frequent words used by the respondents. Although the respondents answered open-ended questions, many used similar terms to describe the four issues (e.g., "self-interest" for corruption and "terror" for security and peace). This allowed us to guide the computational analysis toward detecting the topics raised by the respondents according to their own terminology.

We used the guided-LDA approach to analyze the media and the Facebook corpora separately. We used separate topic models to analyze news articles and politicians' Facebook posts as they differed in terms of language and terminology. We set the number of topics for the politicians' Facebook corpus at 100 and for the news corpus at 250 (which is far more diverse in content). The computational method produced two lists of topics that appeared in the news and Facebook corpora (one list per corpus). Human coders inferred a label for each topic (e.g., "Unemployment," "Benjamin Netanyahu's legal affairs") by reading representative texts and identifying significant keywords that belonged to it. Each text (either a single Facebook post or article) received a score for each topic that ranged from 0 to 1, indicating the extent to which a topic appeared in the text. For each text, we aggregated the topics pertaining to our four issues of concern. For example, topics like "Unemployment" and "Health system" were joint together to a general "socioeconomic issue." We aggregated the scores of the news and Facebook texts on a weekly basis. For example, a weekly score of 0.09 for the corruption issue in the news corpus indicated that, on average, 9% of the coverage in that week pertained to this topic from among all topics covered in the media.

Index

Note: Page numbers in **bold** and *italics* denote tables and figures, respectively. References to endnotes show both the page number and the note number (206n3).

Abbas, Mansur 32, 45, 133, 238, 241, 251, 254; and Netanyahu 45, 133
Abu Shehadeh, Sami 44
agenda 3, 69, 71, 82, 92, 99, 198, 238, 252, 253, 273–4; agenda congruence 260, 265, 267; agenda-setting 259; citizens' agenda 259, 261, 262, 265–7; conservative agenda 251, 252; election campaign agenda 44, 45, 77; foreign affairs-security agenda 36, 111, 251; liberal agenda 133; media agenda 5, 13, 36, 40, 45, 259, 261–3, 265–8, 272, 273, 275; Netanyahu's agenda 77, 100, 101, 125; news agenda (*see* media agenda); policy agenda 195; politicians' agenda 5, 45, 259, 262, 264–7, 281; pragmatic agenda 252; progressive agenda 109; public agenda 5, 36, 45, 77, 248, 259, 260, 269, 263, 266, 272, 274, **280**; right-wing agenda 5, 13, 266, 267, 273–5; social agenda 30; socio-economic agenda 45, 191, 196
Agudat Yisrael 29, 30, 73n3, 218, 229
alternate prime minister 3, 4, 18–19, 42, 43, 49, 72, 83
anti-Netanyahu bloc 4, 9, **12**, 13, 14, 17, 42, 44, 72, 83, 89, 114n2, 132, 176–80, 183
Arab citizens: electoral projections 167; influence on politics 9, 24, 45, 238–42, 248–9, **250**, 251–2, 254; and Netanyahu 105, 106, 110, 112; *see also* Arab voter(s)

Arab party/parties: candidate selection 242; in coalition 4, 23, 24, 28, 48, 91, 104, 106, *169*, 173, 176, 178, 182, 247, 252, 253; government formation 33, 107, 129; joint list 35, 24; personal 229; polls 36; trust in 245, **247**, 249, **250**; votes and seats 9, 37, 238, *243*, 244, 253
Arab politicians 5, 239
Arab public 5, 24, 106, 112, 238, 239, 247–9, 253, 254
Arab turnout *see* turnout
Arab vote(rs) 36, 44, 108, 244; breakdown of vote **243–6**, **253**; electoral projections 167, 178, 187; and Netanyahu 46, 252; stands **250**, 247, 252; *see also* Arab citizens
Ariel, Uri 29
Ashkenazi, Gabi 31, 43
Ashkenazi(m) 108, 114n7, 192–4, 196, 204–6, 206n3
Attorney General: attacks on 102, 104, 107, 120, 126–34; and Netanyahu's legal affairs 28, 32, 39, 119, 125–34, **145**, 148–50, 152n1, 155n30; *see also* Mandelblit, Avichai

Babiš, Andrej 20–1
Balad: bloc affiliation 264; disqualification 40; government formation 38, 248, 249; in The Joint List 31–2, 35, 44, 234, 241–2, 251, 252; in joint lists 221; leadership selection 44; *see also* Balad-Ta'al; Ra'am–Balad

284 *Index*

Barak, Aharon 125
Barak, Ehud 99, 111, 152n3, 220
Barbivai, Orna 31
Barakeh, Mohammad 241, 256n10
Barkat, Nir 29
Basic Law: Israel–Nation State of the Jewish People, 27, 100, 106, 122
Basic Law: The Government 24n1, 42, 142, 144, 145, 150, 154n17, 155n30
Basic Law: The Knesset 24n2, 43
Begin, Benny 43, 114n2, 125
Begin, Menachem 43, 57, 60, **66**, 67, 101, 102, 105, 114n2
Ben-Ari, Michael 32
Ben-Barak, Ram 31
Ben-Gurion, David 102
Ben-Gvir, Itamar 32, 220
Bennett, Naftali: government formation 48; Jewish Home 29; joint list 220; judicial system 130; and Netanyahu 35, 45, 101; New Right party 29; personalism 58; prime minister 4, 19, 49, 119, 182, 191; Yemina 6, 43
Bennett-Lapid coalition *see* Bennett-Lapid government
Bennett-Lapid government 13, 19, 22, 24, 49, 152n1, 195, 254, 274; *see also* 36th government
Bibi *see* Netanyahu, Benjamin
Bishara, Azmi 239, 240
bloc vote **12**, 86–7, **87**, **88**, 89, **90**
Blue and White (Kahol Lavan) 15–16, 30, 32, 39–40, 43, 114n2, 108, 191; Arab vote *244–6*, 253; and Arab parties, 249; bloc **12**, 83, *93*, 264; candidates 31, 44; election campaign 36, 164; electoral projections 168, **169**, 170, 174, *175*, 176, 179, 180, 182; ethnic vote 196, 198–9, **200**, 201, *203*, 204, 205, *210–12*; in government 3; government formation 38, 48, 195; joint list 16, 226, 232; personalization and personalism 31, 60, **61**, **62**, 62, 64, 67, 72; personification 89; polls 30–2, 36, 39, 40, **169**; sociological affiliation 191–3; split 8, 15–16, 42, 45, 132, 182, 191, 195; votes and seats 8, 9, **10–11**, 32–3, **34**, 36, **37**, 38, 40, **41**, 42, **47**, 47–8, 107–8
Bolsonaro, Yair 20
budget *see* state budget

campaign *see* election campaign(s)
candidate selection 28–31, 35–6, 39, 44, 215, 222, 242; and personalization 55–6, 58, **58**, 60, 70, **70**; *see also* primaries
Central Elections Committee 9, 39, 61, 213, 216, 221; allegations of ballot fraud 21, 46; disqualifications of candidates 32, 36, 40, 46; election integrity and administration 36, 44
class voting 5, 18, 108, 190–6, 198, 204–6
cleavage(s) 17, 18, 187, 204, 205, 263; Ashkenazim-mizrahim 204; identity 17, 18, 80, 192; right-left 42, 263; social 17, 204, 205
coalition agreement(s) 18, 23, 42, 123, 191, 195, 252
coalition crisis(es) 3, 28
coalition negotiations 4, 15, 23, 74n10, 130, 163, 165, 254
coalition (predicted) 167–8, *169*, 169–71, *171*, *172*, 173, 176, 178, 180–2, 187
Conscription Law 28, 127
Corbyn, Jeremy 106
Corona virus pandemic *see* Covid-19 pandemic
corruption 3, 5, 28, 38, 110, 121, 132, 151, 154n20; and the agenda 32, 36, 262–4, 267–9, **268**, **269**, 270, 275, 276n9, 282; and public opinion 129, 177
Covid-19 (pandemic): 8, 40, 42, 44–6, 105, 111–13, 149, 195, 252; and the agenda 262, 265, 267, 269, 276n10; and mass protest 21; and the establishment of Netanyahu-Gantz government 42, 132
crisis of democracy 20, 77, 92n1; *see also* democratic backsliding; democratic deconsolidation
crisis of parties *see* parties, crisis of

Dayan, Moshe 220
"Deal of the Century" 39
dealignment 15–17, 220, 234
Degel HaTorah 29, 30, 44, 218, 229
democratic backsliding 4, 5, 20, 21, 22, 78–80, 91–2; *see also* crisis of democracy; democratic deconsolidation
Democratic Camp (Hamachane Hademocrati) **10**, **12**, 35, 36, **37**, 38, 39, 184n5, 245, *245*

democratic culture 79, 80, 85, 91, 92
democratic deconsolidation 79, 91, 92; *see also* democratic backsliding; crisis of democracy
Democratic Israel (party) 35, 39, 220
democratic values: and Netanyahu 4, 14–15, 21; personification of 55, 77–8, 80–9, *84*, *85*, *87*, *88*, *90*, 91, 93n5, *97*, 275; public support in 15, 21, 78–80, 92
Derech Eretz 42, 43, 220, 232
Deri, Arye 30, 60, 131, 141–3, 146, 150–2
Deri-Pinhasi doctrine 141–3, 146, 150, 151
direct election(s) of the prime minister: and joint lists 220–2, 231, 235n6; and Netanyahu 77; personalization and personalism 67, 70, 214; and sanctions against Prime Minister 144, 154n17; split vote 8
Duterte, Rodrigo 21

effective number of parties **7**, 8, 221, 234
Eldad, Dan 131
election campaign(s) 4, 20, 28, 120, 121, 164, 166, 192, 206, 215; agenda 260, 267, 268, 269, 273, 275; election campaign 1981 193; election campaign 2015 101, 121, 126; election campaign Arab parties 238, 244–6, 248, 251, 252, 254, 255n6; election campaign April 2019 29, 32, 104, 105; election campaign September 2019 36, 104, 107; election campaign 2020 39–40, 109, 168; election campaign 2021 43–5, 105, 106, 110, 112–13; media and the election campaign **268**, 273; Netanyahu's election campaigns 100, 101, 102, 104–7, 109, 110, 112–14, 121, 122, 125–8, 130, 131; and personalization 54, 57, 80–1
elections (past): elections 1949-2021 *227–8*, *230*; elections 1949 217, 235n7; elections 1951 217, 222; elections 1959 235n7; 1961, 222; elections 1965: 60, 226; elections 1973 108, 222; elections 1977 17, 57, 60, **66**, 67, **68**; elections 1981, **68**, 190, 193, 220; elections 1984 63–4, **68**, 71, 222, 226, 235n7; elections 1988 **68**; elections 1992 33, 57, **66**, **68**, 229, 231, 235n6; elections 1996 **68**, 220, 222, 235n6; elections 1999 8, 67, **68**, **69**, 70, 77, 93n3, 99, 220–1, 226, 229, 235n5, *243*; elections 2003 15, 33,

40, **68**, *222*, *243*; elections 2006 16, 28, **66**, **68**, *222*, *243*; elections 2009 **66**, **68**, **69**, 123, 229, *243*; elections 2013 61, **69**, 93n3, 101, 220, 241, *243*; elections 2015 3, 29, 35, 62, 63, **66**, **68**, **69**, 93n3, 100, 101, 108, 121, 126, 129, 194, 217, 233, 242, *243*
electoral system 3, 6, 16, 23, 62, 63, 71, 214
electoral threshold **7**, 8, 16, 177, 181; and the Arab parties 241, 242, 244, 252; in April 2019 elections; 28–31, 33, 49n2; and joint lists 213–15, 217, 218, 221, 222, 226, *227*, 231, 233, 235n4; in September 2019 elections 35–6, 174; in 2020 elections 38, 39, 41, 49n3; in 2021 elections 43–8, 232
electoral volatility **7**, 8, 14–16, 41, 197, 206, 220
Elkin, Ze'ev 132
Erdoğan, Recep Tayyip 21, 164
ethnic politics 18, 109, 190, 191, 193, 194, 205, 206
ethnic voting 5, 9, *188*, 190, 191, 193–7, 199, 204–6, **212**, 276n4

Facebook: and personalization 56, 61–3, **61**, **62**; and politicians' agenda 263, 264, **269**, 276n6, 281; and Netanyahu, 114n10
Feiglin, Moshe 29, 35
former Soviet Union (FSU) 82, **87**, 98, 198
former USSR *see* former Soviet Union
fragmentation 8, 23, 45, 215, 221, 234
"French Law" 132, 150, 154n22, 155n29

Gabay, Avi 31, 35
Galant, Yoav 29
Galon, Zehava 31
Gantz, Benny: alternate prime minister 3, 8, 19, 43, 49, 132, 245; electoral projections 168, *168*, 174, *175*, 176, 178, 180, 182, 183; establishment of Blue and White 30, 31; establishment of Hosen Yisrael 30; Fifth Dimension affair 132; government formation 38, 42–3, 107, 130, 191, 195, 248, 249, 251, 254, 256n9; personalization and personalism 57, 58, 64, **65**, 67, 71, 72, 220; personification 82–3, 89, **90**, 91; prime ministerial candidate 32, 39, 132; *see also* Netanyahu-Gantz government

286   *Index*

Gesher 30, 35–6, 42, 44, 220, 232; bloc affiliation 12, 28, 30, 42, 49n4, 93n11, 264; and personalization 58, 61; in the polls 30, 33; vote **10**, **34**, 38, 39, 40; *see also* Labor-Gesher; Labor-Gesher-Meretz
Ghnaim, Masoud 241
Ginossar, Yossi, 141–2, 153n10
Golan Heights: US recognition 3
Golan, Yair 35, 39, 67
Gopstein, Ben-Zion 36
Green Movement (the) 35, 220, 232
Gush Emunim 101

Hadash: bloc affiliation 264; disqualification 32; government formation 28, 33, 247; in The Joint List 9, 31–3, 35–8, 44, 234, 241–2, 251; leader and candidates 241–2, 256n10; Palestinian issue 252; and personalization 54, **61**, **62**; votes and seats 9, 38, 241, 242, 252
Hadash-Ta'al 9, **10**, **12**, 32, **34**, 93n11, 242
Haderech Hashlishit 220
Hamas 28, 48, 71, 106, 113
Happy Planet Index 110, 112
Hathi'ya-Tzomet 226
Hatnu'a 31, 220, 235n2, 235n3
Hauser, Zvi 31, 42, 220
Ha'yisraelim 232
Hendel, Yoaz 108, 220
High Court of Justice (HCJ) 28, 49n1, 123, 124, 140; and candidates and parties disqualification; 32, 36, 40, 46; cases relevant to Netanyahu's legal stand 141–6; trust in 123; and Netanyahu 125, 126, 131, 134, 140; *see also* Supreme Court
Histadrut 31
Hobbes, Thomas 113
Horowitz, Nitzan 36
Hosen Yisrael 16, 30, 44, 191, 220, 226, 232; candidate selection 31; establishment 30; in government 9, 42, 45, 72; and personalization 31, 54, 58, 72; *see also* Blue and White
Huldai, Ron 44, 49n5
Hungary 20, 23, 91, 133

identity: Arab 254; Arab Israeli 252; collective 17, 18, 80, 190, 192, 205; ethnic 190–7, 205, 206n1; Israeli 238–42, 244, 245, 252, 254, 255n1; Jewish 17, 239; Mizrahi 108, 109, 206;

Muslim 254; Palestinian 239, 240, 252, 254; religious 192, 206; sectoral 221; social 192, 197, 274; *see also* non-Zionist Israeli identity
identity politics 107–9, 205, 239–41
IDF (Israel Defense Forces) 103, 106, 108, 114n6; Chief of Staff 30, 31, 43, 103; Deputy Chief of Staff 35
Im Tirtzu 101, 102
immunity 39, 131, 140, **145**, 147, 149, 150, 153n7, 154n23, 155n24
impeachment 140, 143, 146, 147
incorporation regime 192, 194, 205
institutional reform 3, 5, 7, 18–19
Intifada (Palestinian Uprising): second 101, 111
Israel Ahat (One Israel) 99
Israel Hayom 99, 100, 114n1, 127, 131, 261
Iran 99, 100, 111, 113, 276n9
Italy 71, 81, 154n23, 215

Jabotinsky, Ze'ev 101–2
Jerusalem: division of 128; mayor 29; "Shabechi Jerusalem" (praise Jerusalem) 108–9; US recognition 27; US embassy 27
Jewish Power *see* Otzma Yehudit
(The) Jewish Home: bloc affiliation 264; candidate and leader selection 29; coalition 27, 42, 194, 195; decline 16, 43; joint lists 29, 35, 38, 39, 233, 235n2; split 29; stand on Judicial system 124, 126, 131
(The) Joint List: bloc affiliation **12**, 93n11; campaign 246–8, 252; disintegration 9, 31, 33, 44, 232, 241–2, 251; disqualification 36; establishment 217, 240, 241; government formation 37, 38, 40, 45, 48, 104, 195, 248, 249, 254; Israeli identity 238, 254; polls 36, 39, 45, 46, 248, 249, *250*; and the LGBTQ 253; reestablishment 9, 36, 173, 238, 241–2, 244; vote 9, **10–11**, 31, **37**, 37, 38, 40, **41**, 41, **47**, 48, *245*, 252, *253*
joint lists 5, 16, 29, 32, 35, 43, 44, 213–37
Judea and Samaria 17, 124, 131, 198; *see also* Occupied Territories; West bank
Judicial system: activism 143; and attempts to limit its power 29, 100–4, 107, 109–10, 114, 119–23, 125–6, 129–31, 133–4, 139, 140, 141; conservatism 17; doctrines 140; review 140, 143

Kadima 16, 74n11, 99, 235n2
Kahlon, Moshe 27, 29, 39, 44, 58, 61, 126, 220
Kasif, Ofer 32, 242
Knesset Elections Law, 1969 216–17
Knesset Speaker 21, 145
Kulanu: bloc affiliation **12**, 33, 93n11, 264; candidates 29, 31; in coalition 27, 29; as "economic party" 44; in joint lists 233, 276n8; and Likud 13, 35, 38, 42, 233; moderation 29; as a personal party 54, 58, 61, 220; vote 8, **10**, 33, **34**, 35

Labor (Ha'avoda): bloc affiliation **12**, 93n11, 264; candidate selection 31, 35, 44; decline 16; defections 35; disqualification 46; joining government 42, 48, 99, 195; joint lists 35, 40, 44, 220, 229; leadership selection 31, 35, 44; personalization 54, 58, 60, **61**, **62**, 67; polls 31, 32, 46; seats and votes 9, **10–11**, 15, 31, 33, **34**, 36, 38, 40, **47**, 47, 48, 193, *253*
Labor-Gesher **10**, **12**, 35, **37**, 38, 39, *245*
Labor-Gesher-Meretz **11**, **12**, **41**, 49n4, 93n11, 232, 245, *246*
Lapid, Yair: alternate prime minister 4, 19, 49, 191; government formation 48, 83, 119, 191, 195; and Netanyahu 122; optimism 183; personalization and personalism 57, 58, 61, **65**, 220; prime ministerial candidate 30, 39, 43, 45, 83, 182; and the social protest 191; Yesh Atid leader 31, 44; *see also* Bennett-Lapid government
Le Pen, Jean-Marie 190
leadership selection 31, 39, 40, 44, 55, 56, 58, **59**, 60, 70, **70**, 215; *see also* primaries
legal responsibility 4, 139, 147
Levin, Yariv 126
Levy-Abekasis, Orly 27, 28, 30, 44, 49n4, 220
Levy, David 30
LGBTQ 251, 253
Lieberman, Avigdor 6, 28, 36, 37, 43, 58, 72, 93n11, 107, 125, 128, 129, 176, 178, 183, 195
Likud: Arab vote *245*, *253*; bloc **12**, 28, 33, 43, 83, 93n11, 119, 132, 151, 264; campaign 32, 36, 40, 104, 107, 120, 128, 164; candidate selection 28–9, 39, 44, 46, 48, 125; criticism of past

leaders 101; defectors 6, 31, 43, 125, 132; election fraud allegations 21; electoral projections 168–70, *169*, 174, *175*, 176–8, 180, 182; and ethnic vote 107, 193–9, **200**, *202*, *203*, 204, **210–12**; and Gesher 30, 44; government formation 6, 38, 42, 72, 126, 191, 252, 253; ideology and policy 17, 101, 112, 126; intraparty conflicts 43, 99, 114n2; joint lists 38, 220, 221, 226, 229, 233, 234; and Jewish Home 29; and Kulanu 13, 27, 29, 35, 38; leadership selection 28, 39, 40, 60, 131; and New Hope 43, 114, 132–3; personalization and personalism 60, **61**, **62**, 64, 67; polls 29, 32, 36, 39, 40, 46; populism 105, 124; rotation government 3, 42, 43, 191; 2015-2020 government 27; votes and seats 8, 9, **10**, **11**, 13, 15–16, 29, 32, 33, **34**, 36, **37**, 38, **41**, 40–2, 45, **47**, 48, 94n17, 107, 108, 119, 124, 129, 130, 132, 144, **145**; and Zehut 29, 38
Litzman, Yaakov 126
Livni, Tzipi 31, 93n3, 123, 220
Locke, John 113

Ma'arach 193, 226, 234
Mada 235n5, 247
Mandelblit, Avichai 28, 39, 119; *see also* Attorney General
Ma'oz, Avi 220
Mara'ana-Menuhin, Ibtisam 46
Marzel, Baruch 36
Meretz: Arab vote 244, *253*; bloc affiliation **12**, 93n11, 264; candidate selection 31, 35–6, 44; decline 16; electoral projections 182; in government 48, 195; joint lists 36, 39, 42, 44, 217, 229, 232; leadership selection 31, 35–6; personalization 54, 60, 67; polls 32, 46; votes and seats 9, **10**, **11**, 33, **34**, 35, 38, 40, **47**, 47, 48; *see also* Democratic Camp; Labor-Gesher-Meretz
Meridor, Dan 114n2, 125
Michaeli, Merav 44
Military Service Act *see* Conscription Law
Mizrahi(m): and Begin 105; definition 114n7; and Netanyahu 109; rift between Mizrahim and Ashkenazim 108, 109, 192, 193; social class 194, 196; support in democracy 82; voting behavior 9, 191–3, 196–9, **200**, 201,

288 *Index*

202, 203, 204–6, 206n3, **210–12**;
see also identity, Mizrahi
Modi, Narendra 20
Morawiecki, Mateusz 20

National Religious Party (NRP) 194,
229, 234
National Statist Movement *see* Telem
National Union-Tkuma 29, 35, 38, 42,
44, 46, 48, 233, 235n5, 264
Neoliberal(ism) 99, 102–7, 109–14, 122,
194
Netanyahu, Benjamin: achievements
110–11, 114; and the Arabs 24,
113, 133, 248, 249, 251, 252; Bar-
Ilan speech 99; Bibi or Tibi 104,
164; candidate nomination 44; and
democracy 15, 20, 21, 78, 80–2, 86–7,
88, 89, 91; early career 101; and early
elections April 2019 3, 28; election
campaigns 19, 32, 36, 39, 80, 81, 102,
104–5, 107–9, 112–13, 128–31, 164,
275; first government 99, 102; former
allies 30, 31, 48; fourth government
19, 27–8; government formation 33,
38, 42, 48, 119, 152, 154n18, 195; and
identity politics 108–10; immunity
131; and Israel Hayom 99, 261; and
the judicial system 100, 104, 119, 122,
125–6, 131, 133–4; "King Bibi" 77, 99,
113; legal affairs 28, 39, 114n1,
119–20, 125–8, 139, 141, 144,
144, 148–9, 151, 152n3, 263,
269; Likud leader 28, 39, 131;
ministerial appointments 35; and
the national religious parties 29,
35, 46; neoliberalism 105, 110–14;
and personification 89; and political
personalism and personalization 4–6,
15, 55, 57, 60, 64, **65–6**, 67, 71, 72,
77, 80; populism 20, 105–13, 121–2,
124, 133; projections (political) 168,
168, 170, 174, *175*, 176–80, 182–3;
public opinion polls 15, 83, 93n3,
129, 155n29; rotation government 3,
9, 18–19, 42, 43, 49, 132–3, 182, 191,
195, 245; second government 99; and
statism 102, 103, 125; and Trump 39,
46, 100, 106; and the ultra-Orthodox
45, 123; and the USA 100; young
advisors 102; *see also* anti-Netanyahu
bloc; Likud; Netanyahu-Gantz
government; pro-Netanyahu bloc

Netanyahu-Gantz government 7–9, 13,
43, 44, 105, 132, 195, 274
Netanyahu, Yair 101, 114n10
New Hope: bloc affiliation **12**, 93n11,
264; establishment 6, 43, 120,
132–3; government formation 48, 183;
personalization and personalism 58,
72; polls 45, 46; votes and seats 8, **11**,
46, **47**, 48, 114, 133, *253*
Nissenkorn, Avi 31, 43, 49n5
Nitzan, Shai 28, 129; *see also* State
Attorney
new media 101, 102, 259; *see also* social
media; social networks
The New Right; bloc affiliation **12**,
93n11, 264; establishment 29;
government formation 42; in joint
lists 35, 38, 220, 232, 235n2; and
the judicial system 130; leader and
candidate selection 29; personalization
and personalism; 58, 220; polls 33;
votes and seats **10**, 33, **34**, 35
Noam **37**, 44, 46, 48, 220, 232, 264
non-Zionist Israeli identity 5, 24,
238–42, 254, 255n1
"Norwegian law" 5, 18–20

Obama, Barak 27, 99
Occupied Territories 99, 103, 254; *see
also* Judea and Samaria; West Bank
Odeh, Ayman 32, 238, 240–2, 247–9,
251, 252, 254
Ohana, Amir 129, 131
Olmert, Ehud 57, **66**, 67, 74n11, 111,
123, 125, 139, 148, 153n3, 155n29
Orbán, Victor 20
Oslo Accords 99, 142, 253
Otzma Yehudit: bloc affiliation **12**,
49n3, 93n11, 264; disqualification
32, 36; joint lists 29, 35, 39, 44, 46;
personalism 220; polls 36; votes and
seats **10–11**, **37**, **41**, 48

parliamentary system 23, 63, 81, 140,
146
participation (political) 7, 21, 24, 43,
166, 173, 179–81, 183, 187, 195, 238;
see also turnout (voters)
parties, crisis of 4, 5, 14, 214, 219–20
Parties Law, 1992 216, 217, 221
Parties Registrar 30, 61, 217, 235n2
party decline 14, 15, 20, 81; *see also*
parties, crisis of

Party Finance Law, 1973 217–18
party identification 14, 17, 54, 57, 67, **68**, 69
party loyalty 42, 144
party system 3, 5, 6, 14–17, 38, 80, 121, 219, 220, 233–4; multiparty system 3, 23, 44, 163
Peretz, Amir 31, 35, 44
Peretz, Rafi 29, 42, 131
personal parties 6, 14, 31, 32, 54, 58, 67, 220, 231, 232, 234; *see also* Presidentialization
personalism (political) 38, 70–3, 78, 80–3, 91; behavioral 54, 55, 57, 64–70; definition and types 53–4; institutional 53, 55–60; media 54, 56–7, 60–4; *see also* Presidentialization
personalization (political) 4–7, 14–17, 20, 23–4, 70–4, 78, 80–3, 91, 92, 93n5, 264; behavioral 54, 57, 64–70; definition and types 53–4; institutional, 53, 55–60; joint lists 214, 220, 222, 231; media 54, 56–7, 60–4, 264; *see also* Presidentialization
personification 15, 21, 55, 77–84, 86–7, **88**, 89, **90**, 91–2, 93n11
Pinhasi, Rafael 141–3, 146, 150–2
Poland 20, 133, 147, 215
Polarization 22, 80, 92, 252, 253, 274, 275
political culture 6, 18, 20, 78–80, 120, 141, 143, 147, 152
political elite(s) 21, 78, 80, 91, 92, 101–108, 121, 183, 193, 259, 261, 273, 274
political personalism *see* personalism (political)
political personalization *see* personalization (political)
political upheaval of 1977 ("the mahapach") 121, 193
political uncertainty 5, 163–5, 170–1, 216
politics of identity *see* identity politics
polls *see* public opinion polls
populism: campaign 32; majoritarian-populist approach 19; Netanyahu as a populist leader 20, 23, 67, 100–2, 105–10, 112–14, 120–5, 133; personalization and personalism 73; populist democracy 27, 120–1; populist mood 144; populist wave 20, 21, 24, 190; speech 57, 67

pre-electoral coalition 214–216, 235
president of Israel: four tribes account 204; government formation 33, 35, 38, 42, 48, 119, 130, 144, 145, 248, 249, 253; pardons 153n10
president of U.S.A. 21, 22, 39, 80, 99, 100, 111
presidential system/regime 23, 71, 82, 89, 92, 140, 146, 147
presidentialization 53, 71, 81, 82, 91, 92
primaries 28, 29, 31, 39, 44, 131, 132; personalization and personalism 56, 57, 60
pro-Netanyahu bloc 9, **12**, 13, 33, 40, 43, 49n3, 49n4, 83, 93n11, 119–20, 132, 133, 176–80, 181, 183; projections (political) 163–76, 180–3, 187
protest: against Netanyahu 21; against violence in Arab society 248; Ethiopian immigrants protest against police brutality 39; social protest of 2011 31, 35, 106, 191, 192, 194, 274
public opinion 5, 7, 21, 84, 92, 150, 166, 180, 241, 245, 263, 275
public opinion polls: Arab politicians' popularity 241, 256n10; Arab public **246**, **247**, 255n5, 255n8; Covid-19 crisis 112; election integrity 21; exit polls *55*, 57, *70*; and electoral projections 166, *169*, 173, 174, 178, 180; ideology 261; and Netanyahu's trial 150; pre-election polls 28–33, 36, 39, 40, 43–6, 48, 226
public responsibility (of senior officials) 139–44, 147, 150, 151–2
public trust, 73; in Arab parties 247; in elected officials 140, 143; in the fairness of elections 21, 24n3; in government 149; in institutions 79, 93n6, 93n10; in media; in Netanyahu 8, 67; in parties 16; in political elites 92; in the Supreme Court 83, 84, *84*, 85, **85**, **97**, 123

Ra'am: bloc affiliation **12**, 93n11, 264; disqualification 32; government formation 4, 24, 48, 49, 106, 133, 182, 195, 252–4; ideology 252–4; and The Joint List 31, 32, 35, 44, 234, 251–4; joint lists 234, 242, 235n5; leader selection 241; votes and seats 9, **11**, 46, **47**, 47, *253*; *see also* Ra'am–Balad; Ra'am-Mada; Ra'am-Ta'al

290 *Index*

Ra'am-Balad **9**, **10**, **12**, 32, 33, **34**, 35, 93n11, 242
Ra'am-Mada 235n5
Ra'am-Ta'al 241
Rabin, Yitzhak 24n4, 40, 57, **66**, 67, 99, 142, 152n3, 174, 247
realignment 17, 183
reform *see* institutional reform
Regev, Miri 124
religiosity 9, 18, 80, 82, 83, 86, **87**, 98, *188*, 190, 197–9, 201, *202*, *203*, 204–6, 206n4, **281**
Religious Zionism (party alliance) **11**, **12**, 46, **47**, 47, 48, 93n11, 112, 133
resolution 922 (government decision) 240, 255n3
Revisionist ideology/movement 99, 101–2, 114n2
right-religious bloc 4, **12**, 12–13, 27, 33, 42, 49n2, 49n4, 72, 120
Riklin, Shimon 101, 108
Rivlin, Reuven 48, 119, 204, 276n1
rotation government 5, 18–19, 23, 72; Bennett-Lapid 4, 13, 15, 19, 23, 49, 182, 191; Netanyahu-Gantz 3, 8, 9, 15, 18–19, 39, 42–5, 49, 132, 170, 182, 191, 195, 245, 249, 251; *see also* Netanyahu-Gantz government; Bennet-Lapid government; 35th government; 36th government
Russo, Tal 31, 67

Sa'ar, Gideon: Likud 29, 39, 60, 131; and New Hope 6, 8, 43–5, 58, 72, 114, 132, 183, 195
Sectorialization 104, 105
Secularism 198–9, **200**, 204
Segalovich, Yoav 31
separation of state and religion 199, **200**
settlers 103, 122–4, 134, 251
Shafir, Stav 35, 39, 220
Shaked, Ayelet 29, 35, 58, 122, 126, 131, 220
Shamir, Yitzhak 101
Sharon, Ariel 33, 40, 111, 139, 152n3
Shas: bloc affiliation **12**, 33, 43, 93n11, 119, 130, 131, 264; in government 27, 42, 142, 193; government formation 38, 42, 123; leader 30; Mizrahi identity 195, 204; personalization and personalism 60, **61**, **62**; polls 29, 36, 45, 46; votes and seats 8, 9, **10–11**, 30, **34**, **37**, 38, **41**, 46, **47**, 48, *245*, *253*
Shehadeh, Mtnes 32, 44
Shelach, Ofer 44

Shibolet publishing house 102
Shmuli, Itzik 35, 44
Smotrich, Bezalel 29, 130, 133
social media 14, 21, 61, 173, 187, 247, 259–62, 268; *see also* Facebook; new media
social network(s) 54, **55**, 56, 61, **61**, **62**, 70, **70**; *see also* social media
Sofer, Ofir 44
Speaker of the Knesset *see* Knesset Speaker
State Attorney 28, 129, 131, 132, 134, 269
state budget 3, 4, 19, 22, 43, 45, 122–4, 131, 132; and the Arabs **246**, 255n2, 255n3
Statism (mamlachtiut) 102, 125, 194
support for democracy 4, 78–9, 85, 86, 91, 92, 93n6, 93n9, 93n10
Supreme Court: appointments 122; opposition to 124, 126, 134; trust in 83, 84, *84*, **85**, 93n6, 93n10, **97**, 114n9; verdicts relevant to Netanyahu's trial, 141, 142, 144, 155n32; *see also* High Court of Justice

Ta'al 31, 32, 35, 44, 58, 104, 229, 232, 242, 251, 252, 264; *see also* Hadash-Ta'al; Ra'am-Ta'al
Telem (of Moshe Dayan) 220
Telem (National Statist Movement) 30–1, 42, 43, 58, 61, 72, 191, 195, 220, 232
34th government 38
35th government 19, 123, 132; *see also* Netanyahu-Gantz government
36th government 22, 119, 238; *see also* Bennett-Lapid government
Tibi, Ahmad 32, 58, 104, 164, 229, 241, 248, 249, 256n10
Tikva Hadasha *see* New Hope
Trump, Donald 20–2, 27, 39, 46, 92, 100, 106, 111
turnout (voters) 4, 7, **7**, 9, 13, 14, 21, **34**, **37**, **41**, 41, 46, **47**, 164, 173, 181, 216, *243*; Arab 9, 33, 37, 40, 48, 183, 238, 241, 242, *243*, 244, 245, 248, 252, 254, 255n5, 256n12
Tzomet **34**, **37**, **41**, **47**, 220, 226

ultra-Orthodox: conscription 28; and Netanyahu 126, 127; sector 9, 28, 30, 122, 123, 194, 204; parties 6, 8, 9, 27, 28, 29, 33, 36, 38–43, 45, 61, 74n9, 119, 120, 123, 129, 169, 182, 219,

276n7; and the supreme court 123, 125; voters 108, 167

uncertainty 5, 163–6, 170, 171, 216

Union of Right Wing Parties **10**, **12**, 33, 93n11

United States of America (USA) 20, 22, 27, 39, 46, 79–81, 100, 106, 108, 147, 163

United Torah Judaism: candidates 30, 44; coalition 27, 42; joint lists 217, 218, 226, 232; polls 29, 36, 45, 46, **47**, 48; and pro-Netanyahu bloc 33, 38, 43, 93n11, 119, 126, 130; social networks **61**, **62**, 276n7; votes and seats 8, 9, **10–12**, 30, **34**, **37**, 38, **41**, 46; *see also* Agudat Yisrael; Degel HaTora

unity government 13, 36, 42, 72, 99, 274; predicted 170, 176, 177

volatility (electoral) *see* electoral volatility

voter's fatigue 7, 21, 41, 42

Walla! (case) 128, 130

West Bank 40, 71, 251; *see also* Judea and Samaria; Occupied Territories

Ya'alon, Moshe (Boogie) 30, 31, 43, 58, 61, 220

Yabarkan, Gadi 39

Yedioth Ahronoth 114n1, 127, 131

Yemina: bloc affiliation **12**, 43, 93n11, 119, 130, 264; in government 4, 6; government formation 38, 48, 182, 191, 195; joint lists 35, 232; personalization and personalism 58; polls 30, 45, 46; split 38; votes and seats **10–11**, 36, **37**, 38, 40, **41**, **47**

Yesh Atid: bloc affiliation **12**, 43, 83, 93n11, 264; and Blue and White 30, 42, 45, 194, 195; candidate selection 31, 44; in government 4, 48; joint lists 232; leadership selection 44; personalization 54, 58, 61–2, **61–2**, 220; polls 30, 46; vote 9, **11**, 16, 46, **47**, 48, 182, 191, **253**, 253

Yisrael Beiteinu: bloc affiliation 6, **12**, 13, 28, 33, 38, 43, 48, 49n2, 93n11, 107, 129, 264; electoral projections 169, 176; joint lists 220; in Netanyahu's coalition 27–8; personalization 58, **61**, **62**, 72; polls 30, 33, 36, 39, 40, 43, 45, 46; strategic position 38; vote 9, **10–11**, 30, 33, **34**, **37**, 37, 40, **41**, 46, **47**, 48, **245**, **253**

Zamir, Yitzhak 140, 151

Zandberg, Tamar 31, 36

Zehut: alliance with Likud 8, 35, 38, 42; bloc affiliation **12**, 93n11, 264; establishment 29; polls 33; votes **10**, 33, **34**, 35, **37**, 38

Zelicha, Yaron 44

Zionist Camp 16, 31, 194

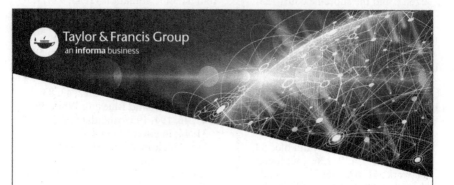